ZAPOTECS ON THE MOVE

❧

Latinidad

Transnational Cultures in the United States

This series publishes books that deepen and expand our knowledge and understanding of the various Latina/o populations in the United States in the context of their transnational relationships with cultures of the broader Americas. The focus is on the history and analysis of Latino cultural systems and practices in national and transnational spheres of influence from the nineteenth century to the present. The series is open to scholarship in political science, economics, anthropology, linguistics, history, cinema and television, literary and cultural studies, and popular culture and encourages interdisciplinary approaches, methods, and theories. The series grew out of discussions with faculty at the School of Transborder Studies at Arizona State University, where an interdisciplinary emphasis is being placed on transborder and transnational dynamics.

Carlos Velez-Ibañez, Series Editor, School of Transborder Studies

Rodolfo F. Acuña, *In the Trenches of Academe: The Making of Chicana/o Studies*

Adriana Cruz-Manjarrez, *Zapotecs on the Move: Cultural, Social, and Political Processes in Transnational Perspective*

Marivel T. Danielson, *Homecoming Queers: Desire and Difference in Chicana Latina Cultural Production*

Rudy P. Guevarra Jr., *Becoming Mexipino: Multiethnic Identities and Communities in San Diego*

Lisa Jarvinen, *The Rise of Spanish-Language Filmmaking: Out from Hollywood's Shadow, 1929–1939*

Regina M. Marchi, *Day of the Dead in the USA: The Migration and Transformation of a Cultural Phenomenon*

Marci R. McMahon, *Domestic Negotiations: Gender, Nation, and Self-Fashioning in US Mexicana and Chicana Literature and Art*

A. Gabriel Melendez, *Hidden Chicano Cinema: Film Dramas in the Borderlands*

Priscilla Peña Ovalle, *Dance and the Hollywood Latina: Race, Sex, and Stardom*

Luis F. B. Plascencia, *Disenchanting Citizenship: Mexican Migrants and the Boundaries of Belonging*

Maya Socolovsky, *Troubling Nationhood in U.S. Latina Literature: Explorations of Place and Belonging*

ZAPOTECS ON THE MOVE

❧

Cultural, Social, and Political Processes in Transnational Perspective

ADRIANA CRUZ-MANJARREZ

RUTGERS UNIVERSITY PRESS
NEW BRUNSWICK, NEW JERSEY, AND LONDON

Library of Congress Cataloging-in-Publication Data

Cruz-Manjarrez, Adriana, 1966–

 Zapotecs on the move : cultural, social, and political processes in transnational perspective / Adriana Cruz-Manjarrez.

    p.   cm. — (Latinidad: transnational cultures in the united states)
  Includes bibliographical references and index.
  ISBN 978-0-8135-6071-7 (hardcover : alk. paper) — ISBN 978-0-8135-6070-0 (pbk. :
alk. paper) — ISBN 978-0-8135-6072-4 (e-book)
  1. Zapotec Indians—Mexico—Hidalgo Yalálag—History. 2. Zapotec Indians—
Mexico—Hidalgo Yalálag—Migrations. 3. Zapotec Indians—Cultural assimilation—
California—Los Angeles. 4. Rural-urban migration—California—Los Angeles. I. Title.

F1221.Z3C76 2013
 398.208997'68—dc23   2012033354

A British Cataloging-in-Publication record for this book is available from the British
Library.

Visit our website: http://rutgerspress.rutgers.edu

Manufactured in the United States of America

*I dedicate this book to Heriberto Avelino
and to the Yalálag Zapotecs*

CONTENTS

ACKNOWLEDGMENTS

I could not have written this book without the exceptional help, trust, and support of many people. First of all, I would like to express my gratitude, appreciation, and respect for *la Gente de Yalálag* who live in Los Angeles, Oaxaca City, and Yalálag. I think of every Yalalteco/a who informed and helped me to develop this project. I am deeply indebted to all of them for allowing me to participate in their community gatherings, for welcoming me in their homes, and for sharing their stories and their joy of life. Warm and special thanks go to my friends Estela Canseco and José Bollo. Estela's support was crucial to carry out this project. I am indebted to her for the time she took to bring me into her community in Los Angeles, for her encouragement to do my work, for introducing me to her extended family in Yalálag, and for welcoming my husband and me into her home. I thank José Bollo for his friendship and unconditional support. I wish to mention that José is not only one of the best Yalaltec-Jarabe dancers in Yalálag and in Los Angeles, but also one of the kindest persons I have known within the Yalaltec community. In addition, his thoughtful ideas, good sense of humor, and remarkable knowledge of his culture have shaped and been fundamental in my work. I thank him for teaching me the art of dancing to the heights.

During the course of this investigation in Los Angeles, I was privileged to work with a great number of Yalaltec families and friends who shared their experiences and stories with me over a period of many years. I would like to acknowledge the generosity and help of Irma, Juan, and Hugo Canseco; Cornelio Aquino; Trinidad Ríos; Gerardo Vasquez; Israel Monterrubio; Bernarda Salvador; the late Chico Diego; Carmen Mestas; Eduardo Molina; Elizabeth Eslava; Octaviano and Elba Mulato; Edith and Renya Cancio; Elia Primo; Juan and Eustolia Ventura; Gerardo Delgado; Josefina Domínguez; Gerado and Oliva Vásquez; Cesar Bautista; Federico Aquino; Elias Bolaños; Noel Ignacio; Ruben Lice; Paula Chimil; Guadalupe Maldonado; Elodia Acevez; Elena Lucas; Irene Miguel; Petronila Vargas; Victoria, Jesus, and Queña Diego; Abundio, Crispin, and Fidencio Acevez; Violeta Chino; Paula Chimil; Hilario Molina; Ema Lucas; Liborio Matías; Aurelio Mulato; Taurino Illescas and family; Rufina Reyes; Silvano Maldonado; Eloisa Fabian; Juan and Severino Montellano; Eufemia Bollo and Juan Bautista; Gladis García Canseco; Norma and Erick Diego; Fredy, Linda, and Juana Fernández; Wendy and Janette Agustin; Erika Maldonado; Anais Diego; Carlos Beltrán; Francisco and Carlos Aquino; Jessica, Carmen, and Reyna Ventura; Silvia, Laura, Daniel, and Javier Mulato; Carlos and Alberto Mulato Vargas; Sheyla Chino; Ana Patricia and Maira Maldonado; Patricia Vicente and family; and Vilma and Magdalena. Thanks to all the musicians of the *Banda Filarmónica de Yalálag* of Los Angeles, the *Zempoaltepetl* brass band, and *La Nueva Imágen* of Los Angeles brass band.

I am also profoundly thankful to a great number of Yalaltecos in Yalálag and Oaxaca City for their hospitality and for their interest in participating in this project. In particular, I want to express my heartfelt thanks to Emilia and Gil Bollo as well as my godmother Alicia and late godfather Juan Bollo. They welcomed me into their homes during my multiple stays in Oaxaca City and in Yalálag and took care of me. My appreciation also goes to late Mario Molina; Rafael Ventura; Cándido Primo, Pedro, Linda, and Doña Tere; Juan Delagado; Tere and Juana Vázquez; Yunitza, Camilo, Arturo and Luis Vásquez; Joel Aquino; Luvia Aquino; Plutarco Aquino and family; Acela Tomas; Maximino Aquino; Alicia Montellano; Adela; Francisco Limeta; Herlinda and Carmen Diego; Senorina; Beremundo Ventura; Juan Diego; Segismundo Molina; Jaime Morales; Justo Pasos and family; Efren Gómez and family; Oscar Cristobal; Juana Méndez; Soledad Revilla; Leonardo Maldonado; Father Adrian Sánchez; Elí Cuevas, Juan Sánchez, and Rene Brito; Marcos Brito; and the students and the professors of *Escuela Secundaria Técnica*, TEBAO, and the Cultural Center *Uken ke Uken*.

This project began as a Ph.D. dissertation in the Department of World Arts and Cultures at UCLA. I wish to express my gratitude to my dissertation committee, who helped shape my early thinking and encouraged me to see this project to completion. I am especially indebted to Ivan Light for his thoughtful comments, support, and guidance throughout this research. I thank Allen Roberts, who enriched my intellectual formation, asked valuable and challenging questions, and made comments on draft chapters. I want to express my appreciation to Colin Quigley, Christopher Waterman and Peter Nabokov, who were involved in this project when I started. I am profoundly thankful to Olivia Cadaval and Daniel Sheehy; when I was a postdoctoral fellow at the Smithsonian Institution, they were important interlocutors in the research process and provided me with very useful insights while writing. My gratitude also goes to Olga Nájera-Ramirez, Norma Cantú, Brenda Romero, Jonathan Fox, Colin Clarck, Paul Scolieri, and Steven Vertovec. They read parts of this research and made valuable suggestions.

I am also grateful to Universidad de Colima, where I found support for my research during the last three years. I wish to thank all agencies and academic institutions that generously supported me with fellowships: CONACYT (National Endowment for the Science and Technology, Mexico), the Smithsonian Institution, UC-MEXUS, DAAD (The German Academic Exchange Service), the Max Planck Institute for the Study of Religious and Ethnic Diversity, the Department of World Arts and Cultures at UCLA, the Phi Beta Kappa Almuni of Southern California, the UCLA Latin American Studies Center, the UCLA Multicampus Research Group on Transnational and Transcolonial Studies, the UCLA Chicano Studies Research Center, the American Organization of States, INBA (National Institute of Fine Arts, Mexico), and FONCA (National Foundation for the Arts and Culture, Mexico).

Con todo el corazón, thanks to my colleague Cindy García, who challenged me far beyond any expectations I may have had for my goals in this research. Thanks to my dear friend Claudia Hernández for her critical comments and *amistad incondicional*. Claudia not only helped me to translate entire citations from Spanish into English, but also made me feel that I was not alone in this journey. Thanks to John Bishop and Jaynie Ali Aydin for helping me to do video during my research. My thanks go to each of them for their help, enthusiasm, and friendship. In particular, I am indebted to Anoosh Jorjorian and Sharon Calandra, who took the time to read this manuscript closely and offered enormous help with the editing. Thanks to Miguel Angel Avila for his help on preparing the images for publication.

I wish to express a special thanks to my editor at Rutgers University Press, Leslie Mitchner. From the very beginning, she was very enthusiastic about this book, and this encouraged me to finish it. I am especially thankful to the anonymous reviewers of Rutgers University Press for their insightful comments. They read this manuscript *very closely* and made excellent and very fine suggestions for the revisions of it.

Thanks to those not directly involved in this research but always supportive and wholehearted: Olga Odgers; Miguel Olmos; Lauren and Larry Hyman; Manju and John Ohala; Pamela Munro; Carolina San Juan; Bob and Olivia Hillman; Celene Navarrete; Felipe Martínez; Carmen Ochoa; Ana María Vargas; Mónica Velasco; Sahyang and Sagang Kim; Lalo Ugalde; Cristina González; Wendy Temple; Alberto Perez; the late Guillermo Hernández; Claudia Russell; Alberto Martín, Verónica de la Torre; Aleks and Enid; Elaine Levine and Evaristo Casanova; Ana I. Zermeño; and Alejandra Aquino. I am truly appreciative of my *Gran Amiga* Paulina Sahagún and her husband Shabaka Henley. Since my husband's and my early days in Los Angeles, they have shared part of their lives with us, generously offered their house, and made our stay in Los Angeles pleasant. Particularly, Paulina's years of experiences as an actress and her incredible knowledge of the history and deep involvement in the Chicano/a community have allowed me to understand the significance of being a Mexican born in the United States and to pay attention to the experiences, complexities, and difficulties that underrepresented communities in the United States have to go through. Thanks to my *comadre* Esther and *compadre* Oziel for their unconditional support and for helping my husband and me to settle in Los Angeles when we first came.

Thanks to my mother Guadalupe García and *mis queridos hermanos* Marcela, Paty, Billy, and Carlos who have been very supportive through these years of studies and hard work. Finally, I am grateful to my husband Heriberto Avelino. This work would have been unthinkable without his love and strong support. Besides listening, reading, and reacting to my work since I started, he has shared very special moments with me. I have enjoyed the beauty of life with him, and his *compañia* and sense of humor have been a great source of encouragement. I am also thankful to him for helping me in every possible way to make this work happen, for making me think about the art of putting things and ideas into words, and for his patience while I finished this study. For all these things, I am so grateful.

ZAPOTECS ON THE MOVE

$$\text{\large ❦}$$

INTRODUCTION

On a day in late November 2000, a Yalálag Zapotec friend of mine, José, invited me to attend a community event in Los Angeles; there Yalaltec immigrants joined together to raise funds for the annual patron saint fiesta of Santiago Apóstol and the reconstruction of the saint's barrio cultural center in the Yalaltecos' home village of Yalálag in Oaxaca, Mexico.[1] When I arrived at a small East Los Angeles ballroom where it was being held, one of three young Yalaltec immigrant men sold me tickets for José, my husband, and myself for twelve dollars each, and handed me flyers about upcoming events for other Zapotec immigrant village communities in Los Angeles. Once through the mandatory inspection by the security personnel, I entered the main room and saw over three hundred Yalaltec immigrants and their children, a Yalálag Zapotec brass band, a DJ, and a tiny temporary altar located on the left side of the room. Walking across the room to find folding chairs to sit with José and my husband, I saw a kitchen and a bar area attended by young Yalaltec women and men. In the kitchen, I learned, women were selling corn and chicken *tamales*, cheese *quesadillas, arroz con leche, gelatinas*, and candies for one dollar each. And men stationed right outside the kitchen offered bottles of water, one dollar each, and cans of Coca-Cola and beer for two dollars.

Around 9:00 p.m., when the DJ stopped playing his set of *salsa, cumbia,* and *Norteño* songs, one of the event organizers took a microphone to announce a performance of the *Danza de Los Mixes* (Dance of Los Mixes) and invited the audience to attend upcoming events for the barrio community of Santa Catarina and the barrio community of San Juan. In the meantime, the Los Mixes dancers appeared in the main entrance of the dance hall, dressed in blue clothes, wooden masks, and leather sandals. The presenter asked children, who were running around the room, to sit with their families to watch the dance performance, and young single Yalaltec men began to pile up in the two doorways. The female journalist from the *El Oaxaqueño* newspaper began photographing the dancers, the brass band, the audience, and the food committee. When the *capitán de la danza* (dance leader) bowed his head to the director of the Zapotec brass band, Zempoaltepetl, the musicians began to play the *son de la entrada* (entrance dance), and the eight Mixe dancers walked into the dance hall and began dancing in two rows in front of a picture of the saint Santiago Apóstol. As the dance came to its end, I asked José about it. "This is the dance of Los Mixes and is performed to honor Santiago Apóstol," he replied. "Look, it's like in Yalálag. My *bi gwlash* are dancing Los Mixes because this is the dance of the patron saint Santiago Apóstol."[2]

While José explained this to me, the brass band started playing the *sones y jarabes Yalaltecos* (social dances), and dozens of couples went onto the dance floor to dance. As I enjoyed listening to the music and watching all the dancers' smooth synchronized movements, I began to ask myself questions that developed over time: How have these long-standing traditions of expressive culture made their way into the United States? Who is responsible for organizing this communal event and for bringing together this crowd, the Yalálag Zapotec brass band, and the dancers? How will the money, raised during the event, be sent to and spent in Yalálag? Who will receive it in Yalálag? What will the patron saint's fiesta in Yalálag look like? What does it means for the second-generation Yalálag Zapotecs to participate in the *bailes* (community gatherings) in Los Angeles? What do Yalaltec immigrants tell their U.S.-born children about these communal events, their culture, and origin? And finally, who are the Yalálag Zapotecs? Where do they come from? How many are there in the United States? What do they do and what are their lives like in Los Angeles? How long have they been in the United States? And how have Yalaltec immigrants and their children experienced their integration into American society? To address these questions, this book examines the history of migration of Yalálag Zapotecs (Yalaltecos) into the United Sates and the multiple activities, practices, and motivations that have connected Yalaltecos in two localities for the last twenty years: Los Angeles and the village community of Yalálag in Oaxaca. To do this, I focus on the cultural, social, and political processes through which Yalaltecos have built a new form of community and examine what impact migration has had on Yalálag Zapotec culture and identity, and on the sending community of Yalálag.

The Yalaltecos are among the many indigenous Mexican immigrants living and working in the United States. They first migrated into California in the first half of the twentieth century and eventually became permanent settlers in Los Angeles. In the mid-1940s, when Yalaltec men were recruited in Oaxaca City and Mexico City to join the Bracero (farmhand) Program, they were hired on short-term contracts to work in the agricultural fields of northern California. But between the late 1970s and the early 1980s, the deterioration of economic and social conditions in Mexico and changes in labor market opportunities in the United States transformed the destiny of this indigenous village community. A new generation of married and single Yalaltecos began to migrate to Los

Angeles to work in manufacturing and the domestic and service sectors. Their improved standard of living and Mexico's lack of social and economic opportunities prompted permanent settlement, family reunification, and family formation in the United States.

During the1980s, when Yalaltecos in Los Angeles had begun to enjoy the benefits of regular employment and financial stability, they organized in different groups to coordinate a series of activities and social events to raise funds to build a basketball court and restore the municipal building in their home village of Yalálag. In 1989, a group of Yalaltecos organized a community social event to collect monetary donations for the patron saint fiesta of Santiago Apóstol and the restoration of the saint's church in Yalálag. A Yalaltec family offered their backyard for this event, and a group of Yalaltec immigrant musicians bought instruments and organized a Yalálag-community brass band in Los Angeles to accompany Yalálag religious performances and social dances and to liven up community gatherings. Since then, Yalaltec immigrants have organized *kermesses* (small fairs), raffles, basketball tournaments, and *bailes* in Los Angeles to raise funds for the Yalálag patron saints' fiestas, and for reconstruction of local churches and the four barrio cultural centers in Yalálag.

In the fall of 2000, when I first participated in one of these events, I was introduced to the transnational life of this Zapotec immigrant village community in Los Angeles and to the social and cultural dynamics, activities, and motivations that have connected Yalaltecos within Los Angeles and to those who remained in their village of origin in Oaxaca. At this time, I was an immigrant myself in Los Angeles doing graduate work in culture and performance studies at UCLA; interdisciplinary research in migration and culture in the United States opened up the possibility of using anthropological, sociological, and performance approaches to understand the complexity of Yalaltec community gatherings (the *bailes*), the transnationalization of Yalálag dance and music practices, and the migration experience of this Zapotec community in the United States.

From November of 2000 on, I began to attend dozens of *bailes* organized by other Zapotec immigrant communities in East Los Angeles who came from La Sierra Juárez and the Central Valleys of Mexico. I became particularly interested in the *bailes* organized by Yalaltec immigrants, and I was surprised to see dozens of Yalaltec families and young single immigrant men and women attending them. I realized that organizing these events required a great deal of communal work and participation, and Yalálag Zapotec religious dance and music for the Yalálag patron saints were central at these events. As I continued to attend the *bailes*, I started to build close friendships with two Yalaltec families and began to experience the intense family and community life of Yalaltec immigrants.

From my participation in the *bailes*, I learned four important things. First, the *bailes* seemed to be very special for the Yalaltec immigrants. These were organized by barrio committees to raise funds for the celebrations of Yalálag patron

saints in Yalálag. Approximately, four months before a *baile* took place, committee members began meeting to organize it. The organizers had to rent a ballroom, invite one or two Zapotec brass bands, and hire a DJ or a *grupo tropical* (a
tropical music ensemble). Yalaltecos who were to perform religious dances had
to pay someone in the community to make their attire, and had to arrange their
personal schedules to attend the dance rehearsals over three weekends at night.
Finally, attendees had to pay approximately twelve dollars for each ticket to participate in the *baile*—not a trivial sum.

The second thing I learned was that José, who invited me to attend that community event in November 2000, had been nominated in Yalálag to do *servicio*
(community work) in Los Angeles for the upcoming barrio event of the patron
saint Santa Catarina in Yalálag; he would also oversee and choreograph the *sones
y jarabes Yalaltecos* performance for the annual festival of La Guelaguetza, organized by the transnational multiethnic Oaxacan Regional Organization (ORO)
in Los Angeles.

Third, the Yalaltec women and men who gathered in November 2000 had
established roots in California since the early 1970s and had let their young children represent the Yalálag Zapotec community in the La Guelaguetza dance and
music festivals in Los Angeles and in Oaxaca. And fourth, dozens of Yalaltec
immigrants, both undocumented and documented, and those who are U.S. residents or American citizens, are accustomed to returning to Yalálag every summer
to celebrate the village's major patron saint, San Antonio de Padua, and the four
barrio patron saint fiestas.

At this point in my research, I had finished my Master's thesis in dance, in
which I proposed that community gatherings, which Yalaltecos describe as *bailes*,
are a context for understanding some aspects of Yalálag Zapotec community formation and the redefinition of group identity in Los Angeles (Cruz-Manjarrez
2001). That is, for the Yalálag Zapotec immigrants, the *bailes* have been something
other than spaces for socialization or collective acts of solidarity with the village
of Yalálag. The *bailes* embody some aspects of this immigrant community's social
life, reflect the trasnationalization of native forms of social organization and the
Yalálag fiesta system of Catholic patron saints, and point to social and symbolic
processes that connect Yalaltecos in Los Angeles and between those in Mexico
and the United States. Although these findings were important in understanding how immigrants reinforce their sense of ethnic identity and group cohesion
in the United States, I was interested in gaining a deeper understanding of the
nature of community and identity formation and the transnational connections
between Yalaltec immigrants and their natal village. Therefore, as I expanded my
research interests, I continued to attend community and family events in Los
Angeles and planned various research trips to Yalálag.

In July 2001, I went to Yálalag in Oaxaca to get to know José's family and their
hometown. I had the opportunity to observe the celebration for Santiago Apóstol

and learned from other Yalaltec immigrants I met by chance in the patron saint fiesta that they were going to take a replica of Santiago Apóstol to Los Angeles. In December 2003, Estela, another Yalaltec friend, her daughter Gladys, her niece Joanna, and I all visited Yalálag for two weeks. On the bus trip from the terminal in Oaxaca City to Yalálag, we met families who reside in Los Angeles. They were visiting their families for Christmas celebrations, and some were coming to organize two *posadas*, that is, two days of the nine-day celebration before Christmas, with the help of their local family members. On December 24, for example, a single immigrant woman, who had made a *promesa* (a sacred vow) to the Niño Dios (Christ child), organized the last *posada* and paid for the village's Christmas Eve celebration. In her role as godmother of the Niño Dios, she offered dinner to all the villagers on Christmas Eve and three meals on Christmas Day at her house.

In the summer of 2004, I attended the fiesta of San Antonio de Padua and, by chance, I met dozens of Yalaltec immigrants and their families from Los Angeles. During the nine-day celebration, my varied observations made me wonder about immigrants' motivations to return to Yalálag and non-immigrants' reactions to the presence of hundreds of visiting immigrants—the village of Yalálag, numbering about two thousand inhabitants, had received around four thousand visitors. Although many of them were Yalaltec immigrants from Los Angeles, quite a few also traveled from northern California, Chicago, Oaxaca City, Mexico City, Puebla, and Veracruz. On June 13, the day of the festival, en route to the church of San Antonio, I saw a parodic dance, described by the local people as *danza chusca*, where Yalaltec non-immigrants made fun of the newly returned immigrants' Westernized appearance and behaviors. Despite such teasing, immigrants were an important part of the festivities: over nine consecutive days, the church's speakers announced repetitive public acknowledgments of immigrants' monetary donations for the fiesta. These included hundreds of dollars and thousands of Mexican pesos donated by immigrants, which meant that everyone attending the fiesta could participate in any event and eat in the *casa del pueblo* (community kitchen) for nine consecutive days for free.

While I was in Los Angeles, I became convinced that the *bailes* were not only very special gatherings for the Yalálag immigrant community but also represented complex social and cultural phenomena. In Yalálag, after my field trips and conversations with local people, I discovered that despite immigrants' continuous economic, social, and cultural participation in family and community life in Yalálag, feelings of family disintegration, community fragmentation, and social disorganization have permeated the lives of non-immigrants. Hence, as I defined the transnational connections and social spaces where Yalaltec immigrants and non-immigrants come together as the universe of my research, I became interested in understanding the impact of migration on those who most expect to be economically and socially benefited: the Yalaltecos in Yalálag. Moreover, questions about the ways in which migration has transformed the everyday lives of Yalaltec immigrants and their children in Los Angeles led me to focus on how Yalaltec immigrants, non-immigrants, and their children have dealt with the fast changes and increasing differences in their understandings and meanings of community, identity, and culture.

In this context, this book examines the impact of international migration on the Yalálag Zapotec community, identity, and culture in both Yalálag and Los Angeles. The ethnographic focus of this study is on understanding the significance of the transnational relationships that Yalaltec immigrants have forged and sustained with their community of origin over the last two decades and the cultural, social, and political processes that have contributed to community formation in Los Angeles. By looking at how social identity is forged and transformed among Yalálag Zapotec immigrants and their children in Los Angeles, this book explores ethnic, national, and racial categories in a specific transnational context. That is, I examine how similar and different perceptions of identity are produced by different social actors across two generations, and how the emergence of new forms of self-identification are constituted within the boundaries and at the crossroad of two operating systems of ethnic and racial classification in the United States, the Mexican and the American. To understand the centrality of cultural performances in transnational communities, this book also examines what happens to cultural practices that are relocated by transnational immigrants in the migratory setting and explores whether migration transforms village cultural practices in the home country. That is, I explore how immigrants and their children have experienced their integration into American society vis-à-vis their changing perceptions of identity and their cultural beliefs and practices of dance, and what kinds of cultural meanings non-immigrants give to the same cultural practices in the ancestral homeland. In order to understand how migration impacts the sense of community, identity, and culture in a group of people that has been identified and identify themselves as a community or *pueblo*, I must begin by discussing how community is generally defined in studies of transnational migration.[3]

The Concept of Community in Transnational Perspective

In the first half of the twentieth century, anthropological and sociological studies on community defined it in terms of a fixed and isolated locality, a homogenous and integrated social entity, and an objective expression of culture (Durkheim 1964; Kluckhohn 1962). More recently, a new body of scholarship shows not only that community may be conceptualized beyond the idea of a physical place but also that its members, who are not quite homogeneous, assert "a sense of primary group belonging" resulting from processes of socialization and the sharing of a particular repertoire of symbolic representations and social practices (Cohen 1985; Pries 2001). In this study, I have chosen to follow the second approach and further elaborate on the concept of community from the perspective of migrant transnationalism (Kivisto and Faist 2009; Portes 2001; Portes, Guarnizo, and Landolt 1999; Vertovec 2010).

In the early 1990s, anthropologists and sociologists proposed the term *transnationalism* to describe the strong social, economic, and political relationships maintained by contemporary immigrants with their families, communities, or countries of emigration. In 1994, the anthropologists Basch, Glick-Schiller, and Blanc-Szanton offered a comprehensive definition of transnationalism to describe the nature of this new global phenomenon: "we define 'transnationalism' as the processes by which immigrants forge and sustain multi-stranded social relations that link together their societies of origin and settlement. We call these processes transnationalism to emphasize that many immigrants today build social fields that cross geographic, cultural, and political borders" (1994, 6). In looking at transnationalism as a new type of social formation, Vertovec (2010) points out that many of today's migrant populations tend to function as transnational communities. Namely, in an era of new global migration movements (Castles and Miller 1998), immigrants engage in long-distance relations with their home communities or countries of origin across the borders of one or multiple nation-states. Their connection facilitated by the development of modern transportation and information technology, contemporary immigrants have access to immediate communication with their families or communities of origin through fax machines, cheap telephone calls, and the Internet. They send cash instantly to their relatives or communities and travel long distances in a few hours or days to visit them (Portes 1998a). In this sense, Levitt (2001b) argues that modern technology has been central in fostering international migration, and in the formation of migrant networks and transnational communities.

In looking at the everyday lives of transnational immigrants, Robert C. Smith (2006) introduces the term *transnational life* to conceptualize the multiple activities, social and cultural dynamics, and political processes that link immigrants and their U.S.-born children in the sending and the receiving countries. He notes that these kinds of links explain how multiple attachments structure and institutionalize a certain type of transnational life. That is, immigrants residing in a specific country engage in transnational religious, political, and cultural activities in the receiving locality and participate in transnational projects in conjunction with their community of origin.

As employed in this book, *transnationalism* is a descriptive and conceptual term used to orient our examination of the cultural, political, and social processes that have contributed to Yalaltec community formation transnationally. In this study I adopt an explanation similar to those explained above, and particularly that of Faist (2000b), seeing transnational community formation as a process in which its members, in this case Yalaltecos, produce a new sense of community based on social and symbolic ties, the sharing of similar interests, and a system of symbolic representations, social norms, and community values that allow them to reconstitute and reimagine their community locally in Los Angeles and transnationally between Los Angeles and Yalálag.

Faist writes that "social ties are a continuing series of interpersonal transactions to which participants attach shared interests, obligations, expectations, and norms" (101). He describes symbolic ties as those "perceived bonds, both face-to-face and indirect to which people attach shared meanings, memories, future expectations, and representations" (102). Building on Bourdieu's (1983) and Putnam's (1993) ideas of social capital, Faist states that social and symbolic ties constitute a form of social capital, namely, "*resources that help people or groups to achieve their goals in ties and the assets inherent in patterned social and symbolic ties that allow actors to cooperate in networks and organizations serving as a mechanism to integrate groups and symbolic communities*" (Faist 2000b, 102).[4] One argument in this book is that social and symbolic ties to the Yalálag patron saints and community provide a context within which transnational life (Smith 2006) is initiated and conducted meaningfully. Moreover, practices of membership (discussed in chapter 2) such as the *gwzon* (reciprocity and mutual support), *servicio* (community service), and *tequio* (communal work) are native social strategies and resources for the social production of community both locally and transnationally. For instance, in Los Angeles, Yalaltec immigrants honor their patron saints according to religious beliefs and the social norms of reciprocity, namely, the *gwzon* of faith. In the *bailes*, Yalaltecos perform spoken prayers, religious chants, and Yalaltec religious dances for the saints in gratitude for the help and support the saints provide. When immigrants organize and synchronize the *bailes* in Los Angeles with patron saint fiestas and send remittances for the saints' celebrations in Yalálag, they (re)create social and symbolic ties that unite Yalálag and Los Angeles in a transnational social space.

Transnational social space is a key concept in this study. Several scholars have used this concept to refer to a limited field of social action that emerges from immigrants' social, economic, and political involvement in their home country or home village and the social, cultural, and political life that also evolves in a specific site of reception.[5] Here, I use the concept of transnational social spaces to explain how those social and symbolic processes that connect immigrants and non-immigrants have contributed to a new imagination of community and a new configuration of social reality for Yalaltec non-immigrants and immigrants and their children.[6] In other words, in order to understand how the transnational Yalaltec community is imagined and created within a transnational social space, it is necessary to examine this community's religious and cultural life as well as the new social positions that migration produces in this social space and the new set of relations that constitute such space. Although he does not address migration studies in particular, Pierre Bourdieu (1990) infers such reconstructive intellectual work when he observes: "My work consists in saying that people are located in a social space, that they are not just anywhere, in other words interchangeable . . . and that according to the position they occupy in this highly complex space, you can understand the logic of their practices and determine, *inter alia*, how they will classify themselves and others" (50).

In this sense, this books argues that to fully understand the meaning of Yalaltec community in relation to migration and the emergence of a new social imaginary of community, one must consider that after seventy years of Yalálag Zapotec international migration to the United States, new meanings, identities, and ideas about community have emerged in novel configurations. Yalaltecos who have been connected transnationally currently occupy distinctive social positions and thus reflect on, experience, organize, and relate to the Yalaltec community in similar and distinctive ways. When I asked Yalaltecos in Yalálag to define their community, many described it in terms of a bounded geopolitical unit and as their ancestral homeland. Some referred to it as a *comunidad fragmentada*, namely, a dispersed community due to migration. When I asked Yalaltec immigrants to identify their sense of belonging, they did so in two ways. First, they referred to their home village in Mexico, because their hometown continues to be their focal point of identification and evokes the history and memories of their community. Second, Yalaltec immigrants also referred to the *comunidad Yalalteca* in Los Angeles because religious, social, and cultural life has produced a new sense of community in the migratory context. When I asked second-generation Yalaltecos about their relationship to the Yalaltec community and sense of belonging, they recognized that their participation in the social and cultural life of the *comunidad Yalalteca de Los Angeles* represents one aspect of their sense of belonging. However, although the village of Yalálag is a referent for their and their parents' ancestral homeland, their sense of community and home are significantly informed by what happens to them in Los Angeles, with whom they relate, and how they are seen by Yalaltecos in Yalálag (see chapter 5).

Although the notion of the community has been transformed among Yalaltecos, and various scholars have argued for the relevance of a theoretical transnational approach, other challenges, community conflicts, and power relations continue to emerge in transnational communities. For example, several studies of Mexican migration to the United States have documented the downside of migration in sending communities. Currently, various *pueblos* or village communities have become *pueblos fantasmas* (ghost towns) due to massive emigration of hundreds of young men and women.[7] Research on family and migration has documented that children and families who are left behind face challenges in parenting and experience family disintegration and psychological distress.[8] A central conclusion of this book is that migration has had a negative impact on the Yalaltec community in Yalálag. Migration has caused social disorganization in the governance system (called the *cargo* system), disrupted family life, and reconfigured social relations on a community scale. For example, in Yalálag, migration has become an expectation for teenage girls and boys, and many have left for Los

Angeles and thus do not comply with communal obligations or participate in the governance system (see chapter 3). In Los Angeles, feelings of exclusion, racism, family disintegration, and pressures to assimilate are so strong among teenage immigrants and second-generation Yalaltecos that some have experienced what Diego Vigil describes as a "multiple marginality" (1994). During my research in Los Angeles, Yalaltecos talked to me about family distress caused by their children's involvement in gang activities. In Yalálag, the local priest told me that a few young teenage migrant boys, who became involved in gang activities in Los Angeles, returned to the village and started to form their own gangs.

Currently, Yalaltecos in Yalálag and in Los Angeles share similar experiences and are spatially connected and affected by way of "social remittances." In her study of Dominican migration to Boston, Peggy Levitt (2001a) introduces the concept of social remittances to describe "the ideas, behaviors, and social capital that flow from receiving to sending communities" (11). I find that this idea offers a useful way of conceptualizing what is socially transferred from Los Angeles to Yalálag and what is expressed in *chusca* dances such as *Los Cholos* (The gangsters) in Yalálag (see chapter 6). Through their dance performance, *cholo* dancers reveal the impact of social behaviors and cultural values remitted from the violent, antisocial, and drug-related gang culture of inner-city neighborhoods in Los Angeles to the village community of Yalálag.

These kinds of distinctive experiences in transnational communities continue to push anthropologists and other social scientists to think of creative ways to describe, interpret, and explain what circulates and is produced in transnational social spaces. They also help us keep in mind that the maintenance of cultural distinction in groups or communities like that of Yalálag Zapotecs, which used to be identified in relation to a specific geopolitical space or in terms of a culture or a fixed collective identity, are conceptually problematic at present. As Akhil Gupta and James Ferguson have wisely written (1992, 7),

> The fiction of cultures as discrete, object-like phenomena occupying discrete spaces becomes implausible for those who inhabit the borderlands. Related to border inhabitants are those who live a life of border crossings—migrant workers, nomads, and members of the transnational business and professional elites. What is the culture of farm workers who spend half a year in Mexico and half a year in the United States? Finally, there are those who cross borders more or less permanently—immigrants, refugees, exiles, and expatriates. In their case, the disjuncture of place and culture is especially clear: Khmer refugees in the United States take "Khmer culture" with them in the same complicated way that Indian immigrants in England transport "Indian culture" to their new homeland.

The significance of transnational life and the emergence of new meanings and understandings of community offer a new way of understanding how the social and symbolic boundaries of community have changed and how they have been continuously produced, negotiated, and reframed. In 1999, in Los Angeles, I saw for the first time Yalaltec immigrants and their children representing the "Yalaltec community" in the dance and music festival of La Guelaguetza organized by ORO. Three years later, I met four second-generation Yalaltecos who had been invited by the Oaxacan government to go to Oaxaca City to dance in the festival of La Guelaguetza with the *delegación Yalalteca*.[9] According to these teenagers, the *delegación Yalalteca* (Yalaltecos from Yalálag representing the Yalaltec community in the festival) did not welcome them wholeheartedly because the Oaxacan government insisted that they be integrated into the *delegación*, and the *delegación* argued that they did not know them. According to the *delegación*, these U.S.-born Yalaltecos did not comply with procedures for group rehearsals and the strict selection process in Yalálag, and thus the dance teacher was unsure about their dancing abilities. In the end, the *delegación Yalalteca* agreed to include them because they believed it would have offended their *bi gwlash* in Los Angeles not to include their children in such an important event.

Describing these incidents is important here because they point to those characteristics that make Yalaltecos aware of their differences and similarities and of the circumstances and motivations that knit them together as a transnational community. In other words, transnational communities today are a product of cultures and identities in constant motion. That is, communities like that of the Yalálag Zapotecs are not and have not been static or entirely homogenous. After three generations of Yalaltec immigration into the United States and within Mexico, Yalaltecos have had to negotiate their differences. They have become different in terms of schooling, religious affiliations, wealth, class, expectations, and the number of languages they speak on a regular basis, among other things (see chapters 3, 4, and 5). However, they continue to identify themselves as members of the Yalaltec community, because they share a sense of historical and linguistic continuity, and a common set of cultural practices that could be said to constitute their group identity.

In looking at distinctive patterns of migrant networks, networks of migrant organizations, and migrant circuits, several scholars have called for new ways of conceptualizing different types of transnational communities. Wimmer and Glick Schiller (2002) bring attention to the use of "methodological nationalism" to characterize a transnational community in relation to a geopolitical unity. Namely, immigrants who migrate from a specific nation-state are usually identified as an immigrant community on the basis of a common origin, history, language, identity, and culture.[10] Levitt (2001b) uses the concept of transnational village to depict another variety of transnational community. According to Levitt, transnational villages function on the basis of three types of cross-border connections: rural-to-urban transnational villages (Levitt 2001a), rural-to-rural transnational villages (Adler 2004), and urban-to-urban transnational villages

(Margolis 1994). She notes that all aspects of social life in transnational communities offer immigrants the possibility of remaining active in their home communities and participating in transnational activities in the receiving locality. Besserer (2002), Kearney (2000), Stephen (2007b), and Velasco Ortiz (2005) introduce the model of a multicentered ethnic community that spans the borders of two nation-states. Immigrants and non-immigrants from the same ethnic group connect various localities in two nation-states on the basis of a shared ethnic identity, language, culture, and history, as well as common experiences of oppression and ethnic and racial discrimination in the country of emigration and immigration. They participate in cross-border projects, are minorities in the countries they come from, and become immigrant ethnic minorities in the receiving countries.[11] These groups tend to organize multiethnic transnational organizations on the basis of their indigenous ethnicity and experiences of social exclusion, exploitation, and racism (Rivera-Salgado 1999; Rivera-Salgado and Escala 2004).

One useful dimension of this classification of transnational communities for my discussion here is that Yalaltecos constitute a type of transnational village. If we consider the history of Yalaltec migration to the United States, we can trace their routes of internal and international migration across three generations (see chapter 1) and the development of Yalaltec migrant networks, circuits, and organizations that have developed in Mexico (Aquino 2010; Bertely 1996) and between Mexico and the United States (Cruz-Manjarrez 2006, 2009; Gutiérrez Nájera 2007). Likewise, we can see that Yalaltecos do not constitute an isolated indigenous immigrant community. In the United States, Yalaltecos are linked to a larger network of Oaxacan indigenous village communities and indigenous migrant organizations. Based on their experiences of ethnic and racial discrimination in Mexico and the United States, Oaxacan indigenous Mexican migrants have developed their localized or community identities into "broader Mixtec, Zapotec, and pan-ethnic Oaxacan indigenous identities" (Fox 2006, 10) with national (Hirabayashi 1993) and international migration. As a result, they have constructed a pan-ethnic sense of an indigenous Mexican identity, and formed a series of multiethnic organizations that knit them together as Oaxacan indigenous migrant communities in the United States. In California, the Yalálag Zapotec immigrants are linked to Yalaltecos in Mexico and to other Zapotec, Mixtec, Mixe, Chatino, Triqui, and Chinantec immigrants, and participate in indigenous migrant organization in the United States. Oaxacan indigenous migrants, who identify as Oaxaqueños in California, come from different regions and village communities of the state of Oaxaca in Mexico, but are all indigenous people and identify as such.

The experience of international migration in villages like those of the Yalaltecos has changed the nature, meanings, and sense of community both locally and transnationally. At present, Yalaltecos see their community spreading out in Mexico and the United States, and they experience it as a dispersed community.

Yalaltecos describe their community in terms of those who reside in Yalálag—the non-immigrants—and those who live abroad—*los migrantes*. To cope with this feeling of fragmentation, Yalaltecos are engaged in reinventing and reimaging their community in a transnational social space. Throughout this book, I use the concept of *transnational community* to describe and analyze what social, cultural, and political processes have brought Yalaltecos together between Mexico and the United States since the late 1980s. I approach the study of transnational community from a processual perspective in which the meanings of community are open to change, and under constant negotiation and continual reframing in "historical contexts of displacement" (Clifford 1994, 308).

IDENTITY AND CULTURE IN TRANSNATIONAL PERSPECTIVE

Sociologists and anthropologists who study migration agree that the formation of transnational communities is linked to the emergence of transnational identities. Castles and Miller indicate that today's "immigration may be able to make a special contribution to the development of new forms of identity. It is part of the migrant condition to develop multiple identities, which are linked to the cultures both of the homeland and of the country of origin" (1998, 296). To understand how the migration experience has contributed to forging multiple identities among transnational immigrants, several scholars have suggested that transnational identities should be conceptualized as a social process (Goldin 1999, Levitt 2001a, Waters 2001a). That is, transnational identities are characterized by their fluidity, flexibility, and changing nature. They are open to change and under constant construction and negotiation (cf. Guarnizo 1997; Hall 1998; Kondo 1990). In her book *Black Identities: West Indian Immigrants Dreams and Realities*, Mary Waters (2001a) uses the term *transnational identity* to describe the multiple identities that migrants develop in the context of immigration. In New York, for example, the black West Indian immigrants, who move back and forth between their countries of immigration and their countries of origin, have come to see themselves as black immigrants according to American racial schemes. In this sense, Vertovec (2001) reminds us that as immigrants settle in a new country, they enter a new system of ethnic and racial relations that make them redefine their identity and develop new ones.

Levitt (2001b) argues that the significance of maintaining transnational relationships and establishing themselves in a new nation-state provides immigrants with multiple memberships. Although Dominican transnational immigrants continue to see Miraflores—their community of origin—as their primary source of self-identification and to engage in transnational family connections, community development projects, and political, religious, and economic affairs, they simultaneously identify as members of a new community in the United States. In this study I adopt a similar approach to examine the impact of migration in Yalaltec identity. I argue that Yalaltec immigrants have developed a transnational identity as a result of their migration experiences and processes of acculturation into Mexican and American mainstream cultures in the United States. Yalaltec immigrants, who have been incorporated into an ethnically segmented labor market in Los Angeles, have come to see themselves as Mexican immigrants despite their historical exclusion from full membership as citizens by the Mexican state and long-standing indigenous resistance to cultural and racial identification as Mexican in the Mexican context. As we will see in chapter 4, this development has to do with the recognition and use of their citizen rights as Mexicans in the United States and the adoption of practices, behaviors, and symbols of Mexican nationalism shared with Mexican immigrants in Los Angeles and in Mexico.

Similarly, Yalaltec immigrants recognize that the fact that they have incorporated some American values and ideas into their everyday lives make them Americanized, and Yalaltecos in Yalálag realize that. When immigrants return to Yalálag, they become a target of criticism for their American manners. In *danzas chuscas* such as *Las Minifaldas*, Yalaltec dancers make fun of immigrant women and men who have changed how they view their bodies and adopted urban lifestyles, such as dressing according to Los Angeles fashion trends or having plastic surgery. As I discuss in chapter 6, behind this criticism is the recognition of changes in immigrants' behaviors, gender ideas and roles, and a critique of those who seem to dis-identify with or bring changes to their community of origin.

From an anthropological and border-studies approach, Lynn Stephen points out that in the United States, Zapotec and Mixtec immigrants, who arrived with their own ethnic, linguistic, historical, and cultural backgrounds, add new values, ideas, and practices from American society into their everyday lives, which help them define "who they are [today] and how they want to live in the future" (2007b, 6). She also observes that Mixtec and Zapotec migrants who have crossed not only regional and international borders as labor workers between Mexico and the United States but also other kinds of borders, such as ethnic, class, linguistic, cultural, colonial, and state boundaries, continue to experience ethnic and racial discrimination within the larger Mexican community in the United States.

Through this investigation of Yalaltec immigrant identities, I found that Stephen's findings resonate with some of my conclusions. The Mexican ethnic and racial relations of *Indios* (indigenous peoples) and mestizos in Mexico work transnationally and influence a socially constructed racial identity as Mexican *Indios* among Yalaltec immigrants in the United States. In other words, as indigenous Mexican migrants, Yalaltecos continue to be discriminated against by mestizo Mexican immigrants and Mexican Americans because *Indios* are not mestizos, and mestizos believe that those they identify as *Indios* are failing to progress and are racially and ethnically inferior. Yalaltecos are indeed Mexican citizens, but are not fully treated as such in Mexico because the concept of citizenship and identity in Mexico has been ideologically fused with the notion of the mestizo national community and identity.

Kearney (2000) notes that the development of transnational identities is constructed within contexts of power, inequality, and cultural differences. In his study of the identity of the Mixtec and Zapotec migrants in California, Kearney finds that Oaxacan indigenous migrants have developed a sense of peoplehood, namely, their indigenous ethnicity. In response to their experiences of ethnic and racial discrimination, exclusion, segregation, and labor exploitation in both Mexico and the United States, Oaxacan indigenous migrants have constructed a multiple identity that materializes in the form of transnational pan-Mixtec, pan-Zapotec, and pan-Oaxacan identities in California and Mexico. When transnational Oaxacan indigenous migrants organize politically in multiethnic immigrant organizations to defend their rights as migrant labor workers and create public collective cultural expressions of themselves as Oaxacan indigenous Mexican peoples in California—as I described from Yalaltecos' participation in the dance and music festival of La Guelaguetza in Los Angeles—they politicize their cultural identities and create an indigenous ethnicity as Oaxacan indigenous migrants in Mexico and the United States.

The emergence of multiple identities in transnational communities is a question not only for the immigrant generation. The new second generation has also developed a multilayered and hybrid identity, which is under constant revision, contestation, and negotiation across different kinds of ethnic, racial, linguistic, cultural, national, and state boundaries. For instance, Glick Schiller and Fouron (2001) observe that second-generation Haitians, who become involved in transnational practices, activities, and organizations in their ancestral homeland, develop a multiple sense of the self that moves between the ethnicities that are created in transnational social spaces: the Haitian American. In looking at second-generation Afro-Caribbeans, Waters (2001b) explains that while some children identify ethnically with their parents' national identity, others develop a pan-ethnic sense of identity as Caribbean or West Indian. Ueda (2002) argues that second-generation Japanese Americans reinforce a sense of Japanese identity when they learn about Japanese culture, history, and language in public schools in the United States. Smith observes that second-generation Ticuanis experience a positive image of their Mexican identity in New York as they form support groups like the Ticuani Youth Group in New York, and visit their families in Mexico. In Ticuani, the second generation finds constructive meanings of Mexicanness such as respect and pride. In New York, negative connotations and stereotypes of Mexicans such as "powerless undocumented workers and dangerous gangsters" (2002, 150) have harmful consequences for some Ticuani children. Wolf (2002) suggests that in contrast to the Filipino immigrants—who are linked to relatives in the diaspora and are "at Home" in the Philippines—second-generation Filipino youth, who may have never been in the Philippines, experience both "Home" abroad and home locally in California. Namely, second-generation Filipinos experience conflicting ideas, values, behaviors, and cultural norms regarding what it means to be a "good Filipino or Filipina" in the Philippines—"at Home"—and in the United States—the other home.

Portes and Rumbaut (2001a) propose that second-generation youth in America have developed three patterns of acculturation: dissonant, consonant, and selective acculturation. The first takes place when members of the second generation acquire English and adopt American ways, but diverge from their parents' English proficiency and Americanization. Consonant acculturation occurs when immigrants and their children become fully assimilated into the American mainstream and dis-identify with their primary ethnicity and culture. And selective acculturation, which influences the development of a transnational identity, occurs when second generations are integrated and participate in the immigrants' ethnic community and maintain their parents' language, but also integrate into the American mainstream.

In my study of the identities of the second generation, I see that there are similar experiences of identification of U.S.-born Yalaltecos with other members of the new second generation. Also, I find some parallels with the conclusions reached by Portes and Rumbaut. There are second-generation Yalaltecos who are not encouraged and are not interested in participating in Yalálag community life, and thus dis-identify with the culture of their parents and Yalaltec community (dissonant acculturation). There are also quite a few youth and children who are raised participating actively in family and community life in Los Angeles and thus identify one aspect of their identity as Yalaltec (selective assimilation). However, unlike Mexican Americans, who usually learn Spanish, the language of their parents, this generation does not learn the parents' mother tongue, Zapotec, and feels discriminated against by mestizo Mexican Americans because they look like Mexican *Indios*. As a result, the internalization of negative views and prejudices about their indigenous ethnicity, combined with the fact that second-generation Yalatecos are raised speaking Spanish and English, has had negative outcomes for them. As I argue in chapter 5, second-generation Yalaltecos have developed a multiple and hybrid identity as Oaxaqueño, Mexican American, Chicano or Chicana, and Latino or Latina, but their sense of self-identification as Yalálag Zapotecs is the weakest.

Consideration that the migration experience's influence on identity does not have the same impact on the immigrant generation and the second generation—as well as on majority and minority immigrant groups—raises a series of questions here. As ethnic immigrant minorities, how do Yalaltec immigrants and their children experience their multiple identities and integration into the United States? How do they see themselves ethnically and racially according to American and Mexican ethnic and racial schemes? And how do Yalaltec immigrants, non-immigrants, and the second-generation Yalaltecos see each other? These are some of the questions I explore in this book.

To bring the significance of culture in action in the context of migrant transnationalism into this discussion, I find that the concept of cultural performance can shed light on the centrality of dance in transnational communities like that of the Yalálag Zapotecs. MacAloon conceptualizes cultural performances as "more than entertainment, more than didactic or persuasive formulations . . . they are occasions in which as a culture or society we reflect upon and define ourselves with alternatives, and eventually change in some ways while remaining the same in others" (1984, 1). Here I adopt an explanation similar to that of MacAloon, seeing ritual and *chusca* dances as a process through which Yalaltec immigrants and non-immigrants stage issues that are currently of great importance and concern for their community: the rapid and profound changes affecting their group identity and culture. Yalaltecos recognize that due to various decades of out-migration, Yalálag and its culture have changed, and that they are experiencing an increasing sense of cultural differentiation as a community. Also, they are aware that religious beliefs associated with the performance of ritual dances are changing in Yalálag and Los Angeles, as well. In Yalálag, old people say that younger generations do not understand the "original" meanings of ritual dances. In Los Angeles, Yalaltec immigrants, who perform ritual dances for Yalálag patron saints, are aware that they give new meanings to the very same dances and perform them in the *bailes* for new purposes: to encourage Yalaltecos born in the United States to participate in community events and teach them something about their culture (see chapter 7). This idea coincides with that of Thompson, that performances are always under constant revision and construction. When performers become aware that their rituals or religious practices "are static . . . or become obsolete, empty of meaning, or eventually die out" (1992, 8), performers change these practices to give them new meanings. Because cultural performance is not a fixed and predetermined entity, a processual approach to cultural performance allows for an understanding that cultural practices are constantly changing and are historically situated in specific time and space.

When I began this research, the performance of *chusca* dances drew me into thinking about the impact of migration on identity. Yalaltecos reflect deeply on the changes that migration has brought to their group identity, and they tend to portray these transformations in jokes and new *chusca* dances. In Yalálag, *chusca* dancers use humorous representation of those immigrants who have changed how they dress, speak, and think. In Los Angeles, *chusca* dancers make fun of their undocumented status and sense of Mexicanness, and lampoon those immigrants who have become "Americanized." To understand this capacity for self-reflection among Yalaltecos, I find that the theatrical concept of the "estrangement effect," explored by playwright and director Bertolt Brecht, may help us to explain what is at stake in *chusca* dances (see chapter 6). Today in Los Angeles and in Yalálag,

Yalaltecos have great concerns about the future of their community. Many of them feel that they will be unable to remain as a differentiated community, due to migration and social pressures to assimilate to Mexican and American hegemonic cultures. As I discuss throughout this book, migration has been a key factor for the Yalaltec community's dispersion and sense of fragmentation; however, transnationalism provides Yalaltec immigrants, non-immigrants, and their children with social, economic, and cultural strategies to organize locally in Los Angeles and transnationally between Los Angeles and Yalálag. This book explores how transnationalism has taken place and describes the impact of migration on Yalaltec identity and culture in the context of transnational migration.

STRUCTURE OF THIS BOOK

This book examines the impact of migration on Yalálag Zapotec community, identity, and culture both in Yalálag and Los Angeles. In chapter 1, "The Yalálag Zapotecs: A Town of Immigrants," I use an ethnographic approach to examine the history of Yalaltec migration into the United States. I describe when, how, and why Yalaltec men and women came to California, based on life-history narratives over five decades of migration into California. Individual and family experiences of Yalaltecos who started the first and subsequent waves of migration into Los Angeles reveal a distinctive pattern of migration, settlement, and community formation in the United States.

In chapter 2, "Building Community and Connections in Los Angeles," I analyze the social and symbolic processes related to border-crossing activities and maintaining homeland ties that inform community formation and the imagination of the Yalálag Zapotec immigrant community of Los Angeles and the transnationalization of cultural practices and native forms of social organization. I discuss how the reconfiguration of practices of membership such as the *gwzon* system of reciprocal aid, community service, and communal participation are forms of social capital that contribute to maintaining community and group identity in transnational settings.

In chapter 3, "Community Life across Borders," I analyze immigrants' participation in the social and religious life of the community of origin in Yalálag. I focus special attention on the village patron saint fiesta of San Antonio de Padua to explore the politics of immigrants' participation and reintegration in the community of origin. Also, I discuss the negative effects of the migration experience in the community of origin in Yalálag, such as social inequality between immigrants and non-immigrants, the introduction of Los Angeles gang culture via migration, and family disintegration.

Chapter 4, "Yalálag Zapotec Identities in a Changing World," investigates how transnational settings and dynamics of migration affect and shape the construction of ethnic, racial, and class identity among Yalálag Zapotec immigrants. I describe why they have come to think of themselves in the United States as Mexican, Indios, indigenous Mexican immigrants, Oaxaqueños, and Latinos. In addition, I discuss why Yalaltecos experience a dual pattern of assimilation into Mexican and American cultures in the United States. I examine why, despite former and present experiences of ethnic and racial discrimination in Mexico, Yalaltecos assert Mexican identification in the United States and adopt behaviors, ideas, and cultural practices from the Mexican mainstream. Finally, I explore the Yalaltecs' ideas, sentiments, and practices that, they confess, make them American.

Chapter 5, "Identities of the Second-Generation Yalálag Zapotecs," covers identity formation of U.S.-born Yalaltecos. I examine the second generation's perceptions of their ethnic, national, indigenous, and socially constructed sense of racial identities. I investigate how and why this generation has developed a strong sense of identity as Mexican American while, at the same time, their sense of identity as Yalálag Zapotec has weakened.

In chapter 6, "*Danzas Chuscas*: Performing Status, Violence, and Gender in Oaxacalifornia," I examine the impact of migration and social remittances on Yalaltec identity, gender, class, and community through an analysis of three parodic dances: *Los Yalaltecos* ("The residents of Yalálag"), *Los Cholos* ("The gangsters"), and *Las Minifaldas* ("Miniskirts"). I explore why Yalaltec non-immigrants have made returning and visiting migrants the subject of these and other *chusca* dances, discussing the significance of using Yalálag Zapotec parodic dances and music to lampoon those who have adopted "American" behaviors or those who have remitted negative values from the inner-city neighborhoods of Los Angeles to Yalálag.

In chapter 7, "Community and Culture in Transnational Perspective," I analyze the performance of Yalaltec identity and changes in the cultural practices of Yalálag Zapotecs within the context of transnational migration. Through a comparative analysis of *Los Huenches* (The dance of our ancestors), I scrutinize the role of cultural performances in the migration experience at the individual and community level. I discuss the relocation and resignification of this cultural practice in Yalálag and in Los Angeles. I suggest that the relocation of this dance embodies struggles over maintaining the community and the reinvention of tradition as these processes generate group identity and shape the social boundaries of community. Further, I argue that contemporary performances of *Los Huenches* in transnational settings incorporate and present the impact of migration in the social lives of Yalaltec immigrants and non-immigrants, while simultaneously continuing the historic purpose of enacting Zapotec religiosity and an expression of hybrid cultural practices that characterize the Yalálag Zapotec culture and identity.

I devote the final chapter of this book to the conclusions. I present a summary of my findings and a discussion of their implications for thinking about the future of the Yalálag Zapotec community in Yalálag and Los Angeles.

❦

CHAPTER 1

THE YALÁLAG ZAPOTECS

A TOWN OF IMMIGRANTS

Zapotec migration into the United States is not a new phenomenon. It started in the first half of the twentieth century and continues until now. In Los Angeles, the Zapotec community is composed of various Zapotec immigrant village communities from the Central Valleys and the Sierra Norte and the Sierra Sur of the state of Oaxaca. This migration includes the earliest immigrants and their U.S.-born children, in addition to recent immigrants with native-born or foreign-born descendants. Yalálag Zapotec migration in California is part of this migratory population movement and reflects its own history and patterns of migration and settlement in Los Angeles.[1] In the early 1940s, the Yalaltecos began to migrate to northern California and then gradually settled in southern California over the past four decades. Currently, the majority of the Yalaltec immigrants live in Los Angeles and, along with their children, they may number more than those living in their village community in Yalálag.

To understand five decades of Yalaltec migration and settlement in the United States, it is important to consider the following facts. Better job opportunities and more attractive wages elsewhere, coupled with Yalálag's high levels of unemployment, poverty, scarce social services and education programs, and inadequate medical services have encouraged Yalaltecos to immigrate within Mexico and to the United States. This migration movement cannot be described as a one-way, direct, and homogeneous process. Some Yalaltecos came to Los Angeles from Yalálag, others from Oaxaca City, while others hailed from Mexico City. This migration comprises a mix of three generations—the *bracero* generation, the children of the *bracero* immigrants, and the *braceros'* grandchildren. This chapter uses an ethnographic approach to examine the history of Yalaltec migration into the United States. By using life-history narratives throughout five decades of international migration, I describe when, how, and why Yalaltec men and women have come to California. Individual and family experiences of Yalaltecos who started the first and subsequent waves of migration into Los Angeles reveal a distinctive trajectory of migration, permanent settlement, and community formation in the United States.[2]

THE PIONEERS: FROM SEASONAL MIGRATION TO PERMANENT SETTLEMENT IN LOS ANGELES

Yalaltec migration into the United States began in the mid-1940s, when a group of American contractors were recruiting impoverished male peasants in Oaxaca City to work in the *Bracero* Program as farm laborers on short-term contracts in northern California (de la Fuente 1949, 35).[3] The program continued until the mid-1960s, and today, a few Yalaltec men in their late seventies and eighties remember their teens, twenties, and thirties as the time when they left Yalálag to work in the California fields as *braceros*. Some of these *braceros* remember that they were employed in Oaxaca City when they were teenagers as domestic workers when they learned about the opportunity to go work in the United States. Others recall being young adults who worked in their corn and coffee fields in Yalálag when their *bi gwlash* (countrymen) who returned from Oaxaca City to Yalálag invited them to go to work in California. Some Yalaltec men and women who are now in their late forties and fifties have memories of their fathers and grandfathers working as *braceros* in California.

Segismundo Molina, who went to northern California to work as a *bracero*, remembers that Yalaltec migration started in the fields of northern California in 1945 with Benito Mecinas, Antonio Fabian, Rubén Fabian, and Pedro Ríos. Cándido Primo, an eighty-one-year-old man who now lives in Yalálag recalls that in the early 1960s, he went to Stockton and Trinidad, California, with two friends to work legally (see fig. 1.1).

In those years, Cándido was married and had one daughter. His plans were to go to the United States to make money to build his house and buy his own land and cattle. As he explains:

> C: In 1960, when I was selling coffee and clothes in the Mixe region, I heard that a group of American contractors was in Oaxaca City again, hiring peasants to work in California. When I returned to Yalálag, I asked my friends Jovillo and Juventino Maldonado if they wanted to go to California. We were a little bit scared of leaving Yalálag because we heard things about World War II. Despite this, we decided to go together. Then, we visited the municipal authorities and asked them for our birth certificates. That was the only requirement we needed to get our contracts as *braceros*. Then, we went to Oaxaca City and from there to Mexico City. I remember that when we arrived at the train station in Mexico City, there were lots of people from all over Mexico who were enlisted in the *Bracero* Program. Among them there were many *bi gwlash* from other Zapotec village communities of the Sierra. When we arrived in Mexicali, the American contractors

Figure 1.1. Cándido Primo,
Yalálag, 2004.

divided all Mexicans into groups and sent us to different places. Jovillo,
Juventino, and I went to Stockton. Other *bi gwlash* went to Sonorita, Texas,
and some to Merced, Salinas, and Woodland in California.

A: How old were you?

C: I was thirty years old. I think that Juventino was about my age and Jovillo
was about fifteen years old. Juventino and I spoke Spanish, but Jovillo did
not. That was hard for him.[4] I learned Spanish in Oaxaca when my father
sent me to work as a *sirviente* (domestic worker). When we arrived in
Stockton, the *mayordomo* (foreman) could not communicate with Jovillo.
The *mayordomo* always laughed at him and asked me to translate. To tell the
truth, it was difficult to decide to go California. Although we knew the kind
of work we were supposed to do, we did not know exactly where we were
heading. When you have a family, it is difficult to leave them behind. I had
my wife and a daughter. I always thought of the hardships they might face
if I did not come back. During those days, one of our *bi gwlash* died in a car
accident in California. That was terrible for his family.

A: Why did you join the *Bracero* Program?

C: My wife, my daughter, and I lived with my parents. My father used to tell me
that I needed to have my own house like any other married man in the village.

Then I thought, "I am going to build a house for my family. I will buy land and have my own little animals." So I went to *El Norte* [the United States]. When I was in Stockton, I worked picking asparagus. We worked from 6:00 a.m. to 7:00 p.m. In those days, the American contractors paid me one Mexican peso each hour. One day, the work ended, but the labor contractors told us that there were lots of jobs in Trinidad. Jovillo and I went together, and Juventino went back to Yalálag. We worked in Trinidad four and a half months picking tomatoes. When there was no more work, the contractors took us to Tijuana. From there, we took the train to Oaxaca, and then a bus to Tlacolula. After that, we walked a day and a half to get to Yalálag. With the money I earned in California, I built this house, bought land, and cattle.

A: Did you go back to California afterwards?

C: No, I did not. When we first went to *El Norte* I was hired. But after those days, there were no more contracts. If you wanted to go to *El Norte* to work, you had to go *contrabando* (without papers) and with the help of the *coyotes* (smugglers). That was very risky. I did not want to worry my family. Some *bi gwlash* did go.

After the *Bracero* Program ended (1964), some Yalaltec men like Cándido returned to Yalálag. Others overstayed their work permits to continue working as farm workers, and about three Yalaltec men moved to the city of Los Angeles to work in the service sector.[5] According to Segismundo Molina, Genaro Vargas, a *bracero*, returned from California to Yalálag in 1960s with an invitation to help Segismundo secure a contract in the *Bracero* Program. In 1960, Segismundo was hired to work in Sonorita, Texas. Between 1961 and 1964, he worked in Merced, Woodland, and Salinas in California. By the end of 1964, when the *Bracero* Program ended, Segismundo decided to move to Los Angeles, where Genaro Vargas was already living with his wife. Segismundo went to Los Angeles because he did not want to work in the countryside. Returning to Oaxaca was not an option for him. In February of 1965, with the help of his friend Genaro, Segismundo found a job as a concierge in downtown Los Angeles. In 1972, when he was economically stable, he sent for his wife and five children, who were immigrants in Oaxaca City at the time:

S: In 1963, I got my green card when the American contractors hired me to go to Salinas. But to tell you the truth, I never liked working in the country-side. So, I began to think that I would go to Los Angeles where my friend Genaro Vargas was living. So, I went to Los Angeles and asked him to help me find a job. Thanks to him, I found a job as a concierge in downtown Los Angeles. In those years, it was very difficult to find a job, particularly, if you did not know anyone. For me, it was even more difficult because I did not want to be a cook or dishwasher. So, I was very lucky that Genaro knew the owner of the building where I worked for thirty-one years.

A: How is it that your wife arrived in Los Angeles?

S: Well, in those days, she was in Oaxaca City with my children. When I became stable economically, I brought her and my children. That was in 1972. When we married in Yalálag, we decided that I would go first to California and then come back to Oaxaca at least once a year to visit her. In Oaxaca, we had our five children and began to build our house. One day, when I returned to Oaxaca, I just told Aida (his wife) that I wanted to have our family together in Los Angeles. We moved with our children to Los Angeles.

California Yalálag Zapotec b*racero* life-history narratives like those of Cándido and Segismundo not only illustrate significant differences in immigrants' plans and individual expectations after the *Bracero* Program ended but they also help to trace the economic causes of migration and changes in the migration patterns of the Yalaltec people who are immigrants in the United States or in diverse regions in Mexico. In the United States, while a few Yalaltec men moved from rural California to Los Angeles, others were returning to Yalálag. In Mexico, while some young Yalaltec men and women were migrating from Yalálag to Mexico City, Oaxaca City, Tlacolula, Morelos, and Veracruz (de la Fuente 1949), others were moving from Mexico City and Oaxaca City to Los Angeles.[6] Some of these immigrants did so to reunite with their families, as in the case of Segismundo, whereas others joined or followed their relatives or Yalaltec friends (Bertely 1996). For example, Elodia was born in 1947, in Yalálag. At the age of twelve, she moved with her parents to Oaxaca City to study and work. A year later, she settled in the *Colonia Roma* in Mexico City, where her older cousins were already working in the service sector. Elodia remembers completing middle school in Mexico City. She worked as a domestic worker to support herself. She also sent remittances to her family in Yalálag and was "enticed" to follow her cousins to Los Angeles. As she recalls:

E: In 1966, when I was nineteen years old, my cousins Emilia and Octavio invited me to go to Los Angeles. Octavio used to say that he was unsatisfied with life in Mexico. He was tired of being poor. So, he learned English, saved money, and went by himself to Los Angeles. At that time, Octavio was doing well with his new job and invited Emilia to come. When Emilia arrived in Los Angeles, she found a job as a domestic worker with Octavio's help. When she returned to visit me about six months later, she persuaded me to join them. When I saw that she had money, a radio, and new clothes, and made more money than what we made together in Mexico City, I decided to follow her. To get to Los Angeles, we had to follow Octavio's recommendations. We took the train to Tijuana, and then got our passports to cross the U.S. border legally. In those days, it was easy to get those passports. I was not required to have a visa. The only thing we were required to do was to go from Los Angeles to Tijuana every two weeks to get our passports stamped. Otherwise, we would be illegal in this country and we preferred not to be. But when President Nixon suspended those local passports, we stayed, working illegally in Los Angeles.

A: So what did you do when you arrived in Los Angeles?

E: Emilia helped me to find a live-in job through her boss. I worked with an American family for six years. They were good people. They paid me $US 110.00 every month and gave me a day off. That was a lot of money. In fact, I should also mention that I got my green card with the help of Mrs. Smith [her employer]. To tell the truth, at that time, I didn't have plans to stay in the United States because I was hoping to save more money and return to Mexico with my family. But, as the years went by I became focused on getting my green card. So, I asked Mrs. Smith to help me fill out my application for my green card, and she requested that the immigration office allow me to work as her domestic worker.

Various scholars have documented that once immigrants begin to settle in a new country, they create social networks and social relationships that further their permanent settlement in the country of immigration and increase the possibility of the arrival of newcomers (Hondagneu-Sotelo 1994; Massey, Goldring, and Duran 1994). Both the Yalaltec *braceros,* who settled in California, and the women and men who began to follow the path of their relatives, siblings, or partners in the late 1960s played a key role in setting down roots and establishing Yalaltec migration routes into Los Angeles. These pioneers provided social and financial resources for the arrival of newcomers. According to Elodia, in the late 1960s, Leo Diaz Molina, Marcela Ríos, Nereo Poblano, Maria and GenaroVargas, who helped Segismundo to migrate, and Jose Allende were already living in Los Angeles. They helped friends and relatives in Yalálag to migrate to the United States. In 1967, Elodia arrived in Los Angeles with the help of her cousins. When Elodia decided to stay in California, she opted for U.S. permanent residency, since her employer encouraged her to do so and supported Elodia's hire. In 1969, when Elodia acquired U.S. residency status, she helped two of her younger siblings to come work in Los Angeles. According to Elodia, the economic hardship in Yalálag and her desire for her siblings to improve their quality of life were important reasons in her decision to help them migrate. Elodia also supported her siblings because she felt alone.

The life stories of Yalaltec immigrants like those of Cándido, Elodia, and Segismundo are framed by the history of U.S. migration policies. In 1942, the *Bracero* Program began as a temporary measure to relieve wartime labor shortages. In 1964, it ended, under the pressure of civil rights and domestic farm workers' organizations that claimed that the program undermined their well-being and labor conditions. However, until 1968, various U.S. employers in commercial agriculture in California sponsored the legalization of hundreds of Mexican farm workers under "the liberal provisions of U.S. immigration laws that prevailed until the Hart-Celler Act took place" (Cerruti and Massey 2006, 41). Changes in the 1965 Immigration and Nationality Act brought about new restrictions in the quota system for countries in Africa, Europe, Asia, and the Caribbean of up to 20,000 visas per year. Although Mexico faced tightening of legal migration, the United States experienced an increase in undocumented Mexican migration (Tienda 1989). Between the late 1960s and mid-1970s, U.S. employers, like those of Elodia and Segismundo, sponsored legal immigration of their employees. In the early 1970s, some of these first U.S. residents covered migration costs to Los Angeles for their relatives and friends. The stories of Cándido, Elodia, and Segismundo illustrate these dynamics as well as changes from rural to urban migration of Yalaltecos in California. They also point to the first patterns of urban settlement of Yalálag Zapotecs in Los Angeles and tell us about the Yalaltecos' migration movements within Mexico and the different migratory routes that brought them into California. Contrary to the idea that Yalaltec men were the first international migrants, the experience of Elodia, Genaro Vargas's wife, and Segismundo's spouse shows that since the late 1960s, Yalaltec women were gradually incorporated into this international migration stream.[7]

SINGLE WOMEN AND MEN, AND YOUNG MARRIED COUPLES, ESTABLISH THEMSELVES IN LOS ANGELES

The 1970s mark a new era in the history of Yalaltec migration into the United States: the descendants of the *bracero* generation constituted the majority of the Yalaltec immigrant population arriving in Los Angeles. They came not only from Yalálag but also from the Tlacolula District in Oaxaca, Oaxaca City, and Mexico City. These Yalaltecos were mostly young single men and women, and a few young married couples who left Yalálag in search of work, education, and a higher standard of living. At present, many of them are in their fifties and early sixties. They describe their childhoods in Yalálag and their youth or first years of marriage spent in diverse areas of Oaxaca and Mexico City, and then in Los Angeles. For example, at the age of six, after the death of his father, Mario migrated with his mother and eight siblings from Yalálag to Tlacolula, a Zapotec village community located between the Central Valleys and the Sierra Norte of Oaxaca. In 1971, when Mario was seventeen years old and finishing high school, he migrated to Los Angeles at the invitation of his teenage friends from Tlacolula, who had just returned to the village fiesta from Los Angeles. Despite the fact that Mario's mother forbade him to migrate, with a few hundred pesos in his pocket and the help of a Tlacolula *coyote,* Mario arrived in Los Angeles with the promise and hope of finding a job and having a place to stay.[8] As he recounts:

> I left in 1971. On a late Sunday evening, when one of my friends told me that he was leaving the next day to Los Angeles, I told him that I wanted to go, too. He asked me if I had money, and of course, I did not. My family was very poor. I

began to work at the age of eight to help my mother support our family. One day, I told my mother that I wanted to go to Los Angeles. I asked her if she could lend me some money, but she did not want me to go to California. Then, I visited a friend of mine. He lent me money to migrate. In those days, I wanted to do something . . . help my family, work hard, have money. I did not want to fail my mother, myself. She worked very hard. We were nine children. Imagine that! When I saw that my friends had money and were helping their families in Tlacolula, I thought I should do the same thing. You know, when you are young, you have dreams . . . you want to do big things in life for you and your family. In Oaxaca, there were no opportunities and life was and is still very hard. That is why I migrated. I can tell you that my mother is now very proud of me.

Mario is now a very prominent and well-off Yalaltec immigrant. Upon his arrival in Los Angeles, he began to work as a cook and went to school to learn how to manufacture security boxes and water vending machines. Over the years, he made money installing telephone security systems and the first water vending machines in Los Angeles. After that, he began to invest in private property. Currently, he owns a few residential apartments and rents them out.

While Yalaltec men like Mario went to Los Angeles with friends from Tlacolula who had previous migration experience into the United States, other Yalaltec women and men came from Mexico City. At the age of eight, Ruben and his older sister, Dora, went to Mexico City to live with their cousins after their mother died; their father had also passed away. According to Ruben, they belonged to a poor peasant family that lacked money to pay for food or education, and their relatives were also poor. They had to migrate to Mexico City because they were the eldest siblings in the family, and Dora had to financially support their younger siblings in Yalálag. In 1974, when Dora was seventeen years old, she married a Yalalteco in Mexico City, and she and her husband decided to migrate to Los Angeles. One day, when Ruben returned from work, Dora asked Ruben whether he wanted to follow her and her husband to *El Norte* or stay in Mexico with their cousins. As he describes:

> Dora got married the same year I came to the United States. One day, she said to me: "It could be great for you and me if you join me and my husband in Los Angeles. From Los Angeles, we could help our younger siblings to come to Mexico City and support them in getting professional careers." Look, when I was a little boy, I began to work in a barbershop to help Dora pay for the expenses of my siblings who remained in Yalálag. In those days, we were the oldest siblings in the family and had a lot of responsibilities. Our younger siblings depended on us. In those days, I used to make thirty pesos a day and a little bit more with my tips. That was not a lot of money, but somehow I could help my sister. When I was sixteen years old, I began to sell newspapers and then encyclopedias to support Dora. As you know, there is never enough

money. That is why I decided to leave Mexico City with Dora and her husband. My brother-in-law had two cousins in Los Angeles and they lent him money for our trip. As soon as we got the money to pay the *coyote,* we left the city.

Today, Ruben has brothers and sisters living in Mexico City. Thanks to Dora and Ruben's economic support, they have degrees in social work, education, literature, and early childhood education. In Mexico City in the 1970s, most Yalaltec immigrant men worked in factories, while women were employed as domestic workers. Many went to work to support their families in Yalálag, and some went to work to support their own studies.

Yalaltec migration into Los Angeles in the early 1970s consisted of two distinct groups of immigrants. The first was made up of young Yalaltec immigrant men and women who left Yalálag and went to Mexico City and Oaxaca City, and then to Los Angeles. The second group was composed of a few married women who followed their husbands who worked as *braceros* in California. In both countries, these Yalaltec immigrants were domestic workers and service and manufacturing laborers. According to Ruben, by the mid-1970s, more than thirty people from Yalálag resided in Los Angeles. Although most of them were young single men and women who migrated to Los Angeles with the help of close relatives such as siblings, cousins, nephews, aunts, or uncles, there were also Yalaltecos who arrived in Los Angeles with the help of Yalaltec friends. Susana, who married Ruben in 1979, came to Los Angeles in 1973 with the help of a Yalaltec girlfriend, whose sister was married to a Yalaltec *bracero.*

In 1972, when Susana was in Mexico City working as a domestic worker to support her mother to raise her younger siblings in Yalálag, she received a letter of invitation from a girlfriend to go to Los Angeles. This girlfriend, who at the time of the invitation was living in Oaxaca City, told Susana that she would meet her in Yalálag on the day of the fiesta of San Antonio de Padua. While Susana was visiting her mother in Yalálag during this fiesta, she met her girlfriend and told her that she would go to Los Angeles without telling her family, since she was a minor. She was convinced that she could earn more money in Los Angeles than in Mexico City, doing the same job. When Susana got to California, she wrote a letter to her mother to apologize for not telling her about her decision to go to California. In that letter, Susana told her mother that she was fine. She was living with a family of *bi gwlash* in Los Angeles. She also explained that her *bi gwlash* had helped her find a job as a domestic worker, lent her money to cross the border, and provided low-cost room and board.

This period of Yalaltec migration into the United States saw the creation and maturation of migrant networks among Yalaltec families and friends in Oaxaca, Mexico City, and Los Angeles, with three significant outcomes. First, through migrant networks, new Yalaltec women and men received help to migrate. They settled and found jobs in the service and domestic sectors in Los Angeles. Second, through friendship and kinship relationships, these young Yalaltecos developed strong ties of reciprocity and social solidarity. Third, because many of these young immigrants were single and tended to socialize within their own ethnic group, they began to marry among themselves (cf. Hondagneu-Sotelo 1994; Massey et al. 1987). During the course of my research, of the thirty-six immigrants I interviewed, eleven had married a Yalaltec immigrant in Los Angeles in the 1970s.

A few Yalaltec men and women who arrived in the mid-1970s were between the ages of fifteen and twenty-one. As they began to connect with each other, some of them became close friends and supported each other, while others married and formed their own families, like Elodia, Susana, and Ruben.[9] Although they had never thought of getting married in the United States and had intended to work for a short time in California, they stayed longer because their lives became tied to their new way of life, jobs, and families. In the following excerpt, Ruben describes what changed his decision to go back to Mexico:

> When our first child was born, everything changed. You no longer think about yourself but acquire a lot of new responsibilities. You begin to look after the well-being of your own family. When they're born, you begin to have big plans for them and invest a lot of money in their health and education. When my children were born, I promised myself to work hard to give them a professional career. Now, one of my daughters is a designer; the other is a professional nurse. When my two older daughters were born, we were illegal immigrants. We had to work hard to provide them with everything they needed. Those days were difficult. First of all, we had to secure our jobs. Secondly, we had to deal with the *migra* [INS]. They were after all illegal immigrants. Just like today. In that situation and with children, you don't want to risk your family. Based on our own history, Susana and I knew that we could not give our children a good life in Mexico. There is a lot of poverty there. You don't have the same opportunities you have in America. Although I have worked as a cook and my wife was a domestic worker for thirty years, we have been able to give our children a better life, with education above all.

Like family formation, family stage migration has specific outcomes during the settlement process and the continuation of Yalaltec migration into the United States.[10] Some of the first young married men and women arrived in Los Angeles together from Yalálag, Oaxaca City, or Mexico City in the early 1970s. A few others came in stages. In 1973, for example, Eréndira immigrated along with one of her brothers-in-law and a cousin-in-law, crossing at Tijuana without a visa. Her husband Miguel stayed behind for a year. When she got to Los Angeles, Eréndira lived with Miguel's oldest brother. During her first weeks in Los Angeles, she found a job as a domestic worker with the help of her brother-in-law. Meanwhile, in Mexico City, Miguel quit his job in an American food factory, General Foods, and went back to Yalálag to inform his parents that Eréndira and his brother were already in Los Angeles and that he was migrating, too. As he recounts:

> In 1973 my brother Raúl was deported from Chicago. When he got back to Mexico City, he came to live with our nephews and my wife Eréndira and me. But since he didn't find his way in Mexico, he told me that he was going back to the United States. One day, he asked me: "What are we doing here? Let's go together." At that time, Eréndira and I were really young and did not have children. And you know, when you're young, you like to try new things and explore new horizons. Then, I asked Eréndira if she wanted to go, and she said yes. But because we were in Mexico City and my parents were in Yalálag, I had to leave a year later. So, I went to Yalálag and let my parents know that we were heading to Los Angeles. Look, in the late 1970s, a lot of young Yalalte-cos came to Los Angeles. We did so because the *braceros,* including my father, had returned to Yalálag with lots of money. The dollar was about 12.50 pesos. That was a lot of money. When the *bi gwlash* came to visit their families from Los Angeles, they had money, new clothes . . . so many things. All the time, they were showing off; that encouraged impoverished young Yalaltec men and women to go to the United States.

From the late 1970s to the mid-1980s, the patterns of Yalaltec migration and the spatial mobility of the Yalaltec emigrants became more dynamic and diverse. Some young Yalaltec single men and women and married men moved back and forth between Yalálag and Mexico City or between Yalálag and Oaxaca City. Others began to migrate directly to Los Angeles and visited their families in Yalálag only occasionally, due to their undocumented status. Some went to Los Angeles and returned to Yalálag until they were granted amnesty in 1986. And others left Yalálag, went temporarily to Mexico City, then to Los Angeles, and after that back to Yalálag. For example, in the late 1960s, Sandra went to Mexico City to work as a domestic worker to pay for her middle school studies and support her parents in Yalálag. In 1971, when she was twenty-four years old, she followed the path of an older brother who lived in Los Angeles, but a year later she decided to return to Yalálag because she did not like the United States. By 1975, Sandra went back again to Mexico City to pursue high school and then a B.A. degree in social work at UNAM (National Autonomous University of Mexico). In early 1983, when she was working as a social worker in Mexico City, she received a phone call from a group of *bi gwlash* in Yalálag who asked her to come back to support the Communitarian Group project (see chapter 3), and she returned permanently to Yalálag.

The story of Sandra's migration is important here because it is representative of three significant changes in the patterns of Yalaltec migration between the 1970s and the 1980s. First, there was a high level of mobility for quite a few young Yalaltec men and women who migrated between Mexico and the United States, and within Mexico and the United States. Second, a few Yalaltec immigrants who came to Los Angeles returned to Yalálag to reunite with their families. And third, young single women increasingly integrated into the international migration process with financing from relatives in the United States for their trip. This last finding coincides with that of Cerrutti and Massey (2006). They point out that throughout the 1970s, Mexican migration into the United States was largely composed of young women whose fathers, husbands, or older brothers came illegally to the United States, with some eventually obtaining U.S. residency and sponsoring the women's trips.

During the 1970s and 1980s, the trend of teenage girls and single women migrating to Los Angeles and settling there grew into an established model of migration. The number of women, who desired to economically support their parents and aspired to become independent, rose significantly. At the age of sixteen, for example, Ursula left Yalálag forever. She migrated to Mexico City because she was ill and had to undergo surgery.[11] During her recovery, she lived with one of her married sisters. Thereafter, she began to work with one of them as a seamstress and sent money to their parents. When Ursula was nineteen years old, she left Mexico City for Los Angeles with the help of a Yalaltec girlfriend. By 1985, Ursula decided to stay in the United States because her labor contractor encouraged and helped her obtain U.S. residency status. As she recalls:

> In the year of 1978, on one of my visits to Yalálag, I told my parents that I wanted to go to Los Angeles. With tears in his eyes, my father told me that despite our poverty, he did not want me to go. My father knew about the difficulties of being an immigrant because he was a *bracero*. He told me that working legally was not the same as working without papers. When he went to California, he went legally. But, because I wasn't going legally and I was a young single woman, he didn't want me to go. I told him that I wanted to go and work to help him economically. I explained to him that I wanted to have my own house and did not want to marry. He was very mad at me. I came to Los Angeles without his permission. In 1985, I went back to Yalálag thinking that it was time to return home. I had enough savings and wanted to be with my family. But to tell you the truth, I didn't feel happy upon my return. I felt that my life had changed in Los Angeles. I became more independent and had my own job. It was very difficult to deal with my father. He became very controlling and authoritarian. Then I thought, "I'm going back to Los Angeles."

Ursula's story of migration to Mexico City and into the United States is representative of two facts. First, some Yalaltecos have migrated temporarily or permanently to Oaxaca City or Mexico City for health reasons. Second, most young single Yalaltec immigrant women who want to become economically independent also move away to avoid family control. Ursula explained to me that upon her return, she was not allowed to go out and visit friends. She even recalled that her father wanted her to wed according to the tradition of arranged marriage. Because Ursula disagreed with her father's ideas about marriage and had different dreams, plans, and money, she went back to Los Angeles. Up until now, working as a domestic worker and babysitter has allowed Ursula to become economically independent and self-sufficient.

In the early 1970s, Mexico experienced economic growth as a result of the oil boom and industrial and manufacturing expansion. The Mexican government promoted large-scale commercial agriculture and favored large producers instead of traditional farmers. Export agriculture provided foreign revenues to finance Mexico's industrialization. In the mid-1970s, however, Mexico entered a financial crisis due to the drop in oil prices worldwide. As a result, Mexico increased its foreign debt and became a net food importer. In 1982, President López Portillo devaluated the peso, and Mexico began to pay high interest rates on its foreign loans. As a result, the Mexican economy contracted, and the livelihoods of thousands of peasant and working-class families across the country were hit. By the mid-1980s, the urban minimum wage fell by 47 percent. As a result, undocumented migration from Mexico into the United States increased to over 1.8 million (Cerrutti and Massey 2004). By contrast, throughout the 1970s, "the dislocations and transformations of the U.S. economy affected the average U.S. workers' standard of living. Wages and salaries fell from 10 percent from 1973 to 1985" (Calavita 1989, 161). While the manufacturing sector contracted, commercial agriculture and the service sector expanded, and a new type of job in the secondary labor market emerged. Between 1970 and 1980, the largest share of low-income and unskilled workers in the United States came from rural areas of Mexico, such as Oaxaca. In California, a great number of *mestizo* and indigenous Mexican migrants went to work in commercial agriculture, and others went into the manufacturing and service industries (Cornelius 1989).

The Rise of (Un)documented Migration and Family Formation

In sharp contrast to the temporary migrant men of the *bracero* era, most of the Yalaltec immigrant men and women who arrived in the 1970s and early 1980s were determined to settle in the United States. One reason for this was family formation and the birth of Yalaltec children in the United Sates. Another reason was family reunification (Chavez 1985; Hondagneu-Sotelo 1994; Massey et al. 1987). And a third, and perhaps most important, reason was the 1986 amnesty for undocumented immigrants. In 1986, the U.S. Congress passed the Immigration Reform and Control Act (IRCA) to legalize the status of illegal "aliens" and to stop the rise of undocumented migration into the United States. As part of this program, the U.S. Congress made a few changes in the annual quotas for immigrants from Cuba and Haiti and underrepresented countries. This created a law that sanctioned employers who hired unauthorized immigrants. That year, it was estimated that about five million undocumented immigrants were in the United States (Ueda 1994), including many Yalaltecos who arrived between the late 1960s and early 1980s. When the U.S. Congress launched amnesty for unauthorized immigrants, the majority of the Yalaltec immigrants I interviewed applied for the legalization and regularization of their migratory status. David, who migrated in the early 1970s, worked without legal authorization in the agricultural fields of northern California. He gained permanent residency through the amnesty program and brought his wife and children from Yalálag under the "family-based" class preference—immigrants reuniting with their families. Rodrigo, who arrived in 1986, secured amnesty when he left Los Angeles to work in Stockton, California, as a farm worker, and his contractor provided him with a letter to apply for late amnesty in 1987.

In the late 1980s, many Yalaltec immigrants became permanent residents through the IRCA. Overall, these new U.S. residents made up two groups. The first was composed of undocumented Yalaltecos who were married and had children born in the United States when amnesty was launched. These couples had already applied for the regularization of their migratory status, but gained permanent residency through the IRCA. Miguel and Eréndira, for example, had wed in Yalálag in 1972 and had made plans to go to the United States for a year and then return to Mexico. In 1976, in Los Angeles, they had their first child and decided to settle in the United States. That year they applied for the legalization of their status, but because the legal process had already taken ten years and they had still not received legal permanent residency, they applied for amnesty in 1986.

The second group of immigrants was made up of Yalaltecos who first applied within the amnesty deadline. They were single men and women and young married couples with no children or with children born in Mexico. While married Yalaltecos' main motivation was to legalize their status because of their children, single men and women also did so because they were determined to settle in the United States. They wanted to work legally and move back and forth between Mexico and the United States. My research revealed that in 1987, although many Yalaltec immigrants regularized their migratory status, others did not. Those who applied for amnesty were interested in becoming legal residents and met the requirements (undocumented immigrants who had been in the United States since January 1, 1982, could apply for amnesty up to one year until May 1987). Timing, intentions to return to Mexico, or their recent arrival influenced those who did not apply. In 1985, for example, Juan returned to Yalálag, and thus could not apply for amnesty at the right time. Others may have filled out their applications, but by the time amnesty was offered, they had no intention of settling permanently in the United States. Although some Yalaltecos did not apply because they were newcomers, others secured their permanent residency by using letters they bought from their employers, labor contractors, and *bi gwlash* attesting earlier arrival. I know one Yalaltec immigrant who sold a supporting letter from his employer to a Yalaltec friend so the friend could apply for the green card.

Throughout the late 1980s, undocumented Yalaltec migration in Los Angeles continued to increase through the expansion of dense migrant networks. In contrast to the family stage migration model of Hondagneou-Sotelo (1994), where husbands migrate before their wives and children, for most Yalaltecos, the move from Mexico to the United States depended on social networks that included friendship as well as kinship relationships. Many of the immigrants of the 1970s and early 1980s set out to migrate into Los Angeles by persuading their older immigrant siblings, cousins, and friends to help them. For instance, in 1982, at the age of fourteen, Fabian came to Los Angeles the first time to work under the aegis of his older sister Alicia. Later that year, he returned to Yalálag because he was a minor and could not find a job. In 1987, Alicia brought Fabian back after visiting her family in Yalálag. Alicia, who was already living in the United States and had acquired U.S. residency through the amnesty program, financed Fabian's trip for a second time. She provided Fabian with housing and food, paid the *coyote,* and found him a job at her worksite. After many years of working in Los Angeles as a domestic worker and gardener, respectively, Alicia and Fabian saved enough money to build a concrete house for their parents in Yalálag. Since the late 1980s, both have covered electricity, gas, and water costs in the Yalálag house. Moreover, they have paid for their parents' health care, and still send remittances regularly to support them. In February of 2009, Fabian got his U.S. working permit.

Like Fabian and Alicia, many young Yalaltec men and women continue to try their luck in the United States and send remittances to their families. Because they have older siblings, relatives, or friends in Los Angeles, hear about employment and education opportunities for U.S.-born Yalaltecos, and witness the ongoing rise in unemployment and poverty in Mexico, emigration from Yalálag, Oaxaca City, and Mexico City continues to increase. For example, Renata, who arrived in Los Angeles in 1979, has helped five of her six younger siblings, as well as cousins and nephews, to immigrate to the United States. According to Renata, after her father died in Yalálag, her mother was left with seven children. Although Renata's mom used to harvest corn, beans, pears, squash, coffee, and sugar cane for her family's sustenance, there was no money left for education, health insurance, and clothing for her children. As a result, Renata and her older brother Julio, the oldest siblings, migrated to Los Angeles to support their mother economically. Over time, Renata's four younger brothers asked her to help them migrate either to Oaxaca City or Los Angeles because no options existed in Yalálag for higher education or job opportunities. As one of seven children, Renata supported one of her younger sisters to go to Oaxaca City to complete middle school, high school, and then a B.A. in education. She also paid for three brothers and another younger sister to travel to Los Angeles. While she helped two brothers find jobs in restaurants and one sister in domestic work, she also became responsible for the education of her younger brother, Gabriel, who came to the United States at the age of fourteen. As she recounts:

> All my siblings asked me to help them migrate. They used to work very hard in the countryside and help my mother at home. All of them were good shepherds, wood carriers, and farmers, but didn't want to be that for their entire lives. However, not all of them wanted to study either. That is why I only supported my sister Sofia to go to Oaxaca City to study. She was the only one in the family interested in pursuing an undergraduate degree. The good thing about my siblings is that all of them like to work. Thus, I helped Fernando, Julio, Remedios, Octavio, and Gabriel to come to Los Angeles. When they came here, they lived with my husband and me. We found jobs for all of them. But when Gabriel arrived in Los Angeles in 1991, he was fourteen years old and it was so hard for us to help him find a job. So, my husband and I told him that we would send him to school. Then, he completed middle school, high school, and college in Los Angeles. Unfortunately, although he wanted to go to the university, he could not. He is still illegal.

Although most Yalaltecos have left Yalálag with the idea of returning, the reality is that, over the years, they have remained in the United States. Some have regularized their migratory status, while others have not. Two particular aspects of the Yalaltec migration in the late 1980s stand out. Married immigrant men who left children and wives in Yalálag returned permanently to Yalálag. And some immigrants with U.S.-born children raised in Los Angeles returned to Yalálag, Mexico City, or Oaxaca City, but remigrated to the United States. After working several years in the United States, for example, Pedro, Juan, and Patricia returned from Los Angeles to Yalálag to reunite with their families. They had worked two or three shifts and saved money to renovate their houses and open small family businesses in Yalálag to make a living. They went back because they disliked the lifestyle in the United States and wanted to join their families in Yalálag.

In contrast, Tomas, who arrived in Los Angeles in 1986 and became a U.S. permanent resident in 1987, returned under different circumstances. Even though he could support his two U.S.-born children and wife in Los Angeles and was working three jobs to rent an apartment for his family, the financial burden was overwhelming. A single income, even from multiple jobs, based on minimum wage, was not enough to support a family of four. Since he wanted to provide his children with a better education and healthier social environment, and did not want them to live in overcrowded apartments in Los Angeles, he went back to Mexico City with his family in 1990. Tomas still goes back and forth between Mexico City and Los Angeles. In the United States, he works as a cook or in the construction industry and sends money to his family. When he returns to Mexico, he is usually unemployed. Currently, Tomas owns a house in Mexico City. As for his two oldest children, born in the United States, one is a medical doctor in

Oaxaca, and the other recently finished high school and reemigrated to work in Los Angeles. Tomas's two Mexican-born children are still in elementary school, and his wife takes care of them.

Agustin is another immigrant who went back to Oaxaca City with savings and the idea of raising his three U.S.-born children in Mexico. As Agustin and his wife watched their children growing up in Los Angeles, they were concerned that their children could become involved in drugs or gangs due to the lack of parental supervision or bad influences. In the United States, then, as now, Yalalte-cos lived in segregated areas and worked up to three shifts to cope with family expenses, and were forced to leave their children unsupervised at home. After two years living in Oaxaca City, Agustin took his wife and children back to Los Angeles, at their urging, because they did not adjust to the way of life in Oaxaca and economic conditions worsened in Mexico.[12]

In the late 1980s, President Carlos Salinas de Gortari redirected the course of the Mexican economy, driving the country into prolonged political and economic crisis. Salinas de Gortari reduced restrictions on imports, opened up the privatization of large state-owned industries, and encouraged foreign investment. In 1992, during the Bush administration, he signed the North American Free Trade Agreement (NAFTA), which promotes a free market and free-trade policies. In 1993, the presidential candidate of the ruling party (PRI), Luis Donaldo Colosio, was murdered. On January 1, 1994, when NAFTA was implemented, the *Ejército Zapatista de Liberación Nacional* launched its uprising in Chiapas. On September 28, the PRI secretary general Jose Francisco Ruiz Massieu was assassinated in Mexico City. By the end of 1994, Mexico reached the limit of its foreign exchange reserves and announced the devaluation of the peso. According to Villareal, "by the end of 1994, Mexico faced a currency crisis, putting pressure on the government to abandon its previous fixed exchange rate policy and adopt a floating exchange rate regime. As a result, Mexico's currency plunged by around 50% within six months, sending the country into a deep recession" (2011, 16). Under the government of President Ernesto Zedillo (1994–2000), Mexico faced more economic and political instability. The national poverty rates and inequities between rich and poor increased. Attorney General Antonio Lozano Gracia, a member of the Partido Acción Nacional opposition party, was appointed by President Zedillo to investigate the political crimes of 1994. As a result, in February 1995, Raúl Salinas, the older brother of former president Salinas de Gortari, was accused of the assassination of Francisco Ruiz Massieu as well as illegal enrichment, drug trafficking, and money laundering. Meanwhile, in January 1995, President Zedillo declared that Mexico was in a deep economic crisis, which he described as an "economic emergency." He announced a rescue plan that included new opportunities for foreign investment, rescuing the banking system at taxpayers' expense, and "moderated borrowing" from the United States. During the Clinton administration, the International Monetary Fund provided the

Mexican government with an emergency financial package of US$50 billion in loans (Cameron and Tomlin 2002). Zedillo's rescue plan also included the sale of key state-owned companies and an increase in "the value-added tax, budget cuts, increases in electricity and gasoline prices to decrease demand and government subsides, and tighter monetary policy" (Villareal 2011, 17). Zedillo's austerity plan represented a dramatic sacrifice for the poorest Mexicans and middle-class families, who experienced declining income.

By the end of the 1990s, NAFTA had had few positive effects on Mexicans and Mexico's overall economic development. Mexican exports in electronics, automobiles and auto parts, and garments and textiles represented 70 percent of total Mexican exports. However, socioeconomic indicators did not reflect an improvement in the "GDP per capita, employment, income distribution, and wages" (Center for International Finance and Development 2001). Berg et al. point out that in Mexico, employment in the informal sector increased from 38.4 percent in 1990 to 41.8 percent in 2003. They also note that "informal employment, measured as the percentage of workers who are not protected by formal labor regulations and thus do not receive any social benefit, constituted 48.7 percent of the working population during the 1991–1999 period, according to data from the National Employment Survey" (Berg et al. 2006, 28). As a result, many Mexicans saw migration into the United States as an inviting survival strategy.

NEW TRAJECTORIES AND STORIES OF YALALTEC MIGRATION

Between the 1990s and mid-2000s, both new and old patterns of Yalálag Zapotec migration arose. In Los Angeles, newcomers were mostly impoverished young single men and women from age fifteen to their early twenties, as well as adult women with foreign-born children, married couples with foreign-born children, and couples with no children. The 1990s saw new changes in the migratory routes as well as a decline in emigration from Yalálag to Oaxaca City and Mexico City. Yalaltecos began to migrate mostly from Yalálag itself to Los Angeles. Other first-time immigrant families arrived in Los Angeles from the states of Morelos and Veracruz. Yalaltecos born in Oaxaca City and Mexico City integrated into the international migration process. And a few Yalaltecos born in Yalálag migrated within Mexico to the cities of Hermosillo, Sonora; Tijuana, Baja California; Guadalajara, Jalisco; Puebla, Puebla; and the states of Durango and Mexico. In these cities, they found jobs in the service and domestic sectors and in manufacturing. For those in the United States, although most Yalaltec immigrants lived and worked in Los Angeles, a few moved permanently to New Jersey, northern California, North Carolina, Texas, and Wisconsin.

As mentioned above, in the 1970s and 1980s, many Yalaltecos had migrated and settled in Mexico City, where some started their families. Many received financial support for academic pursuits from older siblings in Los Angeles. Currently,

there are a few Yalaltecos in Mexico City and Oaxaca City who are quite successful lawyers, doctors, musicians, dentists, architects, and entrepreneurs. However,
others have emigrated to Los Angeles due to the lack of educational opportunities and secure and well-paid jobs and a declining standard of living in Mexico.
In the 1990s, the constant decline in the peasant economy, the restructuring of
agricultural production, changes in agricultural policies, and a continuing lack
of state and federal investment in education, health programs, and social security
in the state of Oaxaca pushed Yalaltec peasants, merchants, and housewives to
emigrate internationally. The Yalaltecos who had settled in Cuernavaca, Morelos;
Playa Vicente, Veracruz; and Mexico City in the 1980s immigrated to Los Angeles
in the early 1990s due to the negative effects of Mexico's economic crisis; many
complete nuclear families also migrated to Los Angeles (cf. Massey et al. 1987).

Consequently, the earlier pattern of younger siblings following their older siblings, cousins, and friends underwent two significant transformations. First, in
addition to young men and women who followed their older siblings, complete
families were arriving in Los Angeles from Yalálag and other urban centers in
Mexico. Second, parents reuniting with family members—who were U.S. citizens,
permanent U.S. residents, or in some cases undocumented migrants—moved
permanently to Los Angeles.[13] In 1992, for example, Eduardo was unemployed
in the city of Cuernavaca, Morelos. When his debts increased, he and his wife,
Cristina, decided to immigrate with their two sons to Los Angeles. With the help
of Cristina's sister Maria, Cristina and Eduardo left Mexico. Maria, who had been
living in the United States since the 1970s and became a legal resident through the
1986 amnesty program, helped Eduardo and her sister Cristina pay for the *coyote*
to bring the entire family and hosted them for three years. Upon arriving in Los
Angeles, Eduardo's son Ivan entered first grade, and Manuel enrolled in the first
year of middle school. When Eduardo and Cristina gained economic stability
and their children felt more adjusted to living in the United States, they decided
to rent an apartment for their own family. Until now, Eduardo has been working double shifts in restaurants as a dishwasher or as a cook. Cristina has been
a full-time domestic worker and takes care of their sons. According to Eduardo
and Cristina, they do not regret having immigrated to the United States. Despite
the adversities of being undocumented immigrants and knowing the multiple
sacrifices their children have made to succeed in the United States, they feel that
their lives are much better in Los Angeles than in Mexico.

The example of Cristina and Eduardo's family-unit migration is not unique.
In the midst of the 1990s, when the economic crisis hit Mexico, a good number
of Yalaltec nuclear families migrated to Los Angeles. They could no longer rely on
their salaries or low wages and had to develop new survival strategies. Like earlier single or newly married immigrants, these complete families, like Eduardo's,
came to the United States because they could count on financial assistance from
relatives and friends who were already settled in Los Angeles. Since migrating

with dependants is an expensive and risky enterprise, immigrants have tended to lend money to newcomers and share their residences for periods lasting a few months to several years. In a similar vein, immigrant men, with previous migration experiences to the United Sates, immigrated with wives and children. For example, Mariana and Marco left Yalálag with their two children in 1991. As Marco recounts:

> We came to the United States to provide our children with a better education and to earn enough money to buy a house in Oaxaca City. When I came back from Los Angeles in 1979, I had some savings and began making *huaraches* (traditional sandals). It was quite a good period. There were not many sandal makers in Yalálag, and I had a lot of customers in neighboring villages. Then, at that time, I fell in love with Mariana. So when I wanted to marry her, I had to work hard for the wedding because weddings are quite expensive in Yalálag. In 1985, we married and a year later we had our first child. But, when we had our second child, I started to feel that we didn't have enough money to raise our children and didn't have our own house yet. As time went by, I felt that our economic situation was not good at all, and my family was feeling the same. Believe it or not, at times, I had no money to buy food or clothes for my family. Then, I asked Mariana if she would call her sister in Los Angeles and ask her if she could help us get to Los Angeles. Fortunately, Mariana's sister helped us come.

As mentioned above, the pattern of mothers and fathers following or reuniting with their older children to Los Angeles is also characteristic of the last fifteen years. In 1985, Nancy migrated with her husband from Oaxaca City to Los Angeles. Although she sent monetary remittances to her parents in Oaxaca City, her income was mainly spent on her own family's education and living expenses in the United States. In 1999, when economic conditions deteriorated for Nancy's parents and younger siblings in Mexico, Nancy's father, Abel, asked her to lend him money to bring Nancy's mother and his two sons to Los Angeles. With financial help from Nancy and her husband, Abel brought his family and began working as a janitor in a Korean supermarket. Nancy's mother and younger sister took on domestic work, and at times, they babysat. Nancy's youngest sixteen-year-old brother was enrolled in middle school.

An important pattern to mention when describing the Yalaltec migration in the 1990s is that quite a few young women came to Los Angeles when they married a Yalaltec immigrant man. Yalálag is a Zapotec community with a high degree of endogamy and a long tradition of arranged marriages. In the first half of the twentieth century, the majority of marriages were arranged between two families. Currently, although most young men and women are expected to date, court, fall in love, and decide on their own to marry, a few young women still wed in accordance with the practice of arranged marriage. Since the late

1960s, migration has played a key role in transforming marriage practices. These changes can be analyzed by dividing them into three groups. First, there are married Yalaltec women who migrated to Los Angeles or within Mexico. They did not choose their partners and did not engage in any sort of relationship prior to marriage. Parents of the bride and groom arranged the marriage and planned the entire wedding ceremony. The second group is composed of single women who migrated to Los Angeles and then married a Yalaltec man either in Yalálag or in Los Angeles without family intervention. When immigrants decided to marry in Yalálag, they usually asked their families to help them prepare for the wedding celebration before they arrived to wed. The third and most recent pattern is that of young immigrant men who contact their parents in Yalálag and ask them to look for a wife. Despite women's increasing opposition to marrying in accordance to the tradition of arranged marriages, various immigrant men and families in Yalálag continue to sustain and promote this practice. Additionally, the constant and higher levels of immigration among single men to Los Angeles has left a high proportion of single women in Yalálag either "available" for marriage or left out of the marriage market (cf. Brettell 2003). In December of 2003, while conducting fieldwork in Yalálag, I attended a wedding between a twenty-one-year-old woman and a twenty-eight-year-old immigrant man. I was told that the bride was "so lucky" to get married because in these days many young women are *quedadas* (spinsters) due to men's high levels of migration. A friend of mine described the bride as lucky because, despite the fact that she was already "old," she was chosen to marry.

Elisa, who is now thirty-two years old and has two U.S.-born sons, describes her experience of coming to Los Angeles after she married:

> Like many other women, I left Yalálag after my mother married me off to an immigrant man. Here, many young single men head to *El Norte* to work, and then come back and marry. Women face many injustices. Some women who left Yalálag with their parents or relatives somehow do not have to cope with this tradition. Others have convinced their parents not to force them to marry a man whom they don't know. Traditionally, many women in the village comply with the traditional practice of arranged marriage. In the last ten years, many immigrant men have chosen a young woman in Yalálag. They go to Los Angeles for a while and return to Yalálag to marry. Men say that when they feel lonely, they need to create their own family or that they want a woman. Then they call or write their relatives in Yalálag and ask them to look for a young woman. At times, when immigrant men come back to the village fiestas, they themselves choose their wives. In my case, my ex-husband called his mother to tell her that he wanted to marry me. So, his mother talked to my parents and they prepared the wedding. In June 1998, my husband came back from Los Angeles and married me. I told my mother that he was a stranger to me and that I did not want to marry him. But traditionally in my village, many women

have been married off without their consent and then go to the United States. So, I met my husband the day of my wedding and a month later, he brought me to Los Angeles.

Although Elisa may appear as a passive follower of her husband, for many women—including Elisa and her sisters—these family arrangements represent the only route to Los Angeles. Among the twenty-five women I interviewed, six arrived in Los Angeles in the 1990s after their parents married them off to an immigrant man in Yalálag. This was part of the 1990s pattern of young men migrating to Los Angeles and then coming back to Yalálag to marry a young woman, a distinct mode of migration for women.

Between the 1990s and the early 2000s, Yalaltec migration into Los Angeles mainly comprised the *braceros'* grandchildren. Among them were young men and women from peasant families in Yalálag as well as Yalatecos holding a B.A. degree who migrated in the 1970s and 1980s to Oaxaca City and Mexico City. At present, the b*raceros'* grandchildren are between their late teens and thirties. Some have professional careers in, for example, business administration, accounting, dentistry, and Latin American Studies. Romelia, for example, is one of three siblings who migrated to Oaxaca City to complete high school and then a B.A. degree in accounting. Between 1995 and 1999, her parents, who own a little butcher shop in Yalálag, supported her financially to finish her studies in Oaxaca. Between 1999 and 2001, Romelia worked as an accounting analyst in an accounting firm that paid her the minimum wage. Despite having a job, she could not make ends meet on that salary and, thus, could not move up socially and economically to help her parents. As a result, she decided to migrate to Los Angeles in 2001, because she knew that she could make more money as a domestic worker or babysitter in the United States than as an accounting analyst at home. When she arrived in Los Angeles, she lived with an aunt who helped her find a job. A year later, Romelia helped her oldest sister come to the United States.

I met Angelica and Alberto in 2001. Both had come to the United States to work. To my surprise, I found that both were born in Los Angeles, but raised in Mexico. When I asked Angelica about this, she said that she and her oldest brother Marcos were born in Los Angeles but raised in Mexico City because it was too expensive for their parents to support their family in the United States. Angelica also mentioned that her father provided her and her siblings with a house and education in Mexico City, but he was absent most of the time because of work. According to Angelica, her father, who has a green card, has moved back and forth between Mexico and the United States because he cannot earn a good living in Mexico City. In 2005, Angelica was eighteen years old and arrived in Los Angeles with her father. Since then, she has lived with one of her aunts and three cousins. Angelica came to Los Angeles with the idea of studying at college and finding a job. In order to achieve her goals, she had to attend school to learn English and work to save money to pay for her own education. As she settled in the United States, she realized that being an American citizen because of her birth facilitated her job search. However, she cannot pursue a college degree or attend university, because it is too expensive. Since she is already an adult, she must cover her own expenses.

Alberto was born in the United States in 1992. When he was a baby, his mother decided to return to Yalálag. There, he completed elementary and middle school. In 2001, he decided to go to Los Angeles to live with one of his uncles for a year, but returned to Yalálag because he found it difficult to adjust to the American way of life. In 2004, he went to Los Angeles again because he wanted to work and have his own money. Currently, he lives with relatives and works in restaurants as a dishwasher or cook.

Luis is another young immigrant who, at age twenty, went to work in Los Angeles between March 2003 and December of 2006. His path of migration, however, was quite different. He was born in Mexico City and held a B.A. in business administration. His parents had married in Yalálag, and in the mid-1980s, they had migrated to Mexico City. When Luis arrived in Los Angeles, one of his aunts provided him with room and board, and an uncle helped him find a job in the restaurant sector. Luis considered the possibility of staying in the United States. However, he preferred going back to Mexico City to graduate. Currently, Luis lives in Mexico City and works for his parents. They own a dry-cleaning business.

Until now, poverty, lack of employment, a marginal social position, a declining standard of living, and scarce health care services and education programs have characterized five decades of international migration into the United States for young Yalaltec men and women. More recently, the culture of migration, which has developed among the younger generations of Yalaltecos, has caused teenaged Yalaltecs to think of migration to El Norte as something necessary and unavoidable. That is, today's increase in migration into Los Angeles is not casual or accidental. It goes along with social and economic conditions as well as ideas and beliefs about migrating. Massey et al. (1994) and Smith (1995) have proposed the notion "culture of migration" to describe the institutionalization of behaviors, values, expectations, and ideas that propel immigrants to migrate. This culture of migration is related "to the spread of consumerism and immigrant success that itself generates more emigration. Migration becomes an expectation and a normal part of the life course, particularly for young men and increasingly for women" (Massey et al. 1994, 737–738). Smith suggests that in the case of Mexican migration, "rather than attenuating, the links between members of many Mexican sending communities and their U.S.-residing counterparts may increase over time through the institutionalization of migration as a way of life and the subsequent carrying out of joint projects by the U. S. and Mexico members of the community" (1995, 24).

Since the early 1990s, the fiesta of San Antonio de Padua in Yalálag has been the time when many young teenagers leave for the United States. According to local middle school and high school principals, it is lamentable to report the high number of students who leave every year after the fiesta of San Antonio de Padua. It should be noted that not just any teenager can leave Yalálag. Usually, an adolescent is required by his or her family to earn a middle school diploma in order to migrate to Los Angeles. The high school principal noted that middle school students tend to finish their studies, but in contrast, high school students often drop out to go to Los Angeles.

Over five decades, migration has increasingly become part of the expectations of young Yalaltec men and women. Return migrants continue to provide economic and social resources that facilitate migration for newer generations to settle in Los Angeles. Since the early 1990s, the fiesta of San Antonio de Padua in Yalálag has been the time when many teenagers leave for the United States. Local middle school and high school principals report that the high number of students who leave every year after the fiesta of San Antonio de Padua is lamentable. It should be noted that not just any teenager can leave Yalálag. Usually, an adolescent is required by his or her family to earn a middle school diploma in order to migrate to Los Angeles. The high school principal noted that middle school students tend to finish their studies, but in contrast, high school students often drop out to go to Los Angeles. While the fiesta of San Antonio de Padua has played a significant contextual role in bringing together immigrants and their families, it also represents a crucial moment in the process of family disintegration. According to the people of Yalálag, this fiesta has marked the departure of many local teenagers who leave their families behind but reunite with relatives in the United States. Interest among many teenagers in getting their middle school diploma perpetuates the desire to migrate, and threatens the social cohesion of dozens of Yalaltec families. In August 2004, I gave a talk in the middle school in Yalálag. After discussing Yalaltecos' experiences of migration in Los Angeles, I asked these eighth-grade students (thirteen/fourteen-year-olds) how many were interested in migrating to Los Angeles. To my surprise, two-thirds of the group (forty-five students) confirmed that they were waiting to finish school to migrate to the United States. They pointed out that they have relatives in Los Angeles, and most of them count on moral and financial support to pursue their goals.

Contemporary Yalaltec migration into the United States has progressively developed, starting with pioneers working on short-term contracts who return to Yalálag; progressing to family formation, permanent settlement, and acquisition of U.S. residency and American citizenship; and augmented by the constant arrival and permanent residence of undocumented immigrants who are steadily incorporated into the U.S. labor market and American society. The arrival of newcomers has evolved due to the maintenance of dense family and community networks with satellite communities in areas within Mexico such as Oaxaca City, Mexico City, Morelos, Veracruz, and more recently Puebla, Durango, and the state of Mexico. Namely, unlike the first immigrants' experiences into the United States, contemporary immigrants integrate into their extended families in Los Angeles, participate in extended family life, and integrate into the U.S. labor market through family and friendship networks. These networks have also provided information about jobs, housing, and transportation and have made migration to the United States an imperative fact of economic life in Oaxaca, Mexico.

At present, there may be more than four thousand Yalaltecos in Los Angeles.[14] Many older immigrants, who formed families and brought their relatives to Los Angeles in the 1980s, have already legalized their migratory status in the United States. Some have, in fact, bought property and are thus losing hope of (and perhaps interest in) returning. In addition, the growing number of second-generation Yalaltec Americans has become another factor discouraging a return home. Consequently, permanent settlement and the constitution of complete Yalaltec families in the United States are two of the factors that have contributed to the emergence of the Yalaltec immigrant community of Los Angeles. This is the focus of the next chapter.

⚘

CHAPTER 2

BUILDING COMMUNITY AND CONNECTIONS IN LOS ANGELES

On a late afternoon in June 2005, while I was conducting an interview with my Yalaltec friend Fabian at the university housing at UCLA, he told me the following Yalaltec joke about the arrival of the Yalálag patron saints in Los Angeles.

> Santiago (San Santiago Apóstol) goes to Los Angeles to make money to fix his old house in Yalálag. Once he repairs it, he suggests to Rosa (Santa Rosa de Lima) that she accompany *him* to Los Angeles so she can renovate hers. Then, Rosa goes to Los Angeles works hard, begins to repair her house, and tells Santiago that *she does not regret* having gone to Los Angeles *with him.* After Rosa and Santiago leave, Juan (San Juan Bautista) visits Catarina (Santa Catarina Mártir) and tells her that Santiago and Rosa *went to L.A. together!* He is hesitant, but asks Catarina, "Hey, why don't you come with me to Los Angeles? We can have *a good time* and could make money and fix our houses." But Saint Catarina walks away, startled and surprised by San Juan's offer. But San Juan visits her again and persists, "If you do not want to stay behind and look like Toño (San Antonio de Padua), you should come with me. Look, Toño is lazy. He just likes receiving charity from Los Angeles. He likes spending all the money on his fiestas. He does not like working. He will never fix his house." Catarina says, "Well, if you say that you are going to help me to renovate my house and *we are going to have a good time,* then let's go!"

At first hearing, I thought, "This joke is more than just a joke." Of course, the joke may not have any significant meaning for the reader, or it may represent only a humorous story. However, I find that the narrative of the joke about the saints provides an exceptional record of the social and cultural processes that have contributed to Yalálag community formation in the United States.[1] Throughout this narrative, the saints embody the social and economic forces driving Yalálag Zapotec migration to Los Angeles. The back-and-forth movements of the patron saints in the joke—which vaguely point to the shift from circular migration to one of permanent settlement in the United States—and the ongoing connections that immigrants like Santiago, Rosa, Juan, and Catalina have built with their home community—reflect the social, cultural, and economic dynamics that constitute the transnational life of the Yalálag community that has developed between the city of Los Angeles in the United States and the village of Yalálag in Mexico.[2] More important, embedded in this funny story is one crucial aspect of what Yalálag Zapotecs describe as "their way of thinking and behaving as a community," and what I define as a system of practices of membership that have facilitated cooperation and communal action in the social and symbolic construction of the Yalaltec immigrant community in Los Angeles.

Using the saints joke as a context in which Yalaltec people use humor to narrate their history of immigration into the United States, I examine Yalálag community formation in Los Angeles through the transnationalization of the Yalálag barrio patron saint fiestas and three Zapotec forms of social organization—*gwzon* or *guelaguetza*, communal service, and communal participation. I use these four names to represent typical immigrants throughout.

Yalálag Barrio Patron Saint Fiestas in Los Angeles

San Juan Yalálag, also called Villa Hidalgo Yalálag, is a Zapotec village located in the Sierra Norte of Oaxaca, Mexico (see fig. 2.1).[3] Archeological evidence indicates that isolated groups were established in Yalálag long before the Spanish arrival during the sixteenth century (Alcina F. 1993; Chance 1989).[4] As related in Yalaltec oral traditions, Yalálag was "founded by two Zapotec families, one originating from Tlacolulita, and the other one from Mitla. The first family settled in what today we know as the barrio of Santa Rosa de Lima, while the latter in the barrio of Santa Catarina Mártir" (de la Fuente 1949, 18).[5]

Around 1524, when the Spanish conquerors arrived at Oaxaca, they found the Valley and the Sierra regions at war. In the Valley, the Mixtecs were engaged in hostilities with the Valley Zapotecs, and the Zapotec lordships struggled for power among them (Chance 1978). The Sierra Zapotecs were fighting both the Chinantecs and the Mixes (Chance 1989). In 1525, when the Spanish entered the Sierra, the Dominican priests arrived with them. While the Spaniards sought to take control of the Zapotec, Mixe, and Chinantec villages and gain political and economic power in the Sierra region, the Dominican priests began the process of proselytization. Under the rule of the Spanish Crown, the Dominicans traveled around the Sierra to organize the founding of the first congregations. They built the first churches in the region, initiated classes of catechism, and administered the sacraments. In 1526, the town of Villa Alta, located 29.8 miles from Yalálag, was established as a mountain outpost between the Mixe and Zapotec borderlands to put an end to the warfare in the Sierra and gain political and economic

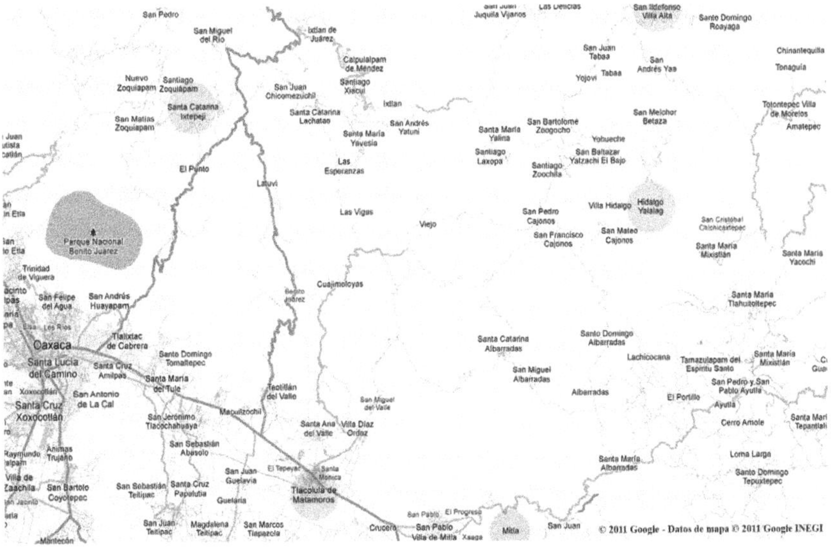

Figure 2.1. Localization of Yalálag in the Northern Highlands of Oaxaca, Mexico.

power in the region (Chance 1989, 17).[6] In 1563, due to Yalálag's strategic location in the region, a large congregation was established and an *encomienda* was founded (Chance 1989, 75).[7]

Following the architectural and residential patterns of colonial Spain, the Spanish colonizers used the Spanish grid plan to design the town and divide the village of Yalálag into four barrios. The four barrios, where the highest and lowest houses were separated by a drop of two or three thousand feet, were named for Catholic saints: Santiago Apóstol, Santa Catarina Mártir, San Juan Bautista, and Santa Rosa de Lima.[8] According to Chance, "*Barrios* were clearly older in the Sierra, the first mention of them is coming from Betaza in 1703, several decades before the appearance of *cofradías* [lay brotherhoods for maintaining the church].[9] Perhaps *barrios* were introduced by the Dominicans as a means of organizing worship for the saints, then were reshaped in *cofradías* by the secular clergy in the second half of the eighteenth century" (1989, 171). In a similar line of thought, Aguirre Beltrán (cited in Young 1976, 194) suggests that the planning of the barrios in colonial times throughout the Sierra was probably an administrative strategy to collect both the royal tribute for the Spanish Crown and the church tithe.

Under the colonial regime, in 1777 the Yalaltec village and each barrio obtained the *Títulos de Composición de Tierras y Aguas* (property titles) for their land, and the geopolitical boundaries of the barrios were defined (de la Fuente 1949, 20).[10] By the end of the nineteenth century, each barrio began to differentiate itself on the basis of economic activities. The people of barrio Santiago made sandals and manufactured hats from palm tree fronds. In Santa Catarina, weavers and seamstresses became known for their production of clothing. In San Juan, Yalaltecos were distinguished as good agricultural workers, and the residents of the barrio of Santa Rosa de Lima became popular as musicians and dancers. Although each barrio developed its own economic activities, together they began to form the basis for the Yalálag economy. Currently, one can trace these economic activities in each barrio, but one cal also find shoemakers, weavers, musicians, dancers, and agricultural workers all over the village. There are, as well, new economic activities related to the creation of small businesses such as bakeries, *tortillerias* (tortilla stores), *tienditas* (little stores), *carnicerias* (meat markets), *fondas* (small restaurants), and stationery shops.[11]

At present, the four barrios represent geographical and political units as well as religious and cultural institutions that constitute the village of Yalálag.[12] Geographically, Santa Catarina covers a vast portion of Yalaltec territory, but has little water. Santiago enjoys plenty of water but has less land than Santa Catarina. San Juan has the smallest population of the four barrios, and Santa Rosa occupies the smallest portion of land. Politically, Yalaltecos have rights and are obliged to participate in the "traditional government," constituted by a system of public positions or *cargos* and the *barrio-cargo* system. This form of government relies on indigenous political, civic, and judicial structures that regulate the social and political life of the Yalálag community.

Culturally, the barrio landmarks, places of worship, and religious life combine to mark the social and symbolic boundaries within the village. Each barrio has its own building for worship, its own patron saint, its own religious fiesta, and its own *casa del barrio* (neighborhood cultural center).[13] For instance, the barrio Santiago has its own church for Santiago Apóstol and *casa del barrio*, and celebrates the saint on July 25. Socially, each Yalalteco has developed both a sense of barrio community and a sense of identification with the barrio patron saint. Each Yalalteco is defined socially and culturally as a barrio citizen because he or she has obligations and rights within his or her barrio community and has built a relation of reciprocity and faith with the barrio patron saint.[14]

In Los Angeles, this sense of barrio identification and the barrio community boundaries of Yalálag continue to be very significant. Although the four barrios are no longer geopolitical entities, linked to a specific place in Los Angeles, they have been redefined through the social work and communal service of the Yalaltec immigrants for the barrio patron saint fiestas and the restoration of the *casas de los barrios* and the barrio churches to which they belong in Yalálag. As described in the saints joke, immigrants like Rosa, Juan, Catarina, and Santiago have repaired their houses in Yalálag. Also, they have funded the barrio patron saint fiestas and the reconstruction of the four *casas de los barrios*, the barrio churches, and the saints' chapels.[15]

Since the late 1980s, Yalaltec immigrants have done so through the organization of community events, known as the *bailes* (Cruz-Manjarrez 2001, 2005,

2009).[16] By *baile* I refer to a community gathering for occasions such as the celebration of the patron saints of Yalálag and regional holidays in Los Angeles. In 1989, in East Los Angeles, Yalaltec immigrants from barrio Santiago organized their first *baile* to finance the fiesta of Saint Santiago Apóstol in Yalálag. The *baile* took place in the backyard of a Yalalteco's house. Tickets cost five dollars, and organizers also sold Yalaltec food such as tamales, *atole*, Yalaltec bread, drinks, and beer to raise more funds. A group of musicians organized a Yalálag Zapotec brass band to liven up the community gathering. Besides playing the traditional Yalaltec dance and music form called the *sones y jarabes Yalaltecos*, the brass band accompanied a group of *danzantes* (dancers), who performed the religious dance of *Los Negritos* to revere the celebrated patron saint.

In 1991, Yalaltecos of barrio Santa Catarina organized a second *baile* to build the *casa del barrio* and to finance the barrio fiesta in Yalálag. According to the barrio organizers, the *baile* was held in a ballroom in downtown Los Angeles, and the committee collected six thousand dollars. In Yalálag, the barrio leaders used this money to pay for various services for the saint's celebration. These included the participation of local and visiting brass bands and tropical music groups, the manufacture of fireworks, the preparation of free food for all visitors and local people attending the fiestas, and the total cost of power and water supply. In the last ten years, Yalaltec immigrants have funded the construction of a new kitchen area, a basketball court, and a dance hall in all the *casas de los barrios*.

During the nineties in Los Angeles, barrio participation and interest in carrying on *bailes* increased. Each barrio began to organize its own *bailes*. Four Yalaltec brass bands emerged: San Juan Yalálag in 1990, Alma Oaxaqueña in 1991, Banda Zempoaltepetl in 1998, Banda Filarmónica de Yalálag in 1998, and Banda Nueva Imágen in 2000.[17] And the *bailes* began to evolve in such ways that they became attached to the native calendar of the patron saints of Yalálag. Originally, the celebrations of the Yalálag patron saints in Los Angeles were carried out months before the barrio fiestas in Yalálag in order to collect money and send it for the preparations of the fiestas or the reparation of the saints' church (Cruz-Manjarrez 2001). But today, they take place during the same month that the patron saints' fiestas take place in the home village, and if possible on the same day. To be more precise, in Yalálag, the fiesta system is regulated by the Yalálag Zapotec ritual calendar consisting of six Catholic festivities: two communal fiestas and four barrio celebrations (de la Fuente 1949). The two communal fiestas, which are planned by representatives of the whole community, are the fiesta of San Juan Yalálag in February (a week before Carnival) and the fiesta of San Antonio de Padua on June 13. The four barrio fiestas, exclusively planned by barrio committees, are San Juan Bautista on June 24; Santiago Apóstol on July 25; Santa Rosa de Lima on August 30; and Santa Catarina Mártir on November 30. In Los Angeles, the immigrant community has reconfigured and transnationalized this

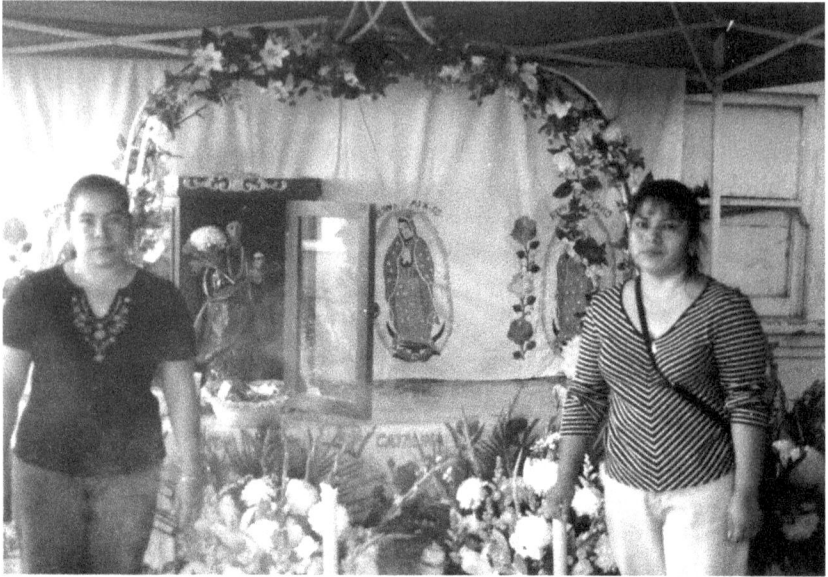

Figure 2.2. *Barrio* committee members organized a *baile* upon the arrival of the image of Santa Catarina Mártir in Los Angeles.

fiesta system honoring the Catholic patron saints, though it is composed of only one communal fiesta, San Antonio de Padua, and the four barrio celebrations.

It is important to note that the *bailes* dedicated to local patron saints in Los Angeles have been crucial in forging the transnational life (Smith 2006) of the Yalaltec immigrant community. The *bailes* have warranted immigrants' continuing membership in both their barrio communities in Yalálag and the immigrant community in Los Angeles. Also, they have provided the basis for redrawing the social boundaries of the four barrios from within and for constructing a sense of home away from the homeland. Between 2001 and 2004, for example, each barrio acquired its own *imágen del santo* (the image of the *barrio* patron saints). Yalaltecos brought these *imágenes* from Oaxaca City to Los Angeles. Santiago Apóstol arrived in Los Angeles in 2001; San Juan Bautista in 2002; Santa Catarina Mártir in 2003; and Santa Rosa de Lima and San Antonio de Padua in 2004. When the barrio saints came to Los Angeles, each barrio organized a *baile* as if they were celebrating the Yalálag barrio patron saints in the home village. In the case of San Antonio de Padua, all four barrio committees organized a *baile* (see fig. 2.2).

During these communal events, Yalaltec immigrants welcomed their patron saints with rosaries, processions, and Catholic masses, along with the participation of Zapotec brass bands, the preparation of traditional foods, and the performance of Yalaltec religious, *chusca,* and social dances. The performances of religious dances that revered the celebrated patron saints were the same ones performed by Yalaltecos in Yalálag. Dances such as *Los Cuerudos, San José, Los*

Huenches, and *Los Negritos* are considered among the most important performances in the saints' fiestas. Each dance is representative of a barrio and cor-
responds to the patron saints of Yalálag: the dance of *Los Cuerudos,* the barrio
of Santiago; the dance of San José, the barrio of Santa Catarina; the dance of
Los Huenches, the barrio of San Juan; and the dance of *Los Negritos,* the barrio
of Santa Rosa.[18] In the midst of these religious performances of Yalaltec music
and dance, and spoken prayers and Catholic masses offered by an American and
a Mexican Catholic priest, the patron saints were sanctified, as if to symbolically
mark the permanent settlement of the four barrios and the translocation of the
patron saint fiestas of the immigrant community of Yalálag in Los Angeles.

In Los Angeles, the barrio patron saints have become significant not only for
their duplication but also for having redefined the social boundaries of "a distinctive community, in historical contexts of displacement" (Clifford 1994, 308)
and relocation (although in Los Angeles the barrios are not distinct geographical
areas). That is, in the migratory context the Yalálag patron saints continue to
be a point of self-identification for the Yalaltec immigrants. They highlight the
internal differences between the four barrio communities in Los Angeles and
represent a symbol of membership that, today, produces a new sense of primary
belonging in the United States. To elaborate, the transnationalization of the four
barrio patron saint fiestas of Yalálag in Los Angeles has allowed Yalaltec immigrants to imagine their community symbolically and socially from within. In his
article "Global Ethnoscapes," Arjun Appadurai (1996) observes that the imagination of community has become a crucial element in the social life and the
construction of identity of deterritorialized and immigrant communities. Imagining, he says, triggers new social orders and positions, new forms of agency,
and new forms of identification. Theoretically this idea of imagining is relevant
here because the Yalaltec immigrants imagine that they form a community in the
United States because their lives are socially and symbolically connected within
Los Angeles and are simultaneously linked to Yalálag.[19] Specifically, within Los
Angeles, Yalaltecos relate to each other through their shared history, language,
cultural practices, religious beliefs, and ideas—which could be said to constitute
their Yalaltec identity—and the experiences of socioeconomic marginalization
and discrimination that caused them to immigrate into the United States.

In his book *The Symbolic Construction of Community,* Anthony P. Cohen
argues that community is a social entity to which one belongs and identifies
through the process of socialization. Community, he also states, is created
through a "sense of primary belonging" that may extend beyond locality. That is
to say, community is a social construct to which people attach certain meanings
and "commit to a body of symbols" (1985, 16). The Yalaltec immigrants experience this process through the transnationalization of the barrio fiestas and the
duplication of the patron saints, and through a system of symbolic representations and social practices that extend beyond the home village of Yalálag. To put

it differently, the act of imagining as a member of the Yalaltec community of Los
Angeles emerged when Yalaltec immigrants came together to work for a common cause—just as Rosa, Juan, Catarina, and Santiago do in the saints joke. They
came to Los Angeles to raise money to repair their houses and then to support
the reconstruction of the saints' churches and their barrio fiestas.[20]

Many scholars on immigration have argued that most immigrants tend to
create strong social and symbolic ties within their immigrant communities as a
response to feelings of exclusion, racial discrimination, and social marginalization in the new country of residence (Brettell 2003; Clifford 1994, 1997; Grimes
1998; Rouse 1989; Tsuda 2003). In the case of the Yalaltec immigrants, the patron
saint celebrations seem to be an integral aspect of the immigrants' social life for
two reasons. The *bailes* provide a sense of community, and the patron saints
themselves help immigrants to cope with feelings of hardship, fear, concern,
stress, and social alienation from the host society. As Saskia Sassen (1998) and
Xavier de Souza (2004) suggest, in a global city like Los Angeles, immigrants
from different ethnic groups are usually segregated from the host society.
Although different immigrants dwell in the same geopolitical areas, they do not
necessarily interact or know each other, "nor do they structure or define themselves by referring to each other (for example ethnically and culturally distinct
groups of migrant labourers)" (Pries 2001, 5). Yalaltec immigrants, who coexist
and work with Euro-Americans, Guatemalans, Iranians, Salvadoreans, Mexican
mestizos, Koreans, and African Americans, for example, never connect or socialize intensively with outsiders. Thus, active participation in religious and social
activities such as the *bailes* contributes to a sense of community and provides
a context within which transnational life is initiated and conducted meaningfully in the United States. In addition, the *bailes* are a way to deal with a sense
of isolation, exclusion, and anti-immigration attitudes and policies in the larger
society.[21] That is, the *bailes* offer a social space that allows for the integration of
religious and secular activities through which immigrants can identify, communicate, relax, and enjoy themselves.

PRACTICES OF MEMBERSHIP: THE *GWZON*, SERVICE, AND COMMUNAL PARTICIPATION

For the Yalalatec immigrants, following the social and cultural patterns of the
home village to organize the *bailes* involves the social processes that inform the
symbolic construction of the Yalálag community in Los Angeles. But more precisely, celebrating the patron saints of Yalálag according to the norm of reciprocity and shared values such as group participation and social solidarity involves
distinctive ways of building social capital. As in Yalálag, the immigrant community in Los Angeles reproduces three native forms of social organization that
allow them to coordinate as a group and celebrate the Yalálag patron saints in the

bailes as if they were in the home village. They are the *gwzon* or the *guelaguetza*, the barrio organization, and the barrio committees, called *comisiones*. These forms of social organization derive from shared understandings of values and cultural practices of what it means to be community members.

In groups like the Yalálag Zapotec, the value of community is one of the most precious collective goods. The community is, above all, a symbol of cultural identity. It represents the social and symbolic ties, shared history, memories, worldview, language, and cultural practices that link Yalaltecos who share the same kinds of interests, social norms, and values.[22] Particularly, community constitutes "a wealth of (in)tangible social resources in which an individual or a group can access or obtain certain benefits derived from social capital" (Faist 2000b, 111). In Los Angeles, the practices of membership oriented toward the maintenance and reorganization of the Yalaltec community are, in the words of Robert D. Putnam, the social capital "such as networks, norms, and social trust that facilitate coordination and cooperation for mutual benefit" (cited in Rohe 2004, 17).[23] In what follows, I describe how practices of membership, which are embedded in the social work of the Yalaltec immigrants for the barrio patron saint fiestas in Los Angeles, namely, social capital, contribute to the social and symbolic construction of the Yalaltec community in the United States and simultaneously have positive consequences for the Yalaltec immigrant.

The Gwzon

In Los Angeles, Yalaltecos access help or benefit from each other when they participate in the social life of the immigrant community, such as the *bailes*. The *gwzon* (Sp. *gotzona* or *guelaguetza*), which means mutual aid or "giving and receiving," is a Zapotec concept very similar to what social scientists have described as social capital. It constitutes a system of mutual aid that promotes collective cooperation in kinship, friendship, and barrio and community relations. As such, it builds upon preexisting relationships, migrants' social networks, and the value of reciprocity, a value that permeates all aspects of the social life of the Yalaltec community.

From the Yalaltecos' point of view, the *gwzon* is a community value. It represents a set of norms of behavior that have operated inside of their community historically and continue in some aspects in the immigrant community. For Yalaltecos, the sense of community and group identity does not depend solely on a set of shared cultural practices and a common history and language, but is also constructed on the continuing exchange-based obligations to the extended family, the barrio, the community, the *bi gwlash*, and the patron saints. The idea of mutual aid within the Yalálag community derives principally from the self-definition of the Yalaltec individual. Being Yalalteco means complying with certain expectations, obligations, and roles in the Yalaltec community. Also, it refers to the individual's commitment to support or help those who are similar to one another. For example, person A or a group A performs *gwzon* (gives something or

does a favor) for person B or for group B with the expectation that B will recip-
rocate with help in the future. During the celebration of rites of passage such as
weddings and funerals, family members and close friends are expected to help
and participate in these events by means of the *gwzon* (de la Fuente 1949, 120).
Help can be offered or requested in the form of money, goods, moral support,
or labor. For these occasions, some individuals are called to fulfill certain roles in
the ritual event or are asked to do special work because they are obliged to do it.
Obligation here does not mean something to be done through coercion; rather,
it signifies a moral, civic, or religious commitment to someone or something.[24]

Within the community-building process, the *gwzon* contributes to the forging
of social resources within the immigrant community. As I described above, in
Los Angeles, each of the four barrios organizes its *bailes* through voluntary cooperation among the barrio community. Also, the four barrios perform *gwzon* for
each other. As José, a former barrio committee member, explained to me, "each
barrio plans its own *baile*, but the other barrios always offer their support by
attending or helping to organize the barrio event. It is like a *gwzon*. They help us
now. Afterward, we return this help." José means that Yalaltecos from other barrios contribute to the success of their *bailes* by means of *gwzon*. Buying tickets,
consuming food and drinks, participating in raffles, preparing food, or helping
to clean up after the event are acts of solidarity socially constructed as a form of
reciprocity. *Gwzon* also takes place when the host barrio invites other barrios to
perform their own barrio-specific dances to honor the celebrated patron saint—
the same dances as are performed by Yalaltecos in Yalálag. These dances include
danzas chuscas (parodic dances) to liven up the fiesta, and religious dances to
revere the saints. Occasionally, the Zapotec brass bands that are representative
of other Zapotec immigrant communities also perform *gwzon* with the barrio
committees.[25] In lieu of payment, both sides understand that the barrio committee will do something for the brass band in the future. Similarly, Yalaltecos can
accrue social capital by participating in the *gwzon*.

Within the Yalaltec community, there are Yalaltecos who have built a relationship of reciprocity with their patron saints through the practice of *gwzon*
of faith. They revere and celebrate their patron saints in the *bailes*, not only out
of religious devotion but also for help or support from the saints. Participating
and supporting the production of the patron saint fiestas in Yalálag and in Los
Angeles is not simply an act of religiosity. Rather, "it is an act of reciprocity with
the deities," as the Yalaltec historian, writer, and poet Mario Molina, explained
to me.[26] When the Yalaltec immigrants leave Yalálag, for instance, many make
promesas to their preferred patron saints. A *promesa* is a personal sacrifice that
includes the commitment or devotion to contributing to the realization of the
patron saint fiestas. For instance, on July 2004, many Yalaltec immigrants came
back to Yalálag to pay back their *promesas*. They had promised Santiago Apóstol,
for example, to send or bring money for his fiesta if they succeeded in crossing
the U.S.-Mexico border safely. From Los Angeles, other immigrants called their

relatives in Yalálag and asked them to pay for rosaries—to be recited on their behalf—during the nine-day patron saint fiesta. During the rosaries, the *rezadores* or *rezadoras* (a person who prays on someone's behalf) asked the patron saints to protect immigrants from failures and accidents in the United States as well as for their health, stable employment, and general well-being.

In the course of my research in Yalálag, I observed that during the fiestas, the *rezadores* can pray more than ten rosaries a day, due to the numerous petitions from family members of Yalaltec immigrants or immigrants themselves. Also, I became aware that some immigrants asked their families to honor the patron saints by adorning the patron saints' churches with flowers and candles, or by offering twelve *cirios* (Paschal candles) on one day of the fiesta. In recent years, the Yalálag patron saints have received dozens of *cirios* from Yalaltec immigrants, to the extent that the barrio committee fiesta has had to schedule these offerings over the course of the nine days so that all devotees have an opportunity to revere their patron saints. Accumulated candles are stored in the *casa del barrio* to be reused throughout the year.

Acts of reciprocity between the patron saints and the Yalaltec immigrants are very significant: just as the Yalaltecos revere and celebrate the Yalálag patron saints in Los Angeles and rebuild the saints' churches in Yalálag, the patron saints respond to the Yalaltecos. The saints alleviate immigrants' burdens, fears, and concerns, and help immigrants to achieve personal goals. Moreover, the patron saints provide immigrants and their families with comfort and self-confidence in the face of uncertainty brought about by migration. As the poet Mario Molina explained to me:

> No one among my *bi gwlash* is going to tell you this. Many immigrants perform *gwzon* with the patron saints. As a way of *promesa*, some send money to pay for rosaries. Others pay for the religious masses. And, a few pay for the flowers, candles, and all kinds of adornments to be used in patron saint fiestas. Look, all these things are done for a reason. My *bi gwlash* do not do this for free. They do this to be protected from harm and bad luck. In our culture, there is a relationship of *gwzon* between *Yalaltecos* and the patron saints. The patron saints help those who comply with their religious obligations and do not forget their barrio, their village, and their saints. The patron saints are obliged to protect the absentees. There is something very special for our people that you need to know. Some elders who pay to have rosaries recited on behalf of their immigrant relatives also pay someone in the village to perform the ritual ceremony of *petición de vida* [petition of life] and *buena salud* [good health] in sacred places in the Sierra. Look, these acts of faith are, above all, *gwzon* of faith.

The ceremony of *petición de vida* and *buena salud* is individual. It takes place in the Yalaltec hills. Yalaltecos make offerings to the *tierra* (Mother Earth) that include food, candles, flowers, mescal (alcoholic drink made from the agave plant), and money. At times, Yalaltecos pay a *rezador* or *rezadora* to go to the site and pray a rosary on behalf of their beloved family members. The petitioner asks Mother Earth or a venerated patron saint to protect their relatives in the United States from harm and provide them with work. John K. Chance points out that during the early eighteenth century, many Zapotec and Mixe villages performed sacred ritual and sacrifices in homes and *milpas* (cornfields). These were held collectively, though secretly, and "the purpose of these rites was to drawn the entire pueblo together to ask for prosperity, good health, and good harvest" (1989, 166).[27]

Service

The *servicio comunitario*, referred to as communal service or *tequio*, is a practice of membership that has to do with the ideas of group belonging and a series of established civic, religious, and moral obligations to the community. Defining oneself as a member of the Yalálag community is not only inherent in the cultural values and social norms that are implicit in the definition of the group's identity but is also based on the social positioning that each Yalalteco occupies in the political structure and social institutions of the Yalaltec community.[28] In the Yalaltec community, each individual is considered a citizen. Each has civic, religious, and political rights and is required to participate in the communal government.[29] In contrast to the Mexican mestizo communities in Mexico, indigenous people like the Yalálag Zapotecs have their own forms of government, known as the *sistema de cargos* (a system of public service posts), or the *sistema de usos y costumbres*, or the *gobierno tradicional*.[30] This form of government, which relies on indigenous political, civic, and judicial structures, defines community boundaries within the region. It also facilitates the village's social and political functioning through two types of communal work: municipal service and barrio service.

Municipal service appointments consist of twenty-five *cargos* (positions) that are distributed among 170 Yalaltec individuals: 140 *cargo* holders and 30 musicians.[31] Each *cargo* holder works for a period of one year and has the right to serve again in the future. After holding a *cargo* (public post) for two years in the municipal service, a *cargo* holder can ask the communal assembly to run again for a new municipal *cargo*. According to the traditional laws, *cargo* holders are responsible for storing their own food supplies and saving money to cover their basic needs during their terms. Historically, Yalaltec men have occupied these *cargos*; however, since the late 1980s, women have started to participate (Gutiérrez Nájera 2007). According to the social norms of the Yalálag community, all Yalaltecos are expected to serve their community and move up through the ranks to a higher social status on the municipal service.[32]

Barrio service is composed of five *cargos* and develops exclusively in each barrio community. It comprises barrio projects using barrio labor, such as paving the barrio roads. It also includes the organization of the religious fiestas of the barrio patron saints as well as restoration of the barrio churches, chapels, and the *casas de los barrios*. The barrio fiestas are planned and organized through barrio fiesta committees, and the reconstruction of the religious buildings for worship and barrio cultural centers is done through barrio labor, known as the *tequio de barrio* (collective work). These *cargos* are hierarchically structured and are voluntary, and Yalaltecos acquire status and respect for their work.[33] Barrio service is separate from the *cargo* service in the municipality. However, if someone is doing *cargo* service in the municipality, he or she is exempt from barrio service during his or her term. It is important to mention that although serving the barrio is an obligation, it is not required if someone wants to run for a *cargo* in the municipal service.

In Yalálag, the value of serving in the municipality and in the barrio is associated with the ideas of group cohesion and also with that of social stability. Those who comply with their obligations contribute to the maintenance of their community, cultural values, and social institutions. Those who fail to fulfill their communal or barrio obligations create social disorganization, alter the functioning of social institutions, and threaten the ideals of social solidarity and ethnic distinctiveness. To prevent social disintegration and communal disorganization, Yalatecos have created a system of penalties based on local laws and social norms. For instance, when a Yalaltec neglects to serve his or her barrio or community, then the barrio or the community penalizes him or her morally and administratively. Morally, a Yalaltec loses respect and social prestige within the community. The community tends to point out the faults of those who do not comply with their obligations, often through gossip. If an individual shirks municipal service, he or she will lose political rights such as voting in the municipal elections and participating in the communal assembly. Those who do not participate in the communal assembly may be fined by the municipality. Refusal to pay can result in jail time.[34]

For barrio service that has to do with the production of patron saint fiestas, sanctions are primarily moral. For instance, the barrio community will put those individuals on the spot. Sanctions will consist of indirect disapprovals for their selfish actions and of public statements such as "they never participate," "they are lazy and irresponsible," or "they are bad Catholics." In cases involving the development of barrio projects, sanctions will lead to monetary penalties. If someone does not follow or comply with the social norms, then the social bonds that link him or her to the barrio community will be at risk. In this sense, an individual's failure to participate in reciprocity and the social life of the barrio or community will lead to his or her own marginalization.

In the context of Los Angeles, barrio service has become an essential aspect of immigrant community formation. It has contributed to the social reorganization of the four barrio communities and has provided a context for the emergence of a transnational social space. Faist writes, "Transnational social spaces are combinations of ties, positions in networks and organizations, and networks of organizations that reach across the borders of multiple states. These spaces denote dynamic social processes, not static notions of ties and positions" (2000c, 191). As mentioned above, since the late 1980s, Yalaltec immigrants such as Catarina, Santiago, Rosa, and Juan began to organize *bailes* to collect money to improve local services in Yalálag, like the reconstruction of the municipal building, the elementary school, and the main plaza (Aquino 2002, Cruz-Manjarrez 2001). As a result of economic success and the increasing impossibility of homecoming, Yalaltec immigrants continued to nurture their desire to help their home village permanently.

Little by little, their engagement extended to the barrio fiestas. Thereafter, they started to sponsor the restoration of barrio churches and the *casas de los barrios*. In the process, immigrants like Catarina, Santiago, Rosa, and Juan began to reorganize their four barrio communities (the barrio system) and reconstitute the *cargo* system at the barrio level to serve their community of origin. Since then, the four barrio committees in Los Angeles have been structured in the same way as the barrio committees in Yalálag, and Yalaltec immigrants have engaged and complied with their *barrio* obligations locally in Los Angeles and transnationally in Yalálag. In Los Angeles, each barrio has three committees that plan and organize the *bailes*: the fiesta committee, the food committee, and at times, the sport events committee. Each of them is composed of five *cargo* holders: a president, a secretary, a treasurer, and two assistant committee members.

As in Yalálag, these *cargo* holders in Los Angeles work for a period of one year.[35] But more important, the improvement of communication technology and modern transportation has been central to maintaining long-distance transnational relations between the barrios in Yalálag and Los Angeles (cf. Harvey 1989; Rouse 1991; Smith 1995, 2006; Vertovec 2004). Barrio committee members in Los Angeles, who are officially nominated in barrio assemblies to serve the community of origin, now receive their *nombramientos*, appointments, by fax or mail from the barrio committees and the municipal authorities in Yalálag. Sometimes, when the barrio committee members return to Yalálag to visit their families or to participate in the patron saint fiestas, they pick their appointments up in person. The *nombramiento* is an official document issued, sealed, and signed by the municipal and barrio authorities in Yalálag. It describes the tasks—meaning the communal service—that the barrio committee members are expected to do in Los Angeles. The *nombramiento* also names the person who is supposed to carry out the service or task and indicates when the appointment starts and ends. In addition, a list of all committee barrio members of Los Angeles is displayed in the main office of the municipal building of Yalálag throughout the year.

I emphasize the reinscription of the barrio-*cargo* system in community formation for three major reasons. First, Yalaltec immigrants like Catarina, Santiago, Rosa, and Juan have overcome the risk of falling apart as a community and of feeling uprooted from their community of origin through barrio service. Second, they have reconstituted their community in Los Angeles on the basis of existing organizational structures—the barrio system and the barrio service—and the communal value of service. And third, Yalaltecos have continued to comply with their barrio obligations because they think of themselves as Yalaltec citizens and are aware of their rights and obligations to their community. However, it is clear that serving in Yalálag is not the same as serving in Los Angeles, or serving in Los Angeles on behalf of the home village. In Yalálag, one complies with obligations and follows social norms to reassert one's membership; to secure civic, political, and social participation and rights; to reinforce the social and political boundaries of the village; and to foster social stability of the Yalálag community. In Los Angeles, at the individual level, serving the community constitutes a form of social capital that can be exchanged for help or used as a way to garner social prestige. Also, serving means complying with civic and religious obligations to Yalálag to maintain one's rights as a citizen in Yalálag. At the group level, serving is meaningful because of its value as a collective good through which the barrio committee members facilitate the reaggregation of their community and connect Yalaltecos in social and organizational networks in both Los Angeles and Yalálag.

In this new context, it is clear that the value of service has broadened and strengthened social relations between Yalaltec immigrants and non-immigrants as well as among immigrants. Additionally, the barrio committee members have contributed to building social capital for immigrants. Currently, however, the experience of migration is causing some Yalaltec immigrants to consider ways that Los Angeles barrio committees and the value of community service could be used to address issues that affect immigrants and their descendants in the United States, including social and economic problems. Gerardo, a barrio committee member, spoke to me about this:

> We have thought that it would be a good idea to organize as a community to resolve social problems that affect us in the United States. I do not know if I should say that, unfortunately, our community concentrates most of its efforts on religious affairs and on helping our *pueblo*. Do not get me wrong. I think it is important that we organize as a community in Los Angeles to resolve problems regarding our immigration status and the bad experiences we have in this country. We need to know about our rights on the job and create outreach programs that help our teens to deal with drug problems and gang violence. There are various problems that need to be addressed: domestic violence, alcoholism, and health problems. Many people do not speak English. We need to do something about all these things. It would be a good idea to have a nonprofit organization in our community. But so far, our community is not there yet.

To sum up, Yalaltec immigrants such as Catalina, Juan, Santiago, and Rosa have been engaged in organizing locally in Los Angeles and transnationally between Los Angeles and Yalálag through existing native forms of social organization, communal values, and relations of trust. Much of this organization has responded to the idea of organizing socially through the value of service. Service related to producing the barrio saints' fiestas has promoted the reconfiguration of social relations, cultural values, and social institutions that define both a new sense of community and specific transnational "spatial-positional relations" (Pries 2001, 16) within the Yalálag community. To put it differently, service or serving the patron saints and the community has contributed to the creation of a transnational social space (Faist 2000b) where all social actors and their new structural-social positions contribute to the senses of group identity, the institutionalization of transnational life (Smith 2006), and maintenance of community in Los Angeles and between Yalálag and Los Angeles.

Communal Participation

In Los Angeles, Yalaltecos conceive of working for and participating voluntarily in the *bailes*—communal participation—as a moral and religious obligation to the patron saints and their community. That is, community members owe the community and are responsible for the betterment of their group just by virtue of membership in this social unit and participation in community life. One of the most notable aspects I have observed in the *bailes* is precisely the communal participation by the members of the four barrios. As in Yalálag, each barrio organizes its own *baile* in Los Angeles through voluntary cooperation. Four months before a *baile* takes place, the barrio committee members begin meeting to organize it. Personal word-of-mouth invitations start circulating among Yalaltec immigrants. The president of the barrio rents a ballroom, and the committee secretary and treasurer invite one or two Zapotec brass bands and hire a DJ or a *grupo tropical* (a tropical music ensemble) to liven up the *baile*. While the *grupo tropical* might be there primarily for entertainment, the brass bands are an essential part of the ritual aspects that take place in the *baile*, such as Catholic processions, masses, rosaries, and the performance of religious dances. The *vocales* (barrio committee assistants) usually ask the local newspaper, *El Oaxaqueño* or *El Imparcial*, to print an announcement of the *baile* within the Zapotec immigrant community in Los Angeles. Also, they make phone calls to their *bi gwlash*, urging them to buy tickets for the *baile*. Sometimes, however, the *vocales* go door-to-door among their *bi gwlash* requesting donations for the preparations and selling tickets for the *baile*.

In the *bailes*, a religious dance is usually performed to commemorate the celebrated barrio patron saint. Every weekend for three months prior to this event, eight male volunteer *danzantes* along with the *maestro de la danza* (dance teacher) meet in a *bi gwlash*'s house to rehearse. Usually, the *danzantes* are immigrant volunteers who have previous knowledge of the dance to be performed. When U.S.-born Yalaltec teens join the dance for the first time, the dance teacher is in charge of teaching them the steps and choreographies. When the dance includes female characters, they are chosen from a waiting list that is managed by the barrio committee members or the dance teacher. For instance, the dance of San José and the dance of *Los Huenches* include female characters: the *Vírgen María* in the dance of San José (barrio Santa Catarina) and Santa Rosa de Lima (barrio Santa Rosa) or the Yalaltec woman in the dance of *Los Huenches* (barrio San Juan). In Los Angeles, these female characters are usually U.S.-born Yalaltecas whose ages range from ten to seventeen years old. However, at times, men can play these characters. A week before the *baile*, in the late afternoon on a Saturday, the Yalálag Zapotec brass band and the *danzantes* come together to rehearse the dance. Each barrio committee invites its community to attend the dance rehearsal. While the *danzantes* and the musicians rehearse the dance and music performances, barrio committee members sell tickets for the *baile*, and a group of volunteer women offers *atole*, *tamales*, and traditional bread from Yalálag to the guests. At the end of the rehearsal, the guests thank the barrio committee members in person for the invitation. Before the *danzantes* and musicians go home, the committee members invite them for dinner and organize rides for those without transportation. According to the barrio committee members, the success of the *bailes* reflects good coordination among committee members, but perhaps more important, it is a testament of how the people of their barrio and the rest of the immigrant community cooperate and participate voluntarily.

For many Yalaltec immigrants, participating in the *bailes* is significant because it is tied to their need to assert their sense of group belonging as Yalaltecos through acts of religiosity. That is, some Yalaltec immigrants work for the *baile* to fulfill a *promesa*—a personal sacrifice that includes the commitment of participating for the patron saints on the day of their fiesta. In the *bailes*, for example, some women volunteer to sew the attire worn by the *danzantes* as a way to fulfill a *promesa*. Others prepare food to be sold in the *baile*. Some Yalaltec men are in charge of selling drinks and buying supplies for the *bailes*. They also give rides to the dancers or musicians and sometimes transport the brass band members' instruments. In sum, the work carried out for the commemoration of the patron saints is considered for some a sacred duty and a blessing in itself.[36] As Remedios, one of the most active volunteers of barrio Santiago, stated, "I am participating in the planning of the celebration of Señor Santiago because this is the *fiesta del santito* (the patron saint festivity). I am from the barrio of Saint Santiago. Therefore, I have to participate and serve the *santito*."

In this sense, communal participation in the *bailes* is a way to symbolically construct a sense of community and home away from the homeland. In addition, as argued above, it represents a way to deal with feelings of exclusion, isolation, and exploitation experienced by the Yalaltec immigrants. The sense of home that derives from communal participation produces meaningful experiences of place (cf. Feld and Basso 1996) and gives Yalaltec immigrants a dignified and recognized presence in the foreign context. Mario Molina, the Yalaltec immigrant and poet who lives in Oaxaca City, reflected extensively on Yalaltec immigrants' motivations to participate in the *bailes* in Los Angeles, Oaxaca City, and Mexico City. It is worth quoting Mario's reflections at length:

> I think that we participate in the *bailes* because the foreign land is not your home. Somehow, through the *bailes*, we feel at home without being at home. The need to talk to someone who speaks your own language, or just to remember together, or being informed about the recent events of Yalálag help us lessen the sadness we feel in a foreign country and the nostalgia for our village.
>
> Living in a foreign country is very hard. For the Yalalatec immigrants, there is always a need to reinforce both our identity and the links that bring us together in a foreign land. Participating in the *bailes* helps us avoid dying in the monotony, that is, in the oblivion, the invisibility. For us, city life is quite different from the way of life we are used to living. In Yalálag, one was accustomed to walking freely in the village. Yes, there is a lot of freedom there. One feels safe. In Yalálag, there are no walls. One can walk from one house to another. The patios are interwoven. It is as if they were a web of paths through which one can move back and forth at will.
>
> But in a foreign land, everything is different. Here, fences mark the physical boundaries where people live. Everyone lives in his or her own world. There is no communication. Nobody cares about you. You are here to work, day and night. These situations make us feel anxiety, fear, and uncertainty. At times, one feels lost. In the foreign land, everything is different. You do not have friends. You feel that you do not breathe the same air. The mountains and the pathways are different.
>
> It is like I said in my book *Lulá Ke Dillé*: "The church's bells do not speak in Zapotec." Yes, our bells speak our language. Once the church bells ring in Yalálag, one knows if someone died or is getting married, or if a *bi gwlash* is coming from the North [Los Angeles], or if the fiesta is going to start, or if there is a communal assembly. The bells are part of our language.
>
> However, when one arrives to the city, one does not know what those other bells are saying. We do not know their language! To live in a new land is difficult and the process of adjustment is hard. I think that the *bailes* unite us. They allow us to feel free. When you encounter your own people, you feel safe. It is like being in Yalálag.[37]

Thus, when the Yalaltec immigrants participate voluntarily in the *bailes*, they know that they are alive not only in the immigrant community but also in the home village. For example, in Yalálag, during the barrio fiestas or the barrio assemblies, a list of the names of the Yalaltec immigrants who participated in the *bailes* in Los Angeles is read publicly. During the nine-day celebration of the barrio fiestas, barrio committee members announce the amount of money sent from individuals in the barrio community in Los Angeles on the churches' loudspeakers. The list includes the names of the immigrants who bought tickets for the *bailes* and the names of those who sent individual monetary donations. Those who sent their donations and remained in Los Angeles are informed via telephone (mainly by family members) that their names were read during the barrio fiesta. Consequently, when Yalaltec immigrants such as Santiago, Catarina, Rosa, and Juan return to Yalálag to visit their families or attend the fiestas of their barrios, they know that the home community is aware of who participated and complied with their communal obligations and who did not. In this sense, participating in the *bailes* is a social and symbolic act through which Yalaltec immigrants perform their mutually supportive ties to maintain connection to their community in both Los Angeles and the home village.

It is important to note that refusing to participate in the *bailes* and moving away from the immigrant community is possible. There are immigrants who do not partake in the *bailes* and do not feel committed to their home village or the immigrant community (cf. Cohen 2004). According to barrio committee members, a few Yalaltecos do so because they do not care about the community. Others move away from their community because they look down upon it and feel more Americanized. When these people show disinterest, they tend to be criticized or overlooked upon their return to Yalálag and within the immigrant community. Thus, when they request help from their *bi gwlash* in Los Angeles or in Yalálag, it may be denied. Eleonora, who was a committee member of barrio Santiago in Los Angeles, described her experience in this regard:

> Look. In the Yalaltec community, it is expected that everyone participates and serves both the village and the patron saints. If you do not, let's say, you may be in trouble. I have served my village because of the faith I have in *el santito* (little patron saint) and because I do have obligations with my barrio. But, whether I liked or not, I have served my village because at some point you need help from the municipality or the village people. For instance, my father, who is an old man, lives by himself in Yalálag. All my sisters and brothers live in Los Angeles, and none has plans to return. And of course, my father does not want to come to the United States. But, look, if my father needs something, I can call someone in the village or in the municipality and ask for help.

When I met Eleonora in Yalálag in June 2004, she also observed: "This year I came to Yalálag because I want to sell my property. I have already talked to the *síndico* and the municipal president about it. Fortunately, I can sell it now. To tell the truth, I was lucky to get all my documents in order. I think that if I had not served this year in the barrio committee in Los Angeles, I would not have made it." This year, Eleonora was elected in a barrio assembly in Los Angeles. Thereafter, she was officially appointed in Yalálag to be the president of her barrio in Los Angeles for that year. In other words, taking part in and working for the community shows that one has complied with his or her community responsibilities and, thus, has contributed to the maintenance of social norms and the idea of community. But if you do not hold up your end of the *gwzon* as a community member, you alienate yourself and will be criticized. As Coleman (cited in Portes 1998b, 7) suggests in his study of social capital, "the mechanisms that generated social capital such as reciprocity expectations and group enforcement of norms" can have harmful effects when one keeps apart from one's group.

Yalaltecos know that their individual participation in the *bailes*, be it voluntary or in barrio committees, not only provides important sources of social capital but also grants them public recognition in both Los Angeles and Yalálag. Public recognition of an individual's efforts is one of the most valuable assets in the Yalálag community. It represents one of a few ways in which the community pays back and honors its members for their individual work and commitment to the Yalalatec community—its social institutions, social practices, cultural values, history, and people. Individual voluntary participation can be taken to mean that according to the logic of *gwzon*, the Yalaltec community will return its moral and economic support and bestow its public recognition only on those who contribute in the reproduction of Yalaltec community transnationally.

Over the course of my research in Yalálag, throughout the weeklong masses for the barrio fiestas, I heard Father Adrian thanking Yalaltec immigrants by name for their continued economic participation and moral support for the saints' celebrations. As I mentioned above, in Yalálag, during the barrio and community fiestas for the saints, a list of the names of the Yalaltec immigrants who participated in the *bailes* in Los Angeles is read publicly over a P.A. system so that the entire community knows about it. In Los Angeles, these public acknowledgments have the same meaning. In July 2001, in the middle of a *baile*, Gustavo, a committee member of barrio Santiago, took the microphone to remind us of the main purpose of carrying out that *baile*: to get money for the barrio celebration in Yalálag. He also said, "Thanks to all you for contributing to the realization of this *baile*. Your support is very valuable and important for the fiesta of our barrio." He added: "Special thanks to Gerardo and his family for letting us use his house for free."

In 2001 and 2004, I experienced two examples of the most breathtaking expression of feelings in both Los Angeles and Yalálag: the social recognition when someone dies and has done meaningful work for the community. Most Yalaltecos believe that community members manifest their deepest respect and honor the *bi gwlash* when they die. Family name, economic position, gender, profession, and even personal conflicts or social tensions or disagreements with the community—these no longer matter. "When someone dies," a friend explained to me, "one forgets about harsh feelings, political differences, or personal problems. What matters once you pass away is what you did for your community." In other words, the greater involvement one has had with the community, the higher expression of prestige and social solidarity.

On July 2001, professor Jeremías Ríos, founder of many Zapotec brass bands in both Mexico and the United States, passed away. A native of the barrio of Santa Catarina, *maestro* Jeremías became famous for his compositions of diverse Zapotec dances, known as *sones* and *jarabes*, as well as Zapotec waltzes, *danzones*, overtures, and marches. Before his arrival in the United States, he spent much time teaching music in different Zapotec villages in the Sierra Juárez, Oaxaca City, and Mexico City. In 1994, he founded the first Yalaltec brass band in Los Angeles, known as Bhen Gualhall (Echoes of Yalálag). Until his death, he conducted the brass band of the immigrant community of Zoochina of Los Angeles and kept training other Zapotec immigrants to form new brass bands. The following excerpt from the newspaper *El Oaxaqueño*, published in Oaxaca and distributed in Yalálag and Los Angeles two years after Professor Jeremías died, shows the importance of his communal participation and the tribute that the Yalálag Zapotec community paid back:

> Marginalization, unemployment, and poverty in the Sierra are three of many reasons that have caused immigration of hundreds, if not thousands, of Zapotecs. Among them are dozens of musicians. Today, there are Zapotec villages in La Sierra that lack their own brass bands because of the continuing expulsion and massive migration of Zapotecs to the United States. Today, we want to acknowledge Jeremías Ríos' efforts and love for his *bi gwlash* and for our music. Thanks to his communal work, a great number of brass bands have formed in the United States. Thanks to Jeremías, our music has been preserved.
>
> Like many other Zapotec immigrants, Jeremías Ríos was accustomed to returning the day of the fiesta of Saint Antonio of Padua. Here, he used to direct the *banda municipal* [the municipal brass band], *Guacuell Kee Yoo' Lhao.* Unfortunately, Professor Jeremías is no longer with us; however, we want to honor and remember him for his work. These thoughts are for him. Thanks to his service and his music, the identity of the Zapotec community has and will prevail.[38]

During my fieldwork in July 2001, I became aware of Professor Jeremías's death when his body arrived in Yalálag from Los Angeles. During the vigil that day, the Yalaltec brass bands Uken ke Uken, the Banda Autóctona, and the Nueva Imágen got together to perform at his funeral. In the middle of spoken prayers and religious chants, the brass bands performed religious music while some women intoned funeral chants. All night, a group of women and men volunteered to prepare coffee and offer bread for all in attendance. The next morning, before the burial, a big procession led the body around the four barrios. Surrounded by funeral music played by the brass bands, dozens of men, women, and children, who carried white gladiolas and Paschal candles, accompanied Professor Jeremías on his last walk. Before reaching the cemetery, the procession stopped by the principal church of Yalálag, San Juan Yalálag. While the casket was placed at the main altar, Father Adrian approached us and expressed his condolences to the professor's family. After Father Adrian blessed and sprinkled holy water on the body, Professor Jeremías's relatives came in front of the altar to thank the community for its support. When we arrived at the cemetery, the family thanked us again for our attendance. When the brass bands started to play, Professor Jeremías was buried, as if he were returning to the core of the highlands. After this event, a big meal was served in the professor's house for the guests, family members, and friends. During the following nine days, a rosary was organized on his behalf. It included the performance of religious music and chants, spoken prayers, and offerings of food. The meal and burial were paid for with monetary donations collected in Los Angeles.

In Los Angeles, community members say that those Yalaltec immigrants who move away from the community or those who scarcely participate in community life are not supposed to be honored or remembered. However, although the community may decide to manifest its collective indifference, it may choose to express its solidarity. To be part of the Yalálag community, be it in Yalálag, Oaxaca City, or Los Angeles, is to have a place, a dignified presence, and an identity, in this case the Yalaltec identity.

In February 27, 2004, Salomón Matías passed away in Los Angeles. Although he was never a barrio committee member and attended the *bailes* only once in a while, on the day of his funeral, the community was there for him and for his relatives. Although Matías's sons could not be reached in Mexico, his niece and various Yalaltecos took care of the funeral. A week before the funeral rite, personal invitations to attend the funerary event circulated by word of mouth among Yalaltec immigrants. On Thursday night, before the wake, dozens of Yalaltec men and women were called to help prepare food such as tamales, chocolate, coffee, *caldo de res* (beef broth), and bread. On Friday night, at least five hundred Yalaltecos gathered at Pico Union in Chico Diego's backyard. For several years, Diego, the president of the Zempoaltepetl brass band, offered his home to Yalaltecos for these types of events as well as family and barrio fiestas. Among those gathered were the Zempoaltepetl brass band, dozens of Yalaltec families, single men and women, teenagers, and a group of volunteers who were in charge of offering hot drinks and food the entire night. Surrounded by white gladiolas, Paschal candles, and incense, a simple brown coffin with Matías's remains rested on the patio the whole night. Around 8:00 p.m., two *rezadoras* and a group of women, who knelt in front of Salomón's coffin, led a series of prayers accompanied by the Zempoaltepetl brass band.

After Father Joseph, an American priest who offers religious services for the Oaxacan community of Los Angeles, led a mass and blessed the body with holy water, a long line formed to bid a personal farewell to Matías. While some Yalaltecos stopped for a moment to grieve over the corpse, others continued on to offer condolences and money to Matías's relatives. That night I was told that monetary donations, left in a small sealed box, were collected to pay for the funeral expenses: food, flowers, candles, folding chairs, tables, power supply, water, the mass, and cemetery services. At times, such money is used to pay for travel expenses when the corpse is buried in Yalálag. According to the social norm of reciprocity, participants offer money as a way of *gwzon* to the deceased's family. And then, the family, who keeps a record of the donor's names and the amount of money offered, is expected to pay back this help in the future.[39]

This funeral was carried out in a way similar to funerals in Yalálag. On Saturday morning, around 10:00 a.m., amid religious music and chants, candles and white gladiolas, a group of eight Yalaltec pallbearers carried the casket to the funeral carriage. When the funeral cortege arrived at the cemetery, Father Joseph, who was already waiting, offered his last blessings. Afterward, some of the attendees spontaneously gave funeral speeches. Some thanked family and community support. Others expressed their grief for the loss of Matías. When the casket was then lowered into the ground outside of a garden of the Angelus Rosedale cemetery, a group of women began to throw white gladiolas on the coffin. When the burial was over, most family members, friends, and guests reorganized to go back to the house for a meal. Later that week, a novena was given on behalf of the deceased.

The funeral ceremonies I have just described provide good examples of the tribute that the community offers its members in return for their communal participation. Also, they reflect the strength of communal bonds and the emphasis the Yalálag community gives to both social solidarity and the value of the Yalaltec individual. During the Matías's funeral, Karla, a second-generation teenage girl, said to me that the big meals and the entire funeral are very important in her community because they remind her of the atmosphere of the *bailes.*

Sometimes I feel that funerals look like a *baile.* Really! During the funerals, you always see a big crowd of *paisanos* (*bi gwlash*). The same people, who participate voluntarily in the *bailes,* the same people, who come to the funerals. It's funny, but to me a funeral looks like a *baile.* Of course, people do not dance. But, unlike the *bailes,* I think, the funerals are very special. I do not know exactly why? You know, there is something in the Yalaltec community that amazes me: My *paisanos* are very united. When they come to a funeral, they help the family of the deceased with money. During the wake, the *paisanos* volunteer to prepare food. Like in Yalálag, men serve coffee, *atole,* and bread. My mom, for example, always comes to cook and help with the cleaning. You know after the whole ceremony is finished, there is so much to clean and eat. There is something that I like the most, people always bring tons of white gladiolas. All of them are very supportive. When the corpse needs to be sent to Yalálag, they raise funds. Really, it is like the *bailes*. All of them work as a team.

In sum, since the late 1980s, in Los Angeles, Yalaltec immigrants have organized dozens of community events, the *bailes*, for the betterment of their barrio communities. Economically, culturally, and morally, they began to support the realization of the four barrio patron saint fiestas and the reconstruction of the saints' churches and the *casas de los barrios* in Yalálag. In the process, they started to institutionalize a type of transnational life that included bringing new replicas of the four barrio patron saints from Oaxaca to Los Angeles, celebrating the barrio patron saints according to cultural, political, and religious patterns of the homeland, and working transnationally with barrio committee fiestas in Yalálag.

In Los Angeles, the value of serving and participating in the *bailes* for the barrio fiestas in Yalálag has been fundamental to community formation, with the reconstitution of the barrio fiesta system and the barrio *cargo* system as key native cohesive social institutions. While Yalaltec immigrants have continued to participate in the *bailes* to fulfill their communal obligations through barrio public posts, they have also taken part in them because this is a way to deal with feelings of exclusion, isolation, and racial and ethnic discrimination (for a detailed discussion of this topic see chapters 4 and 5). Likewise, just as acts of religiosity to Yalálag patron saints have been socially constructed as a form of reciprocity and religious devotion, so has communal participation produced a sense of communal belonging. To be exact, communal participation has allowed Yalaltec immigrants and their U.S.-born children to imagine that the Yalaltec community also exists in Los Angeles. For Yalaltec immigrants such as Santiago, Catarina, Juan, and Rosa, participating in the *bailes* contributes to the forging of social resources, namely social capital, for their community in Los Angeles; in addition, working for the barrios and the saints in Yalálag facilitates cooperation and communal action in the maintenance of two collective goods transnationally: the group identity and the community. In the next chapter, I discuss the significance of immigrants' participation in the most important religious fiesta in Yalálag and the impact of migration in the social life of Yalaltec non-immigrants.

❖

CHAPTER 3

COMMUNITY LIFE
ACROSS BORDERS

During the celebration of the major mass of San Antonio de Padua on June 13, 2004, in the village of Yalálag, Father Adrian spoke, saying: "We must thank all the people who have made possible the fiesta for San Antonio de Padua. This fiesta could not have been done without the collaborative work between local people and immigrants who live in Oaxaca City, Mexico City, Veracruz, Puebla, and the United States." After the mass, the priest invited all in attendance to participate in the blessing of the bullring.[1] On my way there, I bumped into all kinds of people taking part in the activities. I saw immigrants from Los Angeles and their families, including dozens of children I had already met in California, who were running around with their cousins and friends or playing electronic games. There were also hundreds of Zapotec, Chinantec, and Mixe visitors from neighboring and distant towns. They were looking for a place to sit and watch the religious and parodic dances in the basketball court. Dozens of families were waiting inside the bullring to watch the blessing of the horsemen and bullfighters, the bulls, and the bullring.

The bar was crowded with immigrant and local men drinking beer. Food, candies, flowers, drinks, and religious souvenirs were sold in stalls located next to the church and on the main street. Behind the bullring, there was a platform for one of the Zapotec brass bands that was livening up the fiesta. The highlands echoed as the church bells pealed and fireworks exploded, announcing the blessing of the bullring. Immigrants, residents, and visitors kept quiet as Father Adrian, a thirty-eight-year-old Zapotec man, walked around the bullring and sprinkled holy water to bless one of the major events in the fiesta of the patron saint.

This scene is more significant than it appears on the surface. The Yalaltec people believe that three facts distinguish the fiesta of San Antonio de Padua. First, this saint is a great miracle worker, who protects Yalálag's people, the cattle, and harvest. Second, San Antonio looks after the well-being of the immigrants. Third, for his feast day, many immigrants return to thank the patron saint for his help and to visit their families, making this the community's most important event. Since the 1990s, the fiesta of San Antonio de Padua has been realized not only through the participation and service of local people but also through collective and individual donations sent by immigrants in the United States. For the 2004 fiesta, immigrants' donations paid for food and entertainment for approximately four thousand people, a professional bullfight show, and public transportation for two guest brass bands. Immigrants reintegrated into their former community roles as musicians, dancers, cooks, bartenders, or volunteers. For nine days, public acknowledgments of the immigrants' participation and support were repeated at all community events and activities, such as the *baile*; the donation of bulls, pigs, and *cirios* (Paschal candles); and the horse races, bullfights, and basketball games. At every mass, the priest in his sermon, and even parishioners, publicly welcomed and thanked immigrants for their continued participation in the fiesta and asked God to take care of those who served in the fiesta committee (*comisión de festejos*) as well as those who worked to form the first hometown association in Los Angeles, the Unión Yalalteca.

In the context of the fiesta of San Antonio de Padua, this chapter examines why immigrants' reintegration in the social and religious life of Yalálag has evolved and endured, and why immigrants and non-immigrants have reorganized transnationally through the most important festivity of the village. Understanding the significance of the fiesta of San Antonio de Padua and its relation to the formation of the Unión Yalalteca—the first Yalaltec hometown association in Los Angeles—requires a background in the religious and political life of the Yalaltecos from a historical perspective. In what follows, I outline the significance of Yalaltec religious thought and immigrants' current relations with the church in Yalálag.

RELIGIOUS LIFE AND THOUGHT IN YALÁLAG

In Yalálag, Catholicism continues to dominate in the village, while the community's social life centers on Catholic fiestas. Currently, Yalaltecos define themselves as very Catholic and invest much time, energy, and money in religious activities and patron saint festivals.[2] In contrast, from the end of the sixteenth until the eighteenth centuries, Yalaltecos fiercely resisted forced conversion to Catholicism. In 1556, when Dominican friars arrived to the Sierra, the Zapotecs practiced an animist religion, which held that the universe was created by the Supreme Being and was regulated and animated by natural forces such as "lightening, sun, earthquakes, fire, and clouds" (Chance 1989, 151). To begin the proselytization process for all Indians, Dominicans traveled around the Sierra and settled in a few villages. Between 1568 and 1622, the friars built the first congregation in Yalálag, due to its proximity to Villa Alta and the road to Antequera (Chance 1989).

In the seventeenth century, while the Spanish attempted to crush all Indian resistance and demanded as much food, gold, and cotton as possible for their subsistence from all Zapotec villages, the Dominicans likewise tried to crush resistance and built churches, initiated catechism classes, and administered the sacraments. Due to Indian resistance to adopt the conquerors' religion, the Zapotecs were victims of physical punishment: "penalties of sixteen to eighteen lashes were administered to male offenders by the *fiscales* or church *topiles* (police) for such infractions as . . . failing to attend mass, rosary, recitations, or *doctrina* classes . . . [and] disrespect of the curate" (Chance 1989, 158). In 1735, a group of Yalaltecos was taken to civil court trials in Villa Alta for idolatry.[3] Yalaltecos were accused of the: "abominable crime of idolatry, superstition, witchcraft, divination, and slaughter of creatures that natives of the town of San Juan Yalálag have executed by offering their demon nefarious sacrifices among other things commonly practiced in their idolatry: blood, hearts of said creatures [animals], ministering their flesh to the *Principales, Governador, Alcaldes, and Regidores* of said town."[4] In the 1880s, during Bishop Gillow's visit to the Sierra, he was informed that Yalaltecos still performed private Indian worship at home and sacrificed turkeys and dogs in the cornfields (Chance 1989, 162).

In the second half of the seventeenth century, despite the elimination of native religious practices and the Catholic Church's constant stigmatization and condemnation of these beliefs, the Zapotecs began to mix elements of their native religion and integrated them with the religion of the colonizer. They revered community cults and dedicated them to Catholic saints. During religious celebrations at homes and cornfields, they secretly performed sacrifices that coincided with Catholic fiestas. In the second half of the eighteenth century, the Spanish friars saw that converting Indians to Catholicism no longer posed a problem, but aspects of syncretized Catholic worship were out of control. As Chance points outs: "community patron saints become much more important objects of devotion. But fiestas for the saints had become much more than religious occasions; they were celebrations of community identity, power, prestige vis-à-vis other communities." The majority of Zapotec villages in the district of Villa Alta, to which Yalálag belonged, "celebrated seven or eight fiestas a year (not including the smaller *barrio* feast days), with priests always in attendance for at least part of the proceedings" (Chance 1989, 169).

By the middle of the twentieth century, the Church still did not consider the Yalaltecos genuine Catholics because they continued to practice "pagan" beliefs and carry out religious ceremonies in accordance to the ancient Zapotec ritual calendar. De la Fuente (1949) observed in the 1940s that the Church not only promoted prejudice against the Yalaltecos' beliefs and their religious practices, but it also weakened indigenous religious leaders and transformed their practices. For example, under this system, the Church continued to impose its religious ideology and consolidated Catholic beliefs. Yalaltec religious leaders such as priest-shamans lost their religious rank and became known as both *hechizeros* (sorcerers) and *rezadores* (someone who says spoken prayers). Similarly, the Church recast the ancient

Zapotec gods, who lived in hills, rivers, and caves, as demons, devils, and ghosts. Currently, all the Zapotec gods have been forgotten and their ceremonies, too; however, there are still some rituals, religious practices, and ancient beliefs that are syncretized with those of the Catholic God, saints, ceremonies, and beliefs (Alcina F. 1993, Kearney 1972, Molina 2003, Nader 1969).

At present, the religious life of the Yalaltec Catholic population is very intense. Throughout the year, the Yalaltec people celebrate dozens of Catholic fiestas in accordance with the Catholic calendar. Among the principal patron saint fiestas are those of San Juan Yalálag and San Antonio de Padua, as well as the four barrio patron saints. The minor celebrations are those of the Holy Week, San Juan Degollado, the Virgin of El Rosario, the day of Santa Cruz, the Day of the Death, Christmas, the *posadas* (the nine-day celebration before Christmas), Christmas Eve, and New Year's Eve, among others. In Yalálag, the "good" Catholics are characterized as those who fulfill their religious obligations to the Church and the patron saints. While the majority of older people attend church almost every day and especially on Sunday mornings, younger generations are constantly pushed to participate in religious activities. Older people usually encourage teenagers and children to attend religious masses and follow the doctrine, beliefs, and rituals of the Catholic Church. Some are motivated to join the brass bands or the religious dance groups that perform in patron saint fiestas. There are quite a few teenagers very active in productions of religious rituals and festivals. In the last five years, the "religious school," organized by the village's priest, has come to play an essential role in introducing younger generations to Catholic dogma. On Saturday evenings, a group of teenage girls catechize and teach the basics of the life of Jesus Christ to children between five and eight years old. Others coordinate groups of girls and boys nine and ten years old to prepare them for their first communion. The priest and the pastor train the church's choir, El Grupo Juvenil, composed of talented teenaged Yalaltec musicians and singers, who accompany the mass.[5]

The village of Yalálag has Catholic churches, chapels, and *capillitas* and *ermitas* (small chapels). The churches and barrio chapels are located in the village, and the *capillitas* and *ermitas* are either in the village or in the Yalaltec hills. The main churches are those of San Juan Yalálag, San Antonio de Padua, and Santiago Apóstol. The three barrio chapels are those of Santa Catarina Mártir, San Juan Bautista, and Santa Rosa de Lima. The *capillitas* are the ones of the Cristo de los Siete Viernes (Christ of the Seven Fridays) and San Alejo.[6] According to Yalaltecos, the Church of San Juan Bautista, also known as San Juan Yalálag, and the *santuario* of the Virgin of Guadalupe, located on Guadalupe Hill, rest on pre-Hispanic religious sites.[7] Similarly, the chapel of La Cruz Viva and a great number of small chapels in the hills were built on pre-Hispanic religious sites. When de la Fuente (1949) carried out his ethnographic research, he documented that the Yalaltec hills, the caves, the spring, the stars, and the Cruces Vivas (trees whose shape looks like a cross) were still considered sacred entities. Currently,

Yalaltecos call these trees *Cruces Vivas* (living crosses) because they believe that their power is similar to the Catholic cross.

In the course of my research, I found that the elders and some adults believe that there are places in the highlands that were created and are still inhabited by supernatural beings. Among them are the *radg be?* (The Hill Where the Wind Cuts), and the Hill of San Antonio, the latter known today as the Cerro Brujo (Bewitched Hill). According to de la Fuente, the ancient Yalaltecos named this hill "The Hill of the Lord of Animals and Deer." However, the Catholic Church renamed this hill first after San Antonio de Padua and later called it the bewitched hill. At the end of the nineteenth century, the Yalaltecos practiced religious rituals on this hill. They asked the lord of animals and deer for rain to ensure good harvests and a plentiful food supply and for protection of the animals (de la Fuente 1949, 265).

At present, most of these pre-Hispanic beliefs have disappeared, and the younger generations have stopped performing rituals related to Mother Earth and visiting these sacred sites. Some sacred sites and ritual practices did not vanish, however, because they were mixed with Catholic beliefs. Some elders still conceive of the hills, certain stones, and springs of water as having magic powers.[8] And perhaps most significant, some of them continue to perform sacred ceremonies that are associated with ancient beliefs. For instance, some Yalaltec peasants carry out agricultural rituals in their parcel of land or on San Antonio Hill. In such religious ceremonies, the Yalaltec peasants make offerings to Mother Earth and ask a *rezador* to say a Catholic rosary on behalf of the deity. The aim of these ceremonies is to thank Mother Earth for what Yalaltecos have taken from her and to ask the patron saints to protect the coming harvest.[9] In July 2001, I visited the chapel of the Virgin of Guadalupe, which is located at the top of Guadalupe Hill. A Yalaltec friend of mine showed me where some Yalaltecos make offerings to Mother Earth in front of the chapel. She then explained to me that Yalaltecos perform a ceremony in which they dig holes on the soil to offer food and mescal, and sacrifice animals such as hens and roosters for Mother Earth. When we entered the chapel of the Virgin of Guadalupe, she performed a *limpia* (spiritual cleansing) for her sons and me.

Another example of the permanence of native beliefs that are syncretized with Catholicism is the saint who appears in the village and the highlands. Yalaltecos believe that San Antonio de Padua, who is syncretized with the god of the hills and the animals, appears in the village in the form of a child. Once in a while, the saint leaves his temple to visit Yalálag and neighboring villages. Besides watching over the villagers, he also goes to the countryside to care for the animals.

In Yalálag, there is a collection of church organizations known as the *comisiones de la iglesias*. Among these organizations are: the *comisiones de festejos* (fiesta committees), the *comisiones de obras* (church reconstruction committees), and the *comisiones de las iglesias* (church committees). These committees are usually composed of five committee members: a president, a secretary, a treasurer, and two *vocales* (committee assistants). The church committees of Saint Antonio de Padua and San Juan Yalálag are made up of a president, a secretary, a treasurer, and four *mayordomos*. The latter are representatives from each of the four barrios and are appointed by the municipal authorities to work one week per month in these churches during twelve months. According to the local customary laws, these committee members are chosen every year in the annual community assembly. It is expected that all Yalaltecos participate and comply with these responsibilities (*cargos*) out of duty to the village and the patron saint. Barrio fiesta committee members are appointed in barrio assemblies as well.

The major responsibilities of *comisiones de festejos* are to plan and organize the patron saint festivities; the *comisiones de obras*, to reconstruct the churches; and the *comisiones de las iglesias,* to clean the churches, sell candles, ring the church bells, and protect the building and all religious objects against misconduct and robberies. In the past ten years, the *comisiones de festejos* and the *comisiones de obras* have received funds from Yalaltec immigrants in Los Angeles, Oaxaca City, and Mexico City to renew the churches and chapels, improve the barrio cultural centers, and produce the patron saint fiestas. But unlike these church committees, the reconstruction committee of the Church of San Juan Yalálag works with the local priest because it is the only church that has religious authority. Recently, Father Adrian has started to work with the first Yalaltec hometown association in Los Angeles, the Unión Yalalteca, to carry out the *Reconstrucción del templo de San Juan* Yalálag.[10]

All religious fiestas are organized and planned by the *comisiones de festejos*, common to many Mexican indigenous communities. Unlike the patron saint fiestas in metropolitan or mestizo areas, the religious fiestas the Sierra "are organized by members of the villages and not by the Father," as Father Adrian explained to me. In Yalálag, the fiesta committees organize their patron saint fiestas and ask the municipal authorities to officially invite the local priest to perform the religious ceremonies. Although the priest does not intervene in the organization of these religious festivals, his role is highly important. Before the fiesta committees start the planning and organization of religious fiestas, the priest officiates at mass and blesses the committee members in special ceremonies. In addition to administrating the sacraments during the patron saint fiestas, the priest also conducts the novenas, rosaries, and the *maitines* (religious chants and music played a day before of the fiesta). He blesses the cowboys and bullfighters as well as the bullring and the animals—bulls and horses—that will be used in the traditional bullfights. Finally, he is in charge of welcoming the guest bass brands that come from neighboring Zapotec villages or Oaxaca City to animate the patron saint fiestas. The significance of the priest in these celebrations is not only related to his religious authority and myriad religious functions but is also associated to the success of the fiestas in their entirety.

(Im)migration and the Church in Yalálag

In the last two decades, the importance of the Catholic Church has increased and almost superseded practices and beliefs of pre-Hispanic origin. National and international immigrants have significantly contributed to its presence and dominance of ideology, practices, and values. The immigrant community of Yalálag in Los Angeles has raised thousands of dollars for the reconstruction of the main churches, chapels, and the four *casas de los barrios* (barrio cultural centers). The increasing number of new benches in the churches is due to immigrants' individual or family gifts to the patron saints and the church. Summers and winters, the priest works constantly because many immigrant men return to Yalálag to marry (see fig. 3.1).[11] In addition, immigrants provide economic support to their families in Yalálag to celebrate ritual events such as baptisms, confirmations, communions, *XV años* (known in the United States as *quinceañeras*), weddings, and funerals.[12] At times, second-generation teenage girls or young immigrant women from the United States go to Yalálag to celebrate their *quinceañera* or to marry. These celebrations include a mass and a huge family gathering. When a Yalaltec immigrant dies in Los Angeles and the family decides to send the corpse to back to the village, the priest will perform a mass and offer a blessing before the immigrant is buried.

   Another way that Yalaltec immigrants have enhanced the position of the local church is through economic and social participation in religious holidays. Many immigrants return every year to organize one of nine *posadas* (a Christmas festivity that lasts nine days before Christmas Eve) to honor or pay a *promesa* (a sacred vow) to the Christ child. According to Yalaltecos, the increasing number of immigrants interested in hosting a *posada* has obligated the local priest to keep a notebook with pages and pages of names of immigrants and villagers who have promised the Christ child to hold a *posada* in coming years. An important point is that the *posadas* have become more elaborate over the years. Villagers claim that fifteen years ago, the *posadas* were very simple. Today, however, immigrants spend hundreds of dollars on them. Although Yalaltecos think the importance of the *posadas* has not changed, nevertheless, villagers make greater efforts to save enough money for the production of these events. As a result, the expenses for the fiesta have climbed due to the influence of immigrants, pricing them at the upper reaches for those who stay in Yalálag. In December 2003, I attended three *posadas*. The first one was organized and paid for by a local family. The second and the third ones were organized by local families and paid for expatriate Yalaltecos. On the December 23, my friend Estela and her sister Irma from Los Angeles, and her brother Alberto from Oaxaca City helped their mother to organize one of the *posadas*. Estela's mother received the *peregrinos* (Joseph and the Virgin Mary) and prepared a meal for approximately three hundred guests.

   On December 24, Catalina, a single immigrant woman who resides in Los Angeles, invited me to attend the last *posada*. In her role of the godmother of the

Figure 3.1. Yalaltec immigrants return to Yalálag to get married, 2004.

Niño Dios (Christ child), she offered a huge meal to the entire village. Catalina's relatives and friends helped her to cook hundreds of tamales, loaves of bread, tortillas, pots of *champurrado* (a drink made of corn and chocolate) and coffee, and *caldo de res* (beef stew) as a *gwzon*. Catalina paid the *rezadores* to say rosaries on the 24th and 25th, and asked the priest to celebrate the *misa de gallo*—a mass held on December 24 in the church of San Juan Yalálag. Days before Christmas Eve, she placed a huge altar in her mother's courtyard to host the sacred images of the Virgin Mary, Saint Joseph, and the *Niño Dios* that belonged to the Church of San Juan Yalálag. The altar included outdoor Christmas decorations brought from Los Angeles, such as lights and a two-foot Santa Claus. To offer lunch on Christmas Day, the godmother had to buy an extra cow since she had run out of food the night before. On the night of the 25th, she hired a tropical music band and a Yalaltec brass band to liven up the *baile* (popular dance event) that was held in the main plaza.

   In the last four years, social relations among the priest, the villagers, and the immigrants have improved significantly—a contrast with previous years. Father Adrian, who arrived at Yalálag in February 2003, has developed good relations with the residents. According to Yalaltecos, the local priest is highly respected and maintains a good reputation. Unlike former priests, Father Adrian tends to remain neutral in local politics, works hard for the Catholic community, and behaves irreproachably. Based on de la Fuente's ethnography (1949) and on my own field research (2000–2004), I became aware that the Yalaltec people are known for their contentious relationships with former priests. The reasons for this are multiple. De la Fuente found that Yalaltecos did not like Catholic priests because the latter used to condemn and forbid their native rituals. Some priests were seen as lazy and exploitive because they made their living out of Yalalte-cos' contributions and did not want to work in the countryside to produce their own food supplies and comply with their community obligations. Even more scandalous, some Catholic priests were kicked out of the village because they liked women and drank too much alcohol. Father Adrian seems to have developed good relationships with the Yalaltec people, however, because he makes an effort to get along with the villagers, involves the younger generations in church activities, and began a major project for the Catholic community: the Church of San Juan Yalálag reconstruction. Additionally, since he is Zapotec and offers religious masses in Zapotec and Spanish, he has gained sympathy among the Yalaltec community. During one of my interviews, Father Adrian mentioned that older women and men, whom he described as monolingual or more fluent in Zapotec, like him because he preaches the Word of God in their native language.[13]

Likewise, the recent relationship between some immigrants and the priest has started to flourish. For some immigrants and second-generation Yalálag Zapotecs, the priest has come to play an important role as a spiritual counselor. For immigrants residing in the United States, the priest offers to receive long-distance calls from Los Angeles to provide personal and emotional support, and spiritual guidance. According to Father Adrian, immigrants' relatives visit him not only to talk about their own concerns or fears regarding the migration experience of their families, but also to arrange international phone calls between the priest and immigrants. During one of my interviews, Father Adrian mentioned the following:

> At times, immigrants call me to talk about their problems. Some of them tell me about their adversities and ask me for advice. When I talk to them, I ask them about how they are doing. I never forget to ask about their plans in the future. It is always good to remind them why they are in *El Norte*. I try to orient them and make them feel that they are not alone. I remind them about their village and the importance of their families. At times, some immigrants abandon their families. But others come back or are in constant contact. This year, some of them came to the fiesta and visited me. Those who could not come sent money for the reconstruction of the church. I have to mention that I understand perfectly their feelings. I was an immigrant myself. Because of the poverty I experienced in my village, I migrated to Los Angeles. I know why people leave their places of origin. I know how it feels not knowing English, having to find a job, and being in a foreign land. In *El Norte*, life is quite monotonous. You are there to work. In addition, there are a lot of bad habits. You know: drugs, alcohol, violence, and the gangs. These experiences are very stressful for our immigrants. When they call me, I try to give them some comfort.

The priest has also come to play a central role in the community by providing moral advice and spiritual help to Yalaltec immigrants and second-generation teens that have become involved in gang activities. Sometimes when these teens ask for help to withdraw from the gang life of the streets, they are brought back to Yalálag to heal. Father Adrian offered me the following example:

> On two occasions, two teenage boys came and talked to me about their life as gangsters. One of them came from Los Angeles. The other came from Oaxaca City. Both described to me all kinds of experiences they had in the gangs. I told them that they could spiritually heal. I advised them to go and live and work with their grandparents in the countryside. I took one of them to his grand-parents. We talked a lot. I know that it was very hard for them to stop drinking alcohol and taking drugs. I know that one of them made it. He is doing fine. I asked him to help me with some teens, who have become involved in the local gangs. Here, in our village, we have started to have these problems. One of the ways in which we can do something about this problem is by asking ex-gang members to help me to orient newer generations.

At present, the relationship between the priest and the Yalaltec people is in good shape. As a result, the transnational relationships between the Yalaltec immigrants, the saints, and the church have developed in three important ways. First, immigrants have enhanced the position of the saints and the church through economic donations and religious participation. Second, immigrants have transformed their community of origin through economic participation in the social and religious life of the village of Yalálag. And third, the experience of Father Adrian as an immigrant himself to Los Angeles has been both a key factor in understanding the immigrant experience and a key ingredient in facilitating transnational religious and ritual life maintained in the community. Because religious fiestas bring immigrants and non-immigrants together, and because immigrants have contributed to the construction of a transnational social space (Faist 2000c; Pries 1999) through religious activities, I will focus on the discussion of the most important patron saint fiesta of Yalálag: the fiesta of San Antonio de Padua.

Transnational Fiesta

The fiesta of San Antonio de Padua, protector and owner of the cattle and the hills, is the most important communal festivity in Yalálag.[14] It is celebrated from June 3 to 15, but the planning and organization starts on January 1 and ends in the middle of August. Throughout Yalálag history, San Antonio de Padua has not been the major patron saint, but he has become the most important saint of the village. In Yalaltecs' recollections, San Antonio de Padua became the most important saint in the village due to the hundreds of miracles he performed in Yalálag and in neighboring towns.

The fame of San Antonio de Padua, which increased around the late 1940s, was due a number of reasons. First, the continuing conversion of Yalaltecos to Christianity was an essential factor in reinforcing the saints' role in the village. In the second half of the twentieth century, the Catholic Church began to circulate beliefs about San Antonio's powers and aligned them with the attributes of the Zapotec lord of the animals and deer. Like the Zapotec god, San Antonio became the protector of the cattle, who had the ability to make lost animals and things appear (de la Fuente 1949). Consequently, the Zapotec god that Yalaltecos venerated in the Bewitched Hill became syncretized with the image of San Antonio.

When I interviewed Father Adrian in Yalálag in June 2004, I asked him why certain saints exist in the village and some are more famous than others. He explained that San Antonio is famous in Yalálag and other countries because he had the fortune to cross many regions around the world and disseminate the Word of God. Also, people have had much faith in him because people identify with the saint's characteristics. San Antonio was humble. He went to the countryside to talk to peasants about the life of Jesus Christ. "If you teach the Yalaltecos about the life of Saint Thomas of Aquino, they are not going to identify with him. He was not a peasant. He was a philosopher, a geologist, and a wise man. Remember, San Antonio is an intermediary between Jesus Christ and his believers. And more important, he has certain attributes that no other saints have."

Another reason for the importance of San Antonio is that he became associated with the Zapotec god, who was also revered as the provider of rain, good harvests, and luck, because the religious fiestas of both deities coincided with the celebrations of the agricultural rituals of the Yalaltec people. Another factor was that the Bewitched Hill, which the Church considered a pagan place, was renamed the Cerro de San Antonio (de la Fuente 1949, 266). Again, because of San Antonio's novelty and power in the village, in the late 1940s the Yalaltec people built a chapel to honor him despite the opposition of the local priest. When the chapel was finished, a group of Yalaltec shaman-priests inaugurated this sacred building with a religious ceremony. Finally, in the mid-1960s, when the political differences among the villagers diminished, the Grupo Comunitario (discussed below) used this fiesta to reinvigorate the value of community work and community participation (Aquino 2002).

Since the 1990s, San Antonio has become the protector of the immigrants. The Yalaltec immigrants have much faith in him because they believe that San Antonio has helped them to cross illegally the U.S.-Mexican border, and find a job, and get United States residence or American citizenship. As I mentioned in chapter 1, in the mid-1980s and the early1990s Yalaltec migration increased significantly, and many young immigrants legalized their migratory status and brought their families to live permanently in the United States. As a result, it is now customary that on the day of the fiesta, hundreds of immigrants, documented or undocumented, return to Yalálag from the United States to honor and thank

San Antonio for his help. During the nine-day saint fiesta, immigrants comply with their sacred vows to San Antonio and participate in all religious and secular events, such as religious masses, rosaries, the *bailes*, the *convíte*, the *calenda*, the *maitínes*, the racehorses, the traditional and professional bullfights, the brass band and basketball competitions, the *octava*, and the donation of bulls, pigs, and *cirios* (Paschal candles).[15]

On June 13, the day of the saint's fiesta, Yalaltec immigrants celebrate San Antonio in a very special way. They attend the *mañanitas* (birthday song) for San Antonio, the *Misa de Aurora,* and the blessing of the corral. They bring new clothes for San Antonio to wear on this day and hang on their arms one-dollar or one-hundred-pesos bills, and the *milagros* (small status of San Antonio de Padua made of wax). They make monetary *promesas* (cf. Brettell 2003; Levitt 2001a) to the fiesta committee that range from fifty pesos to over a thousand dollars, and provide flowers, candles, incense, new tablecloths, fresh tamales, ears of corn, *champurrado* drink, and bread to decorate San Antonio's altar and his church. During the morning procession, some carry the image of San Antonio around the church. Others take in their hands large copal burners (*incensarios*) to purify the saint and the church. And some play religious music in the brass bands for the *mañanitas,* the procession, the religious masses, the performance of religious dances, the *convíte*, the *calenda*, the bullfights, and the *bailes.*

The significance of immigrants' religious and economic participation in the saint fiesta cannot be ignored. Religious participation has been the key access for immigrants' reintegration in their community of origin. In particular, economic participation, which is more than just monetary offerings, has been a form of symbolic capital through which immigrants assert and negotiate their continued membership to their community of origin and symbolically pay back the patron saint's help. In other words, the fiesta of San Antonio facilitates immigrants' continued involvement when they return to Yalálag. And, countering the threat of imminent social disintegration of the village of Yalálag because of the increasing immigration of younger generations to the United States, the fiesta of San Antonio allows for the reunification of immigrants with their families and their community.[16]

Immigrants' monetary *promesas* have become essential in the transformation and reinvigoration of religious fiestas.[17] Two decades ago, the fiesta of San Antonio was smaller and less sophisticated, although the duration was the same and it was organized in accordance with the very same secular and religious events. In recent years, however, thousands of dollars and pesos are spent on it, and new activities have been incorporated that, over time, have become institutionalized as part of the village's "tradition." For instance, fifteen years ago, it was not common to prepare free food for four thousand people.[18] The fiesta committee invited only neighboring brass bands as a *gzwon* to enliven the celebration. Currently, in addition to local and visiting brass bands, the fiesta committee invites Yalaltec immigrants residing in Oaxaca City to bring their own brass band and

dance groups to participate in the fiesta. To bring these guests, the fiesta committee makes special arrangements and pays private transportation for them.
Immigrants donate hundreds of dollars and pesos as well as domestic animals
such as turkeys, goats, and young bulls for the winners of basketball competitions, the *jaripeo* (traditional bullfight), and the horse races. The priest takes
advantage of the fiesta and organizes raffles of a thousand tickets to raise funds
for the reconstruction of the San Juan Yalálag church. Previously, celebrants did
not spend thousands of dollars to watch a professional bullfight show. Today,
the fiesta committee pays for a professional bullfight show in addition to the
traditional one.

Members of the second generation, born in Oaxaca City, Mexico City, and Los
Angeles are part of these changes, as well. They perform the religious and social
dances and participate in the village's brass bands. Since the mid-1990s, the fiesta
committee has hired tropical music groups for the *baile popular*, which bring the
latest pop music hits that include salsa, *cumbia*, and *ranchera* songs; Spanish and
English rock; *norteño* music; and hip-hop and rap.[19] In the *bailes*, locals are not
only introduced to these new rhythms, but immigrants and second-generation
teenagers teach them the latest dance styles performed in Mexico City, Oaxaca
City, or Los Angeles.

The transformation of the fiesta of San Antonio seems to be the result of a
series of social changes caused by both the impact of migration in Yalálag and
the return of hundreds of immigrants, and the changes in both the moral and
social orders (Griswold 1994, 63) to which immigrants and non-immigrants have
been continuously exposed. In the fiesta of San Antonio, both the *promesas* and
the donations, forms of symbolic and economic capital, have been the driving
forces that contribute to and facilitate changes in the fiesta of San Antonio. But
the sophistication of the fiesta, the institutionalization of new activities, and the
restructuring of certain events also result from the need to allocate the surplus of
financial capital. The more money the committee members receive from immigrants, the more work, projects, and activities they have to plan, organize, and
invent for the Yalálag community.

Likewise, by restructuring the fiesta, non-immigrants and immigrants test the
boundaries of their social, gender, and generational differences and thus redefine
the boundaries of their community. In this sense, the fiesta of San Antonio therefore may be understood as the most important context for social reintegration
and for the reinvention and negotiation of group identity. For example, playing
rap, salsa, *rancheras*, Spanish and English rock, and Zapotec music in the *bailes*
is not a random selection or combination of pop and folk. The production of a
new soundscape represents a cultural response to new social orders within the
Yalaltec community.[20] As Griswold suggests, "cultural innovation—the production of new meanings [and practices]—emerges as a response to incipient anomie" (1994, 63).[21] To be exact, the reinvention and reelaboration of the saints'

fiesta reorient the Yalaltec people and give them "their bearings in the new circumstances" (Griswold 1994, 63). The return of hundreds of immigrants and reinvention of this fiesta are particular features of this historical moment.

At present, the fiesta of San Antonio de Padua constitutes a transnationalized social space (Glick Schiller, Basch, and Blanc-Szanton 1992; Portes 2000). That is, immigrants' economic, religious, and social participation in the fiesta brings to the sphere of Yalálag those social and symbolic processes that produce a new imagination of community (Appadurai 1996), those new social positions that migration creates in this transnational social space (Faist 2000b), and those new relationships that comprise such space. To be exact, each monetary *promesa* sent from Los Angeles for the saint's fiesta, each dollar or peso donated to the *casa del pueblo*, along with any kind of social work done for the fiesta or any kind of participation in religious and secular events redefine the social boundaries of community and place the fiesta at the center of transnational community life (Smith 2006). In the following section, I discuss the significance of transnational community reorganization and the politics of immigrants' participation in the fiesta.

THE POLITICS OF THE HOME VILLAGE AND
IMMIGRANTS' PARTICIPATION IN YALÁLAG

Historically, indigenous immigrants from Oaxaca in the United States have organized collectively to support productive and development projects or to participate in local politics and religious life.[22] Yalaltec immigrants, however, have sponsored only religious activities and church projects in Yalálag. As described previously, the immigrants' return coincides with the religious calendar of the patron saint fiestas, and they invest much time and energy in Los Angeles to raise thousands of dollars for the patron saint fiestas and reconstruction of the main churches, chapels, and the four *casas de los barrios* in Yalálag. What accounts for this concentration on religious causes? A key factor is long-term political divisions in Yalálag that have impeded the formation of a migrant association or an HTA (a Yalaltec community organization) in Los Angeles that could contribute to and work with local authorities' and community leaders' efforts to improve Yalálag infrastructure and communal services.[23] That is, immigrants' participation has been concentrated on religious aspects because Yalálag politics have restricted other forms of participation.

The origins of political conflicts in Yalálag date back to the 1910–1920 Mexican Revolution. During the government of Porfirio Díaz (a native of Oaxaca), Mexico experienced an era of prosperity and economic growth as well as an epoch of social repression and increasing polarization between the ruling elites and indigenous peoples and masses. Díaz promoted the construction of the railroad system, roads, and dams, and allowed foreign investment for industry. Between 1880 and 1905, Oaxaca City became an important political and administrative center, and the Oaxacan regions of La Cañada, the Isthmus, the Coast, the Mix-teca, the Sierra, and the Valley went through a process of industrialization and financial development. Dozens of mining and textile industries were opened, two railroads and a port were built, and commercial agriculture was introduced.

In 1907, Mexico suffered a deep economic crisis. The poor were dispossessed and exploited, and Indian communities lost their lands (Young 1976).[24] Food prices doubled, the production of food crops declined, and political unrest in the country increased. Díaz's conservative administration grew unpopular among the emerging middle class, the proletariat, the peasantry, the politicians, and intellectuals. In Oaxacan Isthmus and La Cañada, dozens of mining and textile workers were laid off. American and English mining companies in the Sierra were closed, and the Bank of Puebla absorbed the Bank of Oaxaca (Chassen 2005). Between 1906 and 1908 in Mexico City, the Oaxacan brothers Ricardo and Enrique Flores Magón organized the first national movement to depose the Díaz dictatorship (1876–1911). In Oaxaca, Angel Barrios, who was accused of conspir-ing against Díaz, led the Magonista Rebellion. In 1909, control of Oaxaca was divided into two groups. The first was composed of those who sympathized with President Díaz and governed Oaxaca. The second group was made up of those who opposed Díaz's regime and supported the revolutionary cause of Francisco I. Madero. When Madero was organizing the revolutionary movement in the coun-try, hundreds of Oaxacan indigenous sympathizers joined his Partido Antireelecci-onista (Anti-Reelectionist Party). Upon Madero's visit to Oaxaca in 1909, the Club Central Antireelecccionista de Oaxaca was founded (Martínez M. 2005). In 1910, when Madero arrived in Chihuahua from exile to campaign for his presidential bid, the first Maderista uprisings in the Oaxacan regions of La Cañada, the Zapo-tec Isthmus, and the Valley, and the Mixteca took place (Chassen 2005).

In 1911, Francisco I. Madero became president of Mexico, and Porfirio Díaz left the country after signing the Treaty of Ciudad Juárez. In Mexico City, Madero intended to reconcile the nation by appointing both Díaz's supporters and his own followers as members of his cabinet. At this time, Oaxaca was ruled by Emilio Pimentel, a Porfirio Díaz sympathizer who had Maderista enemies within his administration (Martínez M. 2005). In Oaxaca, Zapotec *pueblos* in the Isth-mus and Teotitlán del Valle and Tlacolula, and *pueblos* in Tuxtepec and the region of La Cañada identified with Madero's cause. In contrast, the Zapotec pueblos of the Sierra that made up the Fuerzas Defensoras del Estado (military forces of the Pimentel government) were controlled by the Porfirian general Guillermo Meixueiro, General Isaac M. Ibarra, and the caciques (Kearney 1972). In 1912, a group of Maderista deserters, who arrived at Yalálag from Tlacolula claiming loyalty to General Guillermo Meixueiro, stole money from the wealthy.[25] After several confrontations between these deserters and Yalaltecos, the latter killed them with the support of people from the Zapotec community of Zoochila (de la Fuente 1949, 22).

Between 1910 and 1926, there were numerous massacres and reprisals in the Sierra communities. In 1910, most of the Sierra Zapotec communities supported the Díaz regime. However, there were a few who sympathized with the revolutionary cause. The Sierra region, controlled by Díaz's supporters, suffered economic stagnation, social disintegration, and political instability. In 1914, the Oaxacan Sierra saw yet another era of social instability (de la Fuente 1949, Kearney 1972, Young 1976). Two major political forces—the Soberanistas and the Carrancistas—sought to expand their political and military control and gain support throughout the entire region from the Zapotec, Mixe, and Chinantec *pueblos*. The Soberanistas (1915–1920), an Oaxacan elite group in power, had as their main agenda making Oaxaca an independent state. They opposed the Maderista and Carrancista political movements. They defended the Constitution of 1857, but in 1920 during a government meeting in Oaxaca they recognized the Constitution of 1917 (Ruiz C. 2005). The Carrancistas, in turn, were a political force affiliated with Venustiano Carranza, a leader of the Mexican Revolution and the Anti-Reelectionist Movement of 1910. In 1914, Venustiano Carranza became the president of Mexico.

By 1915, the Carrancismo gained many followers in the Oaxacan Coast, the Isthmus, the Valley, and some communities in the Sierra, such as Yalálag. Central Mexico was dominated by Francisco Villa's and Emiliano Zapata's *ejercito campesino* (peasant army). In 1916, the Carrancistas, who identified themselves as División 21, arrived in Oaxaca. They deposed the Soberanist government and incarcerated legislators and representatives of the judicial system (Ruiz C. 2005). In 1917, the Mexican Constitution of 1917 was drafted. Guillermo Meixueiro, the first commander-in-chief of the División Serrana and a Díaz supporter since 1912, escaped from the Soberanist village of Ixtlán to the Soberanist community of Villa Alta.[26] At this time, Yalálag and most Sierra pueblos were completely enmeshed in this revolutionary conflict. Yalaltec community leaders and villagers began to divide along affiliations with these two major groups. While the majority joined Carranza's cause, a minority identified with the Soberanistas (de la Fuente 1949; Equipo Pueblo 1988). In 1920, President Carranza nominated Carlos Tejeda for governor of Oaxaca. Alvaro Obregón, who was campaigning for the national presidency, broke relations with President Carranza. In the Sierra, the Soberanos expressed their support for Obregón. Obregón signed an agreement with the Brigadas Serranas and promised them political control of the Oaxacan state if he won national elections. The Confederación Liberal de Oaxaca and other political parties were formed to support Obregón's nomination (Ruiz C. 2005).

In Yalálag, political tensions continued until the late 1920s, during which time Yalaltecos experienced a series of violent internal conflicts that led to the formation of the *cacicazgo* Yalalteca (1929–1979). The *cacicazgo* is a sociopolitical institution ruled by a cacique and controlled by the state government. The Yalaltec cacique works on behalf of the Mexican government and ruling elites, either directly or by association. He secures political and social control of his own village and is inextricably linked to members of the political party in power. The cacique usually seizes power first in the village. He may then associate with rulers or village followers to maintain his power (Aquino 2002). As mentioned earlier, in the early twentieth century, the Sierra was controlled by two Porfirian caudillos, General Guillermo Meixueiro and General Isaac M. Ibarra. They held military and political power in the Sierra with the help of caciques (Chassen 2005, Kearney 1972).

Since the beginning of the twentieth century, the succession of *cacicazgos* in Yalálag has been characterized by two features. First, each cacique has been associated with or represented by the economic and political interests of certain groups or individuals.[27] For example: the Soberanistas vs. Carrancistas; the progressives vs. the conservatives; the Municipal Committee of the Institutional Revolutionary Party (Comité Municipal del PRI) vs. Yalaltec Peasant Committee (Comité Campesino Yalalteca); the Community Group (Grupo Comunitario) vs. The October 11 Group (La Coordinadora 11 de Octubre); and most recently, the Institutional Revolutionary Party (PRI) vs. Democratic Revolutionary Party (PRD). Second, because Yalálag has been historically divided into two political forces, each cacique or group in power has counted on the support of at least one-third of the local population. In most cases, entire families or particular individuals have defended local caciques because of their political affiliations, economic interests, or family connections. For example, in 1924 the cacique Enrique Valle took political and military control of Yalálag with the help of his Carrancistas allies. The Yalaltecos who supported the Soberanistas escaped to surrounding Soberanist villages because of increasing violence and political persecution. In 1927, the "great associations" and "great confederations" as well as the first unions were formed to prevent the federal government from getting supporters from Oaxaca and the Sierra (Arellanes M. 2005). With the founding of the Confederación de Partidos Socialistas de Oaxaca, Álvaro Obregón created alliances with the Oaxacan caciques in the Sierra and congressional representatives. He wanted to secure his own political power in Oaxaca in hopes of winning presidential reelection in the following term.

In 1928, Obregón was assassinated, and President Plutarco Elías Calles founded the PNR (Partido Nacional Revolucionario). In 1929, Enrique Valle, who was in exile, returned to Yalálag and, with the support of the Oaxacan government that then supported President Calles, founded the first political party in Yalálag, known as the PNR Municipal Committee (Comité Municipal del PNR) (Aquino 2002, 38).[28] Valle abolished the communal assembly and the Council of Elders (Consejo de Ancianos) and reinstituted a new form of political organization along with leadership and practices modeled after the state government.[29] In 1932, many of the country's regional parties disappeared. In 1933, the PNR became the national party.[30]

In 1936, Soberanistas Antonio Primo Fabian and Eucario Vargas Tico returned to Yalálag from exile. They killed Valle and took over the municipality. Rather than installing a new form of leadership and liberating their village from Valle's political and social control, however, Primo and Vargas established a new kind of *cacicazgo.*[31] They took control of the village and augmented their own economic benefits and social privileges (Equipo Pueblo 1988). In the midst of these political conflicts, other important events took place: class differences increased among the villagers, and the ruling group and wealthy families began to promote ideals of Western "progress" and "modernization." In the early 1940s, Yalaltecos categorized each other as rich or poor. The rich were Yalaltec families who owned vast areas of land, had access to cash resources, and were middlemen in the distribution of coffee, locally produced cloth and leather sandals, and services in the Sierra. Some of them were literate and controlled public posts and the municipality. The poor were subsistence farmers who were predominantly illiterate. Some worked as peons for the wealthy.

By the late 1940s, Yalaltecos were divided between the progressives (*progresistas* or *castellanizados*) and the conservatives (*rústicos* or *cerrados*). The progressives, who believed in Western "progress," thought that the suppression of their native language and the transformation of their religious beliefs and local traditions would contribute to the social betterment of their group. They considered Yalálag society to be illiterate, uncivilized, and lagging behind social progress and technological development. Specifically, the lack of competence in speaking Spanish and the "rustic" way of life were perceived as signs of social disadvantage (de la Fuente 1949). The conservatives, who defended their local ways, fought against the progressive leaders and opposed these changes. They demanded respect and recognition for their history, native values, and traditions. In Yalálag, there was a saying that rejected schooling and underscored the significance of working in the countryside: *Para que vas a la escuela, si no vas a comer libros!* (There is no reason to go to school. We are not going to eat books!).

With Mexican Independence in 1810, Mexico had been faced with the challenge of economic, political, and social modernization. Benito Juárez's regime (1858–1872) established equality of indigenous people before the law and education free of dogma. Under Díaz's government, the minister of education, Justo Sierra (1905–1911), argued that "the transformation of indigenous class to a progressive 'class' was possible through education . . . primary instruction was to be the first step toward enlisting the Mexican native in the great work of national progress" (quoted in Gutiérrez Nájera 2007, 87). In Yalálag, since the beginning of the twentieth century, Western ideology concerning education, modernization, and social progress has been crucial in shaping the idea of becoming educated, civilized, and progressive. In the 1920s, under the nationalist ideas of progress, the Mexican government created the state program Misiones Culturales (cultural missions program) to bring about progress by implementing public education. In 1926, the first elementary school teachers arrived in Yalálag. In 1930, Yalálag had its first Yalalteco directing its first elementary school (Gutiérrez Nájera 2007). De la Fuente points out that by the end of the 1920s (when the Soberanist movement declined), the Serrano chiefs got together in Yalálag. In a meeting, they agreed that "each pueblo has the freedom to choose progress or stagnation . . . From now on, everybody is free to do whatever they want. Over the years, it will be seen how much we have progressed or not" (1949, 23).

The end of 1950s saw the start of political turnover, and a few progressive leaders were appointed in the municipality. Schooling at the elementary and secondary levels was instituted. Some Yalaltec teenagers from wealthy families began to migrate to Oaxaca City and Mexico City to pursue professional careers. In the early 1960s, a few men migrated to Oaxaca City or Mexico City to work as construction workers or servants, and some joined the Bracero Program to be employed as agricultural workers in the California fields. In 1969, a group of progressive leaders, who opposed the PRI cacique and wanted to abolish it, in turn, formed the Yalaltecan Peasant Committee (Comité Campesino Yalalteca). The new Yalaltecan Peasant Committee became a member of the National Peasant Confederation (Confederación Nacional Campesina), which was controlled by the PRI but allowed members to reach the state government. In 1974, the Comité Municipal del PRI and the Yalaltecan Peasant Committee agreed to form a coalition government. However, the Comité Municipal del PRI remained in power and appointed a new local PRI cacique to lead the municipality. Meanwhile, the Yalaltecan Peasant Committee gained political recognition among the villagers and began to implement a series of cultural activities and social programs to contribute to the betterment and social reorganization of their community. Between 1964 and 1979, a course on modern agricultural techniques improved the village's agricultural production and promoted self-sustenance among the Yalaltec families. A Parents' Board (Asamblea de Padres de Familia) was instituted and served as a role model in reconstituting the Communal Assembly and the Council of Elders. The planning and revitalization of the fiesta of San Antonio de Padua provided the basis for social reorganization and communal participation (Aquino 2002).

In 1980, the Yalaltec Peasant Committee changed its name to the Communitarian Group (Grupo Comunitario) to run in local elections against the Comité Municipal del PRI. Most Yalaltecos were ready to participate in local elections. They were registered to vote and had their voter identification cards. However, days before the elections, the state government suspended them, fully aware that two-thirds of the Yalaltec population was ready to vote for change in the municipality. As the months went by, the cacique took back control of the municipality and impeded local elections. In response, the Communitarian Group organized peaceful demonstrations to reactivate the local elections. On December 31, 1980, the Group occupied the municipality and demanded that state and local governments form a coalition government, which the PRI and the Communitarian Group did in 1981. However, three months later, the PRI representatives withdrew because they did not want to comply with the communal service requirement and new laws. These conflicts exacerbated political differences among the villagers, because one-third of the population favored the cacique and the other two-thirds supported the Communitarian Group.

In 1986, the municipal brass band, composed of local musicians divided between these two fractions, decided to withdraw from the municipality. According to Aquino (2002, 175) and de la Fuente (1949), the municipal brass bands have represented a crucial organism within the municipality's organizational structure. After withdrawing, the members formed an independent brass band and organized a new political group: the Yalálag Indigenous Group (Grupo Autóctono de Yalálag). Again, the separation of the municipal brass band initiated a new era of political tensions and social divisions among families, friends, and political forces. For nineteen years (1979–1998), the Communitarian Group remained in power. None of the PRI followers participated directly in the local government. Thus, as the Communitarian Group gained political control of the municipality, it took advantage of its new sociostructural position to implement various community projects. Among them were reinforcing their indigenous identity through the revitalization of the Zapotec language and cultural practices and reactivating practices associated with community service. They also formally reinstituted the Communal Assembly and the Council of Elders, and created political and social links with indigenous organizations at the regional, state, and national levels to hold communal assemblies on a regular basis to discuss future projects and the destiny of the community.[32] They reconstructed the municipal building, and built a water drainage and supply system and a new middle school and kindergarten.

By the end of 1998, the October 11 Coordinating Committee (*Coordinadora 11 de Octubre*) was founded to remove the Communitarian Group from local government. This new political faction, composed of a few dissidents from the Communitarian Group, members of the PRI, and the Yalálag Indigenous Group (almost 40 percent of the population), took over the municipality and blocked all local elections for the rest of the year 1998. In December 1998, the Communitarian Group organized a march to take over the municipality peacefully. However, upon arriving to the municipal building, both political factions became involved in intense fighting with weapons. At that time, the diverse political forces could not come to any agreement, nor were they interested in discussing problems. Moreover, the Oaxacan state government offered little help to resolve these conflicts, and the local population had to cope on its own. Consequently, the people of Yalálag remained divided and their internal differences increased.[33]

Political factions have not been able to negotiate their political and ideological differences, reach accords, or propose common projects for the betterment of their community. Although some of these factions are pacifist, this does not mean they are open to negotiation. Others are intolerant and aggressive and promote violence. Perhaps most important, the PRI has the support of the state government. It controls various Sierra communities by means of *cacicazgo* and continues to dominate political life and institutions in Yalálag. For instance, under the system of indigenous laws known as *usos y costumbres*, voluntary public servants are not entitled to a salary for their municipal service or work. In Yalálag, however, some officers have received salaries even though this violates their customary laws. Between 2000 and 2001, there were two frustrated attempts to hold democratic elections. The persistent political divisions and the struggle for power between the Communitarian Group and the October 11 Coordinating Committee led to the death of one civilian, thirty arrests, and injury of fifteen Yalaltecos. Since then, the October 11 Coordinating Committee has remained in power. The Committee has brought in administrators from other areas in spite of the *usos y costumbres*, which require that Yalaltec citizens fill local posts (Aquino 2002; Gómez 2005; Ruíz Arrazola 2000).

Yalaltec political conflicts are nearly a century-old phenomenon. Currently, as some Yalatecos explained to me, the local government is far from reaching an accord, and potential violence still looms. Yalálag is a small village, currently numbering 2,112 inhabitants (INEGI 2010d), and struggles for political power have caused enmity between entire families and friends. Yalaltec immigrants have not remained neutral in these conflicts; they have been part of them. Some immigrants continue to support the Communitarian Group or the October 11 Coordinating Committee from abroad, while others have escaped to the United States because of violent clashes between the two. Immigrants' political affiliations in Yalálag have influenced whether or not they decide to get involved in community activities or projects in Los Angeles that sponsor development projects in Yalálag. For example, between 1982 and 1989, a group of Yalaltec immigrants who sympathized with the Communitarian Group formed an organization called La Comunidad Yalalteca de Los Angeles. Based on the idea of *tequio* (communal work), they collected money for the reconstruction of the municipal building. Immigrants with other loyalties feel they cannot organize in Los Angeles to support their home village and do not work in conjunction with the municipal authorities, due to their political preferences and divisions in the community. Mr. Daniel, one of the first immigrants who settled in Los Angeles, explained:

> Despite the distance and the years, many *bi gwlash* continue to take political sides. I think this is the main reason preventing us from forming a communal organization that works in conjunction with the municipality. That is why no one talks about home politics in Los Angeles. I think that this is very sad for our community. There are other immigrant communities that work together and organize activities to sponsor projects for their communities of origin. For example, in Zoogocho, the immigrant community of Los Angeles repaired the

main plaza, the municipal building, the church, and the elementary school. They gave money to the municipality to pave their downtown. Thanks to the immigrants, the Zoogochenses have a power supply. But in Yalálag, forget it. We are divided. Of course, we do support our patron saint fiestas. This is very important for the Yalaltec individual!

As a result, religious activities and fiestas have been the only avenue for immigrants to integrate into their community of origin and organize in the United States. Throughout the 1990s, Yalaltec immigrants were allowed to create truly transnational community-based organizations—the barrio organization—in order to fulfill two needs in the community of origin: to reintegrate immigrants, and to repair and restructure the *cargo* community system. Currently, in Yalálag, migration's impact on the *cargo* system, also known as traditional government, is negative. Migration has increasingly become part of young Yalaltecos' expectations. Returning and visiting migrants continue to provide economic and social resources that facilitate newer generations' efforts to migrate and settle in Oaxaca City, Mexico City, or the United States. As a result, it has become difficult for younger generations to comply with their civic, religious, and political posts.

Nevertheless, unlike mestizo Mexican immigrants, indigenous Oaxacan immigrants do return to their home village to comply with filling religious and public posts, known as *cargos,* as a part of their community obligations and as a way to justify their continued membership and rights.[34] In the last fifteen years, Yalaltec immigrants have complied with their moral and religious obligations to their community by sponsoring community projects related to church activities and religious festivals. As I have said, immigrants cannot be required to come back to Yalálag and fill public service positions because of the difficulties related to their undocumented status, permanent residency in the United States, and the political situation and dynamics in the village.[35] However, the Yalálag community's current economic status shows that increasing immigration to Oaxaca City, Mexico City, and the United States has affected the *cargo* in significant ways.[36] The *cargo* system represents and maintains the sociopolitical structure of the Yalálag community, and due to the migration process, it is now partially in decline. To counteract this decline, some religious positions are now open to immigrants, and they have responded positively.

In June 2003, for the first time, two immigrants in Oaxaca City were allowed to fill religious posts for the 2004 fiesta of San Antonio de Padua. These immigrant men formed the San Antonio Fiesta Committee (Comisión de Festejos de San Antonio) along with one Yalálag resident. According to Efrén Gómez, the local fiesta committee member, the municipality invited Justo Pasos to serve as the president of the committee and accepted Oscar Cristóbal's petition to serve as a secretary due to the shortage of candidates for *cargo* posts in Yalálag. Cristóbal knew that no one in the village wanted to be secretary, so he traveled all the way from Oaxaca City to offer his services to the Communal Assembly. Cristóbal said that he became interested in filling this religious post because he wanted to fulfill a *promesa* to the patron saint.

In the opinion of the fiesta committee members, younger generations have stopped participating in these *cargos* because they have either migrated to the United States or have become less interested in taking part in community service. The majority of the younger population is extremely drawn to migration or is already living in Los Angeles. But lack of interest among young adults is also attributed to the fact that filling a religious *cargo* post causes financial and emotional stress. Committee members must stop work, and therefore must save an adequate supply of money and food for a year without income. Under current economic conditions, it has become increasingly difficult for younger generations to comply with such responsibilities. Older generations, who could fulfill these *cargos,* cannot or do not want to undertake this responsibility again, because of age or health problems. Many have already complied with their communal duties more than once.

At present, immigrants and non-immigrants have transformed how the *cargos* are filled. For example, Pasos, who lives and works as an architect in Oaxaca, could not stay in Yalálag for the first six months of his term. Instead, he offered to hire a "peon" in Yalálag to do part of his service. He also committed to being present during the weeklong celebration and to pay for and supervise the peon's work permanently. Cristóbal, who is a retired state employee and had more available time for his service, offered to commute twice a month from Oaxaca City to Yalálag to take care of his duties. The only local committee member was Gómez, who was elected during the 2003 community assembly on the same day that Cristóbal was appointed. Gómez had the greatest responsibility in overseeing fiesta preparations. Because only he was living in Yalálag, he had to coordinate and supervise several activities. Organizing this fiesta is a huge responsibility and includes quite a few events and activities. Organizers must also collect the monetary donations and keep a record of them. On this occasion, in addition to planning the nine-day celebration for 4,000 participants, committee members coordinated part of the reconstruction of the Church of San Antonio. Weeks before the patron saint fiesta took place, they hired local construction workers to paint the church, and supervised the construction of a platform for the brass bands and a wall in the rodeo area. Despite the frequent absence of two of the committee heads, the fiesta was very successful because of good coordination and the entire committee's hard work during the fiesta.

To further strengthen the communal system, new forms of social organization and organizational networks have arisen in Oaxaca City, Mexico City, and Los Angeles in recent years. In Oaxaca City, there are three community-based associations that produce their own patron saint fiestas and participate in the village fiestas. They are: the Fiesta Committee of San Juan Bautista (Comisión de festejos San Juan Bautista), the Fiesta Committee of Santa Rosa de Lima (Comisión de festejos de Santa Rosa de Lima), and the Fiesta Committee of the Virgin Santa Cecilia (Comisión de festejos de la Virgen de Santa Cecilia). In Mexico City, there are the Yalaltec Youth Community of Oaxaca (Comunidad Juvenil Yalalteca de Oaxaca) and the Civil Association of Yalaltec Residents in Mexico City (Asociación Civil de Yalaltecos Radicados en la Cd. de México). Both organizations organize community gatherings to celebrate the Yalálag patron saints. They also participate in multiethnic organizations to create alliances with other indigenous organizations. According to community leaders, the main goal of these organizations is to reinforce their social and cultural ties as Yalaltec immigrants in Oaxaca City and Mexico City.

In Los Angeles, Yalaltec immigrants have organized the following associations: the four-barrio organizations, known as the *comisiones de los barrios*, and the Unión Yalalteca. The former are informal organizations known only among Yalaltecos that maintain strong social and economic relationships with their corresponding barrio committees in Yalálag, but not with other transnational migrant associations and organizations. Since the late 1990s, these barrio committees have coordinated community gatherings to raise funds for the four-barrio patron saint fiestas in Yalálag and for the reconstruction of the barrio churches and chapels, basketball courts, and cultural centers in Yalálag. These activities and projects are sponsored and supported by L.A. barrio committees and have generated much social and symbolic capital. The sheer number of barrio events—and the capital thereby accumulated—has been crucial to constitute the Unión Yalalteca (see fig. 3.2).

In the summer of 2004, representatives of the four-barrio committees gathered to discuss the creation of the Unión, the first town association in Los Angeles. During the meeting, the four-barrio committee members reached three agreements: the Unión Yalalteca, established to raise funds for the reconstruction of the Church of San Antonio de Padua in Yalálag, would begin brainstorming projects for the immigrant community; the Unión would join the U.S.-Oaxacan migrant association of FOCOICA to take advantage of the Mexican federal/state co-investment program, "Three for One," to implement the Church project; and the Unión would foster social ties as a community in Los Angeles, thus presenting a united front to the community of origin.[37] In this manner, the Unión Yalalteca has sought to move beyond the internal political differences among Yalaltec immigrants and gain official recognition in Yalálag. In the past, there were a few attempts to form an HTA in Los Angeles.[38] However, Yalaltec immigrants could not agree to such an association because they could not leave behind political conflicts rooted in their community of origin. As a result, the community of Yalálag was not represented in or affiliated with any Mexican indigenous organization in the United States.[39] Furthermore, the immigrant community could not form an HTA because it would have to be approved in Yalálag. In other words, the constitution of any Yalaltec transnational community-based organization, as

Una labor destacable

La organización yalalteca fue reconocida por el presidente Fox, por el gran trabajo realizado en el programa 3x1.

Frida Negrete
LOS ÁNGELES, CA.

EN TAN SÓLO DOS AÑOS, los migrantes de la comunidad de Yalalag han logrado ver hecho realidad un sueño que permaneció "dormido" por más de 18 años: construir un Centro de Atención y Rehabilitación al Adolescente (CARA), que es una clínica de usos múltiples; terminar la primera etapa de edificación del módulo deportivo San Antonio, e iniciar el proyecto de la construcción de un auditorio municipal.

Estos trabajos se realizaron apoyados por el Programa 3x1.

La labor de los migrantes yalaltecos recibió un reconocimiento por parte del presidente Vicente Fox, en su última visita a Los Ángeles.

Gerardo Vásquez, presidente de la Organización Yalalteca, conformada por seis integrantes más, recibió un reconocimiento por parte del presidente Fox en una reunión realizada en un lujoso hotel de la ciudad.

Vásquez cuenta que los trabajos se han logrado realizar a través del apoyo de los yalaltecos migrantes que radican aquí en la ciudad de Los Ángeles.

A través de tardeadas y torneos deportivos, este grupo de migrantes logró recaudar en dos años un monto de 34 mil dólares, recursos que se han repartido en las diferentes obras sociales que se han realizado en su pueblo.

Hace dos años se creó la organización, y con ella surgió el deseo de lograr una meta pendiente que, desde hacía 18 años, se tenía marcada.

Vásquez cuenta que luego de comenzar a recaudar los primeros fondos, escucharon acerca de

los méritos que tenían para recibir apoyo del programa 3x1.

"Nos acercamos a las autoridades en el Consulado, para que nos explicaran, y también hablamos con gente de Zacatecas, para que contaran su experiencia; así podimos lograr esa meta en poco tiempo...", dice el presidente de la organización.

Recibir el reconocimiento del presidente Fox fue una satisfacción que, según Vásquez, no es sólo un mérito para la organización sino para todos los yalaltecos.

"Esto nos motiva a que sigamos

adelante, y que le echemos ganas a realizar más proyectos, porque si uno se lo propone, sí se puede...", expresó.

Vásquez dijo que nunca dudaron del proyecto 3x1, porque al mismo tiempo que se enteraron de su existencia, conocieron los beneficios que éste brindaba.

"Desconfianza de las autoridades siempre se ha tenido, por las experiencias de engaño que hemos vivido; pero en esta ocasión pensamos diferente y de manera positiva, y eso fue lo que nos ayudó a lograr los cambios"

Vásquez mencionó que el programa 3x1 es realmente un beneficio social que nada tiene que ver con la política del gobierno federal, estatal o municipal.

"Ojalá que todas las organizaciones que quieran ayudar a sus comunidades también tomen beneficio del programa, porque es una manera de que se realicen más proyectos...", agregó el presidente de la organización.

EL OAXAQUEÑO Gerardo Vázquez, de la comunidad de Yalalag, fue uno de los dirigentes que recibió reconocimiento de manos del presidente de México.

Figure 3.2. Long-distance state-sponsored transnationalism, Unión Yalalteca.

for the barrio committees, depends on official recognition by the Yalálag municipality and the barrio representatives. During the 1990s, a few immigrants who
belonged to the October 11 Group restored the basketball court at the Church of
San Antonio without permission from the municipal authorities and the communal assembly. As a result, the villagers destroyed it.

At present, the municipal authorities of Yalálag have agreed to authorize the
Unión Yalalteca because it does not support any political party or political project in the village. More important, the Unión Yalalteca is sponsoring a community project that does not interfere with home politics: the reconstruction of the
Church of San Antonio of Padua. To complete this project, the Unión Yalalteca
aims to collect $US500,000. Currently, the L.A. four-barrio committees are rais-
ing funds by organizing *bailes* or *kermesses* (community gatherings) and raffles.
The Unión has been collecting additional funds through community events
organized by FOCOICA and other associations.

In 2005, the *Unión* participated in the indigenous dance and music festival of
La Guelaguetza organized by FOCOICA. In addition to dance and music presentations, the planning committee organized a food stand to sell Yalaltec food and
collect donations. In the same year, the Oaxacan dance troupe Centeolt invited
the Unión to participate in the celebration of El Día de los Muertos, held in
Hollywood Forever Cemetery. They performed the *Los Negritos* religious dance
and sold food to raise funds at the event. Rivera-Salgado and Escala suggest that
transnational organizations such as FOCOICA and community-based organizations "have come to incorporate [immigrants] as social and political actors in
the United States" (2004, 172). These organizations have provided indigenous
immigrant communities with information and social and financial resources
in Mexico and in the United States that would be difficult for immigrants to
obtain on their own. The Mexican government has its own interest in exert-
ing some control over their nationals living abroad (Kearney 2000), which has
resulted in the creation of state programs such as "Three for One," a program
that other Mexican immigrant communities use to implement communal projects (Fitzgerald 2000, Goldring 1998, Fox and Rivera-Salgado 2004). This program was created in 1999 and stipulates that federal and state governments will
match every dollar that HTAs provide for community development projects.
Unión Yalalteca plans to raise funds to reconstruct the Church of San Antonio
de Padua in Los Angeles, then triple the money with federal and state funds. This
project includes various goals that will be accomplished in stages. Among them
are: reconstructing the church's building and basketball court; fixing the water
pump; building new seats for the bullring, an area with rooms for dress rehearsals, public restrooms, and a multipurpose room; and replacing kitchen supplies
such as dishes and plates as well as the stove from *la casa del pueblo* (the town
kitchen). In June 2004, the Unión Yalalteca raised $US8,000 to defray expenses of
the fiesta of San Antonio. However, since it was too late for the fiesta committee

in Yalálag to spend these funds, the Unión Yalalteca committee members invested this money in reconstructing a section of the Church of San Juan Bautista and paving the church's patio.

Without a doubt, the migration experience has caused Yalaltec immigrants and non-immigrants to create new forms of participation in Yalálag. Because of tensions within home politics, national immigrants have been permitted to take religious posts in order to reestablish the community system and reinforce social, economic, and cultural ties among Yalaltecos who live across the migrant circuit. To this day, religious participation continues to be the primary forum for social participation and immigrants' reintegration in Yalálag. Community organization and the organizational practices in Yalálag and Los Angeles, which have been influenced by local experience and a history of political conflict in Yalálag, have also served as a social platform to consolidate the Yalaltec transnational community and to repair the *cargo* system. To put it differently, the migration experience has presented immigrants and non-immigrants with the challenge of reorganizing as a community in Yalálag, in Oaxaca City, in Mexico City, and in Los Angeles, but collaborative efforts between truly transnational migrant organizations, municipal authorities, and non-immigrants have helped Yalaltecos to reinvent new forms of community. Many Yalaltecos define their community as a *comunidad dividida* (divided community) due to the long history of political tensions. Certainly, Yalaltecos seem to have different ideas on how the community should function, and political leaders have had different visions of what Yalaltec *usos y costumbres* should be (cf. Gutiérrez Najera 2007). However, Yalaltec immigrants who have been outside of Yalálag for a long time have come to play a central role in unifying their community through religious activities and projects. Particularly, political conflicts in combination with the long and complex record on the reconstitution of the community outside Yalálag have been responsible for the creation of new transnational community organizations and the revitalization of religious life and ritual activities across borders. In sum, prior to migration, religious thought and the fiesta of San Antonio in Yalálag were structured differently. Today, the migration experience has made immigrants and non-immigrants give new meanings to their religious beliefs and community life. San Antonio de Padua has become the protector of immigrants with the increase in immigration in Yalálag.

On the one hand, immigrants have made this fiesta the most important event in their lives because their success, prosperity, and social well-being are rewards of their reciprocal relationship to San Antonio. On the other hand, this fiesta is highly significant for immigrants and non-immigrants because it allows for family and community reunification and the construction of transnational social, economic, and cultural connections within Yalálag, and between Yalálag and Los Angeles. It is a fact that religious activities have provided virtually the only route for Yalaltec immigrants in other parts of Mexico and the United States to remain connected to their home community. Other types of organizing focused on political participation across borders has proven impossible given the deep and historically entrenched political divisions that have permeated the community in all locations. Immigrants' desire to reintegrate into their home village is subjected to the social dynamics of Yalálag as well as a process of negotiation between immigrants and non-immigrants. Non-immigrants need immigrants' social and economic support, as migration weakens the *cargo* system and creates community social disorganization in Yalálag. Immigrants also need to come back to Yalálag because this is the place where their sacrifices and accomplishments are publicly valued, and for that, they symbolically earn communal recognition for a fiesta that is denied in Los Angeles. Thus, these kinds of transnational relationships and the reinvention of their native forms of social organization maintain a sense of community life that extends to a transnational community settled between Los Angeles and Yalálag.

❖

CHAPTER 4

YALÁLAG ZAPOTEC
IDENTITIES IN A
CHANGING WORLD

Zapotec, or *ben'zaa*, means "people from the clouds." Being Zapotec, according to the Zapotecs, signifies the collective identity of people who are born within this group and behave, affiliate, and act according to Zapotec mores.[1] The Yalálag Zapotecs use three terms to distinguish themselves according to region. Those who live in El Valle are usually referred to as *ben raghe*, which means "people from the city" or "shirt people." Zapotecs who reside in the isthmus are identified as *ben' yeze*, which means "people from the salt hill" or "people from the isthmus." And Zapotecs who reside in La Sierra are named *ben reje*. Since the pre-Hispanic era, the Zapotecs have lived in small towns or settlements in these three geographical areas (Whitecotton 2004). When the Spanish conquerors arrived at Oaxaca in 1521, they came to know these regions as Las Zapotecas (Chance 1989, 8). Anthropologists and linguists agree that Zapotecs are not a homogenous ethnic group. Each Zapotec community is distinguished by its own way of dressing, customs, music, food, religious fiestas, and dances. However, Zapotec language, native forms of social organization, and a common sense of peoplehood as Zapotecs constitute today the most important features through which they can be identified as a group.[2]

In Los Angeles, these regional and linguistic differences among Zapotec immigrants are still meaningful. However, in response to the experiences of migration and permanent settlement in the United States, Zapotec immigrants have reconceptualized their ethnic identity as Zapotecs and have started to consider new ones. In this chapter, I explore the ways in which international migration has shaped the sense of ethnic and racial identity of the Yalálag Zapotec immigrants. The goal in this chapter is to provide a deeper understanding of how migration experiences and new contexts of power and cultural difference alter the meanings of identity and how transnationalism, as a set of social and cultural processes, contributes to the emergence of a multiple, flexible, and fluid identity of Yalaltecos in Los Angeles.

The Logics and Complexities of Ethnic and Racial Identification

Life in a foreign country and travel between emigrant-sending and immigrant-receiving communities have been crucial in the shaping of ethnic and racial identities for Yalaltec immigrants. Upon permanent settlement in the United States, the Yalálag Zapotecs not only become more aware of their ethnic, linguistic, historical, class, gender, and religious differences, but are also challenged by their own perceptions of self and established definitions of their collective identity. In Los Angeles, as Yalaltecos encounter people from different nationalities, creeds, languages, skin color, physical characteristics, class, and ethnic backgrounds, they become more aware of their own distinctiveness. Also, as with any other immigrant population, Yalaltecos learn that they are not necessarily identified or recognized on the basis of their premigration identities. In the United States, they enter the American system of racial and ethnic stratification, which assigns them new ethnic and racial labels. In addition, as they incorporate in an ethnically segmented labor market, they learn to use the U.S. state-defined categories and the popular conventions concerning race and ethnicity (cf. Glick Schiller 1999; Oboler 1999).

According to the U.S. Census Bureau, indigenous Mexican migrants are ethnically Hispanic or Latinos and racially American Indians. In the United States, Latinos or Hispanics constitute an ethnic group, not a race. They are persons of Cuba, Mexico, Puerto Rico, Central and South America or "other Spanish culture or origin regardless of race" (Ennis, Ríos-Vargas, and Albert 2011). Hispanics can identify as members of any race because "the U.S. government, and more specifically, the U.S. Census . . . does not have a single criterion or principle to determine different races. Rather, they currently use several, for example, national origin, tribal affiliation, and membership, and physical characteristics" (Rodríguez 2000, 41). In the U.S. Census Bureau, there are six options for race identification: White, Black, American Indian and Alaska Native, Asians, Hawaiians and Pacific Islanders, or "other race" (Humes, Jones, and Ramírez 2011). Under this logic, Yalaltecos are racially classified as American Indians and ethnically as Hispanics of Mexican origin, namely, Hispanic American Indians (Huizar Murillo and Cerda 2004).[3] According to the 2010 census, 1,190,904 people of Hispanic origin said they were American Indian or Alaska Native. Of these, 685,150 said that American Indian was their only race (Humes, Jones, and Ramírez 2011).[4] In contrast, the Mexican census identifies them as indigenous populations (INEGI 2010b). Language and indigenous self-identification are used to account for the total number of speakers in each ethnic group (INALI 2011). Race is not used as an official label to characterize indigenous people or mestizos.[5] However, since colonial times, Yalaltecos and other indigenous groups have been racially and culturally classified as *Indios* or members of the *raza india*, in contrast to the Mexican mestizos or the *raza mestiza*. In Mexico, social scientists identify indigenous peoples as ethnic groups or ethnic communities.[6]

What is puzzling about the idea of Yalaltecos being identified as Mexican, Latinos or Hispanic, and Hispanic American Indians in the United States? Why is it important to mention the significance of the Mexican system of ethnic and racial classification in the context of U.S.-Mexican migration? As mentioned above, once immigrants settle in the United States, they enter the U.S. system of ethnic and racial classification. Likewise, they reconfigure the meanings of their identity ethnically and racially because they come to the United States with different understandings of race and ethnicity and with their own racial and ethnic hierarchies. In the case of the Yalaltec experience, the following considerations are important. First, in the last three decades, Mexican migration into the United States has become a multiethnic and multiracial process. Before the 1980s, Mexican migration was mainly composed of Mexican mestizos. Currently, indigenous Mexican migrants constitute the largest share of Mexican immigrants arriving into the United States. This demographic change not only shows the reconfiguration of Mexican migration into the United States but also points to different processes of immigrant incorporation.

Second, in the United States, Yalaltecos assert Mexican identity as Mexican migrants despite their historical exclusion from full membership as citizens by the Mexican state and long-standing indigenous resistance to cultural and racial identification as Mexican in the Mexican context. Yalaltecos are Mexican citizens, but are not treated as such because the concept of citizenship in Mexico has been ideologically fused with the notion of the mestizo national community. However, upon settlement in Los Angeles, Yalaltecos have come to see themselves as Mexican according to the U.S. ethnic and racial system. In the United States, "Mexican-ness is simultaneously [a] national, racial, and ethnic" identity" (Fox 2006, 41) and is widely treated as a racial identity (Fox 2006; Rodríguez 2000; Stephen 2007b). As indigenous Mexican migrants, Yalaltecos are racialized by non-Mexicans in Los Angeles as "Mexican" along with Mexican mestizo. When Yalaltecos work for white Americans, they are perceived as Mexican mestizos, not as Zapotecs or indigenous Mexicans. When they interact or work with other Spanish-speaking immigrants including Salvadorans, Guatemalans, Colombians, Spaniards, and Peruvians, they also identify themselves as immigrants of Mexican origin. However, as in Mexico, in the United States Yalaltecos continue to be racialized by Mexican mestizos as *Indios* along with other indigenous populations, because *Indios* are not mestizos. That is, the Mexican ethnic and racial system that works in Mexico operates transnationally in the United States. As Lynn Stephen notes, "indigenous migrants in the United States have become and continue to be a racialized category within the Mexican immigrant community" (2007, 212).

Third, according to Yalaltecos, when U.S. surveys ask them about their ethnicity, the first thing that comes to their mind is their collective identity as Zapotec. However, they respond by saying that they are ethnically Mexican because there is no ethnic label or box on the U.S. census form where they can mark their ethnic identity as Zapotec. Here, Yalaltecos are not thinking in terms of U.S. census terminology. They are appealing to their sense of ethnic community and the "ethnic group" category used in Mexico as Zapotecs, because their sense of group identity continues to be "based on a claim to historical autonomy and perceived cultural or physical traits that are emphasized as a primary source of identity and recognized internally as well as externally" (Stephen 2005a, 19). Yet most of my Yalaltec informants told me they never write in "Zapotec" under the category "Other" because it is difficult to figure out what they are supposed to answer. When they are presented with the various options that appear on the U.S. census forms, it becomes confusing to mark just one category. As a male informant said: "I chose Latino. I could have said that I am Hispanic, too. But, since I don't really know what the differences are between these terms, I just said that I am Mexican." Although most Yalaltecos say that they are 100 percent Zapotec and indigenous whether they live in "Mexico, China, or the Netherlands," they cannot avoid defining themselves ethnically as Mexican in the United States because Mexican is the default category used to identify all immigrants coming from Mexico, regardless of ethnic identity or socially constructed sense of racial identity. Yalaltecos have also come to see themselves as Mexican and Latinos beyond their choices in the U.S. survey, as I discuss below.

Kearney (2000) points out that indigenous Mexican migrants reinforce their sense of Mexicanness as they relate today to the Mexican state through Mexican agencies that provide services to the Mexican immigrant community in the United States. In my interviews, undocumented Yalaltec migrants mentioned that as Mexican citizens in Los Angeles they have certain rights and benefits. When they look for a job, an apartment to rent, or are asked at school where they are from, they use the Mexican ID *matricula consular* issued by the Mexican consulate in Los Angeles to as identification. With this ID, they also open bank accounts, buy alcoholic drinks in the supermarket, obtain health care services, access official documents related to children's issues, and identify themselves upon return to Mexico and avoid paying taxes (IME 2005).[7] Some mentioned that they also used their Mexican ID known as *credencial de elector* to vote in the presidential elections of Mexico in 2000. One undocumented immigrant told me that under certain circumstances he used to carry his Mexican ID as a way to prove his identity: "When I left home, I made sure to bring my *credencial de elector*. If something happened to me when crossing the U.S.-Mexican border, I would have something to be identified as Mexican." Similarly, as the Mexican state creates new policies, establishes bilateral agreements, opens cultural institutes, engages indigenous migrants in Oaxaca state politics, and expands its control over Mexicans abroad through state programs like "Three for One" and the Paisano Program, Yalaltecos become absorbed within the logics of the nation-state in the United States. According to Basch, Glick Schiller, and Blanc-Szanton (1994), this process can be conceptualized as an expansion of a "deterritorialized nation-state building."

In Mexico, Yalaltecos do not struggle to be culturally Mexican. They demand full membership as Mexican citizens, including their right to be culturally different. As Zapotecs, they have a history and cultural legacy that dates back to the Mesoamerican Classic Period (100–900 c.e.) (Whitecotton 2004). Since the late nineteenth century, the Yalálag Zapotecs and other indigenous groups have been pressured to assimilate to mainstream mestizo Mexican culture, language, and society. They have resisted embodying the ideal of the Mexican citizen, namely, the Mexican mestizo, and blend into a homogenous national culture. As a result, they have been excluded from the national imaginary as Mexican and denied full membership rights.[8] But in Los Angeles, Yalaltecos have come to identify themselves strongly as Mexican and share some aspects of Mexican culture with mestizo Mexican migrants through their acculturation and participation in Mexican nationalist culture and discourses in the United States.

BECOMING MEXICANIZED

Yalálag Zapotecs, like other indigenous peoples, are treated as aliens in Mexico, and their history, cultural legacy, and patrimony are not part of the national discourses of identity and culture. In the United States, however, Yalaltec immigrants, who see themselves as members of an ethnic minority in the country of emigration, identify as Mexican because they are learning to be Mexican through their migration experience. To be precise, it is not that Yalálag Zapotecs are becoming less Zapotec. Rather, they are becoming Mexicanized in the United States.

In the course of my research in Los Angeles, I realized that Yalaltecos do not define their identity as Mexicans solely because American society perceives them racially Mexican or because they have been, to some extent, unable to challenge the hegemonic discourses of a national identity.[9] Rather, they are developing a sense of Mexicanness from practices, ideas, behaviors, and symbols of Mexican nationalism shared with mestizo Mexican immigrants. For instance, the emergence of national sentiments and the internalization of national symbols—the Mexican flag and national holidays organized by the Mexican consulate in Los Angeles—and the flow of Mexican mainstream popular culture and information have contributed to the shaping of a Mexican identity among Yalaltec immigrants. All of my Yalaltec informants mentioned that they had never experienced such a deep pride in their Mexicanness before migration. Some pointed out that they became more aware of their identification as Mexicans in the United States because of the "cultural similarities" they have found with other immigrants who hold the same identity. The following excerpt shows how a Yalaltec friend came to understand himself as Mexican in the migration context, and how he restructured his understanding and social positioning in relation to other Mexicans in the context of emigration and immigration:

> J: In the United States, I am Mexican because here we are all Mexican. If I traveled to another country and someone asks me where I am from, I would say that I am Mexican, and I will show my Mexican flag. [As J was saying this, he opened vigorously his arms as if he were showing me an imaginary flag. We began to laugh.] Among Mexicans who live in the United States, I say that I am Oaxaqueño. In Mexico, I would say that I am Oaxaqueño of the Sierra Juárez. But if people ask me about my origin, I would say that I am Zapotec of Yalálag. Let me explain to you. Here, in the United States, we become more proud of being Mexican. Among Mexicans, I am proud of being Oaxaqueño. And among Oaxaqueños, I feel proud of being Zapotec. In the United States, I feel very proud of being all of them.
>
> A: But, what are the differences between you and me if we are both Mexicans? Are we the same kind of Mexicans?
>
> J: Yes. We, you and I, are Mexicans, but from different races. For example, we are la raza Zapoteca. But you are part of the raza mestiza.
>
> A: Did you think of yourself as Mexican before coming to the United States?
>
> J: Not really. I just knew that I was a Yalaltec. I never thought of myself as Mexican until I came here.

Glick Schiller (1999) and Tsuda (2003) suggest that some ethnic minority immigrants have come to understand themselves as national ethnics after migration. Early anthropological and sociological research on the identity of immigrant populations in the United States points out that local identity was the starting point for group identification for immigrants residing in foreign countries. At the beginning of the twentieth century, European immigrants who came to America identified with their regional and local identities. Later, they acquired a national identity, which was created in the United States (Glick Schiller 1999; Thomas and Znaniecki 1920). Among the Yalaltecos, although there is consciousness of the ethnic, historical, linguistic, and racial differences between Mexican mestizos and indigenous Mexican peoples in the context of immigration, they tend to reproduce and reelaborate the "contradiction of differentiation and unity" that articulates the Mexican nation-state in the context of immigration. As Kearney suggests: "we are all one, but [at the same time] we are internally differentiated into class, gender, and race" (1991, 65). In other words, even in the context of international migration, the project of the nation-state has been to create a common sense of identity as Mexicans among different ethnic groups and resolve the contradictions that it causes.

For Yalaltecos, learning Spanish in Los Angeles represents one of the most meaningful practices of Mexican identification. Zapotecs speak Zapotec.[10] But in the United States, Yalaltecos learn Spanish first instead of English because they are surrounded by a large number of speakers of Spanish. They work with Mexican immigrants and live with Central and South Americans in Koreatown.[11] At times, they work for Mexican Americans or Chicanos who speak Spanish. Some of them mentioned that even many Americans prefer speaking Spanish to them because they like to practice their Spanish. Yalaltecos explained to me that although they learned Spanish in elementary school, and some of them had improved it in middle school, they never felt good at Spanish.[12]

Twenty-five of thirty-six Yalaltec immigrants I interviewed said that their linguistic competence in Spanish was very poor before their arrival in the United States. According to them, they were able to read and write Spanish, meaning hand-copying and repeating the words of written materials, but could neither understand what they read or communicate. Since the 1990s, first-generation Yalaltec immigrants have been fully bilingual: unlike former generations, they speak Zapotec and Spanish before migration to the United States. This means that for over twenty years bilingualism in Zapotec and Spanish is a norm among Yalaltec people between ten and sixty years old. As in Yalálag, in Los Angeles, Yalaltecos continue to speak Zapotec among their *bi gwlash*, relatives, and friends because they choose to use their mother tongue. However, those who have children in the United States speak Spanish to their children.

The majority of my informants reported that they have not learned English despite living in the United States. Five of thirty-six Yalaltecos consider themselves good at English because they enrolled in community colleges or high schools and have taken classes in English as a second language. According to them, their language skills are now good enough for them to communicate, understand, and read a little bit of written English. When they arrive in Los Angeles, they speak more Zapotec than Spanish. But they said they were silent most of the time upon arrival because their Yalaltec relatives or friends worked, and they had no one to interact with. Many scholars suggest that English language acquisition is necessary for immigrants' assimilation and integration. It is both part of the adaptation process in their new environment and a way to seek acceptance from the host society. The five Yalaltec immigrants who said they learned English at school said they have been able to find better jobs and obtain better salaries as a result. However, thirty-one of my interviewees are illiterate in English and are only competent in Spanish. The questions that arise here are: Why do Yalaltecos become more fluent in Spanish in the United States? Why do they speak Spanish and Zapotec instead of Zapotec and English? Why not learn English if this is the dominant language in the country of immigration? Most Yalaltecos I interviewed explained that the inability to speak Spanish proved to be a major barrier in the United States, and most asserted that they should improve their Spanish before trying to speak good English. For them, Spanish fluency facilitates acquisition of English and expands job opportunities. Fabian, who is bilingual—Zapotec and Spanish—explained to me why he thinks that speaking Spanish has been more important for him and many of his *bi gwlash* than learning English:

> F: One of the major obstacles we have in this country is speaking Spanish. Look, to learn English, you have to speak and read Spanish first. For us, this is a double challenge. If we cannot speak Spanish well, how are we expected to speak good English? I really felt ashamed of not being able to speak Spanish when I came here.
>
> A: But why do you think so? I would assume that you should be more concerned with learning English, no?
>
> F: No. Look, because I speak dialect [Zapotec], I can communicate with my *bi gwalsh*. But because I could not speak Spanish when I arrived in this country, I could not communicate with other people, and it was not easy to find a job.
>
> A: But why not learn English? This is the language spoken in the United States, isn't it?
>
> F: I think that we have to learn Spanish first. Look, if you need a dictionary to find a word in English, there is no Zapotec-English dictionary. I told you, although I could read Spanish, I could not understand what I read. But, because I speak Spanish now, I can look for a word in a dictionary and understand what it means in English. Do you see my point? Now, I can understand what is going on, and I have a job.

There are three factors that facilitate the acquisition of Spanish in the United States: first, of course, previous knowledge of Spanish that Yalaltec immigrants bring with them plays a crucial role in improving their Spanish proficiency. Second, there is a large Spanish-speaking community that resides in Los Angeles, which would be different if they resided in Ohio or Kansas, and the Yalaltecos' daily interaction primarily with other Spanish speakers makes Spanish fluency an immediate priority. But the third factor is that because Yalaltecos become "Mexican" in the United States and see themselves as members of Los Angeles Mexican community, they also become disciplined within the practices and discourses of the Mexican nation-state. As Fox suggests: "indigenous Mexicans can access 'full Mexican-ness' to the degree that they give up their language and commitment to ethnic autonomy. . . . Less than full command of the Spanish language is another powerful mechanism for exclusion from equal membership in Mexico's national polity and imaginary" (2006, 42).

To Mexicans in the United States and in Mexico, Zapotecs are not Mexicans, culturally, historically, and linguistically speaking. In common usage, Zapotec is not even considered a language within the language hierarchy in Mexico. Most indigenous people describe their native languages as dialects, whereas Spanish is considered a language. Therefore, due to the pressure to assimilate and prove that Yalaltecos have incorporated into a higher-status group (Mexican) in the eyes of American society and other immigrant groups, they emphasize Spanish acquisition and fluency. Additional pressure comes from the stigmatization that Yalaltecos experience for speaking a non-language, that is, a "dialect," which has caused some Yalaltecos to refuse to speak their native language in public places or teach it to their children.[13] All Yalaltec immigrants I interviewed consider that the Zapotec language *no sirve aquí* (is not useful here). Of course, another factor impedes Yalaltecos from improving or learning English: most of them do not have time to go to school to learn it. But again, it is a combination of factors that leads Yalaltecos to believe that it is more important to acquire Spanish than it is to learn English. Further, Yalaltecos who have experienced discrimination because of their native language tend to discriminate against their peers. Fabian elaborated on these incidents:

> I do not feel ashamed of my *dialecto* (dialect). But, I have a lot of *bi gwlash* who feel ashamed of it. Many of them hide that they speak *dialecto*. For instance, if I meet a *bi gwlash* on the bus or on the street, I usually speak to them in *dialecto*. But, there are some who refuse to speak it. If they speak to me in Spanish, I keep speaking in Zapotec. Some of them prefer using Spanish, and I know why: if other people listen to us speaking our dialect, they laugh at us. Do not think that only Mexicans do that, but also Salvadorans and the Guatemalan mestizos, but not the ones who are Mayas. They usually say: *Ya viste a los Oaxaquitas?* (Can you see and listen to those little people from Oaxaca [meaning Indians]?) And they begin to make fun of us.

Although most Yalaltecos think that learning Spanish is more important than learning English, there are a few trilingual Yalaltecos who prefer using English to the extent that they even stop speaking Spanish to their children. On the other hand, there are some who feel that speaking Spanish makes them not only members of a higher class or ethnic group—the Mexican—but equal to Mexican immigrants and Mexican Americans.

This process of Mexicanization of the Yalaltecos is also reinforced by the continuous flow of Mexican mainstream popular culture, which is facilitated by mass media and telecommunication technology. Although Yalaltec immigrants were not completely isolated from Mexican mainstream popular culture back in Mexico, they have reconnected to it more strongly in the United States. In Yalálag, they listen to a limited number of radio stations that play a certain type of Mexican popular music. But in Los Angeles, several radio stations play a great variety of Mexican popular music in Spanish. For example, some programs play music from the 1950s and 1960s, in particular the Mexican *rancheras* and *boleros* that many Yalaltecos like to listen to. A few Yalaltec immigrants have also started to use the Internet to download free music in Spanish. There are also TV channels that have programs such as soap operas, the Mexican edition of *Big Brother*,

El Gordo y La Flaca, *Ventaneando*, *La Academia*, and talk shows that Yalaltecos watch on a regular basis. They are informed and updated about current events in Mexico by watching Mexican news programs. Every Sunday morning, a program airs simultaneously in Oaxaca City and Los Angeles that plays music from different regions of Oaxaca and offers news of events from the state.

In Los Angeles, a transnational culture of the Mexican mainstream circulates back and forth between Mexico and the United States. This culture is composed of shared social practices, values, and ideas that have influenced the lives of Yalaltec immigrants in the context of immigration. For instance, as result of contact with the Mexican mestizo population in the United States, Yalaltec immigrants have incorporated the non-indigenous rite of passage called *XV años*. Known as the *quinceañera* in the United States, this is a rite of passage into young womanhood celebrated at the age of fifteen. This rite is composed of a religious ceremony in a Catholic church, and a series of secular enactments that occur during a social gathering that celebrate and signify that the young girl has gone through the physiological and psychological changes that allow her to behave as a young adult. Among these secular rituals are "the waltz of *la quinceañera*" with her father and *padrinos* (godfathers), "the last doll dance," "the father's speech," and the "cutting of the cake."

Although Yalaltecos could have incorporated this female coming-of-age ritual within their system of cultural practices in Mexico, they did not, but they did adopt it in the United States. Like many Mexican American mestizas, U.S.-born Yalaltec teen girls have been celebrating their fifteenth birthdays in mainstream Mexican fashion for the last fifteen years. However, unlike Mexican American teens, U.S.-born Yalálag Zapotec women or the 1.5 generation girls (those who emigrated as children) have experienced a series of significant social changes in terms of gender relations and ideology related to the celebration of the *quinceañera*.

In Yalálag, there has been a long tradition in which the passage from social puberty into womanhood resulted in an arranged marriage. Most women in the village used to marry between the ages of twelve and sixteen, under the assumption that they could raise a family as soon as they were capable of sexual reproduction. The *quinceañera* was thus not part of the rituals of the life cycle for Yalaltec women because most of them were married before they reached fifteen. Although today teen girls in Yalálag do not marry at the age of twelve, some do marry when they reach fifteen. Also, some girls are allowed to marry as soon as they finish middle school. In contrast, in Los Angeles, U.S.-born Yalálag Zapotec women do not marry until or after they turn eighteen, and Yalaltec immigrants have incorporated the *quinceañera* as part of the rites of passage of teenage girls.[14]

The acculturation of Yalaltec immigrants into the Mexican mainstream is not only represented by the acquisition of certain Mexican values and ideas but is also reflected by the actual performance of specific social practices. Yalaltecos have acquired a series of bourgeois social conventions that are akin to the social conventionalities of middle-class conservative Mexicans. Unlike the ideas and values of womanhood that remain among a few Yalaltec families in Yalálag, Yalaltecos in the United States not only believe that teen girls reach adulthood at the (relatively) late age of eighteen but also that they should wait until they attain a certain maturity to be married. Today, the celebration of the *quinceañera* among Yalaltec immigrants demonstrates compliance with social conventions that require that the girl be a virgin and has reached her age as a respected female adolescent. In her investigations into the effects of the migration process on the sending community, Peggy Levitt (2001a) argues that non-immigrants and immigrants become more mutually dependent because of "social remittances" that flow between receiving and sending communities, and because of the ways immigrants impact the social life of non-immigrants.[15] This finding is in line with my research. In the last fifteen years, Yalaltec teenage girls in Yalálag have also started to celebrate their *quinceañeras* because immigrants have promoted this social change.

Cultural practices and social changes that Yalaltecos have adopted in the United States have moved back and forth along the same migrant circuits (Rouse 1989) and social networks. For example, in December 2003, in Los Angeles, a Yalaltec friend who was the *padrino de invitaciones* (a relative who offers printed invitations for the families' guests) of a young girl invited me to attend his niece's *quinceañera* in Yalálag because he knew that I was planning to go there. During my research in Yalálag in summer 2004, Agustín, another immigrant friend invited me to attend his niece's *quinceañera*. On this occasion, my friend directed one of the brass bands that played a waltz he had composed for the girl. Ana, the *quinceañera*, who was born in Los Angeles, had asked her parents to go to Yalálag to celebrate her *quinceañera* with her grandparents, part of her extended family, and friends. The religious ceremony took place in the main church of the village and the fiesta, which lasted three days, was held in her grandmother's home. Ana's *quinceañera* in Los Angeles lasted only one day, however. In Los Angeles, Yalaltec immigrants have not only appropriated this ritual but have rearranged it to reflect a particularly Yalaltec taste. For example, unlike the Mexican American celebrations, the *quinceañera* of Yalaltec immigrants is an event that occurs at the center of the community's social life. In addition to the extended family, a large number of *bi gwlash* are involved in the production of the fiesta. They assist the parents of the *quinceañera* with the preparation of traditional food and the manufacturing of the Western dress and souvenirs. In their role of godmothers or grandfathers, they donate goods (alcoholic drinks, tortillas, the cake, etc.) and money (to pay for the ballroom, the rental of folding chairs, the DJ, and the brass band), or help to choreograph the girls' waltz. Although the *quinceañera* fiesta usually takes place in private ballrooms, at times, some *bi gwlash* lend their homes. As a rule, the *quinceañera* is regaled by one of the three Yalaltec brass bands. It is customary to play the traditional social dances called the *sones y jarabes de Yalálag* that give the party a distinctive flavor.

Becoming Americanized

In the United States, a common assumption remains: there is an American main-stream culture into which immigrants must assimilate to be fully incorporated. Indeed, both Americans and immigrants believe that there is something called Americanness that serves as a reference for self-identification and as means for incorporation. However, this assumption calls for a closer understanding of what it means to be American and how ethnic Americans and new immigrants define their sense of Americanness. In the case of the Yalaltec immigrants, I find that they feel that they are becoming Americanized while still reinventing their cultural identity as Yalálag Zapotecs. In the course of my research, none of the Yalaltecos I interviewed considered themselves American, regardless of their status as American citizens, U.S. residents, or undocumented immigrants. Yet most agree that they have adopted some of the ideas, values, and behaviors of the American mainstream. Some young Yalaltec couples who are expecting a baby search for names for their children that have an equivalent in English and Span-ish as a way of integration: Anthony-Antonio, Peter-Pedro, Mary-Maria, Laura, Daniel, and so on. A friend of mine whose baby is one year old said to me: "I do not consider Angel American yet, even though he was born here. But, I think that at some point he will become a Mexican American. . . . We chose this name because it is sounds similar in English and Spanish. He can use both." Some Yalaltec parents use the American parental technique of "time out" to discipline their chil-dren when they misbehave. Some Yalaltec families celebrate Thanksgiving and Halloween with relatives or *bi gwlash*. In November of 2002, a Yalaltec family invited me to celebrate Thanksgiving at their home. During the celebration, we ate turkey, pasta, and pumpkin pie. In November of 2003, I helped to decorate the "Day of the Death" altar (*Día de los Muertos*) and participated in a Hallow-een dance party in the backyard of a Yalaltec family that offers its house in Pico Union for Yalálag community events.

For some Yalaltecos, becoming American implies behaving and believing one-self to be culturally American. Yalaltecos mentioned to me that there are *bi gwlash* that "feel" and "behave" American because of two main reasons. First, they are liv-ing legally in the United States and feel American because they are American citi-zens. Second, there are Yalaltecos who deny or feel ashamed of their ethnic origins as Yalaltecos. As a result, they imagine themselves as members of a higher-status group—the American—and look down on their *bi gwlash*. In this context, behav-ing or trying to pass as an American is common for some and becomes a severe target of criticism and cause for conflict. Yalaltecos who behave in American ways and choose a more assimilationist approach into the American mainstream are criticized when they try to flaunt social mobility and treat their *bi gwlash* with contempt. Yalaltec immigrants condemn their *bi gwlash* who attempt to "pass" as American for their efforts to be "culturally" different from their group and their belief that they have been accepted into the dominant group (cf. Tsuda 2003). On one occasion, a Yalaltec friend invited me to her daughter's birthday party. While I was having dinner, my friend introduced me to her brothers and sisters-in-law. As dinner progressed, I realized that the uncles and aunts of the birthday girl not only addressed their children, nephews, and nieces in English, but also spoke to each other in English. Over the years, I became aware that Yalaltecos disapprove of others who prefer to speak English in front of their *bi gwlash* to distance themselves from their peers and demonstrate that they belong to a higher-status group. Yalaltecos believe that this type of code switching is also a sign of shame or refusal to acknowledge their cultural identity as Yalaltecos. There are some Yalaltec women and men who endeavor to reproduce U.S. styles of dress and behavior to show that they comply with American standards. Some women, for example, dye their hair in various colors—from blonde to light brown to highlights—and they wear their hair shorter than the Zapotec norm, which is down to their lower back and is a sign of beauty. Also, these women like to wear mini-skirts, close-fitting pants or skirts, pantyhose, shirts or dresses with spaghetti straps or without sleeves, and high heels. They carry themselves with a certain degree of confidence and tend to be liberal, yet some pay for cosmetic plastic surgeries such as Liposuction, nose reshaping, and eyelid surgery to look less *India* or Mexican.

During my longest stay in Yalálag, I observed how some Yalaltec female immigrants are particularly censured because their behaviors and appearance do not conform to the social and cultural norms of the village. Yalálag is a small town located in the highlands of Oaxaca. Most of the people—90 percent—live on steep mountain slopes, and they usually walk on unpaved roads to reach their homes. Women wear a traditional sandal (*zapatilla Yalalteca*), manufactured in Yalálag. It keeps their feet fresh and facilitates comfortable walking in the hills. However, when some Yalaltec immigrant women return to visit their families and attend the community patron saint festivals, they wear high heels, bring their flashy, revealing clothes, and even apply makeup. Ironically, most times, immigrant women end up buying *zapatilla Yalalteca* because of their greater comfort.

For Yalaltec men, it works in the same way. Many adopt a more urban-oriented fashion. Some assimilate into what is considered to be a negative identity, the *cholo*—represented by gang fashion. (Many young male Yalaltecos who like dressing in the *cholo* outfit are not *cholos*, however, nor do they think of themselves as *cholos*.) Yalaltec immigrants describe the *cholos* as liking to wear baggy pants, loose T-shirts and jackets, and athletic shoes. Some completely shave their heads, get tattoos, and wear jewelry—necklaces, earrings, and nose rings. In Los Angeles, the real Yalaltec *cholos* are usually censured within the immigrant community for three reasons. First, they assimilate into a negative minority of Los Angeles. The *cholos*, who are mostly Mexican American gang members, represent a lower-class ethnic identity, and a move down on the social ladder of the host society. Second, the fact that these young men assimilate into a negative minority in the host society undermines the Yalaltec immigrant community's ideology of success. Third, performing a negative identity on top of an already stigmatized identity—the Indian—results in a double shame for the immigrant.

In Yalálag, the deterritorialized performance of an American identity has become a serious target of criticism when individual immigrant men or women attempt to introduce ideas, behaviors, and values that are completely foreign. The most visible examples are public behaviors that immigrants perform during their visits to the village. In summer 2004, two female immigrants decided to put leashes on their dogs and walk them around the village. In Yalálag, no one treats dogs as domestic pets, so this attracted attention and caused a lot of gossip. In contrast to American middle-class homes, in Yalálag dogs have well-established roles within the household. For example, they accompany men to work in the countryside and guard the house where they live. Dogs are always free to roam around and never are taken for a walk. Therefore, the decontextualization of this type of action and the alteration of social behaviors on the part of Yalaltec immigrants have caused a good deal of gossip and mockery that often travels back to Los Angeles. During a community gathering in Los Angeles, a friend of mine pointed out the two young women who had recently walked the dogs in front of her mother's place in Yalálag. Because these young women went too far by Yalaltec standards in their American ways of behaving—by trying to reflect a certain degree of upward mobility and cultural assimilation into the "civilized" American mainstream—and because gossip also circulates between Yalálag and Los Angeles, they were mocked in Los Angeles, as well.

For the Yalaltec immigrants, "being American" or becoming Americanized has also to do with gaining American citizenship, as Ursula explained to me: "I am an American citizen since 1998. This makes me feel a bit American. But to tell the truth, I have never felt from here. I do not consider myself fully American as other Yalaltecos do. *Me siento más de allá, de mi pueblo* (I am from there. I belong to my village)." Yalaltecos who are American citizens expressed to me that despite having an American citizenship, they feel treated as second-class Americans. There are Yalaltecos who think that becoming Americanized has to do with upward mobility or a change in their social status. That is, becoming American means improving the quality of life and having access to opportunities that Yalaltecos cannot not have in Mexico. Daniel, a Yalaltec man, mentioned that he has become American and feels Americanized because the United States has provided him with economic resources to improve his standard of living and offer a better life to his children who were born in Los Angeles—education, food, clothes, and a better house. He commented that because of his lack of trust in the Mexican government and the socioeconomic marginalization he experienced back in Mexico, he became an American citizen.

In sum, here, Americanness means mainly adopting American behaviors, ideas, and habits. All my interviewees openly admit that they have become Americanized, but they also confess that they hold a sense of Yalálag Zapotecness.

OLD AND NEW RACIAL IDENTITIES

In Los Angeles, Yalaltec immigrants experience racism from their condition as *Indios* and urban poor immigrants. They learn that they "are not 'white,' nor 'mestizos,' nor fully 'Mexican'" (Kearney 2000, 186). The social and cultural boundaries between mestizo Mexicans and the Yalaltec immigrants continue to remain significant in the United States. Mestizo Mexicans and indigenous Mexicans reorganize transnationally as independent communities on the basis of their local and regional identities, hometown associations, and political interests. Mestizo Mexican immigrants are mostly lower class, are racially characterized as mestizos, and have their own local traditions. In Los Angeles, they come from western, northwestern, and central areas of Mexico. The Yalaltecos mostly interact on a daily basis with Mexican mestizos from the states of Zacatecas, Michoacán, Jalisco, Guanajuato, Colima, and Puebla. The Yalaltecos, who are lower-class peasants before arrival in Los Angeles, come from a rural village of the Sierra and have reorganized as a community. They have formed their own hometown association and are affiliated to the Oaxacan multiethnic association FOCOICA, on the basis of their indigenous ethnicity (see fig. 4.1).

As mentioned above, in Los Angeles, Yalaltec immigrants not only continue to use their premigration racial and ethnic schemes to talk about their identity but have also learned to use the American system of racial and ethnic categorization to describe their sense of identification. According to their premigration racial relations and imposed racial labels, some Yalaltecos define themselves positively as members of *la raza India* (the Indian race) because their ancestors were Indians, meaning natives of their homelands. During an interview, Daniel, a Yalaltec immigrant, said that he considers himself and his wife to be part of *la raza India*: "We are proudly Oaxacan Indians. I come from Oaxaca and have my own language and culture."

Yalaltecos say that they identify positively as *Indios* because this is an umbrella term that embraces all indigenous people who live in Mexico, in the United States, and in the Americas. On the other hand, Yalaltecos spoke about their struggle to move away from the negative meanings, stereotypes, perceptions, and ideas that this racial identity has held since colonial times—that they are inferior and remnants of the past, with backward languages and customs. They mentioned that in Los Angeles they feel more discriminated against by mestizo Mexican immigrants than any other group because mestizo Mexican immigrants use the term *Indio* to look down on them. According to the Yalaltecos, the word *Indio* is not a native term. It does not exist in the Zapotec language and is rarely used among indigenous people, although in some contexts indigenous people do use this label to describe and vindicate their racial identity as *Indios* to build identification and political alliances with other native peoples (Kearney 1995; Velasco 2005). However, mestizo Mexican immigrants use the term *Indio* to discriminate against indigenous peoples and claim that mestizos are racially and culturally superior. To be an *Indio* in the

Figure 4.1. Yalaltecos performing in the Guelaguetza, Los Angeles. Photo by José
Bollo Primo.

Mexican context, whether in Mexico or the United States, is to be an undifferentiated *Indio*. It does not matter what ethnic group indigenous people belong to,
how they identify themselves, or what language they speak: they are simply *Indios*.
Throughout history, *Indio* has been a social construct whose origin dates back to
the colonial period. Currently, it is used among Mexican mestizos as synonymous
with social and cultural backwardness, stupidity, stubbornness, provincialism, and
ignorance. As in the case of Yalaltecos, to be an Oaxacan *Indio* is to be a *yope*, as one
of my Yalaltec friends explained to me:

> In Oaxaca City, we are called *indios yopes*. The Oaxacan mestizos call us that.
> In general, Mexicans are accustomed to looking down on us. For them, an

Indian is ignorant, ugly, fat, short, stupid, poor, dumb, dirty, and backward. And here in Los Angeles, it is the same. Mexican mestizos call us *Oaxaquitas* [little people from Oaxaca], which means pretty much the same.[16]

In Los Angeles, the differences between Mexican indigenous people and mestizos are socially constructed on their sense of racial identification and collective identities. But the majority of characteristics that mestizos use to discriminate against indigenous people—ignorant (meaning illiterate), poor, and technologically "old-fashioned"—are similar to those of the mestizo immigrant population. In the United States, the majority of the mestizo immigrants are impoverished low-skilled workers doing menial jobs. They are poorly educated and come mainly from the countryside. Many perform the same kinds of jobs as Yalaltecos. However, in the United States, mestizo Mexican immigrants continue to racialize indigenous peoples by looking down on their indigenous ethnicity (viewing them as culturally backward though exotic) and racial characteristics (viewing them as ugly, dirty, fat, and short).

The migration experience in Los Angeles has transformed class and social relations between Mexican indigenous immigrants and mestizo immigrants in two significant ways. First, both indigenous and mestizo immigrants have experienced a certain degree of upward mobility. Second, indigenous people have become economically equal with the mestizo population in the United States. A comparison of the socioeconomic characteristics of the mestizo and the indigenous populations before migration shows, unsurprisingly, that the latter had been more oppressed and marginalized. Yet although indigenous immigrants are still at the bottom of the social ladder of American society and are seen as "poor, dumb, and silly" in the eyes of Mexican mestizos, they have attained some success. In the United States, social and class differences between indigenous and mestizo immigrants have been restructured and, of course, it is important to point out that being poor in Mexico is not the same as being poor in the United States. For mestizo immigrants, indigenous people are still treated as *Indios*, even though they may acquire the same social and economic status, have the same socioeconomic opportunities, or do the same kinds of jobs in Los Angeles.

In addition to their racial identity as *Indios*, the Yalaltec immigrants identify themselves as Latinos. In Los Angeles, they have learned to position themselves within American society using official U.S. ethnic categories such as Latino or Hispanic, and have experienced racism from their condition as Latin American impoverished brown immigrants. Like other Latino immigrants, Yalaltecos have become conscious that white Americans and other ethnic minorities see all them and their descendants as homogenous and group them together under the category of Latino. When I asked Yalaltecos what makes them identify as Latino, they said that Yalaltecos share certain commonalities with other Latin American immigrants. They constitute a cheap and exploited labor force. They are willing to work for lower wages and take jobs that white Americans, some Asian immigrants, and African Americans are not willing to do.

Generally speaking, Yalaltecos describe Latinos, especially the immigrant generation, as poorly educated and mostly undocumented, and therefore having few opportunities to succeed. Also, they believe that second- and third-generation Latinos have not been able to surpass their parents' educational background because it is difficult for Latino immigrants to muster the economic resources to send their children to college and graduate school. They mention that one of the major problems the Latino community faces is discrimination from white American society. Yalaltecos believe, for example, that because of discrimination many Latino teens are not accepted in college and graduate programs and therefore end up in the same kinds of jobs as their parents. In particular, they described second- and third-generation Latinos primarily as alcoholics, drugs abusers, criminals, and vandals. A Yalaltec man told me that some Latinos, especially Mexican Americans, Salvadoran Americans, and now some second-generation Yalálag Zapotecs, have shamed the Latino community. Another Yalaltec man explained to me that because of the lack of educational and job opportunities, many young Yalaltecos get into drugs, alcohol, and vandalism. Yalaltec immigrants who defined themselves as Latinos and are American citizens consider themselves second-class citizens. They feel that because they are racialized as Latinos, they do not have the same opportunities and are constantly at a disadvantage compared with other immigrant groups such as Koreans, Jews, and Iranians.[17] As one Yalaltec woman who is an American citizen and has been in California for twenty years expressed it this way:

> Here, the Latino people experience a lot of discrimination, racism. Although we work seven days a week, day and night, and give our best to this society, we will never be treated as first-class American citizens. Yes, I am a U.S. citizen and I pay my taxes and fulfill my obligations. But, in this country, all the Latinos are seen with contempt.

Yalaltecos have learned that there are differences in the treatment of immigrant groups by American society. They see clear marginalization and discrimination toward the Latino community. The ideas of second-class U.S. citizens and the social and economic stagnation of second- and third-generation Latinos are just two of the many forms of discrimination Yalaltecos have experienced. Although many Yalaltecos recognize that there are Latinos who are "successful and quite entrepreneurial," they see Latinos lagging behind white Americans and other immigrant groups. As I explained above, Yalaltecos come to the United States with different racial experiences and views of race, but they also learn that they are classified within the U.S. system of racial and ethnic stratification under new labels. As Laura, a young immigrant woman who arrived in Los Angeles in 1990, said to me: "It is not the same to be called *India* or Latina. I feel really uncomfortable when people call me Indian or *yope*. It is not that I feel ashamed of being from *la raza India*. My origin is Yalalteco and I feel deeply proud of it. But if people call me Latina, it is just different. I do not feel offended by that."

To choose or identify with a Latino identity has given Yalaltec immigrants a new sense of group identification and community (although, of course, they disidentify with negative stereotypes of "Latino" immigrants who have acquired negative behaviors such as drug addiction, delinquency, and murder). The construction of the Latino identity in the United States contains two seemingly contradictory characteristics that push Yalaltec immigrants to identify as such. The first is that the category "Latino" has become a political and ideological symbol and an instrumental identity among Latin American immigrants because it allows for group identification and gives public visibility (Glick Schiller 1999; Oboler 1999). Since the mid-1980s, Latin American immigrants have politically organized under—and therefore identified with—this umbrella term to demand resources, equal treatment within American society, and improvement of their quality of life. They have also created various non-profit organizations under this rubric to assist with or resolve specific needs of Latin American immigrant communities. The second characteristic is that although "Latino" is not a racial category, but rather an ideological construct, Latinos experience a process of racialization (de Genova and Ramos-Zayas 2003).

In Los Angeles, Yalaltecos discover that white Americans, African Americans, Mexican Americans, and American Indians identify them as Latinos or Hispanics, or Mexican. In my interviews, many Yalaltecos pointed out that most Americans do not know anything about the Zapotec people and thus cannot tell the difference between Mexican mestizos, Mexican Indians, Central American, and other indigenous immigrant populations from Latin America, unless the latter is heard speaking their native language. Some Yalaltecos even pointed out that although Americans have visited the state of Oaxaca, where Zapotecs come from, they usually do not know that contemporary Zapotec immigrants in Los Angeles clean homes for them, take care of their children, wash their cars, mow their lawns, and cook and clean for them in a wide number of restaurants in Los Angeles. Moreover, it is assumed that Yalaltecos are just Latinos or Mexican immigrants because indigenous people and Latino mestizo immigrants "look alike."

In Los Angeles, Yalaltecos have also learned to use the U.S. ethnic and racial categories and stereotypes to depict the people they interact with. When Yalaltecos are not able to distinguish people's ethnic background, they tend to use racial labels such as Latino, black, Asian, or white. Most times, it is easier for Yalaltecos to distinguish Salvadorans, Guatemalans, Hondurans, Colombians, Mexican Americans, and African Americans because they work with them or live in the same residential areas. Also, Yalaltecos can differentiate between Jews, white Americans, Koreans, and Iranians because Yalaltecos often work for them. But they cannot identify the origin of all immigrants. For instance, most Yalaltecos perceive Asians as a homogenous community regardless of nationality, language, and class. A good number of Yalaltec immigrants live around Koreatown, and upon arrival they work for Koreans. The commercial area of Koreatown includes Korean businesses and a few Chinese and Thai restaurants, tailor shops, beauty salons, and markets. However, at times, Yalaltecos do not distinguish between Koreans, Thai, and Chinese because for Yalaltecos Asians "look alike."

Yalaltecos identify white Americans as *los blancos* or *los Americanos* and interact with them only through work. Most Yalaltec women I know work for "rich" white and middle-class American families as domestic workers, babysitters, or nannies. Men work as gardeners, cooks, and rarely construction workers. Yalaltecos characterize white Americans as the "rich people." They see white Americans as wasteful and consumer-oriented, but they also describe them as good people and hard working. In contrast to Jewish and Iranian employers, whom they identified racially as belonging to the Jewish race and the Arab race, Yalaltec women emphasized that they like white Americans because most of them pay and treat them well, and value their work. In particular, Yalaltecos like the fact that white Americans are "straight": they are very clear about what they want from their employees. Some Yalaltec women spoke to me about the encouragement that many white Americans have given them to apply for their green card. According to Yalaltecos, Americans usually recommend them to their friends to help them get new jobs or clients, and encourage them to study English or finish middle or high school.

In the course of my interviews, I found that only a few Yalaltecos felt free to express their negative views and opinions about white Americans. Those who said something negative about them referred to American family values and family relationships. For Yalaltecos, it is very striking that American elders live by themselves and receive sporadic visits from their children. They also cannot understand why Americans put their parents in retirement homes when they have worked hard to give their children the best. Another aspect that Yalaltecos criticize has to do with how Americans raise their children. Although Yalaltecos like the fact that Americans are not aggressive or rude with their kids and never beat them, they do not like it that Americans seemingly let their children do whatever they want. According to Yalaltec standards, white American parents do not know how to control their children.

Many Yalaltec families live in the same areas where low-class African Americans reside. In fact, some Yalaltecos said to me that they live in "Africa" because most of their neighbors are *morenos*, that is, African Americans.[18] When I asked Yalaltecos if they interact with African Americans, they said that they do not relate to them in any way. However, they mentioned that African Americans tend to discriminate against them simply because Yalaltecos look Mexican or Latino. Alicia, who lives in South Central Los Angeles, said:

> *Los morenos* [the African Americans] are very rude and aggressive with the Latinos. On many occasions, on my way to work, I have had to get off the bus

or the subway because they start shouting at me. I do not do anything that bothers them. They just start shouting and I do not know what to say because I do not understand what they say. At times, I feel scared. They intimidate me. I just get off at the next stop. I think that they do not like Latinos.

Yalaltecos seem to be picking up on negative stereotypes and discourses on African Americans. They described the *morenos* as poor Americans who are not "willing to progress" or have stayed behind white Americans and even Latinos. A Yalaltec man pointed out that unlike good Mexican Americans, African Americans and their children do not take advantage of job opportunities and education because they often live on welfare. In sum, the racial perceptions that Yalaltecos have of themselves and other groups are not only formed on the basis of negative or positive stereotypes, but also derive from everyday social interactions and premigration and current migration experiences of racialization. In Los Angeles, Yalaltecos experience different kinds of racism. One is the result of a socially constructed racialized difference from Mexican mestizos that continues in the United States. And a second derives from the perceptions of non-Mexicans in Los Angeles who identify Yalaltecos as Mexican along with Mexican mestizo.

Between Being "Traditional" and "Modern"

Yalaltecos, like other Mexican indigenous people, have embodied one of the most essentialized identities: the indigenous. According to this definition, indigenous people continue to hold a primordial connection to the land and are considered traditional, that is, belonging to premodern societies because their way of life has been "associated with a non-industrial mode of production and a stateless political system" (Hylland Ericksen 2002, 14). However, many indigenous peoples who are peasants and hold particular worldviews about their natural environment have migrated to the cities and have been reconstructing and negotiating what constitutes their new and "old" identities, or modern and traditional ways of life. Unlike other immigrant ethnic groups, who may claim a national identity or identify with a nation-state, the Yalaltecos define themselves as "traditional" and indigenous. But they might better be considered neither fully modern nor fully traditional, but postmodern and transnational (cf. Kearney 1999). Stuart Hall suggest that postmodern "identities are never unified, and in late modern times, increasingly fragmented and fractured; never singular but multiply constructed across different, often intersecting and antagonistic discourses, practices and positions" (1998, 4).[19]

In my research in Yalálag and in Los Angeles, I realized that Yalaltec immigrants and non-immigrants have long engaged in a continuous process of reflection on the perceptions of their social identity as modern and traditional (cf. de la Fuente 1949). Before coming to Los Angeles, some Yalaltec immigrants defined themselves as traditional and conservative. Others described themselves as modern and progressive. The former interpreted the exposure to city life, through migration or trade, and the incursions of schooling, Spanish, and technology into the village of Yalálag as major threats to their traditional way of life and a form of ethnocide. The latter believed that "being modern" meant homogenization with or assimilation into the mestizo Mexican mainstream, and a form of social progress. The current experience of urban migration to Los Angeles, which has improved the standard of living of Yalaltec immigrants, has de-essentialized and destabilized these social constructs in two significant ways. First, the ideology that indigenous people would become undifferentiated within modern society due to acculturation into the dominant group or because of their socioeconomic incorporation into the Mexican or American working class has not come to fruition.[20] According to the Mexican census, in the last ten years, the population of Zapotecs has grown from 421,796 (INEGI 2000) to 425,123 (INEGI 2010e). I have written that a Yalaltec community leader in Los Angeles calculates that four thousand people identify with Yalálag: "this estimates includes not only the immigrant population, but also Yalaltecos born in the United States" (Cruz-Manjarrez 2001, 48). The 2010 Mexican census reports that 1,241 Zapotecs live in Yalálag (INEGI 2010d).

Second, Yalálag Zapotec identities, formerly conceptualized as a counterexample to modern identities and confined to notions of provincialism and social backwardness, have modernized while still remaining traditional.[21] Since the colonial period and the subsequent formation of nation-states in the Americas, indigenous peoples have been regarded as premodern and peripheral groups. But today, Yalaltecos have moved from the geographic margins to the center and are living according to a modern lifestyle while still maintaining distinctive ways of life, history, language, and culture.

At present, a radical shift in these ways of thinking has transformed the sense of self-identification of Yalaltec immigrants. In the context of international migration, thinking of oneself as traditional and modern at the same time has been complex but possible.[22] For Yalaltec immigrants, being both modern and traditional has allowed Yalaltecos to undo outsiders' social and ideological constructs of their identities and question the outside values imposed on them.[23] For example, previously, if Yalaltecos wanted to "progress," they had to stop speaking Zapotec. At present, being bilingual in Zapotec and Spanish is accepted. Daniel, a Los Angeles immigrant, talked to me about the contradictions he experienced in his home village over the past forty years:

> When I was a child, more than forty years ago, we were prohibited from speaking Zapotec at school. Not only did our professors force us to stop speaking our language but there was a group of people, called *los constitucionalistas* [progressive party], who believed that the village needed to progress. They started all this. But what a contradiction! The other day I watched a video from the *Casa de la Cultura* [cultural center] of Yalálag where people from

the progressive party have been working on various projects to keep our language and our culture alive! Who can understand them! One of my teachers, who banned me from speaking Zapotec and made me pay fines every time she heard me speaking Zapotec, gave a speech at the opening of the cultural center where she talked about the importance of keeping our language and culture alive. Unbelievable!

Another assumption about progress and modernity is that proficiency in the hegemonic language will ease success and, to some extent, acceptance into the dominant society. However, two major difficulties that Yalaltec immigrants have experienced when moving to different cities are their lack of linguistic competence in Spanish or English and the stigmatization of their native tongue. Of thirty-six informants, twenty-seven who migrated in the 1960s and 1970s to Oaxaca City and Mexico City before their arrival in the United States talked to me about the discrimination they experienced because they could not speak the dominant language of the city, Spanish. They also described how their families banned them from speaking Zapotec because they believed that learning to speak Spanish would open the doors of "progress" while their native language would not. Today, all Yalaltec immigrants are bilingual in Zapotec and Spanish. A few have learned English, as well. But if we compare the experience of migrating to Mexico City or Oaxaca City with that of coming to the United States, we will find that in Los Angeles the perceptions and status of the Zapotec language among Yalaltec immigrants has changed in important ways. As noted above, many of my informants who went to Mexico City or Oaxaca City first experienced discrimination because of the use of their native language at school and in public places or because of their lack of proficiency in Spanish. As a result, many stopped speaking their language. Others spoke it clandestinely, at home or when visiting their families in Yalálag. But in Los Angeles, as I have witnessed, one can hear Zapotecs speaking Zapotec on the bus, on the street, at home, and at their community gatherings. A few switch into Spanish or English as needed.

One immigrant woman, Isabel, talked to me about this kind of experience. When she was eleven years old, she won a fellowship in Yalálag to attend middle school in a Catholic convent in the city of Tlaxcala, Mexico. During her days in the convent, she improved her Spanish because a friend helped her with grammar and pronunciation. Three years later, when Isabel was fifteen and finished middle school, she moved to Mexico City to be a domestic worker. There, she could not speak a word in Zapotec because she needed Spanish. Also, the Yalaltec family she was living with did not want to speak Zapotec at all. When she arrived in Los Angeles, she lived with another family of *bi gwlash*. Although she remembers that she saw English words all over and could hear English almost everywhere, at home she just spoke Zapotec. Moreover, when she met some of her *bi gwlash* on the street, they addressed her in Zapotec, and they conversed in it at private fiestas or community gatherings. But because of the ethnic stigmatization Isabel experienced in Mexico and because she used to think that speaking Spanish was a sign of "progress," she believed that her *bi gwlash* in Los Angeles had moved backward twice, and she feels troubled because she cannot understand why her *bi gwlash* are still speaking Zapotec in the United States. Isabel and her husband did not teach Zapotec to their children. In fact, one of her daughters does not speak Spanish well. She prefers English to Spanish.

Although some Yalaltecos still suffer the consequences of previous discrimination, most Yalaltecos feel freer in the United States to speak their mother tongue publicly because the majority of their interlocutors are no longer Mexicans. Isabel's story reveals the constant stigmatization, aggression, and discrimination that indigenous people have experienced because of their indigenous ethnicity. But these stories are also parallel to the contradictions that Zapotec identity embodies. Despite the project of homogenization of the nation-state—that Zapotecs learn to speak Spanish, a "modern" language—Zapotecs still speak Zapotec. Thus, Yalaltecos are Zapotecs because they continue to be linguistically, culturally, and historically different. But, they also see themselves as modernized because they are proficient in the language of a dominant ethnic minority in the United States, the Mexicans.

Because of migration to the cities, Yalaltec immigrants have left behind a way of life that is essentially rural and peasant and have become absorbed within the immigrant working class of the capitalist economy of the urban United States. In contrast to their previous class position and "traditional" way of life, Yalaltecos have accessed modern technology, speak one of the dominant languages in the United States (Spanish), have adopted an urban and modern lifestyle, and are introducing changes in their community of origin.[24] A friend told me a Yalaltec joke that illustrates both the long-lasting contradiction of these differentiated worlds, the modern and traditional, and the complexity of Yalálag Zapotec identity:

> J: Do you know what the similarities are between a cellular phone and a
>   *huipil* (Indian dress of pre-Hispanic origin still worn by Yalaltec women)?
> A: I do not know.
> J: Easy, any Indian can wear ("to use" in Spanish) them! [Laughs]

This joke not only brings to light the ideological constructs that locate technology and the city life as symbols of modernity and progress but it also locates the social self in ways that combine and bring together new and old ways of life. Unlike dominant discourses about *Indio* identities, Yalaltecos see themselves as modern and traditional at the same time. Yet Yalaltecos are negotiating these opposing identities and undoing the fallacy that Zapotec identity is self-contained and inherently inclusive of social backwardness and premodernity. Thus, defining Yalálag Zapotec identity has resulted in a social process full of tensions, conflicts, and contradictions that have been at the core of Yalaltecs' lives. As I already mentioned, the social pressures to assimilate into hegemonic models of "civilization" have led some Yalaltec immigrants to reject their Zapotec identity or live in isolation or secrecy. Moreover, some Yalaltec immigrants view their peers with contempt because they have internalized the dominant ideology of progress and civilization. Of course, I am not claiming that no Yalaltecos have been able to challenge or resist the hegemonic views of their social identities or that they have not found a way to be themselves on their own terms. Rather, I account for the contradictory ideas and discourses that are redefining ethnic identity among Yalaltec immigrants, whom I characterize as postmodern and transnational.

The ideology of progress and success through migration is similar to what Massey et al. (1994) and Smith (1995) have described as the culture of migration, that is, shared values, ideas, meanings, and behaviors that have encouraged immigrants to migrate. In interviews, some informants said they migrated to the United States not only to escape poverty and help their families economically but also because they wanted to progress, another way of thinking of modernity.[25] One contradictory outcome is that Yalaltec immigrants have not surpassed the levels of education they had before migration because they have concentrated on working.

Although the city represents that symbol of progress and modernity, Yalaltecos have had to deal with the contradictions of city and village lifestyles and the knowledge each place produces. Yalaltecos have pride in their rural peasant way of life, their beliefs, and cultural knowledge, but they increasingly undervalue them by judging the city life and education via school as better than the traditional life and education. Yalaltecos I spoke to describe their former way of life in Yalálag as rural and to some extent lagging behind in social and economic progress. Both men and women said that they used to work in the countryside. Most of them used to help with domestic work and with the harvesting of corn, squash, coffee, chili, beans, and sugar cane. Some worked as shoemakers, bakers, musicians, seamstresses, butchers, and merchants.

On several occasions, I heard Yalaltec mothers in Yalálag tell their children to do their best at school if they wanted to make progress and some day have a professional career. Currently, migration has become "an expectation and a normal part of the life course, particularly for young men and increasingly for women" (Massey et al. 1994, 737–738). Yalaltec teenagers who want to migrate to make progress and become more "civilized" must undertake a sort of initiation rite, what van Gennep (1960) might have described as the ceremony in which potential migrant teens are admitted into the immigrant group. Teens can initiate their journey to *El Norte* as soon as they finish middle school.

During my longest stay in Yalálag, I often heard the phrase *se nota que el pueblo ha progresado* (it is obvious that our village, including the people and the town, has progressed) from some Yalaltec immigrants I met in the village. After hearing this expression many times, I asked them to describe the ways their village had "progressed." Most of them described progress as the changes observed in the process of semi-urbanization: introduction of basic services such as potable water, public electricity, telephone lines, Internet, public transportation, and a highway. A Yalaltec man who came to Los Angeles in the 1960s and has traveled back and forth since then described this process as the "modernization" of his village and his *bi gwalsh*:

> When I left Yalálag, we were very poor. No one had water pumps in their houses. I remember I had to walk up to the water tank that was located in the main street. I used to carry two buckets and fill them with water. But, this is past history. At that time, there was no public electricity. The main streets were covered with lots of rocks, dust, and soil. But, as you can see, today they are paved. When I was little, a few families had a power supply. There was no public transportation . . . But now, people have telephones because they can afford it. All families have power and a water supply. That is, *ahora sí se ve el progreso!* (Now, we can see progress!)

Although progress or development is celebrated as something that has finally happened, there is also a concern that rural and traditional ways of life will be replaced by modernity. Yalaltec immigrants are aware that such modernity not only substitutes for what is "premodern" or "traditional" but also destroys it. The thirty-six interviewees regret that the traditional architecture has slowly disappeared. Today, immigrants introduce U.S.-style houses and can afford to construct them. Immigrants have come to realize that they are catalysts for change because they have begun to transform the lifestyle of non-immigrants and introduced technology. In some interviews, immigrants expressed their concern about giving their families in Yalálag new clothes and electronic devices such as blenders, washing machines, TVs, telephones, sewing machines, tape recorders, and so forth. For immigrants, "giving" implies promoting changes in the traditional village's way of life. But they also said that Yalaltecos prefer to do certain things in traditional ways, like cooking, manufacturing traditional clothing and shoes, and making tortillas, beans, *barbacoa*, and so on, even though immigrants have promoted certain types of modernization.

At present, the use and introduction of computers, fax machines, telephone lines, and electronic games has created a sense of modernization that fosters the idea that indigenous people can have access to technology without losing their identity. For many Yalaltecos technological change translates into modernity, as one of my female informants said in Yalálag: "Little by little we have become modernized. Of course, our *bi gwlash* have to do with this. They bring the computers, TVs, VCRs, and so on. Also, we can communicate with our relatives via Internet or by phone." As noted above, the conservative villagers used to believe that incorporating technology would end their traditional way of life. The assumption was that they would become homogenized and their ways of life exterminated. However, technological change has come to be seen as something that can be incorporated into their everyday life and traditional ways without erasing their ethnic identity. In Los Angeles, Yalaltecos think of their modernization as the ability to perform certain tasks adequately and to behave in ways that are particular to the American way of life. When asked to describe what adjustments they had to make to life in Los Angeles, Yalaltecos mentioned practices of daily life, described in terms of modernization. Among them are: navigating the system of public transportation, using electronic appliances, speaking good Spanish and English, making phone calls, opening a bank account, renting an apartment, and, for some, driving a car. In particular, they referred to learning to work according to American standards as an act of civilization.

Another reflection of how much Yalaltecos feel that they have "progressed" is the use and care of their bodies. As suggested by Grimes (1998), the reproduction of mainstream ideologies and middle-class values is usually materialized in the body and the performance of specific bodily acts. At the community gatherings that Yalaltecos organize in Los Angeles, younger generations of immigrant men and women follow American mainstream fashion. They wear middle-class American-style clothes and usually buy them *en las especiales* (on sale). Some also emulate certain bodily movements and attitudes of Latino professional models or actresses from the mainstream media. In contrast, older generations are more conservative but still think they have modernized. As Julieta, a fifty-year-old immigrant woman, described it: "Here, I started to dye my hair and take care of my nails. In Yalálag, I did not wear high heels, but here I do. Of course, you cannot wear them there because it is uncomfortable. But, the city life allows you to do things that you cannot do in Yalálag. Here, one becomes open-minded, like more civilized [laughs]."

Yalaltec immigrants share a conviction that migration to the cities has transformed their way of life in three significant ways. First, it has brought major social and economic changes to the lives of Yalaltecos. Second, it has changed the ideas, values, behaviors, and ways of life of an indigenous peasant population that has stopped being provincial. As a result, Yalaltec identity is more complex today because it fuses a "traditional" and a "modern" way of life. Third, Yalaltec non-immigrants are also experiencing changes as a result of the values, ideas, and technology that immigrants have introduced in Yalálag. However, in contrast to the city-life experiences of Yalaltec immigrants, the life of non-immigrants remains mainly rural.

In sum, the question of identity for Yalaltec immigrants is more complex than it looks on the surface. In comparing their process of self-identification with that of Mexican mestizo immigrants (cf. Goldring 1992, Rouse 1989, Smith 1995), some similarities are clear. For both groups, their sense of identity as Mexican is reinforced in the United States. But for Yalaltecos, their individual and collective identities as Yalálag Zapotecs have become transnational in distinctive ways. Being a Yalalteco combines with the identities they learn, develop, and acquire in the United States such as immigrant, foreigner, Mexican, indigenous Mexican, Oaxaqueño, Latino, and Hispanic American Indian. In addition, their sense of identity as Mexican is not only framed by their Mexican nationality or other links with the Mexican territory but is also based on assimilative practices into the Mexican mainstream culture acquired via migration to the United States. The difference between becoming Mexicanized in the United States and becoming Americanized lies not just in the acquisition of certain values, behaviors, and ideas of the American mainstream; it also derives from the internalization and use of the U.S. system of ethnic and racial categories. While these dominant definitions of identity inform the ways in which Yalaltec immigrants identify themselves, they also materialize a hybrid, contradictory, and complex multi-inflected identity that includes identification with Mexican nationalism, a sense of racialization as Latino in the United States, a legal definition of American through citizenship and residency for some, as well as cultural identifications with some aspects of what is perceived of as "American" life in Los Angeles—and, of course, being Yalálag Zapotecs in new and different ways.

The construction of a transnational identity captures the complex and changing nature of Yalálag Zapotec identity in the immigrant generation. In the next chapter I extend this approach to discuss the ways in which U.S.-born Yalálag Zapotecs construct their identity and how they have developed their sense of self-identification in the context I have described.

❧

CHAPTER 5

IDENTITIES OF THE SECOND-GENERATION YALÁLAG ZAPOTECS

Everyday throughout Los Angeles, second-generation Yalálag Zapotecs negotiate and reframe their sense of identification as American, Mexican, Oaxaqueños, and Yalaltecos.[1] They grow up hearing from their parents that they are Americans citizens of Mexican descent because they are born in the United States and have U.S. passports. Instead of learning the language of their parents—Zapotec––they are raised speaking Spanish and English. And, because they look like the *Indios Oaxaqueños* (Oaxacan Indians) and maintain certain identifying cultural practices of the Yalálag Zapotec people, mestizo Mexican immigrants and Mexican Americans discriminate against them. In this chapter, I explore how second-generation Yalaltecos and the 1.5 generation (those born in Yalálag, but raised in Los Angeles) handle these definitions of their multiple identities and what it means for them to be a Yalalteco growing up in the United States. To approach to these questions, I focus on the perceptions, beliefs, everyday practices, and experiences that inform their sense of identity in terms of nationality, indigenous ethnicity, assimilation into Mexican and American identities, and the socially constructed notions of racial identification.

BECOMING MEXICAN AND AMERICAN

Mexican migration into the United States is composed of both indigenous and mestizo immigrants, who hold a differentiated sense of ethnic and racial identification and have distinctive histories, languages, and cultures. The Yalálag Zapotecs constitute just one of the indigenous Mexican immigrant groups that differentiate themselves ethnically and racially from mestizo Mexican immigrants. In Los Angeles, one may expect that second-generation Yalaltecos continue to highlight these ethnic and racial differences and assert a sense of identity as Yalálag Zapotecs and American. The truth, unfortunately, is not so. Unlike second-generation

Mexican Americans, who assert a Mexican identity and are determined to preserve some aspects of Mexican mestizo culture, second-generation Yalaltecos are giving up various aspects of their indigenous culture and acquiring a sense of identity as Mexican and American.[2]

When I began my research on Yalálag Zapotec identity in Los Angeles and asked Yalaltec immigrants to define the identity of their children, they began by saying that their children are Mexican Americans because they are born in the United States and are part of the Mexican American community. When I asked the same question to twenty-two second-generation Yalaltecos, their replies coincided with their parents.' They began to explain these in terms of how much they feel Mexican and American, and then how much they identify as Oaxaqueños and Yalálag Zapotecs. An exchange between four siblings illustrates this point:

> LUPE [female, 27 years old]: Well, I am Mexican American. But I am not completely Mexican because I was born in the United States. I am saying this because I am very different from Mexicans from Mexico, including my parents and Mexican friends. I feel like being both. But, I feel more Mexican than American.
>
> ENRIQUE [male, 14 years old]: Well, I consider myself an American citizen. But, I am a Yalálag Zapotec too because my parents are Zapotecs from Yalálag. Why I should not consider myself Zapotec?
>
> JORGE [male, 11 years old]: I feel that I am Mexican, American, and Oaxaqueño. But, to tell the truth I feel more Mexican and American.
>
> ALMA [female, 20 years old]: I agree with one of my brothers. I am Mexican and American, but Yalálag Zapotec too. Although I should say that I do not feel that I am very knowledgeable of Zapotec culture and their traditions. Living in Los Angeles makes things quite different. What I mean is that the people from the place where my parents come from are different from me. In this sense, I could not say that I am really a Yalaltec.

In these responses, one observes that the sense of identity of these second-generation Yalaltecos extends beyond one affiliation. They identify as American nationals in contrast to their parents' Mexican nationality. According to the U.S. system of ethnic classification, they identify ethnically as Mexican—namely, they are Hispanic of Mexican origin. They assert an Oaxaqueño identity because this is the regional identification for indigenous Oaxacan migrants and their children in California. They also claim a Yalaltec identity because they define themselves as persons of Yalálag Zapotec ancestry. However, as expressed in their responses, they identify with all these identities, but they do not feel equally competent in Yalaltec, Mexican, and American cultures.

Over the course of my research, I found that most second-generation Yalaltecos recognize an indigenous identity as Yalaltecos, but this is usually linked, sublimated, or even superceded by two types of national identity: American and

Mexican. To deepen our understanding of this kind of reasoning, we need to consider that second-generation Yalaltecos assume that their parents are Mexican nationals and thus they are Mexican too, although most Yalaltec immigrants have only developed a strong sense of Mexicanness in the United States, whereas in Mexico, they identify as Yalálag Zapotec but not culturally and racially Mexican.[3] In California, second-generation Yalaltecos see themselves as a part of two majority Mexican communities—one Mexican, represented by the U.S. Oaxacan community, and the other Mexican American, represented by second-generation Mexican Americans. And their social location as American citizens and their cultural and linguistic competence in Spanish and English languages in Los Angeles emphasize their identification with these two hegemonic identities.

Throughout my fieldwork, I realized that most second-generation Yalaltecos do not speak Zapotec and have low proficiency in comprehension. Some of these adolescents know a bit of Zapotec, and a few of them are able to follow part of their parents' conversation, but are unable to communicate or sustain long conversations. These adolescents learn Spanish as a first language, and later acquire English at school as a second language. All children use Spanish to communicate with their parents, other Latin American immigrants, and relatives back in Mexico. In Los Angeles, they use English outside of family and community contexts, at work and school, and among other members of the second generation such as brothers, sisters, and peers. As noted by Portes (Portes and Rumbaut 2001a), language is one of the most important referents of ethnic identity because it allows individuals to affiliate with a cultural community and "tightens this sense of we-ness" (Portes and Rumbaut 2001b, 113). However, most second-generation Yalaltecos feel it does not make sense to identify fully as Yalaltecos because they cannot speak the language of their parents, Zapotec.

Yalaltec immigrants rely strongly on the Zapotec language, which provides second-generation Yalaltecos continual opportunities for high levels of exposure; however, immigrants do not actively pass their native tongue on their children. Most adolescents explained that their parents do not teach them Zapotec because they are afraid that their language will prevent their children from successfully assimilating into American society. This attitude is grounded in immigrants' experiences when they migrated to Oaxaca City and Mexico City and could not communicate in Spanish, and thus social pressures experienced by Zapotec immigrants in Mexico have had important effects on immigrants' decision to stop teaching their native language to their children. If we consider the status of the Zapotec language in Mexico, we can understand, although not justify, why Zapotec immigrants exert such pressure on their children to learn other languages. In Mexico, it is well known that education policies have privileged the imposition of Spanish as the national language not only to assimilate indigenous people into the Mexican mainstream, but also to weaken their culture and identity, and erase their histories.

In Los Angeles, there is a widespread belief among Yalaltec immigrants that the second generation will be unable to handle three languages and that "linguistic confusion" would make their children fail to acquire Spanish and English.[4] In Los Angeles, Yalaltec immigrants believe that Zapotec is a useless language for their children because it is never used outside of the family and community context. And the pressures of the social environment in which these children move dictate that they acquire the national language of the host society—English. Yalaltec immigrants emphasize that it is mandatory in the United States that their children learn English in order to succeed. In this vein, various scholars have pointed out that most second-generation Americans lose the language of their parents over time (Jones-Correa 2002; Portes and Rumbaut 2001a). They acquire English as the dominant language and prefer English over their mother tongue. But in the case of second-generation Yalaltecos, the mother tongue is not taught, and this is crucial in the definition of an ethnic identity among second-generation Yalaltecos as American citizens of Mexican ancestry. Luisa, a young second-generation Yalaltec girl, discussed these points when I asked her why their parents did not teach her and her siblings Zapotec and how she felt about it:

> I think that my mom was afraid that we could not learn English well. She always told us that it was enough for us to learn Spanish and English because if we learned Zapotec, we were going to be completely confused. Well, but I think that I would like to learn their language because it is part of our culture. My sisters can understand a bit and even speak some words, but I cannot. And I should confess that my Spanish is not very good either. But, I do not know if I could handle three languages. But wait a minute, how can I say that I am a Zapotec Indian, if I just speak English and bad Spanish? O.K. If my parents are indigenous from Oaxaca and I have learned Spanish and English, how can I say that I am an Indian from Oaxaca?

In Oaxaca City and Mexico City, Yalaltec immigrants, like the parents of this girl, have experienced discrimination because they do not speak the dominant language of the city—Spanish. According to the girls' parents, they speak a "dialect," namely, a non-language. As a result, some Yalaltecos have internalized these negative views of their native language and stopped speaking Zapotec to their children for fear of discrimination and exclusion. Stephen notes that second-generation Oaxacan Mixtecs in northern California and Oregon do not want to speak Mixtec, either, because of the "pressures on children to assimilate and specifically to leave behind their indigenous language and identity" (2007a, 215). None of my Yalaltec interviewees and second-generation Yalaltecos sees multilinguism as an asset. In the context of Los Angeles, Yalaltec immigrants and second-generation Yalaltecos interact on daily basis with a large number of Mexican immigrants and Mexican Americans. As discussed in chapter 4, Mexicans and Mexican Americans continue to discriminate against Yalaltec immigrants because speaking Zapotec marks them *Indios*. Thus, for the second-generation Yalaltecos learning Spanish as a first language marks them as Mexican in the United States. According to Gutiérrez (1995), speaking Spanish among Mexican Americans has contributed to a sense of ethnic distinctiveness as Mexican in the United States.

In my conversations with the second-generation Yalaltecos, I found that their definition of a Mexican identity is always constructed in relation to what others represent for them. Waters (2001a) points out that the construction of one's identity is a relational and situational process. One defines his or her identity in relation to what others are. It is also situational because one can hold several identities at once. In my relationship with them, my social location as a Mexican friend always influenced their responses as Mexican. As the interviews developed, this fact became repetitive and crucial for understanding why these adolescents continuously reframed their answers and reinforced their sense of identity as Mexican or Mexican American. In all our encounters, these teenagers identified me as Mexican. My Mexicanness was important for them to establish a common affiliation because, at some point, they collected "me and them" together as Mexicans. When their first response was, "we are Mexicans," I then challenged them to describe in which ways we were distinct. In response, they emphasized the identities I do not have: "well, we are Mexican American because we were born in the United States. And, we are Oaxaqueños [people from Oaxaca, Mexico] because we belong to the Oaxacan community" a sixteen-year-old girl replied.

The recognition of the second generation's Mexican and American ways, as they travel to Mexico to visit their relatives, highlights their sense of identity as Mexican American. Many Yalaltec teens indicated that family members in Yalálag, like their parents in Los Angeles, call them *Americanos* or *pochos* (an individual who is Americanized). This is because in both Yalálag and Los Angeles, switching between Spanish and English signals the identity of a Mexican American. Karla, a twenty-year-old girl, said to me that when she visits her cousins in Mexico City, they make fun of her because her Spanish is a "little bit twisted." Sometimes, she cannot find the right words to express her thoughts because she feels she is thinking in English. Thus, the use of Spanish and English among visiting second-generation Yalaltecos has much to do with why the local people of Yalálag and relatives in Mexico City, Oaxaca City, and Los Angeles perceive second-generation Yalaltecos as Mexican American.[5]

By comparing the way of life between Yalálag and Los Angeles and observing social exchanges between second-generation Yalaltecos and Yalaltec non-immigrants in Mexico, I also became aware of two things. First, for second-generation Yalaltecos their sense of place and belonging is rooted in Los Angeles. They are being raised in the United States and their lives are shaped by their everyday experiences in Los Angeles, not Mexico. Second, there are conspicuous differences in the performance of ethnic identity and the social perceptions that inform the identity of second-generation Yalaltecos as Americans. For example, in 2003, I traveled to Yalálag with six second-generation Yalaltecos and their families for the Christmas celebration. I soon realized that second-generation Yalaltecos do not see themselves as a part of the village community of Yalálag. According to them, they are not used to the Yalálag lifestyle because this is not their social and ecological environment. As a teenage boy said, "it is hard for us to adapt rapidly to the style of life, weather conditions, 'bugs,' food, and, in particular, some of the social dynamics of our relatives and the village's people." On one occasion, a female teenager began to complain about the food, the water, and the mosquito bites. Another one asked her mother if it would be possible to depart earlier for Los Angeles because she missed her home, food, and friends. On another occasion, I asked other visiting second-generation Yalaltec teens if they were having a good time in the village. They said to me that they were already bored because life in Yalálag was too slow, quiet, and monotonous. They also pointed out that Yalaltec non-immigrants see them as outsiders and gossip about them. When I asked them if they could live there, they said that they could visit their families every other year, but never could live in that little village because they would not know what to do and because they already have plans, friends, and activities in Los Angeles. This experience is similar to what Diane Wolf has described as Home and home for Filipino Americans: "For today's children of Filipino immigrants, the Philippines is often right in their home, locally in California, both literally and figuratively" (2002, 258).

In the context of U.S.-Mexico comparison, the act of claiming an American identity among second-generation Yalaltecos is not only based on their reference of their place of birth, nationality, and U.S. citizenship. It has also to do with adopting American behaviors, ideas, and habits. When they travel to Mexico, they become more aware of their Americaness both because they hold American passports and because they behave according to American customs. Genaro, a seventeen-year-old Yalaltec, who talked about his sense of identity as American and his assimilation into the American mainstream, shared these comments:

> I am American because I am a U.S. citizen. I feel American because I speak English. Also, I guess that it is my way of thinking. I think that we [second-generation Yalaltecos] are more individualistic and materialist. I feel that we are more open-minded than our parents. We have fewer prejudices about certain things. For example, talking about sex. What I eat also makes me feel American. I eat hamburgers, pizza, Taco Bell, all kinds of fast food.

The characteristics that distinguish them as Americans not only reflect the way they construct their American identity but also indicate that being "American" is behaving and acting "American." From a second-generation Yalaltec's perspective, being American entails speaking English, adopting American fashions, and behaving and thinking according to American customs. Guillermo, a twenty-seven-year-old man, described significant differences in his way of talking, walking, dressing, eating, and thinking: "When I went to Mexico, I realized that I do things in the American way. For example, I do not cross the streets [only] when the traffic light is green. When I am talking to someone else about a serious issue, I am straight and frank."

Yalaltec immigrants agree with the American-born members of their community that the second-generation Yalaltecos are Americanized. An immigrant man commented the following during an interview with his two sons: "Look, those adolescents, who are born in the United States, are somehow different from us. They are more American. In some respects, we and our children are similar. But, they are more open-minded. They are different. And of course, they are better educated and have a lot of opportunities in this country." Indeed, Yalaltec immigrants recognize that second-generation Yalaltecos have adopted different ways of thinking and behaving and to great extent have learned American values, norms, and ideas. They also point out that being an American implies having American citizenship and the civil rights and opportunities such as education, health insurance, and jobs that go with it.

Although most second-generation Yalaltecos said they feel American because they are American nationals and identify with other U.S.-born Mexicans, they also claimed that they couldn't identify simply as American because this refers to white Americans.[6] In the United States, people use color terms and the names of four continents to refer to "the different races" that constitute the U.S. population: White (Europe), Black (Africa), Red (North America), and Yellow (Asia) (Rodríguez 2000). "In the common sense," White is frequently associated with white people of European ancestry or "European white racial aesthetics" (Rosales 1997). Oboler notes that "U.S. citizens of Mexicans descent . . . are regularly looked upon and treated as 'foreign' presumably because they do not conform the 'White European' image of the U.S. citizen" (1999, 54). From the point of view of the white dominant society, Mexicans have embodied a foreign identity and a negative minority status. Throughout the twentieth century, white Americans have discriminated against Mexican Americans because of their darker racial appearance and cultural characteristics. In the 1960s, Mexican Americans, who identified as Chicanos, "confronted [Anglo-American] racism and self-hate head on, using the slogan 'brown is beautiful' and promoting an allegiance and affect to the Indian-*mestizo* physical features" (Rosales 1997, xix). Currently, Mexicans are seen as poor Hispanics or Latino immigrants regardless of generation—length of stay in the United States, citizenship status, migratory condition, and time of arrival. Two second-generation Yalaltec teenage girls commented on their differences with white Americans in terms of their experience of racialization as Mexican and a sense of alienation as U.S. citizens of Mexican ancestry as follows:

ALMA [female, 20 years old]: I do not consider myself entirely "American." The Americans are the white Americans. We are not Americans in that sense. Above all, white Americans are rich. My sisters and I do not have those privileges. In the United States whether we like it or not, we are Mexicans.

LUPE [female, 27 years old]: Yes, I agree. We cannot say that we are like white Americans. There are always differences between us. Once, I went shopping to a big mall in Irvine. When I was shopping, I felt that I was being watched over. When I paid, I was asked to show three IDs. I felt so discriminated [against]. I thought: why did they do that to me? They do not do that to white Americans. You know, sometimes, white Americans treat you as if you were not from here. Maybe, it is our way of dressing, the way we look, our shoes, our class, or our accent when we speak English.

In listening to these answers, I purposely asked these women to describe what they would say if a European or an Australian asked them about their origin, ethnicity, and culture. Lupe replied: "I would say that I am American. However, when I travel abroad, people do not believe that I am American." Although she explained that while traveling she feels more American than Mexican, because she has to show her American passport, she would definitely describe her ethnicity in term of her parents' indigenous identity and culture, Oaxacan and Yalaltec, and not in terms of her Mexican or American identities. She further elaborated on what she thinks is representative of Yalaltec culture:

I would tell them about my family's origin, our music, that is, the *jarabes Yalaltecos* [Zapotec social dances], and the Yalálag Zapotec brass band. I will describe [for] them the fiestas that are organized in Los Angeles such as the *bailes* [patron saint celebrations] and the celebration of the Day of the Dead. I would tell them that my parents have their own language and come from a village that is located in Mexico. I may explain about the process of making tortillas and preparing *barbacoa*.

In the context of Los Angeles, second-generation Yalaltecos are becoming Mexican and American through a process of ethnicization and racialization, and assimilation to mainstream Mexican and American cultures. But what does it mean for second-generation Yalaltecos to claim a Mexican American identity? I address this question next.

MEXICAN AMERICAN

For second-generation Yalaltecos, becoming a Mexican American signifies assimilation of social behaviors and cultural practices of the Mexican Americans, feeling both Mexican in the United States and partially American, and the act of claiming membership within one of the largest communities of U.S.-born children—the Mexican American. The term *Mexican American* refers to Americans citizens of Mexican descent. Mexican Americans express a "connection to the *mestizo* culture and race forged in Mexico after the arrival Spaniards" (Rosales 1999, 7).[7] As explained above, in Los Angeles, for the second-generation Yalaltecos, the acquisition of Spanish as their first language most prominently defines their sense of Mexicanness. Second-generation Yalaltec adolescents are fluent in Spanish, and it is the main language they use to communicate with their parents, relatives, and other Yalaltecos in Los Angeles and Yalálag.[8] They attend public schools with high numbers of Mexican immigrants and Mexican Americans, and they mostly socialize with them and "communicate in Spanglish." They said that although they interact with African Americans, Chinese Americans, and, at times, with white Americans at school, they feel more connected to teenagers of Mexican ancestry.

The search for Mexican roots is a significant element in the definition of a Mexican American identity. Seven second-generation Yalaltecos said that as they entered undergraduate school, they started taking classes about Mexican history and literature to know more about their "origins." They told me that they have taken Spanish courses to improve their speaking, writing, and reading skills. David, a twenty-eight-year-old second-generation Yalalteco, spoke about the cultural influences, social relations, and experiences that have shaped his sense of being Mexican American:

> I say that I am Mexican American because I have lived within these two systems: the Mexican and the American. I am American because I was born and raised in the United States. All my life, I have studied within the American system of education. In some ways I am Americanized. But, I also say that I am Mexican because of my Mexican background. I have always been exposed to Mexicans and their culture. I speak Spanish. I have committed to learn about my culture. When I was in the university, I took a lot of classes about Mexican literature and history. Specially, I took courses in Spanish and some about Mexican indigenous peoples. I have always been interested in knowing more about my *culture* (my emphasis).

Within the Mexican American community, there is a wide range of social identities that serve as referents for second-generation Yalaltecos and the 1.5 generation: the Mexican, the Mexican American, the Chicano, and the *cholo*. Each embodies a distinctive sense of identity, values, behaviors, attitudes, and positive and negative stereotypes. The Mexicans are described as teenagers who were born in Mexico, but raised in the United States (the 1.5 generation). They are seen as working hard at school and having the immigrant mentality to succeed. The Mexican Americans and the Chicanos are the descendants of Mexican immigrants born and raised in the United States. Mexican Americans include not only members of the second generation but also Mexicans with generations of ancestors in America going back to the late nineteen century (Sánchez 1993). Generally speaking, the differences between Mexican Americans and Chicanos have had to do with their political stance toward their incorporation to American society, their sense of ethnic identification, and relationships to Mexican immigrants. In the early twentieth century, Mexican American activists and various organizations began to struggle for the recognition of their civil rights as American citizens of Mexican ancestry. During the 1950s and 1960s, Mexican Americans asserted "a sense of permanency and a desire to live as the equals of other Americans within Anglo American system—[this] usually occurred in the second or third generation" (Rosales 1997, 252). Mexican Americans saw their social and political integration in American society as a process that implied working within the confines of the existing American political system for social justice (Gutiérrez 1995). Their efforts concentrated on fighting for the betterment of Mexicans born in the United States. Their political support and activism for Mexican immigrants was secondary.

The Chicano identity derives from the Chicano movement that developed in the states of California, Texas, Colorado, and New Mexico within the context of the U.S. antiwar movement and the civil rights movement. During the 1960s and 1970s, hundreds of Mexican Americans organized politically to struggle for equal rights, better education, social justice, and the end of police brutality within the Mexican community. The concept of *Chicano* was associated with a low-class status and the *Indio-Mexicano* identity held by Americans of Mexican ancestry. Mexican Americans adopted the term *Chicano* as a powerful symbol of ethnic pride and social solidarity, and "as an act of defiance and self-assertion and as an attempt to redefine themselves by criteria of their own choosing" (Gutiérrez 1995, 184). Since then, the Chicanos have developed a sense of identity that rejects the ideology of assimilation into Anglo-American mainstream culture and notions of Anglo superiority. This attitude emerged as a political response to their historical socioeconomic marginalization, and experiences of racialization and ethnic discrimination as Mexican. The Chicanismo or being a Chicano has built its sense of identification on "a quasi-nationalist vision of Chicano identity which extolled a pre-Columbian, native ancestry while diminishing or even rejecting their connection with American culture and society" (Gutiérrez 1995, 185). Chicanos consider that their political efforts on behalf of Mexican immigrants should be as important as their social struggle as Americans of Mexican descent.

For the U.S. Mexican community, the term *Chicano* evokes different kinds of identities. For those who know about the Chicano movement, it refers to a politicized and positive identity. In the context of socioeconomic marginalization and ethnic discrimination, it denotes a negative identity. Mexican immigrants and Mexican Americans who dis-identify with this identity use the word *Chicano* interchangeably with the term *cholo*, an identity that refers to low-class Mexican Americans who are gang members or drug abusers. *Cholos* define themselves as

Mexican Americans, but distinguish themselves by their dress style, accent, haircut, and tattoos. Matute-Bianchi indicates that *cholos* are "held in low esteem by other Mexican American students who often express fear or contempt of what they recognize as *Cholo* or 'Low Rider'" (1986, 240). For most second-generation Yalaltecos and Yalaltec immigrants, the Chicanos and *cholos* are Mexican Americans who are rebels, vandals, and even criminals.

During my years in Los Angeles, I learned that the political meaning of the Chicano identity is not familiar to most second-generation Yalaltecos and Yalaltec immigrants I spoke with. However, those second-generation Yalaltecos who assert a Chicano identity do so because they develop this type of identity through schooling. Some of my interviewees said that they learned in school about Chicano history, the Chicano movement, and the political implications of the Chicano identity. Two mentioned that they have acquired Chicano identity as a result of a process of political consciousness that reflects their critical stance of their socioeconomic marginalization and ethnic exclusion and racial discrimination as Mexican in the United States. For example, David said he became a social activist in the Lesbian, Gay, Transgender, and Bisexual (LGBT) community because his work has empowered him and his community. He also mentioned that he asserts a Chicano identity by choice to differentiate himself from Mexican Americans because the latter are more Americanized and lack of a strong sense of Mexicanness. He spoke about how and why he became Chicano:

> When I was an undergraduate student, I lived in northern California. There, I used to identify myself as a Mexican American. But at school, I learned that I was Chicano and Latino. That is, a Chicano is an individual of Mexican descent, who is essentially political. A Mexican American is a Mexican born in the United States without social and political consciousness as Mexican. Chicanos are politicized. I consider myself Chicano because I have been a social activist in the Latino and Chicano LGBT communities. My Chicano friends and I are engaged in various political and social activities in the Latino LGBT and MECHA [Chicano Student Movement of Aztlán] organizations. We spend [the] most part of our life doing social work for our communities.[9]

When I asked David if he would identify himself as an indigenous Mexican, he said that he would. However, he emphasized that he does not introduce or mark himself as Yalálag Zapotec because nobody knows what that is or about their social struggle. Yet he criticized the fact that many Mexicans do not know about the Zapotec people at all. As he commented: "It is easier to identify myself as a Mexican born in the United States, but a Mexican with political consciousness." In contrast to David's experiences, the rest of my twenty-one interviewees refused to identify with the Chicano identity, and particularly with the Chicano political stance. For example, Tomas, an undergraduate young adult, does not consider himself Chicano from a political, social, or cultural perspective. He prefers calling himself an Oaxacan American because he feels that the Oaxacan and American "systems," as he characterizes his Yalaltec and American sides, have shaped his life experiences. Like many other second-generation Yalaltec adolescents, Tomas is strongly engaged within the social, political, and cultural life of the Yalálag Zapotec community in Los Angeles. For instance, he participates in the Benito Juárez Organization, a nonprofit that provides assistance for Zapotec immigrants and their children. In the past five years, Tomas has performed as a trumpet player in one of the Los Angeles Yalálag Zapotec brass bands.

In another interview, two female teenagers mentioned that they do not identify as Chicanas, either. On the one hand, they dis-identify with the negative behaviors of Chicano gangs and their bad reputation (as mentioned, for some Yalaltecos, "Chicano" implies one who is socioeconomically marginalized). On the other hand, they are faced with mixed feelings and contradictory experiences when they are absorbed into Chicano ideology, that is, a political and ideological framework that ignores their indigenous ethnicity as second-generation Yalálag Zapotecs and imposes a homogenous and hegemonic identity as Mexican American. Leticia, a designer in merchandising, was very critical about this issue:

> When I was in high school, my professor of history, who was a Chicana, was giving a talk about the history of the Aztec people. She told us that we were the descendants of them. She also explained that Chicano is a combination of two worlds: Mexican and American. "That is why Americans call us Chicanos," she said. She mentioned that she was doing a study of the Chicano gangs in East L.A. and Boyle Heights. I thought: Chicanos are gang members? I am not, I thought. At that day, I started thinking that I was Latina and Mexican American, but not a Chicana. The professor also explained that we were not Hispanic, either because we were not the descendants of Spaniards. She said that we are descendants of the Aztec people. And I thought, no I am not. I am the descendant of the Zapotec people. But anyway, I had to listen to her class.

Leticia's reflections address several significant issues. First, Leticia makes it evident that her professor has her own political agenda and is conveying a particular ideology in the classroom. Although the teacher's ideology is far from dominant American discourses of identity, she has authority in her classroom to contest the standard American narrative about ethnic identity and reinforce the hegemonic identity of the Chicanos. She is negotiating a history of racism and colonialism by teaching her students that they are Chicanos and, of course, reminding them of their Mexicanness. However, as Leticia suggests, she has her own culture and history as represented by her Yalálag Zapotec ancestry. It is important to mention that the Chicano movement has been strongly influenced by myths, symbols, and discourses of Mexican nationalism. It reinforces the idea that all Mexicans are socially, historically, and culturally similar, and, above all, that they are descendants of the great Aztec Empire. But, for the Zapotec people, this is not the case, as they have their own culture and history that date back before the arrival of the Spaniards in the sixteen century (Alcina F. 1993; de la Fuente 1994; Whitecotton 1985) and the creation of the Mexican nation.

The negative location of Chicano identity takes us to the third point Leticia made. She does not identify as a Chicana because of the negative behaviors and derogatory meanings ascribed to Mexican gangs. However, there are a few second-generation Yalaltecos who are engaged in gang activities and identify as Chicanos or *cholos*. Over the course of my research, I met some of them by chance in community or family events. One of the most visible symbols of their *cholo* identity is their way of dressing. They wear baggy pants, athletic shoes, T-shirts, shaved heads, and tattoos. According to Yalaltec immigrants, the *cholos* are often unemployed and spend a lot of time drinking alcohol and taking drugs on the streets. When I asked second-generation Yalaltecos why some of their peers have become involved in gangs, they replied that the development of gang subculture among second-generation Yalaltecos is the result of the culture clash with both the Mexican and Anglo American communities. It also derives from family stress and disintegration and from economic and social marginalization. Diego Vigil has described this phenomenon in the Mexican American community as the result of a "multiple marginality" (Vigil 1988).[10]

Perhaps one of the most influential aspects that inform second-generation Yalatecos' sense of identity as Mexican Americans is the continuous exposure to Mexican mainstream culture in the United States. Global telecommunications, mass media, and the circulation of images, ideas, symbols, and goods of Mexican mainstream culture provide second-generation Yalaltecos with Mexican identity referents. The hegemonic cultural model goes beyond the national borders of a nation to encompass the transnational (Hannerz 1996, 20–21, cited in Tsuda 2003, 224) and plays a central role in shaping Mexican American identity for second-generation Yalaltecos. For example, the circulation of commodities such as mainstream recorded music, the transnationalization of dance styles, the frequent visits of Mexican popular mainstream artists, and broadcasts of Mexican TV programs and news connect second-generation Yalaltecos to an imagined community (Anderson 1983) of Mexicans.

Despite cultural differences, interests, and social realities, Mexicans, Mexican Americans, and second-generation Yalaltecos share a common set of cultural practices, symbols, and myths. For example, like Mexicans, some second-generation Yalaltecos like listening to Mexican pop rock and ballads. They mention going to the Los Angeles Sports Arena, the Anaheim Sport Arena, and Universal Studios to listen to Mexican pop rock groups such as Café Tacuba, Maná, Jaguares, and Alejandro Lora; ballad singers like Luis Miguel, Alejandra Guzmán, and Alejandro Fernández; *norteño* groups, including Los Tigres del Norte, Primavera, and Climax; *ranchero* singers like Vicente Fernández; and the dance company Ballet Folklórico de Amalia Hernández. They are also fans of Mexican football teams.

In Los Angeles, when I visited some Yalaltec families, I realized that some members of the second-generation Yalaltecos and the 1.5 generation watch Mexican TV programs through Spanish-language channels or cable. For instance, some like watching Mexican soap operas, movies, comedies, and the Mexican edition of *Big Brother*. During my last trip to Yalálag in summer 2004, my friend Isabel, a second-generation nine-year-old girl, told me that in Los Angeles she watched *El Manantial*, a soap opera that was also broadcast on a Mexican channel in Yalálag. In Los Angeles, during community and family events, Yalaltecos and second-generation Yalaltecos like dancing to Mexican salsa, *ranchera* music, and rock in Spanish in addition to traditional styles.

To summarize, the emergence of a Mexican American identity among second-generation Yalaltecos involves their immersion into the Mexican American community and the appropriation of cultural practices and hegemonic discourses that mark them as Mexican Americans. To be precise, second-generation Yalaltecos are becoming Americans by being Mexican Americans.

BEING YALÁLAG ZAPOTECS IN THE UNITED STATES

For some second-generation Yalaltecos, growing up in the United States is difficult. Their parents' low socioeconomic status, the ethnic prejudice toward their indigenous ethnicity, and the racist discourses on the *Indio* identity harmfully affect the sense of Yalálag Zapotec identity among these children. My twenty-two interviewees recognize one aspect of their identity as Yalaltec, but only one identifies himself as Yalálag Zapotec.[11] That is, twenty-one interviewees do not call themselves Yalaltecos, and only one does. Of these twenty-two, eighteen talk about their identity as Yalaltec on the basis of their cultural competence in some Yalálag Zapotec traditions and involvement in the social life of the Zapotec immigrant community in Los Angeles. However, four do not want to describe or recognize any aspect of their identity as Yalaltec because they do not feel culturally competent in Yalálag Zapotec culture and do not participate in Yalálag immigrant community events or interact with Yalaltec immigrants. Enrique, a fifteen-year-old second-generation Yalaltec who recognize one aspect of their identity as Yalaltec, described to me what makes him identify as Yalalteco:

> Certainly, we have our own culture. Mexicans from Jalisco and Sinaloa, for example, have the Mariachi tradition and other types of brass band music. *We* [my emphasis] have our *jarabes* [a dance and music genre], the Zapotec brass bands, traditional outfits, and our food. We also celebrate our baptisms, weddings, funerals, and the day of the Deaths in the Yalaltec way. And the Yalaltec people are very supportive.

In general, second-generation Yalaltec teens describe the Yalaltec culture in terms of these forms of expressive and material culture. But those who assert one aspect of their identity as Yalaltec do so based on their continuing and voluntarily involvement with the Yalálag Zapotec immigrant community and community organizations. For example, in Los Angeles, many teens attend community events and participate in the Yalaltec brass bands that liven up community gatherings, family fiestas, funerals, weddings, *quinceañeras*, and events organized by Oaxacan indigenous organizations in California. According to second-generation Yalaltecos, they like taking part of community and family events simply for the great feeling of affinity and commitment with their family and the Yalaltec community (see fig. 5.1). Other teenagers said that they participate in the performance of Yalálag Zapotec religious and social dances during the *bailes* (community gatherings) to contribute to the success of these events.

Eleven of my twenty-two interviewees said that they enjoy participating in the annual festival of La Guelaguetza that takes place in Los Angeles because they like to represent the culture of "Oaxaca."[12] One teenage girl explained to me that her experience of performing transnationally in the festival of La Guelaguetza in the city of Oaxaca as a member of the delegation of Yalálag made her feel proud and closer to her indigenous roots. In 2002, a few second-generation Yalaltecos went to the village of Yalálag to fulfill social obligations such as dancing and playing music for the patron saints of Yalálag. Also, I observed dozens of children and teenagers attending family and community events and socializing with Yalaltec relatives or friends. These examples refer to what counts as aspects of Yalálag Zapotec identity for this second generation.

Figure 5.1. Yalálag youth brass band. Los Angeles, 2002.

For Yalaltec immigrants, commitment to participation in community cultural life and family events allows second-generation Yalaltecos to be recognized as part of the community. Those Yalaltec immigrants I interviewed said that those U.S.-born Yalaltecos who do not socialize with the immigrant community are not considered Yalaltecos. In other words, despite the Americanization and Mexicanization of this second generation, involvement with the immigrant community legitimizes them as "genuine Yalálag Zapotecs." Mr. Miguel, who has lived in Los Angeles since 1973, outlined this fulsomely:

> Well, our children are Yalaltecos. No doubts about it. Specially, those, who participate in the social life of our community, are Yalaltecos. Although they have been raised here, they have the Zapotec taste in what they eat, and many things they do. Many of them understand our language although they cannot speak it. Let's say that they are 75 percent American because they like eating hamburgers and think as Americans. They learn this new type of life at school, in their exchanges with their friends, and what they do in their jobs.
>
> Certainly, many teens do not care about their origin and culture. Their parents promote this, but what can we do? However, like many *bi gwlash* who feel proud of being Yalaltecos, I have taught my children our traditions, our values, our culture. If you ask my son to dance a *jarabe Yalalteco*, he will do it. You can see that he has the rhythm in his blood and his heart . . . do you remember the Yalálag Zapotec youth brass band? I mean, just listen to those children. They know how to play. They have feeling. My other son, Tomas, likes to play with the brass band Banda Filarmónica de Yalálag. He does this because he likes it.
>
> Let me tell you, recently, I videotaped Joaquin in one *baile*. You know, he was born here. One day he will be the director of the brass band. Look at how he plays! It does not matter that he was born here, don't you think so? He has the Zapotec taste. He is an authentic Yalálag Zapotec.

Most Yalaltec immigrants I spoke with highlighted the perception that those children who participate and interact with Yalaltec immigrants are considered "authentic" Yalaltecos. When Yalaltec immigrants use the expression "authentic," they are referring to two things. On the one hand, they are taking about the community involvement of second-generation Yalaltecos. On the other hand, being an authentic Yalalteco depends on the ability of their children to act in the Yalaltec way, conscientiously continuing the cultural and social traditions of the home community as an assertion of affiliation and identity. As Bonfil Batalla suggests: "the [Mexican] Indian does not define him/herself in terms of a series of cultural traits—dress, language, customs, and so on—that makes him/her different in the eyes of outsiders. Rather, (s)he defines her/himself as belonging to an organized collectivity, a group, and a village that possesses a cultural heritage formed and transmitted through history by successive generations" (1996, 21–22).

As I mentioned above, my twenty-two second-generation Yalaltec interviewees recognize their Yalaltec ancestry, although twenty-one deny calling themselves Yalálag Zapotec. When I inquired why second-generation Yalaltecos might think twice about identifying as Zapotecs or just Yalaltecos, I found that they think that they feel they do not fulfill the models and expectations of "authentic" Yalálag Zapotecs. They consider that they are not "pure" Yalaltecos because their lives are "more" influenced by aspects of Mexican and American cultures. And some second-generation Yalaltecos refuse to think of or call themselves Yalálag Zapotecs because of ethnic and racial prejudices they have toward their indigenous roots. Second-generation Yalaltecos described a "hundred percent Yalálag Zapotec" as a person who was born in La Sierra and speaks Zapotec. They are indigenous people who have suffered extreme poverty and racial discrimination back in Mexico. In all interviews, second-generation Yalaltecos who participate in community life reported that they are proud of the Yalaltec culture. Nonetheless, when they think of Yalálag Zapotec identity in terms of the *Indio* culture or indigenous identity, they tended to dis-identify as Yalaltecos. For instance, when they talked about Yalaltec identity as a marker of Indianness, they refused to recognize that they themselves are indigenous. In contrast, Yalaltec immigrants I interviewed assert one aspect of their identity as *Indios* despite the socially constructed negative stereotypes and racism. Immigrants do so because they recognize that the *Indios* are the native people of the Americas. In an interview, two second-generation teens expressed their clashing opinions:

JORGE: I think that many of us do not want to say that we are Zapotecs or Yalaltecos. Many of us do not want to say it because some people look down upon us because we are Oaxacan Indians. I think that I am Zapotec.

KARLA: Wait a minute. We are not Indians! Our parents are.

JORGE: Look, that is why you do not want to say that we are from Oaxaca. Many of us do not want to feel discriminated [against]. In Los Angeles, Mexicans characterize Oaxacan immigrants as *Indios*. It is common to hear that we, the Indians, are those brown little people, who wear *huaraches, sombrero* [a hat made of palm leaves], and speak a dialect, and come from *los pueblos* [little villages located in the countryside]. To tell the truth, I do not care about what other people think.

KARLA: Well, I think he is rather talking about the expression "Oaxaquitas" [little brown people from the state of Oaxaca]. When people call us like that, I feel bad. I usually confront them and defend my culture and family roots. I feel very proud of being an Oaxaqueña, but I am not an Indian. I know what he is talking about, people say: "Oh yes, if they are from Oaxaca, they are Indians." You know, one feels hurt by these comments.

The difference between these adolescents' opinions is crucial in understanding why eighteen of my respondents, who were deeply involved in community life by the time of this research, refused to call themselves Yalaltecos. Karla's refusal to identify overtly with her indigenous ethnicity is based on these negative and racist views of indigenous people often expressed by mestizo people of Mexican descent she encounters in Los Angeles. In this context, Karla prefers moving away from her indigenous identification as Yalalteca by emphasizing her identity as Oaxaqueña, because the latter blurs her indigenous identity as Yalálag Zapotec. Among Mexicans in Mexico, the Oaxaqueños can be mestizos, afro-descendants, and indigenous, although most Mexicans think of Oaxaca as primarily an indigenous state.[13] However, in California, for Mexicans, to be a Oaxaqueño means to be short, ugly, fat, and *Indio* (cf. Stephen 2007a). In contrast to Karla's sense of identification, Jorge does not deny the origin of his indigenous roots as Zapotec and faces the ethnic and racial prejudices that affect the second generation's sense of Yalaltec identity.

The fact that Yalaltec immigrants describe themselves as a hundred percent Indians or indigenous people has reinforced the idea that second-generation Yalálag Zapotecs are not "really" or "fully" Yalaltecos.[14] In three of my interviews, immigrants said in front of their children that hardship and suffering have characterized the lives of Zapotec people, but not of their children, thus delegitimating their children as Zapotecs. When immigrants spoke about their lives in Mexico, they described their marginal social and economic position, discrimination because of their Indian roots, and their children's ignorance about these issues: "Well, we have provided our children with a different type of life, and better opportunities and life conditions. They have access to education, health care, and a better regime," a Yalaltec man said. Many Yalaltec immigrants tell their children that they are Oaxaqueños and Mexican American because of this discrimination. Also, they tell their children that they are not "really" Yalaltecos because Indians share certain forms of thinking and doing things, unlike second-generation Yalaltecos. For example, Mr. Miguel pointed out that although members of the second generation are culturally and "racially Zapotec Indians," they do not understand "Indian" thought:

> It is true. Our children do not know many things. They cannot. Our life has been hard, and at times very sad. They know about the culture of Oaxaca as represented by its food, language, music, and dances. They are familiar with our religious practices, what music needs to be played during the celebration of weddings and funerals, but they do not know about the *sistema indio* [Indian system]. They do not understand the *gobierno indio* [traditional government], and the Indian people's thought. We, the Indians, do not want to be independent from the Mexican government, but we want to live according to our laws and traditions.
>
> For example, the *tequio* and the *gzwon* are two forms of collective work that are unique in our culture. Everyone is expected to work for our community and help each other. We have our own ways of thinking and living. That is what

makes us different from them [referring to his sons]. We were born and raised within the Indian thought, the Indian system. These U.S.-born Yalaltecos do not know a lot of things about our culture and way of thinking. Of course, it is not their fault.

So immigrants themselves have contributed to the weakening sense of Zapotecness among their descendants. Yalaltec immigrants have led their children to think that embodying a Oaxacan identity is somehow different from having an "authentic" Yalaltec identity. Another relevant issue that second-generation Yalaltecos raised in our conversations was their uncertainty about calling themselves "pure" Yalaltecos. When they mentioned that their blood remains purely Yalaltec, they were positive on their indigenous roots. But when they reflected on their cultural identity and compared it with that of Yalaltec non-immigrants in Yalálag, they did not see themselves as entirely Yalaltecos. As Manuel said: "I am different from Yalaltecos in Yalálag and I do not know if I could call myself an authentic Yalalteco. They are authentic." Likewise, all Yalaltec immigrants I talked to undoubtedly see their children as Yalaltecos; however, they do not know "how much" their children are culturally Yalaltec. In this context, it is common to hear immigrants and second-generation Yalaltec teens employ a percentage system to determine their degree of Zapotecness. Consider the following comments made by three second-generation Yalaltecos and their father:

DANIEL [male immigrant parent]: My children are 50 percent *Oaxaqueños* and 50 percent American.

ALMA [20 years old]: I consider myself one-third Mexican, one-third American, and one-third Zapotec.

LUPE [27 years old]: I think that I am 50 percent American and 50 percent Mexican.

JORGE [18 years old]: I am 50 percent Mexican American, 25 percent Oaxacan, and 25 percent Yalálag Zapotec.

Some 1.5 generation adolescents talked about this issue in the same manner. They acknowledge that some members of the second generation qualify as a hundred percent Yalaltecos because of their cultural competence and closeness to the Yalaltec immigrant community. Manuel, one of the 1.5 generation, said this to me:

I consider Alejandro and Karla almost 100 percent Yalálag Zapotec. Although they were born and raised in the United States and speak good English, they are quite Yalaltecos. They like to socialize with our *bi gwlash*. It is obvious that no one forces them to hang out with the Yalaltecos. If they are part of the Yalaltec community, it is because they like it and feel identified with our culture. These are the images and feelings I have about them. You know, they have our culture in their blood, and they also have chosen to be part of the Yalaltec community. Despite their American accent and nationality, I would say that they are more Yalaltecos than *gabachos* [Americans].

As a result of conflicting images, stereotypes, and ideas of what is to be a "pure" and an "authentic" Yalalteco, in addition to the constant remarks from Yalaltec immigrants about the partial and mixed nature of the cultural identity of second-generation Yalaltecos, an ambiguous sense of an indigenous ethnicity is continually reinforced. The fifty-year-old father of two of male adolescents was very clear about this issue:

> Well, culturally, they are Mexican American because they were born in the United States. But, I always tell them that they are Yalaltecos too because they were born from two Yalaltec people and their family is from Yalálag. It does not matter that they were born in the United States. They continue to be Yalaltecos. I keep telling them: "You are Yalalteco even though you were born here" [he was addressing one of his sons]. Your blood is Yalaltec.

For second-generation Yalaltecos, the process of self-definition develops at the center of emergent ideas of who they are and dominant discourses of their identity. Yalaltec immigrants tell their children that they are Mexican Americans, and particularly Oaxaqueños. And indeed, to some extent, they are becoming Oaxaqueños in the United States. The following excerpt illustrates the opinions of two Yalaltec immigrants in which they renamed the identity of their children as Oaxaqueños:

> DANIEL: My children are bicultural, that is, they are Americans and Oax-
> aqueños. At school, they learn the culture and history of the United States.
> At home, we teach them our customs. My wife has done a lot of things to
> teach them our culture. It was her idea to take them to the dance troupe.
> They love it. Now, they do not want to miss any class or festival of La
> Guelaguetza. In fact, I have thought that they are more Oaxaqueños than us
> because they know much more about the culture and traditions of Oaxaca.
> DALIA: To me, they are Oaxaqueños and Americans. They are similar to us
> in many ways, but they are different too because of their way of thinking.
> They speak English and Spanish, are better educated, but physically they
> are Oaxaqueños.

In Mexico, *Oaxaqueño* is a term that mainly denotes the indigenous popula-tion of Oaxaca. Similarly, in California, for Mexicans, an Oaxaqueño is above all an indigenous person who speaks a "dialect," comes from Oaxaca, and looks like an *Indio*. For second-generation Yalaltecos, there is a growing sense of being Oaxaqueño. For them, Oaxaqueño means being a member of the Los Angeles Oaxacan community, representing the Oaxacan community in ethnic festivals in the United States, and identifying or claiming a sense of belonging to the Los Angeles-Oaxacan immigrant community. For those who perform in the festival of La Guelaguetza, to be an Oaxaqueño means having cultural knowledge of dance and musical practices of the seven regions of Oaxaca: La Cañada, Central Valleys, the Isthmus of Tehuantepec, La Costa, La Sierra, Tuxtepec, and La Mixteca.[15]

As I mentioned earlier, second-generation Yalaltecos do not speak the language of their parents and this influences their idea of not naming themselves Zapotec or feeling fully Yalálag Zapotecs. Tomas, who perform in one of the Yalaltec brass bands in Los Angeles, was one of the Yalaltec adolescents who had this experience:

> I do not consider myself completely Yalálag Zapotec because I do not speak the language of my parents. To some extent, I consider myself indigenous because of our food. Many of our traditions are pre-Hispanic. And we have our music and dances. However, I was not born in Yalálag. When I went there, I realized that my way of thinking and goals are very different. When I socialize with my *paisanos* (*bi gwlash*) I can see our differences and similarities. Indeed, I consider myself a bit indigenous because I was born from two indigenous people. But if someone else asks me about my identity, I would say that I am Oaxaqueño.

After learning how complex and politicized it is to talk about the sense of identity of second-generation Yalaltecos and seeing how the sense of Yalálag Zapotec distinctivenss is becoming lost in this generation, I asked immigrants and their descendants, *De quien va a depender que su cultura e identidad se mantengan?* (On whom will they depend for their traditions and identity to be preserved)? All agree that it will depend mainly on the immigrants' efforts to maintain their language and culture outside of its original context. Since immigrants are considered the "most knowledgeable" about Yalaltec culture and language, and maintain stronger family and social and economic connections in Yalálag and within the immigrant community, they are expected to be responsible for the continuation of their culture. Also, immigrants and their children agree that it will depend on what parents teach their children about their culture and who they are. However, as I observed, despite immigrants' commitment and responsibility to preserve their culture and instruct their children about it, there is a clear determination on the part of the immigrants to tell their children that they are Oaxaqueños, Mexican, *and* American.

For Mexican Americans, however, the second-generation Yalaltecos are Oaxaquitas because they look like the Oaxacan immigrant Indians. For second-generation Yalaltecos, the experience of ethnic and cultural racialization parallels the experience of racism faced by their parents and other Oaxacan indigenous migrants in California. Nagengast and Kearney describe how the experience of racialization has lead to the emergence of a pan-indigenous and statewide identity as Oaxaqueño. As they say: this pan-ethnic identity builds on "the shared

Oaxacan migrant experience of ethno-racial discrimination in north-western Mexico and in California [which] drove the processes of 'scaling up' previously localized to broader Mixtec, Zapotec, and pan-ethnic Oaxacan indigenous identities" (Nagengast and Kearney 1990 cited in Fox 2006, 47). Thus, for second-generation Yalaltecos, the sense of identity as Oaxaqueño is socially constructed as an act of self-assertion and identification with their parents' indigenous culture.

According to my informants, a few Yalaltec immigrants and their children have distanced themselves from the Yalaltec immigrant community because they feel ashamed of their indigenous roots. They want to become American and "better people." These immigrants and their children feel that to be American necessitates moving away from their community, and by doing so they have "progressed." Here, progress means two things. First, it denotes moving up socially and economically despite the real socioeconomic and marginal position that Yalaltec immigrants have in the United States. Second, it means that Yalaltec immigrants and their children have become more "civilized" or "modern" as result of their incorporation into a "modern" society like that in America. In this sense, establishing themselves as "American," and distancing themselves from indigenous Yalaltecos in Los Angeles marks their "progress."

In sum, I argue that second-generation Yalaltecos who are involved in community life in Los Angeles are becoming Oaxaqueños and that their sense of ethnic identification as Yalaltecos is being gradually diminished. For the Yalaltec immigrants, the act of naming their children Oaxacans is very significant. On the one hand, it is framed with notions of "indigenous" roots, blood, and traditions. On the other hand, it blurs the indigenous ethnicity of their children as Yalálag Zapotecs.

Another aspect of the process of self-identification involves socially constructed notions of race; what are the implications of being racially identified as Oaxacan *Indios* and Latinos in the United States?

"WE ARE LATINOS, BUT NOT *INDIOS*"

For second-generation Yalaltecos, the socially constructed ideas of race as *Indios* and Latinos inform their sense of identity in two significant ways. On one level, it marks them as Oaxacan "Indians." On another level, it defines them as Latinos in the United States. As discussed before, the term *Indio* is racial category within the Mexican system of ethnic and racial relations. The term *Latino* is not a racial label in the United States. However, as Rodriguez points out, research on the U.S. census responses on the race question for Latinos born in the United States shows that they "continue to classify themselves and to write in Latino" (2000, 144). When second-generation Yalaltecos talked to me about their sense of racial identification, they started with the *Indio-Mexicano* system of ethnic and racial classification, and then the American. Over the course of my field research, I found that most second-generation Yalaltec teens refuse to identify as Yalaltecos because this identity overlaps and is usually associated with negative stereotypes of their indigenous ethnicity as Indian. According to my informants, Mexican immigrants and Mexican Americans discriminate against them, using their phenotype and indigenous ethnicity as proof of their "inferiority." For example, in Los Angeles, as in Oaxaca, Mexican mestizos have a significant number of popular sayings and jokes to make fun of indigenous people. Miguel, a Yalaltec immigrant, told me that Yalaltecos have been discriminated against because of their height, skin color, facial traits, and size. While I interviewed Miguel and his two sons, he recounted a "typical" joke that Mexicans use to characterize the "Indians" of Oaxaca: "What do a porcupine and an Oaxacan Indian have in common? Well, they are short, fat, ugly, dirty, and have rebellious hair."

The term *Indian,* which began in the sixteenth century to designate all indigenous people in the Americas, served in Latin America to establish a system of racial, ethnic, and social stratification among three clashing groups: the Spaniards and the *criollos* (the colonizers) who stood at the top, the so-called *castas* of mixed blood and the mestizos in the middle, and the *Indios* (the colonized) and the blacks (the slaves) at the bottom of the hierarchy (Bonfil Batalla 1996; Florescano 1999; Wimmer 2002). Since Mexican Revolution times, the self-image of the Mexican mestizo population has been at the top of the hierarchy, with the indigenous at the bottom. The mestizos have been defined as constituting the "national we" and are characterized by their "prominent" Western physical characteristics. As a result, Mexican mestizos have socially constructed the physical characteristics of the indigenous population, Indians, as unpleasant and ugly in contrast with Western aesthetics. As Mr. Miguel described: "If you look Indian, people discriminate against you. According to their standards, you are ugly, short, brown, and stupid. In turn if you are *güerito* [blonde] and have light-brown skin color, then people treat you differently. Ironically, if you are *güerito,* they do not believe that you are Indian, either." Mr. Miguel's point is twofold: On the one hand, Indians cannot be different from their phenotype. On the other hand, Indians cannot contest or modify the "social characteristics" that have constituted the "nature" of their Indian race. In Mexico, when indigenous people are described as stupid and ugly, it means that they are unable to speak Spanish, look dirty, and smell bad. Accordingly, as U.S.-born Yalaltec adolescents learn about these negative images, which are imposed upon their phenotype, they become more aware that some people will discriminate against them just by the fact of having these physical traits. Two sisters described their experiences of discrimination when they realized that their Mexican American peers were discriminating against them because of how they looked:

LUISA: My sister and I have learned that here there is so much discrimination against indigenous people because of the way we look—short and brown.

There is always that distinction between those who are lighter, prettier, skinnier, and taller than us.

ANA: I agree. Now that I am older, I feel a little bit released from these prejudices. When I was a child I never said that I was from Oaxaca. I felt *vergüenza* [shamed]. At this moment, I cannot tell you why I felt that way, but I felt discriminated against. When you identify yourself as Oaxaqueño, people see you as an Indian and in fact they call you *Oaxaquita*.

In this interview, the father of these teenage girls told me that when Ana was in elementary school she used to ask him to drop her off two blocks away from her school. This was because Ana was afraid that her peers would make fun of her dad's appearance. In Los Angeles, as in Oaxaca, there are many terms that Mexican mestizos continue to use to denigrate indigenous people: *Indio, Oaxaco, yope, chuntis* (Indian-looking or behaving), and *Oaxaquita*. The terms *Indio* or *Oaxaco* are used in a pejorative manner to refer to any person born within the Oaxacan community whose origins and physical characteristics are indigenous. Since the beginning of the twentieth century (Montes 1998), the term *yope* has been used to characterize Oaxacan indigenous immigrants who have gone to work in the city of Oaxaca as peons and domestic workers. Currently, *yope* is still used pejoratively by the Oaxacan elite, mainly composed of the mestizo population, to discriminate against indigenous people. Mexican immigrants and Mexican Americans characterize Yalaltecos as Indians, meaning ignorant, stupid, dumb, dirty, and socially backward.

The term *Oaxaquita* literally means "little people of Oaxaca." It connotes that they are insignificant people and representatives of a lower race, not just short or small in stature. Mexican mestizos who live or work in the northern states of Mexico and in the United States, particularly in California, still use some of these terms to discriminate against Oaxacan indigenous peoples, who usually migrate to work in the countryside as farm workers, or in the cities as domestic workers and in the service industry (cf. Esquivel 2012; Kearney 1999; Rivera-Salgado 1999; Stephen 2007b). It is important to clarify that in the United States, Mexicans— but not white Americans—use these pejorative terms against Yalaltecos.

Second-generation Yalaltec adolescents have internalized such negative ideas to the point that they have felt ashamed of both their indigenous origin and their parents. During one interview with four adolescent siblings and their parents, one of the girls recalled: "On one occasion, many of my classmates [of Mexican origin] where making fun of a Oaxacan boy. They called him *Oaxaquito*. I felt that this comment included me. I felt insulted too. At that moment, I thought: 'If we are all the same, why these guys are doing that?' I did not say anything, I was afraid." Although her father replied immediately that he has always inculcated to his children not to be ashamed of their Indian origins, he understands that many children, like his daughter, are not able to confront such situations because of the fear of being ridiculed. Moreover, he mentioned that many second-generation Yalaltecos feel ashamed of their parents because the latter look and behave as Indians, and have a ranching way of life. As a result, when second-generation Yalaltec adolescents meet racist people and cannot deal with their racist attitudes, they tend to hide the indigenous roots (cf. Back 1995, 1996). As one male teenager told me: "I do not consider myself Yalalteco. My parents are the real Yalaltecos, not me."

Although most second-generation Yalaltecos understand that Mexican immigrants and Mexican Americans discriminate against them because of their phenotype, they also reported that white Americans and African Americans victimize them because of their social and racial characteristics as Latino. Most of my respondents said that African Americans discriminate against them because they think that Latinos have come to the United States to take their jobs. They also said that according to African Americans, white Americans prefer employing and dealing with Latino/as because they are hard-working, honest, respectful, and good people. Tomas, a twenty-year-old man, lives with his parents in a neighborhood heavily populated by African Americans. He described the negative ideas and perceptions he has encountered within the African American community: "For low-class African Americans, we take away jobs from them. I think that they feel that we are a big threat to them. And to tell the truth, many white Americans prefer hiring members of the Latino community. Generally speaking, the Latino people are honest and hard workers. I think that African Americans do not like us and are mean to us because of these reasons." In the same manner, the idea that white Americans discriminate against second-generation Latinos is based on the perception that "Latinos draw government funds in the various social welfare programs and take away jobs from citizens," a female teenager replied.

The stereotypes, images, and discourses that white Americans hold of Mexican Americans and the Latino population have also shaped the construction of a racialized identity among second-generation Yalaltecos. On the one hand, my informants assert a racial identity as both Latino and Mexican because they identify as members of these communities. On the other hand, they are aware that white Americans use these labels to characterize them in negative terms and to classify them within a minority group. Aaron talked about the images and negative ideas he has learned while growing up in the United States:

> For the white American, all the Latinos are Third World immigrants. They see us as invaders. For them, it is very easy to spot us. We are the newest immigrants. They think that the Latino community is here to serve them. From watching TV, I have learned how they see us. The Latinos always take the role of domestic workers, immigrants, or working-class people. In this country, the brown people are seen as poor and ignorant people. This is the way white Americans see us.

Currently, many second-generation Yalaltecos assert their identities as Latino or Mexican Americans and do not have trouble acknowledging their social status and "looking" racially Latino or Mexican; however, there are some who prefer to choose an American identification and try to look like white Americans. Accounts of second-generation Yalaltecos wanting to be white are common in Los Angeles. For example, a teenager described how some second-generation Yalaltec adolescents emphasize their whiteness by stressing their American accent when they speak Spanish with Yalaltec immigrants and by dressing in the American fashion. According to my informant, Sara, some second-generation Yalaltec girls like to dye their hair red, blonde, and light brown. They make a point of eating American food, and they and some teenage boys wear blue or green contact lenses. She described that most of these teens and their parents usually move away from the Yalaltec immigrant community because of prejudice they have toward their own culture. For them, acting like a white American means promoting themselves as white American of Mexican ancestry. Also, for these second-generation Yalaltecos, passing or behaving as a white American allows them to avoid racist and discriminatory attitudes against them.

In Los Angeles, second-generation Yalaltecos are engaged in racial discourses with two available systems of racial and ethnic classification: the Mexican and the American. They learn to resist or cope with negative ideas, attitudes, and narratives imposed upon their identities as Mexican/Latino or Yalálag Zapotec/ Indios. For most, claiming an identification as Latino or Mexican in the United States is better than asserting a Yalaltec or an indigenous identity. The former grants a better social status while the latter continues to be at the bottom of the structure and is highly stigmatized within one of the largest communities in Los Angeles, the Mexican. As a result, the second generation's dis-identification with both the Yalaltec identity and the Yalálag Zapotec community is stronger than with that of the Latino community. As one of my informants said: "The Indians are our parents. Here, we are Latinos."

One may conclude that the experiences of stigmatization and racial discrimination as Indios Oaxaqueños have caused second-generation Yalaltecos to disregard their indigenous ethnicity, which most times translates as an Indio identity. They have adopted the regional and national identity of their parents' country of origin—the Oaxacan and the Mexican—as a result of their immersion into the Mexican community. In doing so they have simultaneously taken on and gradually assimilated to a Mexican American identity in Los Angeles. At the same time, as a response to racist experiences from white Americans, they have adopted a Latino identity to distance themselves from white mainstream culture and assert a positive identity within an empowered American racialized minority—the Latino or Hispanic community. It is important to highlight here that Latino is not a racial category used in the U.S. census to identify Latin American immigrants and their descendants under the U.S. system of ethnic and racial classification. According to the U.S. census categories, Latinos or Hispanics can be of any race. However, there is a history of racism and oppression experienced by Mexican Americans and Latin American immigrants that has made them to identify themselves as Latinos (de Genova and Ramos-Zayas 2003; Oboler 1999; Rodríguez 2000).

At this historical moment, the second-generation Yalaltecos are in the process of defining their sense of identity as a generation and individually. This process is highly complex and contradictory, and furthermore is still changing. As Hall suggests: "because identities are constructed within, not outside, discourse, we need to understand them in specific historical and institutional sites within specific historic formations and practices, by specific enunciative practices" (1998, 4). My findings indicate that the construction of their multiple identities is not the result of a free combination of multiple selves. Indeed, second-generation Yalaltecos are empowered to choose how they want to identify, but from above, a series of hegemonic and homogenizing discourses on ethnic and racial identities in both Mexico and the United States shape and produce their perceptions of identity as American citizens of Mexican ancestry, Mexican American, Chicano/a, Oaxaqueño/a, and Latino/a. From below, everyday practices, daily experiences, contact with other peoples, and opinions voiced by their parents, relatives, Yalaltec immigrants and non-immigrants, and peers all influence these perceptions, as well.

Although these youth recognize that one aspect of their identity is Yalaltec, they do not feel a particular enthusiasm to name it. As mention at the beginning of this chapter, just one of my interviewees called himself Yalalteco. Eighteen believe that they do not comply with the characteristics of what constitutes a "real" Yalalteco. But they like to participate in family and community life, and that makes them identify as real Oaxaqueños regardless of the language they speak. Although I maintain that second-generation Yalaltecos are developing a multiple identity—"constructed across different, often intersecting and antagonistic, discourses, practices, and positions" (Hall 1998, 4), their sense of identity as Yalálag Zapotecs is weakest among the others—American, Mexican American, Oaxaqueño/a, Chicano/a, and Latino/a. They have internalized negative views and prejudices about their indigenous ethnicity that make them refuse or minimize their sense of identity as Yalaltecos. Although second-generation Yalaltecos' experiences seem to be similar to what other members of the new second generation have undergone in America (Levitt and Waters 2002; Waters 1990, 2001b), there is much that is unique in the second-generation Yalaltecos' understanding of their identities. These second-generation youth, who are racialized as *Indio*, dis-identify with their Yalálag Zapotec identity and assimilate to a Mexican American or American identities. Some second-generation Yalaltecos experience their assimilation to a Mexican American identity as a move up within the *Indio-mestizo* Mexican system of ethnic and racial relations in the United States. However, for white Americans, African Americans, and Chinese Americans among others, second-generation Yalaltecos are grouped together with Mexican Americans, because they do not notice differences between the descendants of indigenous Mexicans and mestizo Mexican immigrants. For second-generation Yalaltecos, being a Mexican American constitutes today a new type of incorporation into American society. At the same time, it represents a process of becoming Mexican Americans. By being Mexican Americans, second generation Yalaltecos have developed a sense of Oaxacan-ness that makes them different from the rest of the Mexican immigrants and Mexican Americans in Los Angeles.

Yalaltecos are deeply aware of the changes that migration has brought to their culture and group identity in terms of gender, class, and youth identification. During the *bailes* in Los Angeles and the barrio patron saint fiestas in Yalálag, Yalaltecos tend to portray these transformations in *chusca* dances. This is the focus of the next chapter.

CHAPTER 6

❦

DANZAS CHUSCAS

PERFORMING STATUS, VIOLENCE, AND GENDER IN OAXACALIFORNIA

Danzas chuscas are parodic dances performed in indigenous and mestizo villages throughout Mexico, and date back to as early as the 1930s (de la Fuente 1949). In Yalálag, Yalaltec non-immigrants dance Yalálag *danzas chuscas* during patron saint celebrations, a time when many Yalaltecos who have immigrated to Los Angeles return to visit their families. Since the late 1980s, these immigrants have often become the subject of the *chusca* dances. Yalaltec non-immigrants humorously represent those who have adopted "American" behaviors or those who have remitted negative values and behaviors from inner-city neighborhoods of Los Angeles to Yalálag. *Danzas chuscas* such as *Los Mojados* (The wetbacks), *Los Cocineros* (The cooks), and *Los Cholos* (Los Angeles gangsters) comically portray the roles and new identities that Yalaltec immigrants have come to play or develop in the United States. *Danzas chuscas* such as *Los Norteños* (The northerners), *Los Turistas* (The tourists), and *El Regreso de los Mojados* (The return of the wetbacks) characterize Yalaltec immigrants as outsiders and visitors in Yalálag. And the choreography in dances like *Los Yalaltecos* (The residents of Yalálag) and *Las Minifaldas* (The miniskirts) reflect changes in these immigrants' social status, gender behaviors, and class position in both Los Angeles and California. In other words, these *chusca* dances embody transnationally the impact of migration on social, economic, and cultural levels. Through physical humor, immigrants and non-immigrants confront the tensions and uncertainties stemming from Yalálag Zapotec migration into the United States: community social disorganization, social instability, and changes in the meaning of group identity as it relates to gender, class, ethnicity, and culture.

In this chapter I adopt a transnational perspective to examine the ways in which *danzas chuscas* such as *Los Yalaltecos, Los Cholos,* and *Las Minifaldas* embody the impact of international migration and social remittances in Yalálag Zapotec identity, gender, class, and community in both Yalálag and Los Angeles. I begin by examining the dance of *Los Yalaltecos* to explain what causes Yalaltec non-immigrants in Yalálag to make fun of the new social status and upward mobility that Yalaltec immigrants attain after migration to the United States. Then I examine the dance of *Los Cholos*, to reveal the impact of social behaviors and cultural values remitted from violent, anti-social, and drug-related gang culture of inner-city neighborhoods in Los Angeles to the village community of Yalálag.

And finally, I consider a performance of *Las Minifaldas* performed at a Los Angeles *baile*. I analyze how experiences of migration and processes of assimilation into urban lifestyles appear to influence changing gender behaviors, gender relationships, and ideas of sexuality among young Yalaltec immigrant men and women in the context of *Oaxacalifornia*.[1] I argue that *danzas chuscas* provide a staging ground where the struggles over the meanings of group identity, gender practices and ideology, and the incorporation of new statuses and social identities are contested, reframed, and negotiated.

LOS YALALTECOS: THE PROMESAS AND THE PERFORMANCE OF CLASS

The fiesta of San Antonio de Padua—the protector of the cattle and the hills—is celebrated from June 3 to 15. San Antonio de Padua is not the main patron saint in Yalálag, but he has become the most important saint in the village due to the hundreds of miracles he has performed for the Zapotecs in Yalálag and in neighboring towns. More recently, stories of San Antonio helping immigrants to cross the U.S. border illegally and helping them to find a job, and even alleviating immigrants' hardships, have enhanced his position in the village. In the course of my research, I heard various personal stories about the importance of the saint:

> When I went to *El Norte* [the United States], I asked San Antoñito for help. I told him: "I need to go. Please give me a hand. You will see that I will offer you at least a couple of candles for your fiesta. I will pray for you." Then, I put myself in the hands of San Antoñito. Look, in Yalálag, this is our mentality. I knew that he was helping me to cross the U.S. border. I believe that we [San Antonio and my informant] crossed quickly and easily because he was taking care of me. We did not suffer. I was not hungry or thirsty. The border patrol did not catch us.

As a result, it has become customary that on the day of the saint's fiesta, hundreds of immigrants return to Yalálag from Los Angeles, northern California, Chicago, Oaxaca City, Mexico City, Guadalajara, Puebla, and Veracruz to thank him. Yalaltec immigrants return for the saint's fiesta to symbolically pay back the saint's help, as a *gwzon*.[2] For example, while some Yalaltec immigrants promise San Antonio that they will come back to contribute economically to his fiesta, others return to perform a particular service or a sacred vow, known as a *promesa*, to show gratitude for the saint's help. In June 2004, for example, two female immigrants from Los Angeles offered San Antonio the service of adorning the interior and exterior of his church as well as his altar and the arches of the entry door. A friend of mine, who performs in religious and *chusca* dances in Los Angeles, danced in one of the *danzas chuscas* for the whole fiesta as a way to pay a *promesa* he made for the saint. Although many immigrants from the United States return to Yalálag to make their *promesas* to San Antonio, others, including those who cannot return to the fiesta due to economic issues, family concerns, work, or their migratory status (undocumented migrants, for example), have their relatives in Yalálag pay such *promesas* on their behalf. At this particular fiesta, a Yalaltec man in Yalálag paid a *promesa* on behalf of his nephew who was seriously ill in Los Angeles. After the nephew recovered, he sent money to his uncle to buy a cow and offer it for the fiesta.

The Yalaltecos that live across Mexico participate in the saint's fiesta socially, economically, and culturally. That is, it is not only international immigrants who send money or come back from the United States that make offerings to the saint, but national immigrants also pay *promesas* to the patron saint. For example, on this occasion in 2004, two women from Oaxaca City offered to adorn the interior and external areas of the church as well as the altar and the arches of the entry door. A woman from Mexico City sent money to pay a group of construction workers to paint the church for the fiesta. A man who is cattleman and lives in Playa Vicente, Veracruz, offered a cow for the fiesta. A young couple that lives in Oaxaca City on weekdays and comes back to Yalálag every weekend offered another cow and a pig. A brass band director who lives in Oaxaca City directed the Banda Autóctona de Yalálag during the brass band musical festival.

Since the late 1990s, Yalaltec international and internal immigrants have been making monetary donations as a way of *promesa* to San Antonio.[3] Currently, those who immigrate to the United States make monetary *promesas* that range from fifty to a thousand dollars.[4] Those who return from Mexico City, Oaxaca City, Puebla, and Veracruz make offerings from a hundred to a thousand pesos (ten to one hundred dollars). Since monetary donations of Yalaltec non-immigrants tend to be significantly smaller than those of Yalaltec immigrants, Yalaltecos generally supplement their monetary offerings by providing food supplies and offering their labor for the fiestas. Throughout the week-long celebration, it is customary for the fiesta committee to thank immigrants for their monetary *promesas*. Usually, one of the fiesta committee members reads from a notebook with pages and pages of names, the type of currency, and the amount of money each immigrant donated. Through the public address system of San Antonio's church, one can hear such announcements as the following: "Mario Molina from Oaxaca sent 200 pesos. Family Monterrubio from Los Angeles sent 50 dollars. Family Fabian from Mexico City sent 300 pesos. Familia Mulato from Puebla sent 150 pesos. Family Tomas from Los Angeles sent 300 dollars. Francisco Diego from Los Angeles sent 500 dollars . . ." and the list goes on and on until the fiesta is over.

A number of important studies suggest that religious fiestas in the home community facilitate the continued involvement and reintegration of immigrants when they go back to their place of origin.[5] In the case of Yalaltec immigrants, the fiesta is a religious event that allows for the reunification of immigrants with their families and community. On another level, the fiesta redefines the Yalálag community through specific religious practices, as Durkheim (1964) would argue, and actualizes a series of religious beliefs. Monetary contributions and *promesas* for the patron saint also have other symbolic, social, and even political implications in the relationships between immigrants and non-immigrants.

First, immigrants' donations are more than just offerings. They are a form of symbolic capital through which immigrants assert and negotiate their continued membership to their community of origin and pay back the patron saint. Moreover, against the threat of imminent social disintegration of the community of origin, immigrants are contributing symbolically to the maintenance of their community by way of economic participation.

Second, although remittances represent a valuable form of social and symbolic capital for the immigrant community, for some Yalaltec residents, especially political leaders or evangelicals, they do not.[6] They perceive immigrants' economic participation in religious fiestas as a waste of human and economic resources because it does not have a positive impact in the community infrastructure and social development. Thus, immigrants' intentions to make the fiesta more successful do not have the same meaning for all Yalaltec residents. The following excerpt from a resident man summarizes this type of sentiment:

> To me, the fiesta has become a useless way to waste money. We know that the economic situation in the village is terrible. However, the fiesta committee can spend thousands of dollars on fireworks. This year, $20,000 was spent on fireworks. It is unbelievable that all this money is gone in thirty minutes. Just think! How many poor families could send their children to school with this money?

Julia, another informant said: "What makes me angry is that a lot of cows are sacrificed. When the fiesta is over, we do not know what to do with the leftovers. A few years ago, thirteen cows were given to the food committee. It is an absurdity. Who is going to eat the leftovers? We are not used to eating lots of meat. And also look, throughout the year, many families do not have anything to eat. It is a waste of money." Certainly, there is a small group of people in Yalálag who strongly criticize and openly oppose to the excessive waste of capital in patron saint fiestas due to their own political interests and lack of religious orientation. However, to understand why immigrants invest huge amounts of money in religious fiestas, it is important to consider the powerful reasons that have restricted immigrants' social and economic participation in other community affairs: the politics of Yalálag, discussed in chapter 3.

Monetary *promesas* and the influx of money from outside the community have become politicized and thus transformed social relations between immigrants and locals in Yalálag. For example, making donations for the fiesta in dollars or pesos has started to crystallize the ways that class differences within the village have sharpened and how social positions have shifted between immigrants and non-immigrants.[7] Some families have more money than others by way of remittances. Others do not receive remittances at all. And the families that used to be affluent in the village have come to occupy reduced social positions compared with that of the immigrants.

In Yalálag, Yalaltecos have experienced a continuing process of differentiation in terms of wealth, class, and land distribution. Between the 1940s and 1960s, some Yalaltec families began to make money when they became involved as local merchants and coffee traders in the regional and national market (de la Fuente 1994). In the Sierra Juárez, coffee production and cash crops became important sources of wage labor to such an extent that they transformed the local peasant economy from one of self-sufficiency "into a fully monetized economy dependent on the inflow of goods from outside the zone and producing a limited range of products for that 'external' economy" (Young 1976, 295). Yalaltecos who profited from coffee sales began to buy great extensions of land and cattle, and to open little stores, traditional shoe shops, and butcher shops. They began to hire labor in Yalálag and became known as the rich people in town. They employed poor Yalaltecos who had no coffee lands and whose lives depended on a subsistence peasant economy. In her article on the "Sexual Division of Labor," Kathe Young found that the expansion of commercial capitalism in the Sierra Juárez between 1950 and 1970 transformed what was "a relatively undifferentiated society based on a form of communal ownership of land, on exchange labor between kin and neighborhoods and on non-productive investment of the surplus to a stratified society based on private appropriation of land and other resources, and use of wage labor" (1979, 148). Consequently, Zapotecs began to distinguish themselves as the *ricos*, the *pobres*, and the *medios*. The rich had access to cash resources and were "those who employed labor both in agriculture, including coffee production, and in the home, whether permanently or temporarily, and [the poor were] those who provided such labor." The *medios* were those families who "owned land but neither employed nor provided labor regularly, but tended to use unremunerated familial labor or exchange labor" (1979, 144).

In the 1970s, when young Yalaltec men and women began to migrate within Mexico and into the United States, rich Yalaltec teens were sent to study in Mexico City, while poor and *medio* Yalaltecos left Yalálag to work in the domestic and service sectors and industry. As many members of this generation settled permanently in other places in Mexico or moved to the United States, they began to see the benefits of migrating as their social status and purchasing power increased. Those who went to California sent hundreds of dollars to their parents, helped their siblings or friends to immigrate, and saved money to buy products, land, and services in Yalálag. As a result, international migration became a major force in transforming the standard of living and the restructuring of social and class relations among Yalaltec immigrants and non-immigrants.

Those Yalaltec families who enjoyed a high social status and were economically prosperous in the village have seen their social and class position affected by the social status and purchasing power attained by immigrants through their economic success in Los Angeles. Currently, some Yalaltec immigrants in Los Angeles who came from poor and *medio* families work in the same kinds of jobs as those from a higher-status background, and earn similar wages. Some of them own houses in Los Angeles, Oaxaca City, or Yalálag. In addition to paying their own family expenses in California, they continue to send remittances to their families in Yalálag and help them to access products and services that they previously did not have. Today, these newly rich Yalaltec immigrants employ poor Yalaltecos in Yalálag to build new houses for them. Others pay Mixe people to take care of their homes in Yalálag. Those who own land in Oaxaca City pay local construction workers to build new houses for them. Ironically, in Yalálag, some *medio* or poor families have left their work in the countryside because they receive remittances from their family members abroad. Some of those immigrants who recently retired in Los Angeles have come back to Yalálag or Oaxaca City and support themselves through their retirement. So, today, many young Yalaltec non-immigrants find themselves envying immigrants for their economic success and social mobility, to the extent that they become future immigrants. They know that a few years of education, relatives in Los Angeles, and a loan for their trip are enough to immigrate to *El Norte* to change their status and improve their standard of living. According to the principal of the middle school in Yalálag, Yalaltec teens do not like to study "because they are only thinking about going to Los Angeles." The result is that migration has become institutionalized, and young Yalaltecos see it as way to be socially and economically successful.

On my way home from the fiesta in 2004, I overheard a local man drinking beer in a little store tell his friends: *Aquí en el pueblo todos somos iguales. Vengan de donde vengan* ("Here, in the village, we are all the same. It does not matter where people are coming from"). As described earlier, the repetitive public announcements of monetary *promesas* and immigrants' *promesas* reveal, on the one hand, the significance of immigrants' religious participation and the social and economic power they have in Yalálag. On the other hand, they make visible the differences in economic status between international and national immigrants, and between immigrants and the local people.

Additionally, some immigrants take advantage of the fiesta to boast of their new social status by showing off their affluence in public and private spaces. Some immigrants make expensive monetary *promesas* (between $300 and $1,000 USD) to reward the winners of the racehorses and bullfights that take place during the fiestas. Others spend between $5,000 and $12,000 USD to offer San Antonio cows, pigs, Paschal candles, and fireworks. At times, some immigrant men display their new status by buying alcoholic drinks for local men. Some families make expensive donations for the racehorses or bullfights. Women perform their new status by dressing up in the latest L.A. fashions. They are distinguished from non-immigrant women because they tend to dye their hair in light colors, use city shoes, and bring imported clothes for their relatives to wear in the fiesta. According to Teresa, a local woman, such performance of a higher status and economic success is usually interpreted as an act of arrogance and pretension.

> For example, when immigrants come to the fiestas, they like to show off that they have money. Besides spending hundreds of dollars in fireworks and food donations for the fiesta, they think that bringing fancy clothes, perfumes, different kinds of shoes, watches, rings, necklaces, and of course, their video cameras makes them richer and more important. But, what I really dislike about their attitudes is that sometimes they look down upon us.

In Yalálag, locals have contradictory feelings about the wealth that immigrants bring and the ways some immigrants perform their new status and spending power in the fiesta. Local people think that immigrants use the fiesta to compete economically with each other. For example, from June 3 to 12, one immigrant man spent about $12,000 dollars to pay for a cow and Paschal candles (*cirios*) for San Antonio and a family fiesta, which included paying for the manufacturing of fireworks, the ritual activities and ceremonies that accompanied the offerings such as rosaries and a mass, and hiring a brass band. But while immigrants raise their social prestige by bringing money to the fiesta and showing that they have made it in the United States, locals both honor and resent them for it. Villagers react negatively to immigrants' attitudes with feelings of confusion, sadness, anger, or disillusion. They also retaliate against immigrants' behavior in several ways. All of my informants in Yalálag said that the townspeople gossip about the incongruities between immigrants' new socioeconomic status in Yalálag and their everyday lives in the United States.[8] Even though some immigrants conspicuously display the wealth and upward mobility that they gained abroad, in the United States they form part of the working class—and the locals know it. Non-immigrants also critique immigrants in *danzas chuscas* such as *Los Yalaltecos*.

On June 12, 2004, I watched a performance of *Los Yalaltecos* at the San Antonio church basketball court. It included a series of choreographed movements parodying immigrant women and men. With exaggerated hop-step motifs and graceful hip movements, male bodies imitated immigrants' behaviors.[9] During the performance, we laughed at the chubby and burly men because we knew that they were making fun of immigrants' Americanized appearance and attitudes. Currently, clothing is one of the most characteristic ways in which Yalaltec immigrants and non-immigrants differentiate themselves. On nonfiesta days in Yalálag, local women wear a shirt and a skirt or a dress (always falling below the knees). Besides manufacturing these clothes and the traditional *rebozo* (shawl), women wear Yalaltec huaraches (traditional sandals made in Yalálag). Most women braid or tie their long hair. Men wear pants, a shirt with long sleeves, huaraches, and a hat made of palms. In contrast to younger generations, old people are still accustomed to dressing in the traditional fashion. Old women wear pre-Hispanic *huipil* (dresses) and *enredo* (skirts). Some old men wear pants or *calzón de manta* (pants and a shirt made of cotton), a *morral* (a bag made of cotton), Yalaltec sandals, and a hat made of palms. In Los Angeles, in turn, Yalaltec men and women have changed their ways of dressing. On a daily basis, women wear pants, blouses, and skirts and a great variety of shoes for the city. Men dress in pants, T-shirts, baseball caps, and tennis shoes or moccasins. For Yalaltec non-immigrants, the way in which immigrants dress is representative of both city life and assimilation to modern American way of life and ideology.

At the performance of *Los Yalaltecos,* the male dancers playing female characters were dressed like old Yalalteca women with *xhtap* (long skirts) wrapped around their waists and *'ll xha'* (dresses). They also draped *rboz* (shawls) over their left arms, as many Yalaltec women do during social dances. Each "female" dancer wore a plastic mask, painted pink and with blue eyes. Two wore make-up; the others had sunglasses. They wore wigs made of cotton threads that resembled the immigrant women's long, straight hair, but unlike real women's hair, the wigs were dyed in vibrant yellows.[10] The dancers representing male characters also wore plastic masks and were dressed like the old Yalaltec peasants in *calzón y camisa de manta* (a white long-sleeved shirt and white pants made of cotton). Some masks had big moustaches while others had beards, sunglasses, or both. Each "male" dancer also had two women's shawls, one wrapped around his head to cover his hair and the other worn around his arms, in addition to a typical Yalaltec hat made of black wool.

As the dance began, I became aware of how the dancers' physical carriage, the dance movements, and the costuming of the characters were used to ridicule and satirize immigrants' behaviors. For example, as some "female" dancers walked to their spots, they began to blow kisses to the audience and walked as if they were modeling on a runway. Some of the male characters moved their hands over their heads as if they were combing their hair or adjusting their sunglasses. In one of the *sones* (dances or parts), four of the eight dancers formed a circle and moved counterclockwise. As the two female characters began turning, they started to lift their skirts and move their bodies with a peculiar sensuality. The male characters followed the same step motifs, but their movements were more controlled. One of the characteristic movements of the male characters was the energetic swinging of their arms from one side to the other. As their hands were lifted into the air, they began to shake their shawls as if they were asking for the audience's attention.

The dance of *Los Yalaltecos* is one of a series of *danzas chuscas* that are performed during the patron saint fiestas to make fun of the immigrants. According to one informant, Yalaltecos in Yalálag (and, in my experience, in Los Angeles, too) like to make fun of everything. But in recent years, they especially like to ridicule publicly Yalaltec immigrants who adopt an Americanized identity, foreign styles and ideas, and look down on the locals. Victor, a Yalaltec community leader, explains how Yalaltec views, feelings, and attitudes toward immigrants figure into the *danzas chuscas*.

> I do not know what is wrong with the immigrants. But once they get here, they start showing off. However, the villagers are very sharp. If immigrants arrive with new clothes and want to impress the locals, then the *danzantes* (dancers) invent dances to make fun of them during the days of the fiesta. The *danzantes* are very sharp and clever. What they usually do is to choreograph funny movements. They lift their skirts, move sensually, and walk with arrogance. They copy the ways immigrants dress or appear. What the *danzantes* like to do is to imitate and exaggerate how immigrants behave. Sometimes, you can even tell who they are making fun of. It is hilarious.

The dance of *Los Yalaltecos* appears in the saint's fiesta as a social critique of the immigrants and as a performance of the contradictory roles and multiple social positions that immigrants come to play in sending and receiving societies (Mahler 1998). To be exact, the dancers use a combination of native and Western symbols, such as the plastic masks and the shawls, to signal the tensions created between locals and immigrants. In other words, in *Los Yalaltecos* the dancers act out the ways in which immigrants have adopted an Americanized identity, internalized dominant ideologies, and reproduced new power relations and hierarchies within their own community. For instance, they make visible to all the feelings of some immigrants that they are unable to "adjust" or live in accordance with the peasant way of life in Yalálag; more significantly, some members of the second generation use derogatory terms such as *chuntis* (Indian-looking or behaving) to describe Yalaltecs, either immigrants and non-immigrants, who "continue" to typify the peasant and ranching ways of life of Yalálag.

In *Los Yalaltecos*, the costuming, the dance movements, and the gestures of the characters are crucial to understanding the message of the dance. On the one hand, they evoke Yalaltec cultural symbols, such as the way old people continue to dress and the native way of dancing and making music. On the other hand, these dancers mark their bodies with a system of American symbols such as the yellow wigs and a series of specific body movements and gestures to signal the assimilation of immigrants to American values and ideology and nonlocal behaviors. In their portrayal of the immigrants as an assemblage of conflicting images and juxtaposed elements, the locals stage a performance of cultural resistance and a social critique and call upon immigrants to reflect on their behaviors and attitudes.

Undoubtedly, the purpose of this *danza chusca* is not only to entertain people but also to express public critiques of immigrants.[11] That is, *danzas chuscas* are public statements that aim to provoke a destabilizing reaction in the immigrants and bring forward the tensions created between them by their negative behaviors and attitudes. The dance of *Los Yalaltecos* confronts immigrants with their own incongruities: dancers point out the faults of immigrants such as discriminating against their own people and making them feel inferior. To understand this capacity for self-reflection among Yalaltecos, I find that the theatrical concept of the "estrangement effect" may help us to explain what is at stake in *chusca* dances. As a playwright and director, Bertolt Brecht employed subversive humor and the "estrangement effect" in his plays to cause a reflexive effect in his audience. Brecht believed that a particular kind of performance could potentially transform the people who witness his plays (Weismantel 2001, 112). Using Brecht's model of the "estrangement effect," I suggests that this performance appeals to immigrants to recognize themselves in these dances, reflect upon their negative behaviors and attitudes toward non-immigrants, and reform them.

LOS CHOLOS: SOCIAL REMITTANCES IN TRANSNATIONAL SOCIAL SPACES

During the fiesta of Saint Antonio, I was particularly struck by the distinctive presence and participation of Yalaltec teenage boys and young adult men who belong to local gangs. Some had returned from Los Angeles to form their own gangs in Yalálag. Others were local teenagers that joined these *pandillas* (gangs) without ever having traveled to Los Angeles. On June 13, the *cholos* (gang members) appeared during the *jaripeo* (traditional bullfights) and the *baile*. In the bullfights they participated as bullfighters and horsemen and used this public event to show off their virility and reaffirm their presence, power, and rivalry before the village residents and other neighboring gang members. In the *baile* (a nightly popular dance gathering that takes place in the basketball court) they were having a good time. I saw some of them drinking alcoholic beverages in the temporary stands, while others were dancing with teenage girls on the basketball court.[12] Interestingly, these *cholos* styled themselves in the "*cholo* fashion" of Los Angeles gangs.[13] Their heads were shaved, and they had tattoos on their arms, necks, and hands. They wore baggy pants and loose T-shirts, and some sported baseball caps. While some wore athletic shoes almost identical to those worn by L.A. *cholos*, others created a syncretic style of *cholo* by wearing Yalalteco sandals.

The impact of migration in emigrant-sending communities is sometimes far from benign.[14] *Cholo* immigrants, for example, affect their community through "social remittances": the ideas, behaviors, identities, and social capital they bring from the host country to country of origin. In other words, the *cholo* immigrants reproduce negative ideas, stereotypes, "values, and practices that they have been exposed to and add these social remittances to the repertoire [of Yalálag,] both expanding and transforming it" (Levitt 2001a, 55). Additionally, immigrants' assimilation into "the oppositional identities of native [U.S.] racial minorities" serves as a role model to create a new social order and new social identities in their community of origin (Portes and Zhou, as cited in Portes and Rumbaut 2001b; Rumbaut 1999). Thus, the marginal social identities immigrants acquire in Los Angeles contribute to social disorganization and social instability in the emigrant-sending community.

According to my interviewees in both Yalálag and Los Angeles, *pandillerismo* (gang activity) has become one of many severe problems that affect the social life of Yalálag and many other Zapotec village communities of La Sierra Juárez. In the last ten years, gang members—who are either young migrants who have returned to the village or second-generation Yalaltecos—have introduced L.A. gang culture to their native communities. During the course of my research in Los Angeles, I learned that some Yalaltec immigrants have taken their children from Los Angeles to Yalálag to heal them from *pandillerismo* (Cruz-Manjarrez 2006). Although some of these teens are cured with the help of relatives and the local priest, others go back to Los Angeles and return to street life (see chapter 3). When I asked second-generation Yalaltecos in Los Angeles why their peers join gangs, most agreed on a few explanations. As Karla, a twenty-year-old Yalaltec woman from Koreatown, explained: "They become involved in gang activities because they feel discriminated against or because they lack parental supervision. I think that many of our *paisanos* (countrymen) do not have enough time to take care of their children because they work all day long. Thus, I think that these guys like hanging out with the homeboys—*cholos*—or homegirls—*cholas*." The youths also emphasized that social disorientation and a lack of opportunities for some young immigrants, whose status is usually undocumented, contribute to negative activities such as joining street gangs, taking drugs, and engaging in criminal or violent acts (Vigil 1988).

Non-immigrants told me that when the *cholos* began to settle in the village, the community thought they were a temporary problem. They expected the gang members to return to Los Angeles or change their destructive ways. (Gang culture did not exist previously in Yalálag.) They stayed, however, and instead formed local *pandillas* based on L.A. gang culture. Yalaltec immigrant *cholos* continue to identify with their U.S. gangs, such as the L.A. 13 and the 18th Street gangs.[15] They tattoo their bodies and graffiti walls around the village, two of the acts that publicly demonstrate the gang's sense of extraterritorial belonging and transnational loyalty. Although some of the elders could not tell me what the graffiti or tattoos represented, a fifteen-year-old girl had a good understanding of what these gang symbols mean: "I know that some of the *pandilleros* belonged to Los Angeles 18th Street gang. I know that having a tattoo of the number 18 means that they belonged to that *pandilla*. I also know that they like to paint graffiti around the places they like to hang out." The East L.A. 13 and the 18th

Street gangs are of Mexican origin and are settled in various neighborhoods in Los Angeles. Since its beginning in 1959, the 18th Street gang has been composed of Mexicans, but recently Central Americans, African Americans, and Asians, among others, have joined it. Since the late 1990s, the 18th Street gang has grown across Central America and Mexico, and gang members in these regions have kept their loyalties and reproduced the L.A. gang culture in their new settlements. Gang members are usually involved in criminal activities such as murder, rape, assaults, drug trafficking, extortion, prostitution, and robberies.[16] In Yalálag, immigrant *cholos* have also formed new *pandillas* in Yalálag, such as 23 West, that are not affiliated with gangs in Los Angeles. According to the same girl, who wished to remain anonymous for fear of retaliation, the number 23 represents the number of founding gang members. It is important to mention that not all gang members in Yalálag are returnees from Los Angeles who form their own gangs. There are local teens who joined this gang and had not been been to Los Angeles, but absorbed, processed, and redeployed cultural and social ideas, values, and behaviors that arrived in Yalálag from Los Angeles.

Currently, there are no estimates of the number of gang members or *pandillas* in La Sierra Juárez, but it is common knowledge that in the last ten years the *pandillas* have become a threat to the region. According to the Yalaltec villagers and municipal authorities, gang members commit robberies, sell drugs, and kill innocent people. Immigrants and non-immigrants are robbed in broad daylight on public transportation as they travel through La Sierra to reach their villages. Usually, the robberies occur during the six-hour trip between Oaxaca City and Yalálag. My Yalaltec friends say the *cholos* target immigrants because they bring money from the United States for their families.

In Yalálag, the local people describe gang members as *el nuevo mal de la comunidad* ("the new community evil"). In one of my interviews, Pancho, a forty-five-year-old resident, explained to me that locals think the *cholos* "have polluted the younger generations because the only thing the *cholos* do is to teach teenage boys to misbehave, but profitably." At the present time, the increasing presence of gang members in Yalálag has gone hand in hand with the introduction of drugs, acts of violence against the villagers and between neighboring gangs, acts of vandalism, and the recruitment of mostly male youngsters. One of the worst acts of the *cholos* in Yalálag began with the illicit sale of drugs in *la secundaria* (middle schools). According to a school principal, one of his main concerns and the most common complaint he receives from the students' parents is the selling of drugs after school. One of the teachers also mentioned that he has started to talk about the consequences of taking drugs because some of his students are becoming drug consumers. Another teacher described what the *cholos* actually do after school:

> Every day, the *cholos* come here to sell marijuana. They wait for our students on their way home. Unfortunately, a few of our students are very immature. It seems that they do not know that drugs are harmful and may create addiction, so they

try them. In addition, because the school is a little bit far from the village, it is a propitious place for this criminal activity. Look, this a very difficult situation. Many of our students come from neighboring villages to study. They live here on their own and lack supervision from their parents. As for the parents of our Yalalteco students, they cannot come here every day to pick their children up. They work. Before, this was not necessary. Look, what is really sad today is that we do not count on the support of the municipal authorities. Unfortunately, being away from the town center makes our middle school a propitious place to persuade our students to consume drugs or join the *pandillas*.

Currently, the consumption of drugs is not seen as an isolated problem or as the only social problem that causes social instability and violence in Yalálag. Drinking beer and mescal (a distilled alcohol from the agave plant) are other social problems related to destructive behavior and, at times, gang activities. However, it is the *cholos* who smoke marijuana and are accused of harming locals while under the influence of alcohol and drugs.[17] For example, a woman who is an outsider but works in Yalálag told me that she has been sexually harassed by one of the *cholo* leaders. A family who runs a *tiendita* (small store) in the hills suspects that one of the *pandillas* burglarized it when they were away. According to residents, the community has urged the local authorities to do something about *pandillerismo*. However, the authorities have devoted little attention to this problem because of fear and a lack of knowledge or resources to reduce or stop the gangs' crimes.[18]

In the *danza chusca* called *Los Cholos*, dancers tackle the existence of a transnationalized *pandillerismo* and the presence of Yalaltec *cholos* in Yalálag. They represent syncretic cultural stereotypes of the L.A. gang subculture. To invoke the L.A. *cholo* style, male characters deploy symbols like baggy pants, loose T-shirts, athletic shoes, and baseball caps, while female characters sport miniskirts, high heels, and pantyhose. Framed by Zapotec musical sounds and choreographic styles to which Yalaltec *cholos*, immigrants, and non-immigrants alike all dance, the dancers mimic in a comical way some aspects of the *cholos'* manners. At this fiesta, for example, when the eight *cholo* dancers performed at the San Antonio basketball court the *son* (dance or part) *la cadena sencilla* (simple chain), they used the hand sign "Hook 'em Horns." With arms extended to the sides, elbows facing down in a slight semi-flexion, and their index and baby fingers pointing down and thumbs facing forward, they first crossed lines (two of four dancers each), returned, and regrouped to start the *cadena sencilla*. Accompanied by the tune of the brass band, four dancers began moving clockwise and the other four counterclockwise. As they moved forward to "weave [dance] the simple chain," they did a complete right turn with a partner, and then half a left turn to change places. This choreographic sequence was repeated eight times to allow all dancers to reach their starting position.[19]

By using a combination of the hand sign "Hook 'em Horns" and a sequence of a step-hop-point/step-hop-point, hop-step/step, and a step-hop-point, the *cholo* dancers conveyed in a comical performance the community rejection of gang activities and the development of new gangs, as well as the social dynamics and feelings *cholos* engender in Yalálag. The social dynamics include tensions between locals and *cholos* and between families and their troubled *cholo* teens. One of the most important elements in *danzas chuscas* is the multiplicity of narratives they symbolize. When I asked residents what the dance of *Los Cholos* means, they pointed out that this dance is a playful mockery and does not seek to offend. According to one *cholo* dancer I spoke to, the dancers mock the real *cholos* to offer a "lighthearted" social critique of their antisocial behaviors—a critique that the *cholos* experience by watching the *danzas chuscas*. But a community leader explained to me that the *cholos* are perceived in the village as a threat and a shame to the community, and they represent the failure of the American dream. In the context of the fiesta, then, the significance of *cholo* dance performances, as well as the multiplicity of narratives the *cholo* dancers embody, is more complex than it appears on the surface. On one level, the *cholo* dancers use choreographic texts to communicate to the real *cholos*, who usually watch the dance performance during the fiestas, how the locals see, feel about, and perceive them. On another level, the dance performance offers the real *cholos* the opportunity to see themselves from a distance and with a critical eye. Furthermore, this dance provides social and cultural theorists with an understanding of how this Yalaltec community sees itself and how it deals with the migration experiences and assimilation processes of Yalaltec migrant teens and second-generation Yalaltecos, who have been affected by multiple marginality (Vigil 1988) and thus become gang members.[20] Yet *chusca* dance performances create a livable social space for reminding *cholos*, who take part in the fiestas and watch the performance of *danzas chuscas*, that they are Yalaltecos and are part of a community, one that may even be seeking to reintegrate them. The *danzas chuscas* performances, then, constitute a common symbolic language by which Yalaltecos communicate with each other.

LAS MINIFALDAS: GENDER AND SEXUALITY IN
TRANSNATIONAL PERFORMANCES

It is almost 10 p.m. on May 3, 2003, in Los Angeles, and the *baile* is coming to one of its best moments. The rosary and mass are over, and people have had time to buy food and drinks, dance their social dances, and hear Mexican popular music. The dancers of *Las Minifaldas* are ready to perform. Juan, one of the organizers of this community event, announces the dance presentation, and as he invites the adults and their children to be seated to watch the performance, the Yalaltec brass band La Nueva Imágen waits to hear the signal from the *maestro de la danza* (dance leader) to begin to play.

    As the dancers show up in the main entrance of the ballroom, Juan asks the audience to welcome the dance ensemble with applause. As the dancers walk in two lines to the center of the ballroom, members of the audience begin to laugh at the dancers' outfits and their comical presence. The female characters wear colorful blouses, miniskirts, pantyhose, high heels, and blonde and brunette wigs. As they walk into the ballroom, one of them swings her hips sensually from side to side and holds her hands at her waist. The one behind adjusts her sunglasses, and another one waves her hands to greet the audience. The male characters wear long black pants, ties, long-sleeve shirts, hats, and boots. All the dancers wear plastic masks of human faces painted with pink ink and blue eyes and Yalaltec shawls wrapped around their hair. They adjust their ties, vests, and sleeves and begin shouting to emphasize their presence. As the brass band starts to play the *son de la entrada* (entrance dance), the dancers form two lines. As they approach, they slightly lift their arms to their sides, make a left turn, return, and regroup in the two lines to begin dancing.

The appeal and relevance of contemporary *danzas chuscas* such as *Las Minifaldas* rest not only on the dancers' ability to humorously reveal the Yalaltec immigrants' uneasy integration of American and Mexican behaviors, values, and ideas but also on their ability to convey how they perceive, feel, and experience the historical continuities and discontinuities in gender and class relations that characterize contemporary Zapotec life in Oaxacalifornia. In Yalálag, Yalaltec non-immigrants perform this dance, like some other *danzas chuscas*, to tease Yalaltec immigrants who now live in cities and adopt urban ways of life such as that of dressing according to L.A. fashion. In Yalálag, then, local dancers perform *Las Minifaldas* when immigrants return to Yalálag to participate in the patron saint fiesta of Santiago Apóstol. In Los Angeles, the dance of *Las Minifaldas* has likewise been danced to celebrate Santiago Apóstol and to raise money for the saint's fiesta in Yalálag, as well as to "liven up" the *bailes* in Los Angeles. However, in Los Angeles, *Las Minifaldas* underwent a significant change: Yalaltec immigrants took the place of the Yalaltec non-immigrants to make fun of and criticize themselves. When I inquired about *Las Minifaldas*, I learned from Yalaltec immigrants in Los Angeles that they make fun of themselves for the very same reasons that Yalaltecos do in Yalálag. That is, in the comical dance performances Yalaltecos mimic those who have assimilated to urban ways of life, have changed their views of their bodies, and have transgressed the norms and values that regulate their gender behaviors, relations, and ideology.

To understand the meaning of *Las Minifaldas* within the context of the transnational migration and religious celebrations requires the consideration of various factors. These include five decades of migration of Zapotecs from rural villages to the urban areas of Oaxaca City, Mexico City, and California; the development of nascent Zapotec communities in these cities; permanent relationships between immigrants and their community of origin; incorporation of women in the migration process; changing views and roles of gender relations, ideology, and hierarchies; influences of contemporary constructions of sexuality; the impact of popular culture and music; and the transition to an urban lifestyle. As outlined in previous chapters, Yalaltecos began to migrate to Oaxaca City and Mexico City in the late 1940s. By the early 1960s, Yalaltecos began migrating to California. Since then, some migrants have returned to Yalálag while others have moved back and forth between their place of origin and immigration, forming transnational economic, cultural, social, and political ties. The experiences of migration and the multiple processes of adaptation to urban environments have had different implications in gender relations, hierarchy, and ideology and in sexuality for both immigrants and non-immigrants.[21]

For immigrants who are embedded in new gender relations and roles and are exposed to distinctive social constructions of gender and sexuality, the places of immigration have come to represent a new social context for assessing and transforming sexuality and their gender values, ideas, and behaviors. Those who try on new gender and sexual behaviors, internalize new gender norms, or are forced to acquire new roles often face opposition, critique, and mockery from their families and communities. Although not all Yalaltecos are conservative, on the basis of my research in Yalálag and Los Angeles, I will risk characterizing the majority of the Yalaltecos I know as conservative. By this I mean that their community values and ideologies of gender and sexuality are highly influenced by the Catholic Church and include emphasis on family honor, virginity, births legitimized by marriage, monogamous marriage, and heterosexuality.

In Yalálag, gender relationships are structured by specific roles and domestic tasks, and gender behaviors and sexuality are highly monitored by family and community members. Most women do domestic work, take care of their children, and manufacture textiles and clothing, while men work as peasant farmers, construction workers, bakers, musicians, or sandal makers. Likewise, young women, who have access to schooling, are strictly monitored to protect their reputations and "respectable" appearance, while young men have relatively more freedom and control over their sexuality and presentation, unless a man dares to overtly express homosexual traits.

In the transnational Yalaltec community, homosexuality is a taboo and rare to the point of "nonexistence." However, a man is considered homosexual when he acts like a woman. Male dancers performing female characters are considered heterosexual men. Nonetheless, Yalaltecos say that there are "a few men who are in the closet," namely, the homosexuals, who like to perform female characters in *chusca* dances. During the dance performance, nobody knows who the dancers are. The masks, the dress, and the consumption of alcohol allow those men, who look like "homosexuals," to perform freely their "homosexuality." Yalaltecos do not talk about homosexuality among women at all.

Kinship and marriage relationships are patriarchal. That is, women usually remain in the family and their marriage, under the authority of men. In addition to the restrictions of established domestic roles for men and women, women's rights and desires are somewhat undermined by their fathers, brothers, and male authorities. During my research in Yalálag, some young women told me that although they want to migrate to work or study, their parents oppose their wishes or only allow their brothers to do so. Others said that while some young women are free to choose their husbands, others' choices are still subject to their parents' approval. Further, under the tradition of arranged marriage, many families still arrange their daughters' marriages without asking for their opinion.

In contrast, in Los Angeles norms of work, family, marriage practices, spousal relations, household division of labor, and patterns of family authority and patriarchy in sexuality and gender behaviors have changed significantly.[22] For example, men not only learn and are obligated to do domestic tasks that are supposed to be part of women's territories and roles, but they in fact become skilled at cooking, ironing, and cleaning, and most of them work as dishwashers, cooks, and janitors. Some learn how *not* to be dominant and authoritarian, become less macho, and even abandon dominant patriarchal ideologies and behaviors such as beating women and marrying them without the woman's consent. In addition, because many women learn and can exercise their rights, become socially and economically independent, and are removed from family surveillance and patriarchal domination, they have more control of their lives, bodies, and sexuality (cf. Hirsch 2007).

Symbolically, *Las Minifaldas* perhaps best represents these new marked differences. It exposes the reactions and critiques of Yalaltecos whose ideas and values concerning gender and sexuality are shaped by a patriarchal system and the influence of Catholic principles such as virginity, sanctified marriages, childbirths legitimized by marriage, and family honor (Stephen 2002, 52). Like in all *danzas chuscas*, in *Las Minifaldas* four elements connect and convey the assessments by both non-immigrants and immigrants of immigrants' changes in gender identity and ideology, through the clothing, dance movements, music, and exaggerated mimicry of immigrants' public behavior.

The clothing used in *Las Minifaldas* links the meanings of the dance performance with immigrants' new sense of their bodies, the adoption of urban fashions, and above all their new ideas about gender and sexuality (see fig. 6.1). That is, the miniskirts are the most salient feature in the dance because they best symbolize immigrants' new discourses and practices of gender and sexuality and embody distinctive gender positions and ideologies specific to transnational social spaces. Yalaltec men and women I interviewed both in Yalálag and Los Angeles recounted a saying that reflects how townspeople and some conventional Yalaltec immigrants perceive the impact of immigration on gender dynamics: "Migration has emancipated Yalaltec women." Currently, young Yalaltec women who migrate to Los Angeles have more say in the way they live their lives, their ways of dressing, and their marriages and sexuality, and they are economically independent. This does not mean that they sever family ties

Figure 6.1. Dance of *Las Minifaldas*. Los Angeles, 2003.

nor that their relations with their families and communities are smooth. Quite the opposite: they are always challenged and are often at the center of tensions within their families and communities.

Most women in Yalálag are raised to be well-behaved, highly religious, and *muy aguantadoras* ("to put up with a lot") with their husbands. Their parents and close relatives monitor their sexuality to ensure family honor and "respectable and proper" behavior. Make-up is not part of their daily personal care and cultural values, though it has been introduced recently via immigrant women. Its use among few teenage girls is also due to the influence of mass media and the expansion of cosmetic companies. Yalaltec women do not color their hair or cut it short. If young women want to get a haircut, they have to ask their mothers for permission. They wear loose dresses or skirts (usually falling below the knees), loose-fitting blouses with short sleeves, and Yalaltec sandals. In contrast, Yalaltec immigrant women and their daughters in Los Angeles are more flexible with their personal care and with the ways they carry their bodies. They may dye their hair, use make-up, and wear miniskirts, tight dresses and pants, and pantyhose. Many women like high heels. With respect to marriage, two changes are most notable: they date before they marry, and they choose their husbands or sexual partners. Thus, because immigrant women have moved away from family control, live in accordance with urban norms, have tried new behaviors and ideas of gender and sexuality, and carry their bodies in new ways, they are portrayed in *Las Minifaldas* as *mujeres liberadas* (liberated women) and *mujeres de ciudad* (city women).

In the case of the immigrant male dancers, certainly the miniskirts do not represent sexual and family liberation. However, they similarly refer to men's assimilation of urban ways of life and changes in their gender values, roles, and ideology. What we see in the dance is the substitution of rural peasant ways of dressing with urban dress styles. Immigrant men are portrayed as wearing sunglasses, ties, vests, and pants made of cashmere—all considered accessories of city life. More specifically, *Las Minifaldas* refers back to the new gender roles, values, and social norms that regulate immigrants' gender behaviors and relations in the United States. For instance, unlike Yalálag, in Los Angeles if men mistreat women physically, sexually, or psychologically, they can go to jail.

Like all *danzas chuscas*, *Las Minifalda* is performed by eight male dancers.[23] The dance structure is composed of eight fixed group choreographies, each set to a different *son* (or song) and eight steps. The step motifs are a combination of hop-steps and *puntillas* (points), a distinctive pattern of Zapotec dance. According to Romualdo Limeta, a well-known maestro of *danzas chuscas* in Yalálag, the step sequences in *danzas chuscas* draw on basic steps of Zapotec social and religious dances and a few popular dance styles such as polka, *quebradita*, and *norteñas*. There are three defining moments in the structure of the *danzas chuscas*. The first is when the dancers appear in front of an audience and begin to walk to their positions. In *Las Minifaldas*, for example, dancers perform playful mockeries of immigrant men and women that include walking sensually, blowing kisses to the audience, and adjusting their sunglasses, ties, and hats. The second part is the dancing itself. This section is divided into the entering dance, six *sones* (parts or songs), and the *despedida* or *salida* (farewell). The last part is when the dancers leave the performance space. They may leave dancing or walking.

In *danzas chuscas*, music constitutes a significant aspect of the dance performance. It highlights the message of the dance and refers to those modern and Americanized identities that Yalaltec immigrants have developed in Los Angeles and to what Yalaltecos consider popular, urban, modern, and new. *Danzas chuscas* are accompanied by a Zapotec brass band, and because many *danzas chuscas* were developed recently, the music is new as well. The director of the brass band and the dance teacher, known as *maestro de la danza*, always work together to define and compose the tunes, so the music is custom-made for each particular dance. Romualdo Limeta explained to me how this process works in his community. In general, he picks or invents eight tunes, many based on a popular song. In the dance-making process, it is also possible that a dancer offers the *maestro de la danza* tunes and step motifs to create a new *son*. Then, the *maestro de la danza* thinks about the steps and tries to make them fit with each tune. With these elements in mind, he asks the director of the brass band to write the music. As the dance teacher whistles the tunes for the director, he composes the music and matches them with the steps. The significance of the music is based on the images and sounds that it represents. Thus, the dance performance is acoustically framed by a Zapotec soundscape and by modern, urban musical sounds that represent both *El Norte* (the United States) and an urban way of life.

In *Las Minifaldas,* dance, music, and costumes are equally important. During the dance, these elements together materialize complex processes of social change in Yalaltec identity as it refers to gender. In addition, they embody and codify community responses and views of these changes, including social critiques toward those who break the social norms that used to rule their gender behaviors and ideology. As I have argued above, in *Las Minifaldas* dancers represent in comical ways what is socially constructed as urban, different, new, and, more specifically, transgressive. Through dancing, dancers emphasize that immigrants themselves are no longer the same people they were in Yalálag, and confront them with their new gender identity and ideology. This dance, then, confirms changes in the logic and dynamics of this patriarchal system, gender relations, and behaviors associated with Catholic principles among Yalaltecos in Yalálag and in Los Angeles. Finally, perhaps more than any other principle of group cohesion, the dance structure—the steps, choreographies, and bodily movements—stand for the continuities and discontinuities that characterize contemporary Yalaltec identity in transnational social spaces.

In sum, the importance of religious fiestas and community gatherings in the context of transnationalism speak to us about cultural and symbolic processes and social structures that reintegrate Yalálag Zapotecs in Los Angeles, in Yalálag, and between these two "homes." Since the late 1960s, many Zapotec village communities in Oaxaca have experienced high rates of out-migration, and while Zapotec immigrants have reconstituted their communities and formed their own families in the United States, they have remained linked to their places of origin.[24] One of the most important ways that immigrants have reconnected with and reintegrated into their village communities in Oaxaca is through economic and religious participation in patron saint fiestas. By sponsoring and taking part in them, they have reinforced their community ties and complied with their communal responsibilities and religious obligations to the most important Yalálag patron saint—San Antonio de Padua. Simultaneously, however, immigrants have transformed religious fiestas and used them as a context for valorizing their new social status and class position (Goldring 1998).

In Yalálag religious fiestas and in Los Angeles community gatherings, *danzas chuscas* performances reveal and embody the significance of change, conflict, and social remittances in this Zapotec transnational community. Because of the increasing social differences among Yalaltec immigrants, non-immigrants, and second-generation Yalaltecos, I propose that both immigrants and non-immigrants perform *chusca* dances to manifest how they see each other and how they are experiencing the historical continuities and discontinuities that shape social change in gender, class relations, and social identity. In this sense, *chusca* dance performances are spaces of and for self-reflection, and dancers use humorous representations of immigrant behaviors to tackle the uncertainties and fragmentation of their community as well as the consequences of a transnationalized *pandillerismo*. Finally, in the context of the fiesta and in the moment of *chusca* dance performances, the role of humor cannot be disregarded. In the worldview of the Yalálag Zapotecs, humor is *como un costumbre* (part of our tradition). Romualdo Limeta, the well-known maestro of *chusca* dances in Yalálag, said this to me and added, "These dances are like a joke on someone from the community, but nobody gets mad. This is the way we are. We make fun of ourselves."

A religious dance that is associated with pre-Hispanic ritual corn ceremonies and one of the founding myths of Yalálag is the subject of the final chapter.

❦

CHAPTER 7

COMMUNITY AND CULTURE IN TRANSNATIONAL PERSPECTIVE

At present, religious fiestas and cultural practices such as dance and music continue to be as essential to the social life of the immigrant community in Los Angeles as they are to Yalaltecos in Yalálag. In both places, scores of Yalaltecos come together to honor the Yalálag patron saints. The fiestas create special occasions for family reunions, community reorganization, and the collective expression of religiosity. The performances of village dances and music at these community events express the Yalaltecos' religious devotion. They symbolically connect immigrants and non-immigrants, and embody the extraordinary joy of life and the depth of human experience.

The fact that Yalaltecos continue to express their views of the world through these cultural practices in patron saint celebrations in Los Angeles and Yalálag merits for various reasons. Yalaltecos are, above all, music and dance experts, and their dedication to these arts is fueled by the role of these events as socialization opportunities for youth and as a means of communication among people and with their deities. Yalaltecos not only dance as a way of *promesa* for the patron saints in both places, but also choreograph *chusca* dances in Los Angeles and in Yalálag to stage issues that are of great importance and concern for their community at present: their struggles to keep their collective memory alive, their need to express their views on the rapid and profound changes affecting their community, and the efforts of Yalaltec immigrants and non-immigrants to find ways to negotiate their increasing social differences. In this final chapter, I examine the significance of the Yalaltec dance of *Los Huenches* (the ancient Zapotecs) in both the redefinition of group identity and the negotiation of deep shifts in social and cultural life of the transnational Yalaltec community.

LOS HUENCHES: ON THE LOCATION AND TRANSLOCATION OF PERFORMANCE

In Yalálag, the dance of *Los Huenches* derives from historical and mythical accounts of the founding Yalálag village, village patron saint fiestas, and ancestral ceremonies dedicated to the Zapotec goddess of the corn. One of the myths of Yalálag's founding says that, during Spanish colonization, the ancient Zapotecs fled to the highlands. During that time, they formed thirteen Zapotec settlements and founded the villages of Tiltepec and Yetzelálag. In his article, "*Los Huenches:* La danza sagrada del maíz," Yalaltec historian and poet Mario Molina (2003) points out that, according to the oral tradition of Yalaltecos, these settlements evolved into the village of Yalálag. Although the first documented performances are from the end of the nineteen century, the villagers say this dance is pre-Hispanic.

Contemporary performances of *Los Huenches* also have roots in religious festivals honoring the Yalálag patron saints of San Juan Bautista, on June 24, and Santa Rosa de Lima, on August 30, and in nearly obsolete ritual corn ceremonies. According to the Yalaltecos, they used to perform the corn ceremony in the highlands to revere Mother Earth during the fiestas of these two saints. These ceremonies consisted of offerings of food, candles, feathers, and flowers; the sacrifice of hens or turkeys; the recitation of rosaries; and the performance of the dance of *Los Huenches.*

Currently, although these ceremonies have almost vanished, old Yalálag Zapotecs continue to believe that performing this dance is a sacred and magic act and an offering for the Mother Earth and the patron saints. In Yalálag, in the worldview of the Yalaltecos, dancing *Los Huenches* is conceived as a propitiatory act for rain. Also, performing this dance is a religious and symbolic act by which Yalaltecos ask the patron saints to protect the harvest from danger and thank Mother Earth from what Yalaltecos have taken from it. It is believed that dancing *Los Huenches* helps ensure a plentiful supply of corn, sugar cane, beans, squash, and chili crops.

The dance ensemble of *Los Huenches* is composed of various characters: the *huenches*, the Yalaltec woman, Rosa Maria, and a deer *huenche*. The character of the *huenche* plays a central part in one of the founding myths of Yalálag and in the dance. Yalaltecos describe the *huenches* as "the founders of Yalálag." The word *huenche* derives from *wench gure*, "the ancient Zapotecs." As José, a renowned Yalaltec dancer from Los Angeles, said to me: "The village people have a lot of respect for the *huenches*. They represent our ancestors, those who were poor and were searching for our home." In the dance, the *huenches* are the living representation of the *wench gure*, but they are also humorous characterizations of contemporary Yalaltecos in Yalálag and in Los Angeles, as we shall see.

According to Molina (2003), the female character in the dance used to represent the goddess of the corn. However, due to syncretism between Zapotec and Catholic symbols and beliefs, and the imposition of Catholicism, the female presence in the dance was transformed into a dual character: Rosa Maria and the Yalaltec woman. At present, the dance ensemble of the barrio Santa Rosa represents the female character as Rosa Maria, while the ensemble of the barrio San Juan, represents her as a Yalaltec woman. Although the representation of these two characters evidently points to a symmetrical syncretic symbolism, the significance of mixing these two religious systems and their cultural elements is in constant process, and sometimes both women appear together in the dance.

The dance of *Los Huenches* is composed of various parts. It begins with a series of *sones* (parts or songs) dedicated to Santa Rosa de Lima, followed by two *sones* (songs or dances) performed by Rosa Maria or the Yalaltec woman. In the third dance, Rosa Maria performs short segments with four *huenches*, each one dancing in turn with her to salute the four cardinal directions. Each *huenche* approaches the goddess and opens his arms to hold the goddess' hands to begin dancing. They start bending and moving their bodies from one side to the other as they turn slowly around the floor. In next dance, the same four *huenches* begin moving in a square formation with Rosa Maria. This formation walks halfway down between two lines that are formed by the presence of approximately sixty *huenches,* thirty to a line. With the sound of a flute and a drum, Rosa Maria or the Yalaltec woman move back and forth along the lines, while the rest of the *huenches* stand on the line formation. As the music plays, she moves a pink handkerchief with her right hand from side to side as if she were drawing S shapes, to chase squirrels, foxes, armadillos, or badgers off that are potentially harmful to the maize crops. Molina (2003) notes that in accordance to the oral tradition of old dancers, these movements are meant to produce a magic power in which the goddess of the corn protects the harvest from danger. After that, the *huenches* perform a series of dances where they cross between lines, switch between partners, and unfold and refold lines in symmetrical scrolls. Finally, the dance stops while some of the *huenches* present a comical show, including humorous bullfights and short sketches.

Over the course of my research, I learned that the dance of *Los Huenches* started to disappear in the 1980s and 1990s, along with the tradition of going to *ermitas* to perform the corn ceremony.[1] In the summer of 2004, in connection with the fiesta of Santa Rosa de Lima, some villagers became deeply concerned that the performance of the corn ceremony would be extinguished. The leaders of the Yalaltec cultural center Uken ke Uken in Yalálag coordinated with representatives of the Instituto Nacional Indigenísta (National Indigenous Institute) in Oaxaca City and one of the local *Los Huenches* dance leaders to film such a ceremony.[2] They wished to ensure that a permanent record of this dying tradition will be available to younger generations, who have become increasingly detached from this ritual and have "lost understanding" of the purpose of this ceremony.

On August 30, 2004, during the fiesta of Santa Rosa de Lima, a peasant family and the dance ensemble of *Los Huenches* walked to the *ermita radg be?* (The Hill Where the Wind Cuts) to perform the ceremony.[3] When they reached the *ermita,* they made offerings to Mother Earth and performed ritual activities for the patron saint. The *huenches,* the Yalaltec woman, and four girls who each played the character of Rosa Maria in the dance decorated the *ermita radg be?* with white gladiolas, Paschal candles, and incense. Accompanied by music, the peasant family offered food, including *tepache* (a drink made from corn), *pozontle* (a drink made from cacao, corn, and sugar cane), tamales, *caldo de res* (beef broth), *memelas* (a type of tortilla), and mescal to Mother Earth while two male *rezadores* recited a rosary. Afterwards, the *huenches* returned to the village to perform their dance in the chapel of Santa Rosa de Lima.

When the dance ensemble arrived at the chapel, the *huenches,* the four Rosa Marias, and the Yalaltec woman lined up in three rows before the altar of Santa Rosa de Lima.[4] Before the drum and the flute players began, the dancers knelt silently and drew an imaginary cross with their right hand in front of their upper body to salute the patron saint.[5] To perform, each *huenche* was dressed in a shirt and pants stitched from coffee sacks, and most wore hats made of cardboard, *petates* (mats woven from palm trees), or woven baskets.[6] A few wore Mexican palm hats or mariachi hats. Although most of the dancers had Yalaltec sandals, others wore tennis shoes or moccasins. I was told that a few decades ago, it was common to see all *huenches* wearing wooden masks; on this occasion, only a third of the dancers wore such masks. The remaining participants had plastic masks, adapted from those used on Halloween, for wrestling, and by clowns.[7] The four girls who represented Rosa Maria—all between five and twelve years old—were garbed in pink dresses with a handkerchiefs hanging from their waists down their right sides and hats made of pink satin. Their costume included Yalaltec sandals, pink socks, earrings, and small medallions hanging around their necks. The man who represented the Yalaltec woman wore a Yalaltec *huipil* (dress), an *enredo* (skirt), a black mariachi hat, pantyhose, and Yalaltec female sandals. His hair was wrapped with a Yalaltec shawl, and the wood mask that covered his face was painted pink, with large eyes and red lips. When the *maestro de la danza* bowed his head and began playing his flute, the *huenches* stood up and began to yell, jump, and clap before they performed.

When I saw *Los Huenches* performed in the private home of a Yalaltec family the next day, I recalled the performances of *Los Huenches* I had seen in the home of a Yalaltec immigrant in Los Angeles a year earlier.[8] I felt that the performances I observed in Los Angeles were quite similar to the ones I was watching in Yalálag. They were alike in terms of the dance structure, the step motifs, the choreography, and music. But the contexts of the dance performance as well as the portrayal of the *huenches* were somehow bafflingly both similar and different. That is to say, in Yalálag and in Los Angeles, performances of *Los Huenches* continue to privilege its religious location. This dance is performed in accordance with the religious calendar of the fiestas of the Yalálag patron saints, and the primary motivation of performers is to participate is religious devotion. However, the religious context is changing; even in Yalálag, this dance no longer accompanies the corn ceremony as a rule, and some of the young *huenches* I spoke to both in Los Angeles and Yalálag do not know about the role of this dance in the corn ceremony and the significance of the choreographic movements.

During the course of my research in Los Angeles and in Yalálag, I also saw the *huenches* using their bodies, outfits, and performance to make fun of themselves and to express their feelings and views of their experiences of migration in their community. These situations provoked a number of questions for me: What are the differences between performing the dance of *Los Huenches* in Los Angeles and in Yalálag? Why have most peasant families stopped performing corn ceremonies in the Yalaltec *ermitas?* Why has the dance of *Los Huenches* not disappeared if these ritual ceremonies are almost extinct? What do the contemporary props and references in present-day dance performances mean? How do all these elements relate to the myth of the dance and the ceremony of the corn? Finally, what does the dance of *Los Huenches* mean for the Yalaltecos who live in Los Angeles?

As noted throughout this book, migration has been one of the main driving forces causing major changes in the social, cultural, religious, and economic life of Yalaltecos who live in Yalálag and in Los Angeles, and the dance of *Los Huenches* puts aspects of these changes in perspective and focuses them in the portrayals of *Los Huenches* and the parodic segments of the dance. One could argue that Yalaltecos have changed throughout their history and that other factors—such as the conversion of Yalaltecos to Christianity and the gradual assimilation of younger generations into Mexican and American hegemonic models of culture and identity—have also contributed to social, economic, and cultural changes in this Zapotec community. But in the last four decades, migration has been the main factor contributing to the transformation of the Yalaltec community across generations and localities. According to older generations, the value and view of the rural, peasant lifestyle began to change dramatically as a result of migration and schooling. Since the late 1980s, most of the teenage boys have begun to migrate to Los Angeles. While many settled permanently in the United States, others return to the village. At the same time, the ones who have stayed in Yalálag are not encouraged to work in the countryside. In the past, working on a farm was highly praised. People who worked in the fields sustained themselves and their families, thus increasing their value and social standing in the community. But today, rural work is viewed in monetary terms as non-remunerative, and indeed, few Yalaltecos can make a living at it. Many Yalaltec families who receive remittances from their relatives in the United States refuse to work in the fields. Other families who make a living from small businesses, construction work, and the fabrication of local arts and crafts, have abandoned their fields because these jobs provide them with better economic and social benefits.[9] Furthermore, the population of Yalálag is mainly composed of elders, who have stopped working in the fields or receive money from their immigrant relatives.

As a result, the perceptions of group identity have also increasingly diverged between older and younger generations. Currently, Yalaltecos characterize older generations as "the corn generation" and the younger ones as "the migration generation." Roberto, a resident of Yalálag, explains:

> The newer generations have lost much understanding of our past history and the cultural knowledge of our ancient traditions and beliefs. The expulsion of our youngsters to the cities of Mexico and Oaxaca and the United States has deteriorated our way of life and transformed their way of thinking. Today, the community values are at risk. In the past, the village's people depended a hundred percent on the countryside. You could say that we were the people of the corn. Our mentality was linked to the corn, its production, and its rituals. The corn has been our main source of sustenance. But today, everything is different. A lot of families rely on immigrant remittances. Ironically, they prefer going to CONASUPO to buy corn instead of growing it in their fields.[10]

Erick, another elder and a Yalaltec peasant, further elaborated on these issues and the deterioration of the countryside:

> Currently, the countryside is pretty much abandoned. Just take a look at how the underbrush has grown. Nowadays, wild animals such as snakes, puma, and deer have begun to enter the village. In the past, this did not happen. Look, when the peasants work their fields, the animals are away because the fields are clean. But today, it is very sad to see what is happening in the fields and in our village. The younger generations are not interested in working in the countryside. They just want to emigrate or their parents want them to get a professional career. Many people say: "If my children want to progress, they have to leave Yalálag to study."
>
> Look, young Yalaltecos think differently, and their parents do too. The younger generations do not know much about the peasant lifestyle. They do not know how to live according to the old ways. They do not belong to the culture of the corn. If you send them to work in the fields, they do not even know what to do. I think that too many things are becoming lost in our community. For us, the elders, it is very sad to see that the majority of the young people want to emigrate. They feel that there are no options here. They may be right.

Nowadays, education and migration go hand in hand. Both translate into social status and upward mobility and correlate with future earnings. Younger generations of Zapotecs do not recognize the importance of agricultural work because they do not see social and economic benefits from the countryside.[11] Their parents, too, encourage their children to attain a middle-school diploma, at a minimum, and prepare for urban life. Although many elderly Yalaltecs still find a great value in the peasant way of life and tell their children about it, this does not mean that their children send their grandchildren to work in the countryside. The experience of migration of the first migrants has shaped this way of thinking. Since working and living in the cities was a burden for many of them, especially because they were illiterate and did not speak Spanish, Yalalte-cos today encourage their children to study and become literate to adjust to the urban way of life.

Thus, the peasant life is now conceptualized as backward, traditional, and disadvantageous economically and socially. The following example illustrates in the voice of a Yalaltec woman what parents tell their children about being a peasant or working in the field: "If you do not want to go to school, I will send you to watch over the cattle, to load firewood, and to harvest. If not, I will send you to work with the *huaracheros* [sandal-makers]." This clearly implies that if younger generations are better educated, they will obtain better paying jobs and a higher status. But to do that, they must emigrate and study abroad to incorporate into a different social environment. Ironically, being a peasant or artisan is not considered socially and economically worthy among teenagers, but I know old and young Yalaltec immigrants in Los Angeles who have middle school, high school, and BA degrees but work as dishwashers, cooks, gardeners, or domestic workers.

The school system reinforces these ideas. One teacher I spoke with in Yalálag said that, unfortunately, younger generations are taught to leave behind their lifestyle and native beliefs and, thus, look down upon their traditions. The professor said: "What is important for the education system is to incorporate our students into modern society and teach them to think scientifically." Along with the abandonment of the countryside, permanent emigration, and the ideals of progress and modernity, there have been related economic, social, cultural, and ideological changes in this Zapotec community. That is, Yalaltecos have experienced discontinuity and transformation of their native beliefs, ritual practices, and ways of understanding the relationships between nature and human beings, and between human beings and the Yalálag deities.

The penetration of commercial capitalism and schooling has caused dramatic changes in the local economy and way of life of the Zapotecs. Out-migration increased as a result of cash shortage and the development of capitalist relationships in the region. Some of the best fertile maize lands were transformed into cash crops, and others were abandoned. With the introduction of schooling, children's labor in the family's maize crops declined. With the arrival of trucks, muleteer families got rid of their mules and donkeys, and the sale of cheaper subsidized maize began to be substituted for locally produced maize. In addition, "mountain plots which were no longer cultivated became overgrown, rodents (badgers, squirrels, and raccoons) began to increase in numbers and to raid crops on plots once relatively free of them. Yields decreased because of high in-field loss from these rodents" (Young 1976, 233).

In this context, the dance of *Los Huenches* has evolved in several ways into something different from its "original" meaning without losing its religious motivation.[12] To paraphrase Hobsbawn words (2000), Yalaltecos have reinvented their traditions in Yalálag and Los Angeles. In this case, the dance of *Los Huenches* has been resignified in various ways. This dance continues many traditions and beliefs that derive from pre-Columbian and colonial practices and carries them into modern times. It persists as a vehicle for the expression of religiosity and a means of communication with the Yalálag patron saints. That the agricultural rituals have gradually disappeared from the *ermitas* is related to continued Yalaltec emigration and abandonment of agricultural work. Thus, younger Yalaltecos, who do not learn and are not taught to live in accordance with the peasant way of life, have experienced changes in their social and cultural values and ideology. For example, the *huenches* stopped complying with certain ritual requirements to perform in the dance such as an age requirement and fasting. And the spoken prayers and chants disappeared and were substituted with claps, yells, and claps. What can we say about all these changes? I suggest that these performances of *Los Huenches* are at once a continuity and transformation. Yalaltecos who continue to perform the corn ceremony do so because they believe in old ways of doing things, and carry on traditions and ancestral beliefs that are meaningful for them at present: thanking Mother Earth from what they have taken from it and thanking the patron saints for providing a plentiful supply of food.

Schechner and Appel (1985, 2002) and Thompson (1992) indicate that transformation is an essential characteristic and principle of any cultural practice. In Yalálag, dancing *Los Huenches* for the patron saints is indeed a continuation of an ancestral performance that adheres in some ways to its original structure and symbolism. In Yalálag and in Los Angeles, Yalaltecos have incorporated new meanings and narratives to this dance and to their individual performance. The "original" meanings of this dance, which have been gradually lost across generations (dancing for the goddess of the corn, thanking Mother Earth, and dancing to protect the harvest from harm) have become at once a discontinuity and transformation. For some dancers and villagers, this dance is a ritual practice in the social and religious sense. The dance is performed as an offering for Mother Earth and as a propitiatory act. For others, the act of dancing is more a question of a personal *promesa* or an act of reciprocity and a means of communication with the Yalálag patron saints. The following quote from Florentino, an immigrant man from Los Angeles, shows how some contemporary performers offer their dance to the patron saints for different reasons: "A year ago, I promised Santa Rosa to come back from Los Angeles and perform in her fiesta. To tell the truth, she is very miraculous." Florentino is referring to a time a year ago when he was in the United States and asked Santa Rosa de Lima for help. Since she responded to his pleas, he went back to Yalálag to honor her generosity.

When I asked the peasant family that performed the corn ceremony in the *ermita* why they had invited *Los Huenches* to their place, they explained: "We made a *promesa* to the patron saint. We promised him to take the dance to his *ermita*.

Part of our offering was to make the sacrifice of feeding the *huenches* in our place during the fiesta of Santa Rosa de Lima." In the peasant family's explanation, the *promesa* for Santa Rosa de Lima was to feed approximately sixty dancers in exchange of a plentiful supply of corn and the well-being of their family in the coming year. In her study of Yoruba ritual, Margaret Thompson suggests that performances are always under constant revision and construction. When performers become aware that their rituals or religious practices "are static . . . or become obsolete, empty of meaning, or eventually die out," performers change these practices to give them new meanings (Thompson 1992, 8). Changes in the *Los Huenches* dancers' motivations to perform and the translocation of the dance also point to the negotiation of old and new narratives and to the social construction of new ones.

During my field research in Yalálag in August 2004, I was able to interview some of the *huenches* and one of the Rosa Marias filmed performing in the private home of the peasant family that carried out the ritual corn ceremony in the *ermita radg be*? Paulina, a ten-year-old second-generation Yalaltec girl, spoke of her motivations to perform: "When I saw *Los Huenches* in Los Angeles, I told my mom that I would love to dance and represent Rosa Maria. When we came to Yalálag, I talked to her again about my desire to perform with *Los Huenches* when I saw the dance rehearsals of *Los Huenches*. I thought it was cool to perform in the dance. Then, my mom asked for permission to leader of the dance and looked for a seamstress to make my clothes." As I continued my interviews, I asked some of the local *huenches* why they were performing. An old man said that it was an offering for Santa Rosa de Lima. A young *huenche* explained that he participates because he likes dancing *Los Huenches* and participating in the patron saint fiesta, and also because he belongs to the barrio Santa Rosa. Another *huenche* told me that he dances with *Los Huenches* to enjoy himself. Pedro, a man who helped to organize the food and refreshments for the dancers in the peasant's home said: "The old dancers believe that this dance is performed to honor our ancestors and Mother Earth. They have their own beliefs. Before, they went to perform to the hill's chapels. There, they danced and made offerings to the patron saints. But today, the younger generations, perform for Santa Rosa and San Juan as a way of *promesa*."

Without a doubt, the dance of *Los Huneches* crystallizes a continuum between sacred and profane meanings and spaces, and transnational practices that account for a continued relation between the past and present history of Yalaltecos and between old and new narratives of this dance. As mentioned earlier, the dance can be divided in various segments, and concludes with a performance by the *huenches* of comical skits, bullfights, and other amusements. Molina (2003) asserts that the incorporation of these sketches or comical skits in this dance is related to the gradual "loss of meaning" of the original purpose, the imposition of Catholic symbols, the prohibition of native rituals, and changes in the system of Zapotec religious beliefs (cf. Alcina F. 1993). In this sense, he claims that Yalaltecos have corrupted this dance by making it a secularized practice. In contrast to Molina, I contend that although the incorporation of parodic elements in the dance may be seen as inappropriate and bizarre, it embodies a dynamic process where Yalaltecos have reinvented some aspects of the dance and given new meanings to their religious beliefs, performance, and traditions (cf. Hobsbawn 2000). While this performance continues to be an expression of religiosity, Yalaltecos have also invented and incorporated narratives that are significant in their present.

In Los Angeles, on September 8, 2003, I attended a *baile* organized by the barrio San Juan, and approximately ten *huenches* performed a comical bullfight. A man, dressed as a *huenche* wearing a plastic mask, a piece of deer skin, and deer horns, represented the bull. Accompanied by music, three *huenches* appeared, and one walked the *huenche*-deer on leash as if it were a dog. Then, the *huenche*-deer was released from the rope and the other three *huenches* started leading the "bull" back and forth. As this comical "bullfight" evolved, the deer fought with some of the *huenches* until he put them on the floor. Other *huenches* began riding each other while others told jokes in Zapotec. Some *huenches* did unexpected things like playing *salsa*, rap, *cumbias*, or pop rock on portable tape recorders, mimicked skateboarding, or played with mannequins or baby dolls. As the bullfight reached its peak, these *huenches* began to form a human pyramid, and the rest of the *huenches*, who were watching this performance, sang or shouted out responses to the leader's call.

During the course of my fieldwork in Yalálag and in Los Angeles, I asked some of the dancers to explain the deer's role and the reasons for its transformation into a bull. They answered that the deer's role is unknown, and no one knows for sure when this parodic performance came into being. However, Yalaltecos told me that today most old deer hunters kill themselves in the countryside as an offering for Mother Nature. Matilde, a Yalaltec immigrant, described: "The deer hunters sacrifice themselves because they believe that killing themselves is a form to give back to Mother Nature what they have taken from it." Molina (2003) observes that for the ancient Yalaltecos, the deer may have been a sacred animal.[13] According to the elders, at the beginning of the twentieth century, there was a segment in the dance in which the deer *huenche* walked along two lines that were formed by the *huenches*.[14] When the deer moved back and forth between these lines, the *huenches* vowed to revere its sacred presence. However, Molina suggests that around the 1930s, when the livestock and the bullfights were introduced in Yalálag, the deer became a bull because it had lost its past meaning.[15]

After watching the *huenches* in Yalálag, I realized that Yalaltec immigrants in Los Angeles make a conscious effort to reproduce an exact version of this dance and to privilege its religious location. In the *bailes* of Los Angeles, this dance is performed between June and August, in accordance with the religious calendar of the Yalálag patron saint fiestas. A series of religious enactments and objects enhance the sacred dimension of the *baile* and locate this dance as the principal offering for the patron saint (see fig. 7.1).[16] These objects and enactments can include the image of the celebrated patron saint, the setting of temporary altars, the production of processions and Catholic services, and performances of rosaries and sacred music. However, the messages conveyed in these sketches in Yalálag may not be relevant in Los Angeles. In Yalálag, the *huenches* perform

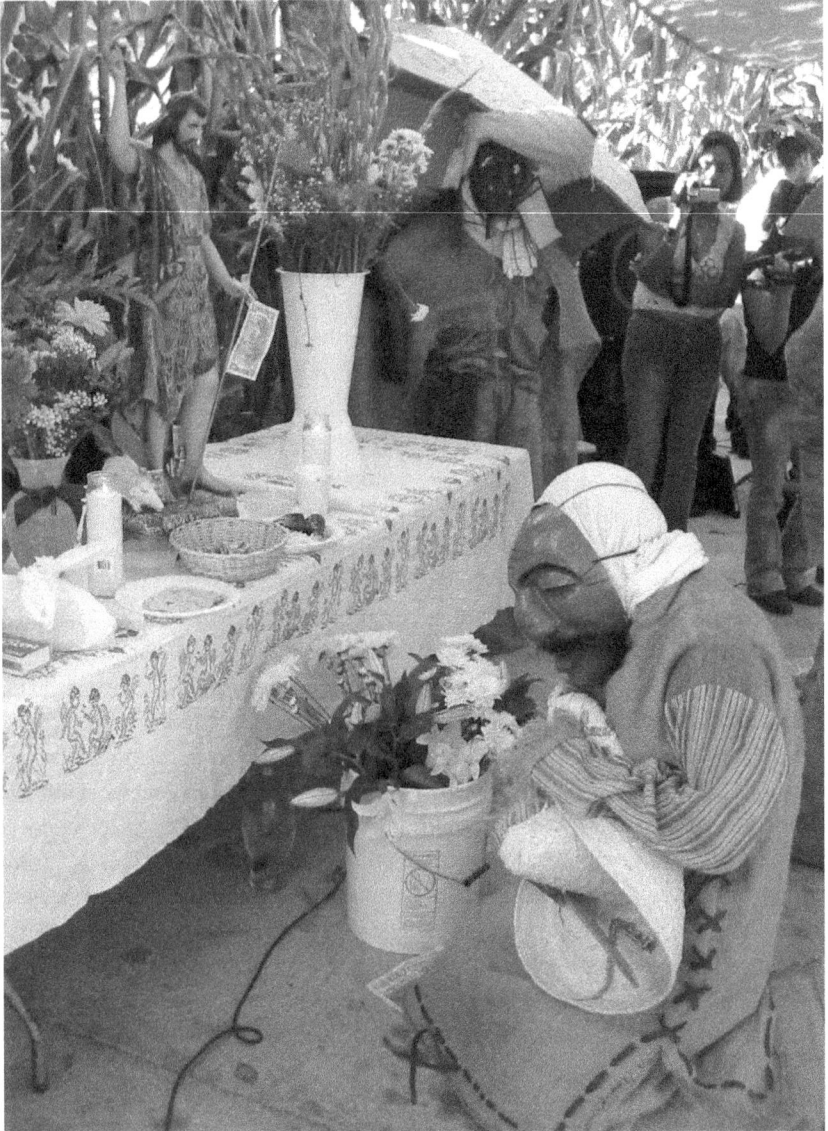

Figure 7.1. *Huenche* honoring San Juan Bautista. Los Angeles, 2003.

comical bullfights, as do the *huenches* in Los Angeles. But they also improvise and do things that do not happen in Los Angeles.

In Yalálag, on August 31, 2004, the dance troupe of *Los Huenches* was invited to have lunch and perform in the private home of another local family. When the dance of *Los Huenches* ended the group movements, approximately ten *huenches* began to improvise a comical sketch of one segment of the religious dances of San José.[17] Following one of the melodies of this dance, an old *huenche* walked into the kitchen of the house and invited the female owner of the house to perform the character of Virgin Mary. As she tried to persuade the *huenche* not to perform this sketch, she was pulled into the yard of her house in the middle of laughter and whisperings. A *huenche,* who was waiting in the yard, offered a chair and an old baby doll to the female owner. While the woman tried to recover from her shameful role, a *huenche* asked her to coo to the doll. A group of *huenches*, who stood up behind her, began singing a lullaby. Other *huenches*, who approached the "virgin," began giving her various kinds of fake gifts. As in the dance of San José, an old *huenche* put a mat on the floor to place gifts that are usually given to the baby who plays the Christ Child. A young *huenche* gave a plastic sack containing dried tortillas and stale bread. Other offered an empty pack of beer. And another one gave the "virgin" a miniature umbrella stroller for her doll. While one the *huenches* began performing a comical dance for both the doll and the "virgin," a couple of *huenches* were conversing in Zapotec. I was told that the *huenches* take advantage of these sketches to say funny things such as news, gossip, or jokes about local people to amuse the people who watch the dance.

When I asked my informants why the *huenches* staged this comical sketch, I was told that they improvise whatever they like to entertain the audience and enjoy themselves. However, I found that these sketches accomplish important work in helping Yalaltecos to demonstrate how they perceive each other, and what their taboos and moral and social values are. These sketches stage a peculiar sense of humor, a kind of self-irony about Yalaltec themselves. As Molina explains:

> Yalaltecos make fun of everything, including the extravagant, the exhibitionist, the conceited person and even those who do nothing. Yalaltecos like having fun and make people laugh. No one escapes them alive. Yalaltecos usually use their imagination and creativity in order to make people feel happy. We are happy people. We try to enjoy life. But also, I should admit that there is a certain kind of sarcasm in our jokes and dances.

In this occasion, these *huenches* made use of a segment of the religious dance of San Jose to make fun of an adult woman by making her play a young maid.[18]

Humor and improvisation are essential elements of this dance as it is currently practiced. In Los Angeles, as in Yalálag, Yalaltecos improvise all the time to give new meanings to and contextualize their performances. In Thompson's sense

(1992), improvising in this dance and staging these comic routines is important because the parody signals ironic differences between the past and the present history of the Yalaltecos, between old and new ways of living, and between old and new narratives in the dances. In this sense, instead of seeing these divisions as a separation of time and meanings of the dance, they mark a continuum between sacred and profane spaces and meanings. I find that the transition between sacred and parodic can be observed in the mix of these elements in the costuming of the *huenches* and in the dance structure. In fact, Yalaltecos use both the terms *sagrado* (sacred) and *chusco* (parodic) to characterize this dance and the multiple meanings, symbols, and narratives that are inscribed in the chore-ographies, the bodily movements, and the costuming of the *huenches*.

As explained at the beginning of this chapter, the *huenches* are both the *wench gure* and the living and comical representation of contemporary Yalaltecos. On the one hand, the *huenches* evoke and reproduce a set of images of ancient Yalalte-cos, those who are part of the mythical accounts of the founding of the village. Yalaltecos say that the *huenches* wear coffee sacks with bottle caps and hats made of cardboard because their ancestors were poor, had nothing to wear, and were longing for their village in the Highlands. The *huenches* are also comical repre-sentations of contemporary village's men, and they enact a particular kind of humor and self-irony. In the dance of *Los Huenches*, in honor of the *wench gure*, the *huenches* wear wood masks that are comical representations of the village's old men that have been characterized as having bad humor or bad temperament. Likewise, the recent use of plastic masks and the incorporation of items, behav-iors, and written statements in the *huenches'* costume (as explained below) are vehicles of communication between the dancers and Yalaltecos in attendance at the religious fiestas. In both Yalálag and in Los Angeles, the *huenches* utilize their outfits and individual performances to criticize and make fun of themselves and to express something that is meaningful for them.

In Yalálag, some examples of these representations, unsurprisingly, include mimicking immigrants in a humorous manner. Some *huenches* carry big suit-cases in their backs to criticize immigrants' arrogance and the ways they flaunt their higher status upon their visits. We have seen how some *huenches* do unex-pected things like playing commercial music on tape recorders or playing with baby dolls and skateboards. As Mario Molina, the Yalaltec poet and historian, described:

> In the *danzas chuscas*, local people imitate immigrants in a humorous manner. For instance, when the dancers perform, they act and dress as the immigrants do. Look, when immigrants return, they arrive to the village driving their big trucks. They come with long hair, showing off their watches, and wearing cow-boy boots and pants, like the *Norteños* [Mexican mestizo immigrants]. And the fact that immigrants feel superior, because they carry lots of dollars, makes the local people make fun of them. That is why the dancers of *Los Huenches*

and other *danzas chuscas* make exact copies of the immigrants, but clearly, in *chusca* manner. Look, the patron saint fiestas are the best time to ridicule immigrants. And for that, you have to be creative. The dancers have to invent new dances, its steps, choreographies, and the music. That is, they have to be clever. They have to feature immigrants in a way that you know who they are talking about. It is amazing. Believe it or not, you can tell!

Similarly, the *huenches* mimic immigrants who have either brought the Los Angeles gang culture to Yalálag or have already become *cholos* (gang members) in the village. When I asked one of my informants why some of the *huenches* had graffiti painted on their coffee sacks and wore nose rings, chains, and black caps, they said that the *huenches* dress in this way to make fun and criticize the gang members who have introduced drugs and new forms of crime and violence in the village. On August 30, when the corn ceremony was performed in the *ermita* of San Martín de Pórres, the gang *huenches* stayed in the town. When I asked my friend Gabriela why this group of *huenches* did not join the group, she replied: "Well, can't you tell it is the *gangster huenches*?" In other words, representing a *cholo-huenche* implies two things. It means portraying and behaving as a *cholo* to criticize the negative behaviors of the real *cholos* (see fig. 7.2).

In addition to portrayals of Yalaltec immigrants and local people, the immigrants who return to Yalálag from Los Angeles to join this dance often use this rite to express freely and comically their political views of U.S.–Mexico relations by writing on their props things like: "Wanted. President Fox, Bush's puppet." In Linda Hutcheon's theory of parody, mimicking someone is an "ironic signaling

Figure 7.2. In the back, young Yalaltecs play the *cholo-huenches*, Yalálag, 2004.

of difference at the very heart of similarity, paradoxically indicating both cultural continuity and change, authority and transgression, involving both creator and partaker in a participatory hermeneutics" (cited in Thompson 1992, 3–4). Just as the gang *huenche* is a representation of real Yalaltec gang members, so the *huenche* who carries a suitcase on his back is a parody of real Yalalatec immigrants who flaunt their status. But even while some *huenches* express their views on politics and ironically signal their position as undocumented migrants, they also refer to the *wench gure*. Above all, as my informant explained: "The *huenches* represent our ancestors."

In Los Angeles, the characterization of the *huenches* follows cultural patterns and understandings of the home village. But the *huenches* of Los Angeles also incorporate meanings, props, and behaviors that are distinctive to their current location and experience. For example, it is common to see that the *huenches* write on their coffee sacks or hats statements such as *Viva Yalálag!*, an expression of immigrants' nostalgia for the home village and a claim of belonging. They also remind the audience of the social positions that immigrants have acquired in the United States. For instance, a *huenche* wrote on his attire, "I am a wetback, so what!," an expression of his identity as both undocumented immigrant and foreigner. Others wrote, *Que viva la Raza!*, an expression of pride and dignity in the midst of a racist and harsh environment. Another one stated, *Soy la Migra* (I am the INS), a statement that parodies the laws, institutions, and discourses that highlight their undocumented status and threaten their social status. And a few of them deploy the statement, *Viva Mexico!*, to mark their status as foreigners and reinforce their identity as Mexican Indian migrants. As I discussed in chapter 5, Yalálag Zapotecs have acquired a strong sense of identity as Mexican in the United States, an identity they did not claim in Mexico.

Likewise, there are parodic and ironic expressions that would not make sense in Yalálag, but make sense in Los Angeles, such as: *Aprende Zapoteco sin Barreras* (Learn Zapotec without barriers). On Spanish TV channels in Los Angeles, there is a commercial that sells a language program to learn English called "Learn English without Barriers" (*Aprende Inglés sin Barreras*). The irony is that Zapotec is a non-written language that is in the process of disappearing among second-generation Yalaltecos. When I asked the *huenche* who wrote this statement on a small poster why he wrote it, he replied:

> I did it to entertain my *bi gwlash* (countrymen) and somehow to copy what happens with the English language. I think that it would be great to have a program that teaches how to learn Zapotec. Don't you think that it would be good to have a program like those of English? But, maybe no one is going to be interested in it. If we had a program like the ones we use to learn English, the newer generation of Yalaltecos could learn our language. I wish they were more interested in learning our language.

The implication is that the Zapotec language is an endangered language and that the newer generations of Yalálag Zapotecs are not learning it.

The importance of changes in gender roles in the dance also reflects how immigrants have tried on new ideas and values in Los Angeles, and how they have contributed to the incorporation of these changes in the home village of Yalálag. In Los Angeles, the recent incorporation of second-generation teenage girls in this dance shows a significant social change. In the past, in Yalálag, the dance of *Los Huenches* was a male-oriented performance. However, in recent years, teenage girls in Los Angeles have been allowed to fulfill the roles of Rosa Maria or the Yalaltec woman, and today, the barrio committee member of barrio San Juan and barrio Santa Rosa has a waiting list that includes the names of second-generation teenage girls who are interested in representing these characters in the coming years. According to Yalaltec immigrants, in Yalálag, the participation of girls or female teenagers in this dance is a copy of the changes that *Los Huenches* have made in Los Angeles. As Levitt suggests, because immigrants remain active in their homeland and become carriers of new ideas, perspectives, practices, values, material goods, and technology, then non-immigrants "try on new gender roles, experiment with new ideas ... to such an extent ... that transnational villages are likely to endure" (2001a, 11).

The act of dancing *Los Huenches* is, then, a cultural practice that embodies a distinctive worldview that encompasses specific religious practices and ancient and contemporary beliefs. This dance also provides an important context for understanding how Yalaltecos have constructed their identity in specific historical and social contexts and how they have reconfigured, reactivated, and resignified their collective myths, religious practices, gender ideas, and beliefs in transnational settings. To summarize, then, this dance embodies some aspects of the impact of migration in the social, economic, religious, and cultural life of Yalaltecos who live in Los Angeles and in Yalálag.

Certainly, the impact of migration is experienced differently in Yalálag and in Los Angeles, and Yalaltecos have choreographed some aspects of this experience and staged issues that are of great importance to them. Because migration has disrupted and destabilized the social, economic, and cultural life of the Yalaltec community, Yalaltecos have used this dance transnationally to reinforce their social and symbolic ties, to negotiate a new meaning of their community, and to redefine their new sense of group identity. The translocation and new uses of this dance expose significant differences and changes in the life of the Yalaltec immigrants and non-immigrants, but also provides some basis for negotiating these differences by reading from bodily texts that they are less divergent. The dance of *Los Huenches* brings them symbolically back together and knits together the damaged social fabric.

✌

CONCLUSION

Migration movements around the world are part of human history. However, what distinguishes contemporary migration movements from previous large-scale migrations are political and ethnic conflicts, natural disasters, and, most notably, the increased social and economic inequalities between people living in the same country and differences between people and countries around the world. Increased interconnectedness of regions and continents in terms of capital flow, communication, free trade agreements, and travel have also been powerful forces behind international migration movements. This has resulted in a backlash, the expression of anti-immigrant sentiments from developed countries; and the enforcement and creation of migration policies to control and restrict the movement of people across national borders have become pervasive.

The late twentieth and twenty-first centuries have culminated in important changes in migration patterns and experiences of migration. Migration movements have come to be more diversified than ever before in terms of gender, ethnicity, class, and age. A great number of immigrants have moved from developing countries to settle in developed countries in North America, Europe, and Australia, as well as in the fast-growing economies in Asia, and these numbers continue to swell. Not only has modern transportation allowed immigrants to travel more rapidly and relocate in new places but communication technology has also kept immigrants connected to their countries of emigration in unprecedented ways and sustained global labor markets and migration flows. Unlike international immigrants of the first half of the twentieth century, contemporary immigrants have been exposed to differing contexts of reception. The descendants of these immigrants have experienced diverse patterns of assimilation or incorporation in the countries of immigration. Not surprisingly, the emergence of new immigrant communities, the development of new cultural patterns and social identities, and the differentiation of connections between immigrants and their countries of emigration or communities of origin have proved to be distinct from earlier migration movements and significant factors in shaping contemporary migration processes.

At this historical moment, international migration is a global phenomenon that raises complex issues, concerns, and questions related to the political, demographic, economic, social, and cultural order; these highlight the crucial role of international immigrants in the global economy (Massey et al. 1998; Portes 2000; Zolberg 1989). Contemporary migrations from remote areas, such as those of indigenous peoples of developing countries in Latin America to rich and developed countries in Europe, Canada, and the United States, are not isolated phenomena. They are part of and respond to processes of economic globalization, which network people and specific localities into new transnational entities, and thereby inevitably transform them.

In this context, this book has offered an analysis of transnational relationships that Yalaltec immigrants have forged and sustained with their community of origin over the last two decades; the cultural, social, and political processes that have contributed to community formation in Los Angeles; and the impact of migration on Yalaltec identity and culture in both Yalálag and Los Angeles. I used an ethnographic approach to describe the history of Yalaltec migration to the United States to contextualize the unique migration patterns and dynamics and the multiple processes that have contributed to the emergence of the transnational community in Los Angeles. I argued that fifty years of international migration from Yalálag to California has led to a fragmented experience of community and identity. Over the last decades, however, Yalaltecos who live in Yalálag and Los Angeles have been engaged in building a new form of community and sustaining economic, social, cultural, familial, and symbolic ties to hold them together as a community. Likewise, Yalaltec immigrants and their children, who have developed multilayered identities in Los Angeles, continue to identify with Yalaltec non-immigrants in Yalálag because they share "cultural structures of commonality."

I have argued that Yalálag Zapotec community formation in Los Angeles primarily results from social and symbolic processes. In addition to economic processes and family connections that link immigrants and non-immigrants, the Yalálag Zapotec immigrant community exists in the social imaginary because Yalaltec immigrants have redrawn the social boundaries of community from within and have re-signified their social relationships and a system of symbolic representations in the context of immigration. I argue that in addition to multiple connections that Yalaltec immigrants have developed with their community of origin, the reconstitution of the four-barrio communities in Los Angeles has been crucial in forging the transnational life of the Yalaltec community. The transnationalization of Yalálag patron saint celebrations have been important factors conducive to community reorganization within, across, and beyond the U.S.–Mexico borders. In chapter 2, I suggested that the synchronization of the

Yalálag patron saint celebrations across national territories has allowed Yalaltec immigrants to symbolically bridge separate places and peoples and transform their imagined community into a community in a fixed location.

In chapters 2 and 3, I discussed how community is not only the sum of a set of shared cultural practices, a common history, and a language, but a more complex concept that embodies social and symbolic ties and practices of membership that connect people across and beyond the borders of two nation-states, the United States and Mexico. For the Yalálag Zapotecs, community is socially constructed on the continuing exchange-based obligations to the extended family, the barrio, the community, the patron saints, and the *bi gwlash*. Membership practices such as the *gwzon* (system of mutual aid), community service, and community participation constitute rich sources of social and symbolic capital that contribute to the maintenance of community and benefit the individual as well as the community as a whole. I also argued that Yalaltecos honor the Yalálag patron saints because they are powerful and provide a source of spiritual comfort. I explored the concept of "*gwzon* of faith" to account for the ties of reciprocity that exist between Yalaltecos and the patron saints. Beyond religious devotion, Yalaltecos honor their patron saints in gratitude for the help or support they provide.

I also presented a discussion on the positive and negative effects of migration in Yalálag. On the one hand, the emergence of new class differentiation and the transnationalization of gang activities have permeated the lives of Yalaltecos in Yalálag. On the other hand, religious celebrations and ritual life have emerged as the basis for transnational organization and the revitalization of Yalálag community life locally and transnationally. The history of political tension and rivalry in Yalálag explains why religious participation has been the primary medium for immigrants' reintegration into their community of origin. While Yalaltec immigrants and non-immigrants are undoubtedly more interrelated than ever before in terms of social, economic, cultural, and family relationships, long-term left/right political conflicts and divisions have impeded Yalaltec immigrants from working with the Yalálag municipal authorities or the community assembly to develop community infrastructure projects. Political tensions are not confined to the home community and are not left behind when immigrants immigrate: conflicts in Yalálag are of greatest importance in Los Angeles because they circulate between Yalálag and Los Angeles (cf. Gutiérrez-Najera 2007) and continue to limit immigrants' participation in their community of origin and to inform immigrants' relations and motivations to participate in community events in Los Angeles.

In the context of immigrant transnationalism (Portes 2001), I argued that Yalaltec immigrants and U.S.-born Yalaltecos have experienced significant changes in their own perceptions of self-identification. They have developed multiple and hybrid identities as a result of their migratory experiences, incorporation of historical and contemporary categories of the Mexican and American systems of ethnic and racial stratification—which have produced specific subjectivities and social positions—and processes of acculturation into Mexican and American mainstream cultures in the United States. I chose the title *Zapotecs on the Move* to remind us that after seventy years of Yalaltec migration in national and international contexts, Yalálag Zapotec identity and culture have changed, and Yalaltec immigrants and their children and non-immigrants in Yalálag have, too. In this sense, I proposed looking at Yalaltec identity and culture as processes, because they have not been unified systems or fixed entities. I argue that although Yalaltecos have been part of the same community and share a language, a history, native forms of social organization, and experiences of oppression, racialization, exploitation, and marginalization in both Mexico and the United States, they have not been homogenous or equal. Over the years, Yalaltecos have differentiated themselves in terms of schooling, wealth, class, gender roles, marital status, religion, age experiences and expectations, social status, migratory experiences, and the like. Currently, transnationalism contributes to an understanding of how international migration alters the meanings of group identity. Also, it provides a framework for understanding the multiple processes that shape the negotiation and reelaboration of group identity in Los Angeles and between Yalálag and Los Angeles.

Although Yalaltec immigrants recognize that their social identity is shaped by migratory experiences and new social locations in Los Angeles and Yalálag, second-generation Yalaltecos' identity is informed by present-day experiences of integration into American society, assimilation into the Mexican American minority, the development of a Oaxacan pan-ethnic sense of identity, and the retention of distinctive Yalaltec cultural practices in Los Angeles. In contrast, although non-immigrants' identities are also subjected to change and reelaboration, other social forces influence and define them (cf. Aquino 2010). What binds together Yalaltec immigrants, non-immigrants, and second-generation Yalatecos and informs the group identity of all, however, is the performance of mutually supportive ties, practices of membership, and involvement in Yalálag Zapotec cultural expressions and community life locally and transnationally.

In this work I have given special attention to the significance of transnational cultural practices. I argued that dancing is more than entertainment or a means of socialization. In comparing the performance of parodic and ritual dances in Yalálag and in Los Angeles, I found that Yalaltecos perform ritual dances in different locations but with the same leitmotif: to honor the Yalálag patron saints and/or ask for their help. Nonetheless, Yalaltecos choreograph new *chusca* dances and include additional meanings and narratives to their individual performances to address issues that are relevant for them locally and transnationally. *Chusca* dancers inform the public transnational cultural space and embody how Yalaltec immigrants, non-immigrants, and the second-generation Yalaltecos see each other and how they are experiencing their historical continuities and discontinuities in terms of class, gender, generation, and national and transnational social identities. In chapter 7, I argued that while the dance of *Los Huenches* remains a collective enactment of Yalaltec religiosity, it also incorporates new narratives and elements that are meaningful to the current experiences of Yalaltecos who live at both ends of the Yalaltec migrant circuit. The dance of *Los Huenches* embodies important aspects of Yalaltec history—the myth of the founding of the village by ancestral immigrant Zapotecs and its history of colonization and evangelization—and continues to play a significant role in the celebration of religious fiestas. However, this dance also refers to the experiences and impacts of migration on Yalaltec community and identity. I suggested that in addition to using this religious performance as a vehicle to communicate with the Yalálag patron saints and Mother Earth, Yalaltecos use this dance to stage issues that are of great importance and concern for their community at present: their struggles to keep their historic memory alive, their need to express their views on the rapid and profound changes affecting their community locally and transnationally, and the efforts of Yalaltec immigrants and non-immigrants to find ways to negotiate their increasing social differences.

The Future of Yalaltec Culture and
Community in Los Angeles and Yalálag

After talking with Yalaltecos in both places about the future of their community and culture, I became aware that although they have resisted all kinds of oppression, aggression, marginalization, and discrimination throughout centuries of colonization, domination, and exclusion, they currently feel that they will be unable to continue as a differentiated community. I heard this concern again and again from Yalaltecos on both sides of the U.S.–Mexican border. In Yalálag, Roberto, one of my informants, said that he thinks that migration has become a key factor in accelerating the extinction of the Yalaltec community in Yalálag:

> Without a doubt, migration has benefited hundreds of families economically; however, it has also weakened our community life, altered our social institutions, and emptied our villages, but it has not destroyed our community values yet. I think that there is no hope for our younger generations to stay in Yalálag. They have changed their perspectives. I think that migration has changed them. Life in the United States seems to be more attractive, I do not know. Of course, there are no options for them here either. There are no jobs or a good education for them. I think that perhaps some aspects of our culture will survive, but our people and our villages will vanish in a few generations. When I say vanish, I mean transformation into something other than what we are. It is like renouncing calling yourself Zapotec. Look, if you think of what has happened to other Zapotec villages such as those of Yaatzachi, Zoochina, Xochistepec, or Los Cajonos, it is very likely that the same experience is going to happen to our community.

Today, these communities are referred as to ghost towns. Thirty years ago, these villages were alive. But nowadays, for example, in Yaatzachi, there are only five elders. There are no brass bands. All the musicians are in Los Angeles. In the village of Xochistepec, there are around forty people left. The government closed the elementary school because there are no children. Other villages such as those of Zoogocho, San Pedro Cajonos, and San Mateo Cajonos are in the same situation, and Yalálag is heading in the same direction. Do you know what not having elementary schools means in these villages? Death. This is the beginning of our community's death. If we do not have children and our adolescents are gone, who is going to reproduce our culture, our people? Many people would tell you that we would become something different, other people. Indeed, we have changed over the centuries. We are different from our ancestors. But we are still the Zapotecs. But, when you realize that those teenagers, who were born in the United States or Mexico City, do not speak our language, and the village and the village people are not meaningful to them, you feel that there will be no continuity.

During my conversations with Yalaltec immigrants in Los Angeles, I asked them about the future of their community and culture in Los Angeles. I constantly heard that the ones responsible for keeping the Yalaltec community alive are the immigrants. Miguel, one of the first immigrants in Los Angeles, elaborated on this:

I think that the Yalaltec immigrants are the ones who will maintain our culture and community in this country. I do not see our children doing that. Based on my experience, I see that as soon as they grow up and become more independent, they leave the community. Many of them do not identify with us. Some of them feel ashamed of their indigenous origin. Even if they want to spend time with us, it is difficult for them, especially, when they have to work and study. It is not like in Yalálag. In addition, if our *bi gwlash* move away from our community and do not teach our children who we are, why we are here, and where we come from, I think that in a few generations, we are going to disappear as a group. I am convinced that we, the immigrants, are the ones who will maintain our culture and community.

In this context I ask: what will happen to the Yalaltec people? What is going to happen with the Yalaltec village if emigration continues to rise? Will Yalaltec immigrants in Mexico vanish through their *mestizaje*, namely, becoming fully Mexican? Will they become homogenized into the Mexican immigrant community of the United States? Will second-generation Yalaltecos become assimilated into the American mainstream? Will the second generation become Chicanos or Mexican Americans? Is it possible to think of a stable Zapotec immigrant community in Los Angeles over the coming years? Will the transnational community of Yalálag become a diaspora?

It is quite likely that there is no one single response or scenario to such a complex set of questions. However, I would venture some possible scenarios. The first is that Yalaltec immigrants will remain a distinctive immigrant community in the United States within the larger Zapotec, Oaxacan, and Mexican immigrant communities through transnationalism. As a result of ethnic and racial marginalization, segregation, and exploitation as indigenous Mexican migrant workers, Yalaltec immigrants will continue to reinforce and reinvent their sense of community and identity as Yalálag Zapotecs and Oaxaqueños in the United States. At the same time, as long as Yalaltec immigrants keep working together to maintain cultural, ritual, and political connections and have common projects with their community of origin and support their families in Yalálag, they will retain a strong sense of community based on their village affiliation and to those multiple localities where Yalaltecos reside.

The second scenario envisages that over the years, Yalaltec immigrants will rename themselves, as did Oaxaqueños and Mexicanos in the United States, blurring their indigenous ethnicity as Yalálag Zapotecs, while at the same time retaining some aspects of Yalálag Zapotec culture. If the community of origin in Yalálag disappears, transnational processes will obviously end. If this scenario becomes real, but the Yalaltec immigrant community remains unified and maintains political connections with the Oaxacan-pan-indigenous community in the United States, and second-generation Yalaltecos involve themselves in community life, identify (at least partially) as Yalálag Zapotecs, and learn their parents' language (as many interviewees mentioned and demanded), the immigrant community and their descendants will become a true diaspora.

With respect to the village of Yalálag, I foresee in the long term that it might become a *pueblo fantasma* (ghost town), though inhabited by Mixe immigrants. As I explained in chapter 3, the Mixes are Oaxacan indigenous immigrants from the Sierra Norte, who settled in Yalálag over the last fifty years. According to the Mexican census (2010b), there are 2,112 inhabitants in Yalálag. Of these, 1,241 are Yalaltecos, 545 are Mixes, and 326 do not identify as members of either of these groups. Again, while Yalaltec immigrants and non-immigrants maintain their social, economic, and symbolic ties, and immigrants have families to visit or are engaged in transnational community life in Yalálag, it is likely that Yalaltec immigrants and non-immigrants will continue to foster their transnational connections. As the Yalaltec immigrants start to organize in Los Angeles to deal with issues that affect their children and themselves as immigrants, they will become a stronger community.

As for second-generation Yalaltecos, I see many of them moving away from the Yalaltec community and choosing to identify solely as Mexican Americans, while others identify as American because of social pressures to assimilate into a higher social status and hegemonic identities. As other scholars have shown (de la Fuente 1958, Aquino 2002, Bertely 1999, Gutiérrez-Najera 2007), Yalaltecos who dis-identify with their indigenous ethnicity tend to move away from their community. This results from the ethnic discrimination and racialization they have experienced as well as the internalization of negative images, values, and ideology associated with their indigenous origin. However, I hypothesize that other members of this generation will become more politicized and oriented toward their Oaxacan pan-ethnic identity and Yalálag Zapotec roots, and claim what I have defined as a second-generation Yalaltec identity. As I argued through-out this book, identity, as process, is always under construction, open to change, ambiguous, and contradictory (cf. Hall 1998, Kondo 1990). Currently, the emer-gence of multiple identities between Yalaltec immigrants and second-generation Yalaltecos enables greater flexibility, permeability, and openness of the boundar-ies of group identity.

International migration presents a challenge in maintaining the transnational Yalálag Zapotec community and defining group identity in the long term, but transnationalism allows Yalaltec immigrants, non-immigrants, and the second-generation Yalaltecos to coalesce and (re)organize locally and transnationally today.

APPENDIX

✦

THE STUDY SITES

I conducted this study in two localities—the city of Los Angeles, California, in the United States and the Zapotec village of Yalálag, Oaxaca, Mexico. In Los Angeles, I spent long evenings and entire weekends in areas where the Yalalteco study participants live and socialize: Koreatown, South Central Los Angeles, the Pico Union, and West Adams districts. According to Yalaltecos, Koreatown became their main area of settlement in the late 1960s. During the 1970s, Koreatown was mainly populated by Korean immigrants, but today's Korean and Thai immigrants have been joined by Yalatecos, other Mexicans, Guatemalans, and Salvadoreans to constitute a diverse ethnic neighborhood. Some Yalaltecos began to move out of this area in the last decade when housing prices in South and East Los Angeles became accessible and better economic conditions allowed them to invest in private property. Unlike the Yalaltecos who still live in Koreatown, the families who are in East and South Los Angeles inhabit residential areas that are highly populated by African Americans, Mexican Americans, and Mexican immigrants from the states of Jalisco, Michoacan, Distrito Federal, and Sinaloa.

At the time of this study, eighteen of the twenty-two participating families lived in Koreatown. Four of them owned a house and fourteen rented modest apartments in small buildings. The ones who rented one- or two-bedroom apartments paid between $700 and $1,200 per month in rent. Usually, families of about four members, who enjoyed modest economic stability and had been in the United States for over ten years, lived in one- or two-bedroom apartments. At times, they shared bedrooms or living rooms with newcomers to support them upon arrival. The four families who own homes stated that after paying rent for almost twenty-years, they decided to purchase a house. Although one family found good prices in Koreatown, three of them got better deals in South Central Los Angeles, Pico Union, and West Adams. These families' homes consist of one- or two-level units with two to four bedrooms, a garden or concrete backyard, and a garage. It is the Yalaltecos who arrived during the 1970s and obtained amnesty under the Immigration Reform and Control Act of 1986 (IRCA) that are the ones who own houses in the United States. Others have built new houses in Oaxaca or Yalálag.

Since the 1970s, Koreatown has remained a Korean commercial area with well-establish physical boundaries and a history of Korean settlement. However, at present, Koreatown is not only well known for its numerous Korean restaurants, shopping malls, bakeries, travel agencies, nightclubs, karaoke, bars, and the Korean Cultural Center, but also has quite a few Salvadorian, Mexican, Greek, Guatemalan, and Oaxacan-owned businesses that include restaurants, markets, coffee shops, bakeries, barber shops, butcher shops, beauty salons, and cleaners. When I began my fieldwork, I went to this area because nearly all of the Yalaltecos I interviewed for this study lived there. But, even as my fieldwork evolved, Koreatown became a significant site to observe. This is the main area where the Yalálag Zapotec community and other Zapotec village communities rent ballrooms or community and church centers to hold their family and community events. Additionally, what I found interesting about Koreatown was that it is still filled with many small businesses owned and run by Zapotec immigrants. These include Yalaltec restaurants, butcher shops, and bakeries, as well as Oaxacan barbershops, record and tape stores, grocery stores, and a few places that offer money-order services to Zapotec immigrants (López and Runsten 2004).

Koreatown is not a little Oaxaca because its population is quite diverse. However, the fact that it is a neighborhood heavily populated by Zapotec immigrants from various Zapotec village communities in the Sierra Juárez and the Central Valleys and has a distinctive ethnic market makes Koreatown a place with a specific social configuration and economic activity. The development of an ethnic market and the Zapotecs' settlement patterns in Koreatown explain this area's transformation into a Zapotec immigrant neighborhood. Perhaps more important, the social use of this space provided me with a site where I understood how the social dynamics of family, community, and the daily lives of Yalaltec immigrants and their children have contributed to the social construction of community.

Conducting fieldwork in the village community of Yalálag required flying from Los Angeles to Mexico City, and then traveling by bus to both Oaxaca City and Yalálag. During my first trips to Yalálag (summer and winter of 2001 and winter of 2002), I traveled six hours from Oaxaca City through the Sierra Juaréz to reach the village, but the trip took only four hours in the winter of 2003, when the Oaxacan government began paving the only road that takes Yalaltecos to Yalálag. By the summer of 2004, when the road was completely paved, the trip took three hours.

San Juan Yalálag, also called Villa Hidalgo Yalálag, is a Zapotec village community located in the Sierra Juárez of Oaxaca, Mexico. Archeological evidence indicates that isolated Zapotec groups were established in this town long before the Spanish arrival in the sixteenth century. Since colonial times, Yalálag has been divided into four barrios. Arriving from Oaxaca City, one enters Yalálag via barrio Santa Catarina. Heading down the main street into downtown Yalálag, one finds the barrio Santa Rosa de Lima on the right side of the hill. Once downtown, the barrio San Juan lies downhill to the left and the barrio Santiago to the right. According to the 2010 Mexican census, the population of this village comprised 2,112 inhabitants (INEGI 2010d). These villagers' principal economic activities are based on agricultural labor and selling local products and crafts such as traditional sandals, traditional attire, and modern clothing.

The municipal building, the church of San Juan Yalálag, the post office, the police station, the main bus stop, a small medical clinic, a basketball court, and a fountain constitute what Yalaltecos define as downtown Yalálag. On Tuesday mornings at 6 a.m. Yalaltecos organize an outdoor market in the main plaza where they sell fresh meat, beans, corn, squash, chili, guavas, banana, *barbacoa* (lamb stew), tamales, coffee, *atole* (a rice-based drink), *pozontle* (a drink made from corn, cacao, and sugar cane), *chicharrón* (fried pork skins), tablecloths, clothes, and shoes. There is one elementary school, one middle school, and one high school for the entire village. Among the main religious buildings are two Catholic churches and four barrio chapels, and one evangelical temple.

Like many other Zapotec communities of the Sierra Juárez, Yalálag is not exclusively filled with old single-level houses made of adobe, but nowadays is surrounded by numerous houses built in the U.S. style. Hidalgo Avenue, which serves as the village's main artery, boasts at least one dozen small stores and a cultural center called Uken ke Uken. Across town, there are at least five stationery shops, two *tortillerias* (tortilla producers), four bakeries, four butcher shops, a water pump, and a dozen small grocery stores. Gang graffiti can be seen on the walls of some of these buildings, and political propaganda hangs on electric poles.

The village of Yalálag is located in the northern region of the state of Oaxaca, which has been described as among Mexico's poorest regions. Currently, Yalálag not only continues to embody five hundred years of social and economic marginalization but also reflects the economic, social, cultural, and political impact of out-migration into the United States. Most Yalaltec immigrants have provided their families with better economic conditions and have consequently changed the economic and social life of this village. For example, economically speaking, several families now own small businesses they could launch with immigrants' remittances. Likewise, young and old men work as construction workers because immigrants have employed them to build or reconstruct their houses and the main religious buildings in the village. Various changes in the social sphere can also be noted. Yalálag has many vacant houses due to out-migration to the United States. All families in Yalálag have relatives living in the United States. Although not every family has electricity in Yalálag, nearly all families have a television, VCR, and radios, all bought with immigrants' remittances. In recent years, most Yalaltec families have access to phone service, and some have Internet. These communication systems have given Yalaltecos in Yalálag new ways to connect with Yalaltecos in Los Angeles. Moreover, a few families have received desktop computers, video cameras, clothes, and washers and dryers as gifts from immigrants from Los Angeles. Conducting fieldwork in Yalálag provided a valuable site for understanding the on-the-ground impact of migration in the Yalaltec immigrants' place of origin and the multiple connections and activities that have linked Yalaltec immigrants and non-immigrants since the former settled permanently in Los Angeles.

The Yalálag Zapotecs of This Study

The Immigrant Generation

The Yalaltec immigrants of Los Angeles represent a diverse group in terms of their time of arrival into the United States, occupational and educational backgrounds, and immigrant status, as well as marital, age, and gender characteristics. Yalaltec migration is rural-urban migration and the Yalálag Zapotec immigrants of this study represent the second and third waves of out-migration from Yalálag into California. Unlike the first wave of immigrants into California—those who came to work as braceros in 1960s—these second and third waves of migrants arrived between the early 1970s and early 2000s. Even though all the immigrant men and women of this study left from Yalálag, the sequence of their stops on the journey to California varies significantly. In the 1970s, eleven of the thirty-six immigrants I interviewed migrated first to Oaxaca City, then Mexico City, and after that to Los Angeles. One couple told me that they first went to Oaxaca, then to Cuernavaca City, and from there to Los Angeles. One man who settled in his youth with his family in the municipality of Tlacolula, in the Central Valleys of Oaxaca, and left with Zapotecs from Tlacolula to Los Angeles; another man who joined the military service in his late teens went to the state of Tamaulipas first, and from there to Los Angeles. Of these thirty-six Yalaltecos, nine were community leaders when I did my research.

All Yalaltecos in this study went to school. Twenty-four completed at least five years of elementary school in Yalálag. Eight of them finished middle school in Yalálag, two of them in Oaxaca City, and two in Mexico City. Only one woman earned her B.A. degree in accounting in Oaxaca City. All of these women and men are bilingual. They speak Zapotec as their first language and are fully fluent in Spanish. Only one woman is completely proficient in English. When I asked immigrants to calculate how much English they speak, they said that they could only understand "basic English" since they did not have enough time to go to school to learn it, and their work has not demanded that they speak it.

At the time of the research, I interviewed thirteen married couples, two single women, and one couple who lived in a consensual union. Of the thirteen married couples, eleven were married in Los Angeles and two in Yalálag. It is important to mention that Yalaltec immigrants continue to be mostly endogamous; the fact that they arrive from different destinations in Mexico has not made them marry outside the Yalálag community. In the same vein, it is interesting to note that I met four second-generation Yalálag Zapotec women who married Yalaltec immigrant men.

The migration status among the Yalaltecos in this study varies and is related to the immigrants' time of arrival in the United States and changes in American immigration law. Nine of the thirty-six immigrants first became residents under the 1986 amnesty program (IRCA), and then became American citizens. According to them, they applied for American citizenship because they realized that they could access better welfare benefits when they retire. Just one man stated that he became American because Mexico had failed him, and he is not planning to live in a country that does not provide security and a stable future for his family. In contrast to the thirteen undocumented immigrants in this study, fourteen Yalaltecos told me that they are U.S. residents, and from this group five women have considered becoming American citizens for the welfare benefits and the possibility of participating in the politics of the country where they live. According to these women, becoming American is not necessarily a sign of abandoning their loyalties to the Mexican nation and their village in Oaxaca. Rather, it is a matter of "convenience," and the only way they can access social, civic, and political rights in the United States.

The Second Generation

The descendants of Yalálag Zapotec immigrants (the second-generation Yalálag Zapotecs) constitute one of the largest groups of indigenous Mexicans born in the United States. With the exception of two teenagers who were brought to Los Angeles at the ages of five and seven (thus the 1.5 generation), nineteen second-generation Yalálag Zapotecs who participated in this study were born in Los Angeles. Six of these nineteen were born in the late 1970s, six in the 1980s, and seven in the 1990s. When I interviewed these young Yalaltecos, nearly all of them told me that they went to public school in Los Angeles. Only those whose parents arrived in the 1970s went to Catholic schools until they entered the university. At the time of my fieldwork, three teenage girls and two teenage boys were still completing middle school. Four young women and four young men were in high school. Two men and two women were doing their undergraduate studies. Among the three who had finished a B.A. degree, two were working as nurses, and one was working as an assistant researcher on a university project. One woman who was working as an assistant manager in a shopping center in East Los Angeles was studying design in a private university.

To my knowledge, all second-generation Yalálag Zapotecs are fluent in English and Spanish, and only one of them had a strong accent when speaking Spanish. Although one might expect that they spoke their mother tongue, the Zapotec language, none of them did. There were two women who confessed to me that despite understanding Zapotec, they could not speak it and were not interested in learning more than they already know. By the time I started interviewing this young second generation, I had already met most of them in community gatherings and family events, and I observed that, although they like to socialize with the immigrant community and their relatives, there were three of them who did not participate in community events at all.

The Non-immigrants and Internal Migrants

During my fieldwork in Yalálag, I interviewed eleven community, barrio, and religious leaders, and twenty Yalaltec residents, of whom one was a pioneer migrant who joined the Bracero Program in the 1960s. Among the twenty Yalaltec interviewees, I found that only one had had no previous migration experience into the United States, but had some in Oaxaca City. That is, nineteen interviewees had been immigrants in Los Angeles in the 1980s or 1990s. When I began to conduct fieldwork in Yalálag, I found that not all of my interviewees were residents of Yalálag. All of them were raised in Yalálag, but four were living in Oaxaca City and two in Mexico City. These six Yalaltecos were attending the major religious fiesta of Yalálag. They told me they returned regularly to visit their parents and other relatives and, at times, to tend to family business. Two of the men who reside in Oaxaca City returned specifically on June 2004 to comply with their community obligations—religious and civic posts—during the fiesta of San Antonio de Padua. At the time of the interviews, the four adult men were in their late forties. Two of them were married to Yalaltec women, one was married to a Zapotec woman from the Sierra Juárez, and one was single. They have been living in Oaxaca City since the late 1970s. According to them, they left Yalálag in their early years to continue their studies or to work to support their families in Yalálag. Currently, one of them works as an architect in Oaxaca. Another is a university professor of education and a poet. Another is retired, and the last one earns his living in a small store. As for the education levels of the other two young immigrant men, one is earning a B.A. in computer science and the other a B.A. in economics in Mexico City at UNAM (Universidad Nacional Autónoma de México).

Unlike the Yalaltecos who went to Mexico City or Oaxaca City to study, the fourteen Yalaltec participants who reside in Yalálag completed at least five years of elementary school in Yalálag. Finally, like the Yalaltec immigrants of Los Angeles, all of them are fully fluent in Zapotec and Spanish. Just the Yalaltec man who worked as a bracero in northern California, is illiterate. Five of the twenty adult men and women were single, one lived in a consensual relationship, and fourteen were married.

METHODS

This study was based on twenty-two months of research in Los Angeles and in Yalálag, between December 2002 and September 2004. Over the course of my research, I used ethnographic methods, semi-structured and open-ended interviews, informal conversations, and participant observation. In particular, my approach drew from Marcus's call for a multisited ethnography that accounts for the "processes and relations which connect locales" (1998, 54) and people.

In Los Angeles, my field research built on previous relationships with Yalaltec immigrants I had met through my master's and doctoral research. Through friendships and close personal connections with two Yalaltec families, I secured introductions to many Yalaltec immigrants and participated in various family events such as weddings, baptisms, *quinceañeras*, and funerals. I also learned much by attending several *bailes*, two festivals of Zapotec dance and music known as La Guelaguetza, more than ten celebrations of the patron saint Santa Cecilia, a commemoration of the Day of the Dead, and the anniversaries of two Yalaltec brass bands. I was fortunate to assist with the production of one *baile*, and I established a *compadrazgo* (godparenthood) with a Yalaltec girlfriend. Participation in these events was crucial to observe, understand, and experience the processes that have shaped community formation in Los Angeles.

After getting to know various extended families and developing closer relationships with Yalaltec immigrants, I was able to set up interviews to trace their personal stories of migration and explore their migration experiences. I explored how they see themselves after migration, and how the second-generation Yalálag Zapotecs self-identify. In addition, Yalaltecos showed me videos that came from Yalálag on patron saint fiestas and family events. I interviewed community leaders and asked them questions about community projects and the organization of community and religious events.

Between June 2003 and April 2004, I conducted thirty-six semi-structured interviews with Yalaltec immigrants, nine with community leaders, nineteen with second-generation Yalálag Zapotecs, and two with two members of the 1.5 generation. For my research on the perceptions of identity among second-generation Yalálag Zapotecs, I used focus groups. I invited three to four teenagers to discuss their views and perceptions of themselves based on a series of questions I designed. Interviews lasted ninety minutes to an hour and twenty minutes, and were conducted in an informal setting. Some interviews expanded to two sessions because their parents arrived at the end of our interviews and engaged in the conversation. I took advantage of these unexpected situations to set up an additional session to discuss how parents and children see each other and experience their identities.

My involvement with Yalaltec friends and immigrant leaders in Los Angeles led to contacts in the village of Yalálag and helped me to build relationships with my friends' families and other Yalaltecos. As I mentioned earlier, I made three short trips to Yalálag in summer 2001, winter 2002, and winter 2003. On these field trips, I accompanied Yalaltec friends and second-generation Yalálag Zapotecs to visit their families in Yalálag during their vacations. We attended wedding celebrations, a couple of *quinceañeras*, the *posadas*, a Christmas celebration, and two patron saint fiestas. In the summer of 2004, I spent three months in Yalálag to conduct research on three patron saint fiestas and document the immigrants' participation. I interviewed twenty-five Yalaltecos, including community leaders and religious and municipal authorities. I also interviewed the principals and students of the local middle and high school. I mostly addressed issues regarding the impact of migration on family and community life and non-immigrants' perceptions on immigrants' participation and return to Yalálag. I was asked to offer English classes and lectures of my research. As part of these presentations, I organized six group discussions with middle- and high school students to discuss the causes and impacts of migration in Yalálag and their perceptions of identity between immigrants, non-immigrants, and second-generation Yalálag Zapotecs. During these months, I also spent two weeks in Oaxaca City doing interviews with four community leaders.

Over the course of my research, many experiences and exchanges with the Yalaltecos in Los Angeles and in Yalálag raised important methodological questions. First, I came to understand that although experiences of migration among Yalaltec immigrants tend to be homogenous, differences emerge in terms of generation and gender. Second, the language I used to conduct fieldwork in Yalálag and in Los Angeles raised an important concern: to what extent did speaking Spanish limit my study and my understanding of the events, interactions, and attitudes I investigated? In Los Angeles, to some extent, it was easy to conduct my fieldwork. As Yalaltecos and I conversed in Spanish spontaneously, we understood each other through a common language. As I discuss in Chapter 4, Spanish is the main language that Yalaltecos use outside of the community context in Los Angeles. When we met, we introduced ourselves in Spanish, and it naturally followed for us to use this language in interviews. In contrast, in Yalálag, although I engaged in Spanish with most of my informants, I had some problems communicating with elders. Since I knew very little Zapotec and some do not speak Spanish, I constantly needed assistance from young Yalaltecos. On some occasions, I found myself isolated and disconnected from what was happening in the village, at private functions or in family conversations. Although eventually I would know what was said, in the moment I could not follow conversations or understand information announced over the speakers at outdoor community events. Of 1,645 Yalálag Zapotec villagers, 1171 speak Zapotec. Of these 1,037 speak Spanish, 127 are monolingual, and 7 are unspecified (INEGI 2005). Zapotec continues to be the everyday language at home, on the streets, and during family and community events.

Third, as a Mexican mestiza and scholar, I always had to negotiate my social position. In Los Angeles, before I began my doctoral research, I spent a lot time with my Yalaltec friends. They became convinced on their own that I liked them and respected their culture and community, which was crucial to conduct my study effectively. In August 2002, a friend of mine and I won third place in a social dance competition, *sones y jarabes Yalaltecos*, at a community gathering. That day, I felt that I had earned the sympathy of the Yalaltec community. It is important to mention that in a Mexican context, most Mexican mestizos (non-indigenous Mexican) discriminate against indigenous people and belittle their culture and communities. Mestizos often highlight class and racial differences to place themselves above indigenous people. Thus, indigenous people are usually reserved and generally distrust Mexican mestizos. But when Yalaltec immigrants learned that I did not behave and identify with the behaviors and values of most Mexican mestizos, they opened up and became interested in helping me to carry out my project.

In Yalálag, Yalaltecos did not initially trust me, either. Although I initially thought their reasons were similar to those of Yalatecos in Los Angeles, I later discovered that their distrust stemmed from their belief that I supported and sympathized with one of the village political groups. As a result, during the summer of 2004, one of the barrio committees expressed their unwillingness to talk to me and banned me from taking pictures or video of one of the patron saint fiestas. Only after the directors of the local middle school and high school invited me to give talks on my research in Los Angeles, and after I taught English classes, was interviewed on Radio Universidad in Oaxaca City, and befriended some high school and middle school students, did Yalaltecos become open.

Fourth, although my research did not center on women's issues, Yalaltec women were crucial to my work. I spent most of my time with them, and they provided perspectives that made me view their community from different angles and reminded me of my gender position. Women brought issues to my attention that I would have overlooked if they had not described their migration experiences and discussed changes in women's ideology, roles, and hierarchies in Yalálag and in Los Angeles.

Doing field research in Los Angeles and in Yalálag was both a touching and a learning experience on both personal and research levels. In both places, I made close friendships through which I experienced the complexities of family and community life due to migration in both places. For instance, while I could move freely between Mexico and the United States, my closest friend could not return to Yalálag when his father lost a leg and became seriously ill. As an undocumented immigrant, he had to stay in Los Angeles at the request of his brothers, who asked him to send as much money as he could for his father's surgery and treatment, while simultaneously keeping alive his dream that one day he would be able to see his father again. Another friend received a call from her sister in Yalálag informing her that her mother had passed away. She decided not to go to Yalálag for fear of being detained at the U.S.-Mexican border upon her return to Los Angeles. She is an undocumented migrant and the mother of one child born in the United States. In Yalálag, as I visited family members of other Yalaltec friends of Los Angeles, I was asked to videotape a friend's mother who asked one of her daughters in Los Angeles why she had forgotten her family in Yalálag and why she did not want to return her mother's calls. When I returned to Los Angeles, this friend accused me of lying to her mother about her life in Los Angeles. I explained that I had simply told her mother that she and her husband worked hard, were doing well, and had a great family. While in Yalálag and Los Angeles, I was unaware that she did not communicate with her family.

At the community level, doing fieldwork in Los Angeles and in Yalálag led me to understand the Yalaltecos through their communal life and activities in two different localities and across two countries. Through the ethnographic materials I collected for this work, I gained insights into this book's subject matter: the struggles in maintaining and reinventing the meanings of community in the context of transnational migration and migration's impact on the group identity and culture of Yalálag Zapotecs within and across these two places.

NOTES

1. *Barrio* refers to a geopolitical and administrative area. Four barrios constitute the village community of Yalálag.

2. *Bi gwlash* is a Zapotec term that means fellow countryman or fellow countrywoman. In Spanish, it means *paisano.*

3. In Mexico, the term *community* has been used to define the ethnicity of a people, for example, the Zapotecs, the Mixe, and the Triques, among others. Also, it has been used to refer to a *pueblo,* as in village or a village community: for example, the community of Yalálag or the community of Villa Alta of the Sierra Juárez.

4. Italics are in original.

5. See Faist 2000b, Goldring 2001, Glick Schiller and Fouron 2001, Levitt 2001a, Smith 2006.

6. Following Durkheim's ideas of social reality, Bourdieu refers to social reality as "a set of invisible relations, those very same relations that constitute a space of positions exterior to each other and defined by their proximity to, neighborhood with or distance from each other, and also by their relative position—above or below, or even in between, in the middle" (1990, 126).

7. See Cornelius and Lewis 2007, Fernandez and Gonzalez 2003, and Smith 2006.

8. See Debry 2010, López Castro 2007, Mahler 2003, Menjivar 2000, and Moran-Taylor 2008.

9. At present in Oaxaca, there are two festivals of La Guelaguetza. Oaxacan indigenous and mestizo communities and the Oaxacan government organize one of them. Since 2007, the dissident social movement of elementary school teachers and the APPO have organized the second one.

10. See Basch, Glick Schiller, and Blanc-Szanton 1994, Fitzgerald 2000, Glick Schiller and Fouron 2001, Mahler 1995, Pessar 1995, and Rouse 1989.

11. In this context, "ethnic immigrant minority" means an indigenous Mexican immigrant group that interacts with other indigenous Mexican immigrant groups and a majority group such as mestizo Mexican immigrants or Mexican Americans.

CHAPTER 1 — THE YALÁLAG ZAPOTECS

1. For detailed description of the history of migration of other Zapotec immigrant communities to the United States, see Bartolomé and Barabas 1986, Cohen 2004, Hirabayashi 1993, Hulshof 1991, Kearney 2000, Klaver 1997, Malpica 2007, Rivera-Salgado 1999, Stephen 2005b and 2007b, Velasco 2005, and Young 1976. Patterns of migration vary as some communities immigrate to different places in the United States, and destinations have changed over time.

2. Except for the bracero generation, throughout this book, I use pseudonyms to protect the identities of Yalaltec participants.

3. After World War II, the U.S. and Mexican governments established the guest worker program, better known as the Bracero Program, under which Mexicans worked in agriculture and transportation and helped to maintain American railways. See Durand 2007, Hernández 2010, Stout 2008, Tienda 1989.

4. Yalaltecos speak Zapotec as a first language. Currently, in Yalálag, there are 2,112 inhabitants (INEGI 2010d). According to the Mexican census (INEGI 2005), 1,171 Zapotecs speak Zapotec. Of this number, 1,037 speak Spanish, 127 do not speak Spanish, and 7 are unspecified.

5. Ueda 1992 and Tienda 1989 point out that thousands of braceros became illegal immigrants, since they overstayed their working permits. In the 1950s, Mexico sent 300,000 immigrant workers.

6. Studies of internal migration in Mexico identify seasonal labor migrants as the Zapotecs and Mixtecs going from Oaxaca to work in the sugar plantations in the state of Veracruz (Hirabayashi 1993; Hulshof 1991; Klaver 1997; Stephen 2005, 2007; Young 1976).

7. These migratory patterns coincide with those of other Zapotec village communities in southern California. See Cohen 2004, Hirabayashi 1993, Hulshof 1991, Klaver 1997, Nader 1969, and Stephen 2005b, 2007b.

8. López and Runsten 2004 and Hulshof 1991 note that quite a few Zapotec villagers from the Central Valleys who were related to Tlacoluleños arrived in Los Angeles via Tlacolula networks.

9. It is common to find that marriage among Zapotec immigrants has remained endogamous in Mexico and in the United States.

10. Hondagneu-Sotelo proposes a typology of family migration to describe the different patterns of families who are coming and settling in the United States: family stage migration, family unit migration, and independent migration (1994, 39).

11. Even now, Yalálag does not have a hospital. There is just one rural clinic that provides basic health care. If someone gets seriously ill, they must travel to Oaxaca City.

12. In her study *Gendered Transitions: Mexican Experiences of Immigration*, Hondagneou-Sotelo 1994 finds that immigrant women tend to develop a desire to stay permanently in the United States. In contrast, men are less inclined to stay permanently in America.

13. Two similar examples of this pattern of migration are found in Hondagneu-Sotelo's 1994 and Cornelius's 1989 studies of Mexican immigrants coming from urban areas and Mexico's main cities into the United States throughout the 1980s.

14. During my research between 2000 and 2001, a Los Angeles barrio committee member suggested that there were more than 4,000 Yalaltecos living in Los Angeles (Cruz-Manjarrez 2001, 48). This estimate included the immigrant population and Yalaltecos born in the United States. Gutierrez Nájera calculates 2,500 according to a census she conducted in Yalálag and Los Angeles between 1998 and 2002 (2007, 66).

CHAPTER 2 — BUILDING COMMUNITY AND CONNECTIONS IN LOS ANGELES

1. Yalaltecos tend to portray themselves in tales and jokes as well as dance performances. Romualdo Limeta, the well-known maestro of *chusca* dances in Yalálag, said to me: "All *chusca* dances and jokes on someone from the community are just a joke, but nobody gets mad. This is the way we are. We make fun of ourselves."

2. Robert C. Smith 2006 uses the term "transnational life" to conceptualize the multiple activities, social and cultural dynamics, and political processes that link Ticuaneses in Ticuani, Mexico, and New York. He notes that transnational links help explain how multiple attachments structure and institutionalize a certain type of transnational life and how the identities of immigrants and their descendants are shaped by their integration to American society and multiple attachments to Ticuani.

3. In the Sierra Juárez of Oaxaca, each Zapotec village has a combination of a Spanish name and a Zapotec name. Most villages' names contain the prefix *yaa*, meaning "hill," and refers to the Oaxacan Highlands. Commonly, the first name is given in Spanish because the Spaniards renamed all Zapotec villages after a Catholic saint, while the second one is given in Zapotec, such as San Juan Yalálag. According to the Yalaltecos, Yalálag means "spread hill," "overflowing hill," or "the sliding hill."

4. There is a pre-Hispanic ball court in the Hill of Guadalupe in Yalálag that indicates that indigenous people were settled there. It is difficult to know about the pre-Hispanic Zapotec society of the Sierra Norte due to the lack of historical documents and systematic archeological studies. However, there are a few colonial documents on the Sierra and scattered information on Zapotec communities that help understand what happened in the region during the colonial period. For more information on the history of the Sierra Zapotecs, see Alcina 1993; Calvo 2010; Chance 1978, 1989; Ríos 1994; Whitecotton 2004; and Young 1976.

5. My translation.

6. In 1556, the Spanish Crown gave Dominicans a royal decree and a thousand pesos to take control of the Villa Alta district (Chance 1989). Currently, Villa Alta is one hour by bus from Yalálag.

7. Kearney 1986 points out that in the early 1530s, the Spanish founded the first *encomienda* in the town of Ixtepeji. Thereafter, they established more *encomiendas* throughout the Sierra to control more Indian villages in the region. Chance mentions that throughout the sixteenth century, the conquerors had to deal with numerous Indian uprisings. To subjugate the indigenous population, ensure payment of tribute, and reward individual conquerors for their efforts, the Spanish introduced two institutions: the *encomienda* and the *corregimiento* (1989, 23). Chance describes the former as "grant of an Indian town or towns, carrying the right to assess tribute," and the second as "jurisdiction or office of a *corregidor*." The *corregidor* was "a Spanish officer in charge of a local Indian district" (Chance 1989, 188).

8. According to Chance (1989, 171), the current traditional geographic distribution of Zapotec communities in the Sierra, including Yalálag (de la Fuente 1949), dates back to the sixteenth century.

9. San Melchor Betaza is 17.6 miles from Yalálag.

10. It is beyond the scope of this study to examine in detail the ethnohistory of the Zapotecs of the Sierra Juárez. For further reading, see Baskes 2000, Chance 1978, Tavárez 2011, Taylor 1972, and Yannakakis 2008.

11. According to the Yalaltecos, most of these small businesses opened recently through migrant remittances. A few others began to develop many years ago.

12. The village is a "face-to-face" community. Everyone knows each other by name, family name, or by sight. This is due to the community's relatively small size, close family and barrio relationships, communal social organization, and the high incidence of village endogamy.

13. At present, the barrios in Yalalag are residential units. In other Zapotec villages, modern barrios are not residential units. Chance points out that "where they exist their function is primarily religious: each *barrio* has a patron saint and a *mayordomo* in charge of organizing and financing the saint's fiesta often taking up a collection from the members" (1989, 171).

14. Although Yalálag is mainly a Catholic village, a few Yalaltecos have converted to Protestantism. According to the Mexican census (INEGI 2010a), there are 1,731 Catholics, 245 Evangelical Protestants, 87 *Bíblicas diferentes de Evangélicos* (this category includes people who identify with three religious sects: Adventistas del Séptimo Día, Iglesia de Jesucristo de los Últimos Santos, and Testigos de Jehova; INEGI 2010c), 41 persons without religion, and 8 without available data . According to a community leader, Protestants and *Bíblicas* are mostly Mixes. They do not participate in Catholic religious celebrations because of their different religious practices. They do not participate in barrio service when this relates to Catholic fiestas. However, they are obliged to comply with certain barrio duties because they are barrio citizens. These include projects such as paving the barrio roads and attending barrio and municipal assemblies. De la Fuente mentions that Catholicism was the only religious institution in Yalálag until the late 1940s (1949, 275). Protestantism was incorporated in the village in late 1960s.

15. In Yalálag, there are three main churches: 1) San Juan Bautista, also known as San Juan Yalálag, 2) San Antonio de Padua, and 3) Santiago Apóstol. In addition, there are seventeen chapels. Among them are the three barrio chapels (Santa Catarina Mártir, Santa Rosa de Lima, and San Juan Bautista), plus four *ermitas* (small chapels). The location of the *ermitas* is based on the four cardinal directions.

16. In Oaxaca City, immigrants refer to these events as *Bailes Serranos*.

17. Jeremías Ríos formed the Alma Oaxaqueña brass band. Today, it no longer exists.

18. *Los Cuerudos* is "The ones in skins," referring to the *cueras*, jackets; *San José* is "[The dance of] Saint Joseph"; *Los Huenches* is "[The dance of the] ancient Yalálag Zapotecs"; and "*Los Negritos*" is "[Dance of] black folks" (as diminutive).

19. Various scholars writing about transnationalism have argued that while immigrants are in the process of adjusting to the host society, they are also linked to their communities of origin economically, culturally, and politically (Glick Schiller and Fouron 2001; Kivisto 2001; Levitt 2001a; Smith 2006).

20. For a detailed ethnography of the *bailes*, see Cruz-Manjarrez 2009.

21. For example, in 1994, the passage of Proposition 187 in California denied services such as education and health care to undocumented immigrants and their children. In December 2005, a bill introduced by House Judiciary Committee chairman James Sensenbrenner (R-WI) introduced the "Border Protection, Antiterrorism, and Illegal Immigration Control Act of 2005" (H.R. 4437), intended to make it harder for legal immigrants to become U.S. citizens. In addition, it criminalizes undocumented immigrants. It broadens the definition of smuggling to include anyone who aids undocumented immigrants. In November 2005, U.S. Congressman Duncan Hunter, chairman of the House Armed Services Committee, called for the introduction of a reinforced fence along the entire U.S.-Mexican border. It would include a 100-meter border zone on the U.S. side.

22. For a more detailed analysis of the notion of social and symbolic ties as constructs of community and as a form of social capital, see Coleman 1988, 1990; de Souza B. 2004; Faist 2000a, 2000b; Light 2004; and Portes 1998b.

23. I am also following Light's concept of social capital as "a set of 'relationships of trust embedded in social networks'" (Light 2004, 5).

24. The institution of the *guelaguteza* has been widely studied by de la Fuente 1949, Kearney 1986, Stephen 2005b, and Young 1976. They describe *guelaguetza* in relation to agricultural production, house construction, and exchange of goods for ritual and ceremonial purposes at the family, barrio, and individual levels in various Zapotec villages.

25. In Los Angeles, there are at least thirteen brass bands from different Zapotec villages: 1) Banda Filarmónica de Yalálag, 2) Banda Nueva Imágen, Yalálag, 3) Banda Yaatzachi El Alto, 4) Banda Yaatzachi El Bajo, 5) Banda Zoogocho, 6) Banda Xochistepec, 7) Banda San Andrés Yaa, 8) Banda Zempoaltepetl, 9) Banda Filarmónica Juvenil Solaga-USA, 10) Banda de Santa Catarina Albarradas, 11) Banda Filarmónica Yohueche, 12) Banda Regional Yatee, and 13) Banda San Jerónimo Zoochina.

26. Mario Molina Cruz has won two awards: the Premio Nacional de Cuento, Mito y Leyenda "Andrés Henestrosa" in 2002 and Premio Nacional Nezahualcoyotl de Literatura in 2006.

27. The Spanish word *pueblo* has two meanings in Mexico. It refers to indigenous communities or ethnic groups (similar to indigenous nations in the United States). It also denotes a village.

28. There are three social institutions that regulate community life in Yalálag: the *cargo* system, the communal assembly, and communal work.

29. According to Aquino, in Yalálag, a Yalaltec man or woman becomes a citizen under the following criteria: He or she must: a) reside in Yalálag and be born within the Yalaltec community; immigrants maintain their citizenship and their communal rights as long as they fulfill their obligations; b) be eighteen years of age, produce their own corn, and be married; c) comply with communal work and public posts; and d) follow and respect community values. All Yalaltec citizens have the following rights as long as they comply with their obligations: a) access to public services; b) the right to participate and vote in communal assemblies; c) the right to participate in the municipality; and d) freedom of speech, of religion, of press, and property (2002, 148). As I argue throughout this book, Yalaltecos do not constitute a homogenous community. They differ in terms of schooling, class, the number of languages they speak, wealth, and religious affiliations. However, all of them are considered Yalaltec citizen as long as they respect their obligations and rights. For a detailed analysis of internal differences among Yalaltecos, see chapters 4 and 5.

30. For a broader discussion on the *sistema de usos y costumbres* see Aquino 2002, Besserer 2002, Bonfil Batalla 1996, Fox and Rivera-Salgado 2004, Hirabayashi 1993, Kearney 1972, Rivera-Salgado 1999, and Young 1976.

31. The *cargo* system is composed of: municipal president (1), *sindico* (1), *alcalde* (1), municipal secretary (1), treasurer (1), *secretario del tesorero* (assistant treasurer) (1), *secretario del registro civil* (1), *regidores de hacienda* (2), *regidores de educación* (2), *regidores de salud* (2), *regidores de obras* (2), *Comité Clinica del IMSS* (Health Care Committee of Mexican Institute of Social Security) (6), *Comité de Agua Potable* (Potable Water System Committee) (7), *Comité Secundaria Técnica no. 95* (Middle School Committee) (7), *Comité de Escuela Primaria* (Elementary School Committee) (11), *Comité de Educación Pre-escolar* (Kindergarten Committee) (3), *Comité de Parroquia San Juan* (Committee of the Church of San Juan) (11), *Comité Capilla San Antonio* (Committee of the Chapel of San Antonio) (7),

Comité de Fiestas Patronales (Patron Saint Fiestas Committee) (7), *auxiliaries* (assistants) (29), policemen (40), and police chief (1); see Aquino 2002, 140.

32. During colonial times, the conquerors introduced the Spanish administrative and political system in the Sierra villages (Young 1976). The conquerors gave a certain degree of autonomy to the Zapotec villages to take care of their own affairs. The Spanish also allowed Zapotec *caciques* or *principales* to participate in some high ranks of this system to help them control Indian labor, collect tribute payments for the conquerors, and "minimize the need for a large bureaucratic apparatus" (142). Men worked in religious *cargos* first and then in the political or administrative posts.

33. Nader (in Young 1976) and Young 1976 point out that service to the community also constitutes a source of social prestige. Service ranks Zapotecs into a single social hierarchy.

34. It is important to mention here that historically Zapotecs have differentiated themselves by class (Chance 1978, 1986; de la Fuente 1949; Young 1976). Currently, in terms of complying with a civic or religious post, richer men or immigrants in Yalálag may pay someone in the village to fulfill his *cargo*. Middle-class or poor men who refuse to comply with their *cargos* and do not have money to pay for a substitute may leave the village to work and return a few months later. Young 1976 describes the same situation in her work on the community of Copa Bitoo.

35. A decade ago in Yalálag, the term for the *cargo* holders lasted about three years. Because it has become difficult to comply with this period, the public posts have become shorter.

36. Cruz-Manjarrez 2005, Mendoza 2000, Rodriguez 1996, and Sklar 2001 offer a detailed description of the meaning of working for or performing as a way of fulfilling a *promesa* among indigenous people.

37. In his poem "Cuando Regrese a mi Pueblo" (When I return to my village), Molina 2004 writes about the Yalaltecos' experience of leaving and then being back in Yalálag.

38. *El Oaxaqueño,* July 26, 2003, 22.

39. In many Zapotec villages, the Zapotecs use *guelaguetza* notebooks to document the amount of money, transactions, or goods that Zapotecs have to give back (cf. Stephen 2005b). In Yalálag and Los Angeles, the barrio committees or the fiesta committees document the amount of money Yalaltecos voluntarily offer for the community fiestas in *guelaguetza* notebooks.

CHAPTER 3 — COMMUNITY LIFE ACROSS BORDERS

1. The bullring, known as the corral, is a fenced area where the bullfights take place.

2. As mentioned in chapter 2, in Yalálag, the majority of Catholics are Yalaltecos. Protestants are mostly Mixes. With the establishment of the first Protestant church in Yalálag (1966), people were divided between Catholics and Protestants. Currently, Protestants do not participate in the religious life of the Catholic population and are not required to comply with religious posts or *cargos* (see chapter 2 p. 79 for further explanation). In the past, there were confrontations between these two groups because converting to Protestantism signaled a rupture with the Catholic Church and implied failure to comply with religious *cargos*.

3. There are colonial documents that describe court trials for idolatry and "pagan" rituals in Yalálag and neighboring Zapotec villages. See Alcina 1993, 167–168; Calvo 2010, 193; Chance 1989, 151–175; de Villa-Señor y Sánchez 1994, 62–63; Zilbermann 1994, 149–151.

4. In the *Auto criminal contra la República de* Yalálag *por idolotría. N, 235, fs. 3. Año del 1735, Archivos de Villa Alta* (de la Fuente 1994, 100). My translation.

5. In Yalálag, this pastor is a married Catholic minister who is not officially recognized by the Catholic Church, but is allowed to assist the priest and give spiritual advice to the Yalaltecos.

6. Between 2002 and 2003, Francisco Diego's family from Los Angeles restored the latter.

7. Archaeologists of the National Institute of Anthropology and History found a pre-Columbian burial site right behind the Church of San Juan Bautista.

8. In July 2004, during a communal assembly, the elders proposed that the villagers take the younger generations to the *manantiales* (where the water springs). According to the elders, the younger generations do not know where the water is born and the significance of these sacred places.

9. Chance 1989 describes the same type of ceremony during the eighteen century.

10. Due to lack of Catholic priests in the village and in the region, there is only one priest in Yalálag. In fact, Father Adrian, who lives in Yalálag, is responsible for offering religious services in six neighboring villages. During weekdays, he travels to these villages to offer his services.

11. Compare Brettell 2003, Fitzgerald 2000, Goldring 1992, Malpica 2007, Stephen 2002.

12. *XV años* or *quinceañeras* are rites of passage into womanhood at the age of fifteen.

13. Father Adrian mentioned that although it is difficult to translate the gospel into Zapotec, he does his best to do it in his sermon. It is important to mention here that the Yalálag Protestants have a Bible translated in Zapotec. The translation was made by the Summer Linguistic Institute.

14. In the late seventeenth century, the Spanish conquerors introduced cattle and *ganado menor* (sheep and goats) and granted Zapotecs viceregal licenses for ranching and herding. In 1694, a license to raise cattle was given to a cacique in Yalálag (Chance 1989, 111). The first mention of a cattle ranch in Yalálag is in 1717 (Chance 1989, 92).

15. The *convite* is a late afternoon procession. To the music of local brass bands, a delegation of children and the fiesta committee walk through the village announcing that the main day of the fiesta is about to start. The procession invites all Yalaltecos and visitors to attend all the events. This procession takes place on June 11, two days before the celebration. The *calenda* is a late evening walk that starts around 8 p.m. and ends at 2 or 3 a.m. Along with the Zapotec brass bands, the residents and the visitors dance through the village as an invitation to the celebration on June 13. *La Calenda* takes place on June 11; in recent years, it also takes place on June 12. The *maitines* is a mass that takes place on June 12. It is accompanied by one of the local brass bands and the church choir. The *octava* is a one-day fiesta that occurs a week after June 13. The fiesta committee organizes a *baile popular*, a traditional bullfight, and a mass.

16. As noted in chapter 1, although the fiesta of San Antonio provides a context for family reunification, it is also the time when many young teenagers leave for the United States.

17. Compare Adler 2004, Brettell 2003, Fitzgerald 2000, Goldring 1998, Levitt 2001a, Rouse 1989, Smith 1995 and 2006).

18. Nowadays, everyone attending the fiesta, that is, locals, visitors, and immigrants, can participate in any event and eat for nine consecutive days for free.

19. The *baile popular* is a nightly social dance that takes place in the basketball court. *Cumbia* refers to a Colombian folk dance form and the ensemble that plays for the dance form. It is very popular in Mexico and Latin America. According to Herrera-Sobek, a Mexican song sung in *ranchero* style refers to the "sartorial mariachi dress, vocal, and performance style, specially if accompanied by a mariachi group" (2012, 201). *Norteña* music is a popular music genre born in the 1940s in the U.S.-Mexico borderlands. It is rooted in

the Mexican Revolution and currently stands as a symbol of Mexican national identity. For a further discussion see Ragland 2009.

20. The concept of soundscape was introduced by R. Murray Schafer in the 1970s to describe the multiple sounds that constitute the social environment.

21. I understand anomie here as the multiple negative effects of the migration process in Yalálag: family disintegration, the decline of social institutions, political division, and increasing emigration of men and women as well as the presence of gangs, the use of drugs, and crime.

22. For a detailed discussion on this topic in Zapotec and Mixtec communities, refer to Fox and Rivera-Salgado 2004, Hinojosa 2003, Kearney and Besserer 2004, Klaver 1997, López H. and Runsten 2004, Martínez-Saldaña 2004, Rivera-Salgado and Escala 2004, Velásquez C. 2004, and Woodman Colby 1998.

23. The U.S.-based Oaxacan indigenous communities have organized two major organizations: the migrant associations and the hometown associations (HTAs). The former are multiethnic organizations composed of Mexican indigenous migrants such as the Zapotec, Mixtec, Chatino, and P'urepecha communities, whose leaders are Mexican indigenous migrants and who collaborate to resolve common problems in the United States. These organizations aim to provide information to indigenous immigrants about their civil rights, changes in immigration laws, and new Mexican governmental programs for expatriate communities. They also offer a social platform for immigrants to organize politically in the United States and reinforce their identities as indigenous migrants, distinct from other Mexican immigrant communities or immigrant groups (Rivera-Salgado and Escala 2004, 106). The HTAs are community-based organizations usually known as *organizaciones de pueblo* (hometown associations), *comisiones de pueblo* (town committees), and *clubs de oriundos* or *clubs sociales comunitarios* (hometown clubs) that primarily provide economic and moral support and participate in the local politics of sending communities (Fox and Rivera-Salgado 2004).

24. In 1856, with the Desamortization Laws of 1856 (*Las Leyes de la Desamortización*), Yalálag lost its rights to communal land ownership, converting all land to private property (Gutiérrez Nájera 2007).

25. The Serrano fortunes, including those of Yalaltecos, were made from coffee production. Fortunes were amassed from trading coffee, not from plantation ownership and cultivation in Yalálag (Gutiérrez Nájera 2007, Hirabayashi 1993, Young 1976).

26. Ixtlán was the main military post for Porfirio Díaz's regime (Chassen 2005, Kearney 1972).

27. Aquino points out that currently Yalaltecos define the *cacique* as an individual who has political and social control over the village and is closely related to the PRI (2002, 39). I also found that some Yalaltecos define the *cacique* as someone who is wealthy, owns land, has political "control" over certain followers, and affiliates with leftist political parties and social organizations. Whether this is true or not, it is important to mention that both definitions have characterized the ways in which the cacique has been socially constructed. Although it is not my intention to question or discard Aquino's definition, it must be pointed out that the cacique is perceived as a central figure in Yalálag's social and political life because this individual has access to powerful positions, stands out among his followers, and owns extensive property. To clarify, some Yalaltec families have become wealthy through successful businesses, but among them, certain individuals have been identified as caciques because they have been in power or represent specific political interests.

28. Young 1976 points out that in the Serrano village of Copa Bitoo, local politicians encouraged some progressive leaders to form a branch of the PNR in the same year.

29. Young describes the same phenomenon in Copa Bitoo. When the PNR was founded, the elders were removed from power. The administrative apparatus and the relationship between municipal authorities and the federal and state governments were restructured (1976, 260).

30. In 1934, President Lazaro Cárdenas changed the name to Party of the Mexican Revolution (PRM). In 1946, President Manuel Ávila Camacho gave the party its present name, PRI, Partido Revolucionario Institucional. In Yalálag, the PRN Municipal Committee became Comité Municipal del PRI.

31. It is important to note that in Oaxaca, people in power—whether governors, municipal presidents, or caciques—have changed political affiliations during their terms. They do so according to their own political and economic interests. This does not mean that some caudillos or political leaders were not loyal to their political and moral principles. This phenomenon has characterized the history of politics in Oaxaca.

32. On the regional level, in the 1980s, the Groupo Comunitario joined AAZACHI (Assembly of the Chinantec and Zapotecs Authorities), ASAM (Assembly of Mixe Communities), and ODRENASIJ (Organization for the Defense of Natural Resources and Social Development in the Sierra Juárez). The purpose was to support and be included in an indigenous organization that worked on behalf of the indigenous communities in the Sierra, by reconstructing public roads, for example. On the national level, in the 1990s, the Grupo Comunitario creates links with the EZLN (Zapatista Army of National Liberation) and the Movimiento Nacional Indígena. They joined the national struggle for communal autonomy and the right to self-determination among indigenous Mexican communities (Aquino 2010). For a detailed discussion about the proposed plan, see Aquino 2002, 52.

33. Aquino 2002 suggests that Yalaltecos lack a common definition for justice, which helps to perpetuate these divisions.

34. Rivera-Salgado 1999 observes that Mixtec immigrant men are expected to return to their home villages to comply with their *tequio* (communal work) commitments as part of their civic obligations. When they cannot comply with civic or political *cargos,* they are allowed to hire someone in the village to fill their public posts. Kearney and Besserer 2004 indicate that in other Mixtec communities, the municipality calls on immigrants who reside in Mexico and in the United States to serve in the local government between one to three years. Woodman Colby found in her 1998 study of returning migration in the region of La Mixteca Alta that, before 1994, Mixtec immigrant men were required to return for three years to fill public posts. Recently, the term has changed due to migrants' increasing dependency on the income that migration provides and the difficulties of moving back and forth between Mexico and the United States. In some Zapotec communities of the Central Valleys of Oaxaca, immigrants have not been summoned back to their village to fill civic, religious, or political positions (Klaver 1997, 189). However, they contribute economically towards development projects and religious festivals in order to demonstrate their commitment to their village and retain their membership and rights. In other Zapotec communities, immigrants return to comply with religious *cargos,* such as the *mayordomo* of the patron saint fiesta. In the village San Lucas Quiavini, for example, the *mayordomos,* appointed in a communal assembly or serving as volunteers, fulfill religious obligations by financing and organizing the village's patron saint fiesta (Hulshof 1991).

35. Immigrants have the right to vote in Yalálag local elections. However, they are not allowed to take a civic or political *cargo* because they do not live there and cannot stay for the term of service.

36. This experience also applies to Mixtec and Zapotec communities (cf. Kearney 2000, Kearney and Besserer 2004, Rivera-Salgado 1999, Velásquez C. 2004, Woodman Colby 1998).

37. Since its inception, the Unión Yalalteca has only concentrated on its first goal.

38. In the late 1980s, there was an attempt to form the first HTA, called Unión Yalalteca of Los Angeles. Because most of its founders supported one of the political parties and its projects, however, Yalaltec immigrants could not support this association.

39. Nevertheless, they did participate in various cultural events organized by indigenous organizations such as the ORO (Oaxacan Regional Organization) and FIOB (Oaxacan Indigenous Binational Front). Among them are the Guelaguetza festivals, the Day of the Dead, and the Catholic festivals of Oaxaca.

CHAPTER 4 — YALÁLAG ZAPOTEC IDENTITIES IN A CHANGING WORLD

1. The Zapotecs are the sixth most populous indigenous group in Mexico. According to the Mexican census, there are 460,695 Zapotecs (INEGI 2010c). The two most populous indigenous groups in Mexico are the Nahuas and the Mayas.

2. De la Fuente 1994, Hirabayashi 1993, Muntzel and Pérez González 1987, Nader 1969.

3. According to the U.S. census, "American Indian or Alaska Native refers to a person having origins in any of the original peoples of North and South America (including Central America) and who maintains tribal affiliation or community attachment. This category includes people who indicated their race(s) as 'American Indian or Alaska Native' or reported their enrolled or principal tribe, such as Navajo, Blackfeet, Inupiat, Yup'ik, or Central American Indian groups or South American Indian groups" (Humes, Jones, and Ramírez 2011, 3). Also according to the U.S. Census Bureau, the "question on Hispanic origin is an ethnicity question and not a place of birth question. . . . It can include people born in Mexico, in the United States or in another country" (Ennis, Ríos-Vargas, and Albert 2011, 2).

4. In the 2000 census, 674,601 Hispanics said they were American Indians or Alaska Natives, either as their only race or in combination with another race. Of this total, 407,073 Hispanics said they were American Indians or Alaska Natives, and that was their only race.

5. This is a racial category that refers to people in Mexico of a mixed race: indigenous, Spanish, and African roots and blood. This category has its roots in the sixteen century, when the Spanish conquerors divided the New World society according to "purity of blood," namely, in terms of their "descent and race" (Wimmer 2002).

6. In Mexico, an ethnic group is a concept used by social scientists to describe a social unit that is historically, linguistically, and culturally different. It is characterized by traditional forms of social organization that have been passed from one generation to another. An ethnic group is a minority that interacts with other ethnic minorities and with a majority group (Giménez 1994).

7. In February 2005, U.S. president George W. Bush and Mexican president Vicente Fox signed a migratory agreement that allows undocumented Mexican immigrants to have a legal ID. "For Mexicans in the United States, IDs facilitate the opening of checking and savings accounts and dozens of other banking transactions; it makes it easier and economic for them to send money to relatives in Mexico along with other practical benefits like being able to attain electric and water services. In some States, the official document serves primarily to obtain a drivers' license," http://www.sre.gob.mx/losangeles/.

8. For a further discussion on the drastic changes in current official discourse on ethnic diversity and multiulturalism in Mexico, see Díaz Polanco 1991, Olivé 1999, Stavenhagen 2008, Wimmer 2002.

9. Tsuda (2003, 246) points out that before migration, transnational minority immigrant communities usually do not assert a sense of national identity. He claims that transnational migrants develop a national consciousness and a deterritorialized migrant nationalism when their communities and connections spread across the borders of two or more nation states.

10. This language belongs to the Otomanguean linguistic family and is related to other Indian languages such as Otomi, Mazahua, Pame, and Ocuilteco. Avelino 2004, Nader 1969, and Swadesh 1949 suggest that Zapotec may not be only one language, but also different languages. The Zapotec language presents different phonetics, morpho-syntactic and lexical features among its dialects, but the number of mutually unintelligible Zapotec languages remains undetermined by the experts. Chance 1989 points out that there are four Zapotec language areas in Oaxaca: the Valley Zapotec, the Isthmus Zapotec, the Sierra Norte Zapotec, and the Sierra Sur Zapotec. He also indicates that in the Sierra Norte, there are four Zapotec language groups: Serrano, Nexitzo, Cajonos, and Bixanos. Yalálag Zapotec belongs to the Cajonos language group.

11. Refer to the appendix for a detailed description of the study site in Los Angeles.

12. In Mexico the official language for schooling is Spanish.

13. Aquino 2002, Berteley 1996, and de la Fuente 1949 discuss how Yalaltecos have internalized a negative image of themselves since the 1950s as a result of racial and linguistic discrimination. As they socialize with Mexican mestizos in surrounding mestizo villages and immigrate to Oaxaca City and Mexico City, they have seen themselves as "ignorant," "uncivilized," "closed minded," and "traditional." In the last three decades, in Yalálag, many Yalaltecos have changed these negative views.

14. The age of consent in the state of California is eighteen, so girls must be eighteen years old before marrying.

15. Social remittances (Levitt 2001) are ideas, behaviors, identities, and social capital that flow from host to sending communities. Immigrants carry these social and cultural resources to their communities and have an impact in the social life of home communities and non-immigrants.

16. *Oaxaquitas* is a pejorative term that denotes the diminutive form used for Indians from Oaxaca. It does not distinguish between ethnic groups. The term *yope* is used to characterize Oaxacan indigenous immigrants that have gone to work in the city of Oaxaca as peons and domestic workers.

17. In contrast to the Yalaltecos, some immigrants such as Koreans, Iranians, and South Asians come with a higher class standing, capital, and education skills.

18. In Spanish, *moreno* means brown person. In the United States, Yalaltecos use the term *moreno* instead of *negro* (black) to describe the racial characteristics of African Americans, since the latter has pejorative connotations.

19. Although I agree that identities articulate several ideas, narratives, practices, elements, and the mixing of codes, I disagree with the idea that identities are experienced as fragmented. Despite the perceptions of outsiders of immigrant cultures, immigrant individuals living in a transnational context may live their lives as integrated selves.

20. For a detailed discussion on the ideology of integration and the politics of cultural assimilation of indigenous Mexican peoples in Mexico, see Wimmer 2002. See Kearney

1999 and 2000, and Rumbaut 1999, for an analysis of the assimilationist model of socio-economic and cultural integration of foreigners in the United States.

21. I follow King's 1995 definition of modernity. King conceptualizes modernity as an invention of the West that emerged during the creation of nation-states. He suggests that the invention of a modern society is associated with the assumption that premodern societies are rural, are technologically undeveloped, and have experienced a certain degree of social backwardness. In contrast, modern societies are associated with industrialization, economic development, progress, technology, and cosmopolitanism. In the same line of thought, Kearney 1999 points out that one of the projects of modernity has been to transform premodern societies into modern groups. Modernity is expected to replace what is rural, traditional, and nonindustrial. One of many assumptions is that peasant societies will transition into modernity, as modern societies have already done.

22. I have to mention that many Yalaltecos still believe that assimilation into the Mexican or American mainstream is synonymous with progress and modernity. Convinced by Western ideas of modernity, they believe they still lag behind the economic and social progress of modernity.

23. I do not want to imply that Yalaltecos have not resisted colonial domination since colonial times. But I want to account for the present-day experiences of the Yalaltecos I have encountered and engaged with.

24. I do not include here all the social and cultural changes that occurred after Spanish colonization.

25. It is important to note that the first and latest waves of immigrants have had differing expectations and ideas of success. Yalaltecos who left their village in the 1960s and 1970s migrated to the United States because of extreme poverty. Although the main reason to migrate was for work, they also wanted to pursue a career. In schooling, 70 percent of my interviewees finished elementary school and about 10 percent went to middle school. In contrast, most of the Yalaltecos who left after 1980 reached middle school, and some went to college. These immigrants told me that they left Mexico because of the lack of opportunities for employment and education in Yalálag, Oaxaca City, and Mexico City, not because of extreme poverty. Contemporary Yalaltecos who come to Los Angeles are not interested in studying. They migrate exclusively for work and better earning opportunities.

CHAPTER 5 — IDENTITIES OF THE SECOND-GENERATION YALÁLAG ZAPOTECS

1. I employ the term "second-generation Yalálag Zapotecs" to refer to the descendants of Yalatec immigrants who are born in the United States. Its fixed, unambiguous meaning refers to the ethnic identity of U.S.-born Yalálag Zapotec adolescents and acknowledges their cultural and historical background. It is important to mention that the "second-generation Yalálag Zapotecs" do not use this term to identify themselves. Depending on the situation, they call themselves Yalaltecos or Oaxaqueños when they want to highlight their indigenous ethnicity with the Yalaltec or Oaxacan community.

2. I use the term "Mexican American" to refer to American citizens of Mexican descent. According to Gutiérrez 1995, the concept of Mexican American identity is complex and within the U.S. Mexican community is highly politicized. For a detailed discussion on these multiple forms of Mexican American identification, see also Rosales 1997 and 1999, and Sánchez 1993.

3. As described in chapter 4, in Mexico, indigenous Mexican peoples are Mexican nationals but have been treated as foreigners and denied full membership as Mexican

citizens because they have not given up their culture, language, and natives forms of social organization.

4. A few immigrants explained that they studied some Spanish at school. The great majority of my informants told me that they acquired Spanish as a second language when they went to work in Oaxaca City and Los Angeles.

5. Most children of Yalaltec immigrants in Mexico City do not learn Zapotec, either. In Oaxaca City, it is more common to find that the children of Yalaltec immigrants speak Zapotec.

6. According to the U.S. census, "White" is a racial label that refers to a "person having origins in any of the original people of Europe, the Middle East or North Africa. It includes people who indicate that their race(s) as 'White' or reported entries such as Irish, German, Italian, Lebanese, Arab, Moroccan, or Caucasian" (Humes, Jones, and Ramírez 2011, 3).

7. This sense of Mexican American identity is different from that of Mexican-American. The latter existed only from the first half of the twentieth century, particularly in Texas. The term "Mexican American" suggests a long historical continuity through generations.

8. Muñoz 1989 and Matute Bianchi 1986 observe that the legacy of assimilationist policies in the United States has made the retention of Spanish difficult for many second-generation Mexican Americans, because the U.S. educational system supports English as the hegemonic and official language.

9. "Aztlán" refers to the present-day Southwest of the United States where the Chicano movement arose (Rosales 1997, 253).

10. The second-generation Yalaltecos, who have become gang members, have joined the following gangs: 18th Street, Harpys, Playboys, Aztlan, and Burlington. These gangs are not Oaxacan gangs. They are made up of Mexican Americans. This information was provided by the second-generation Yalaltecos I interviewed.

11. Stephen 2007a describes a similar pattern among second-generation Mixtecs in Oregon.

12. This is an annual festival of indigenous dance and music founded in 1989 and organized by the Zapotec immigrant communities in Los Angeles.

13. According to the Mexican census of 2000, 42.3 percent of Oaxaqueños identified as indigenous (INEGI 2004).

14. I use the labels "indigenous" or "Indian" in two ways. First, I use them to describe the identity of the Zapotecs as native people of the American continent. Second, I utilize Indian as a racial construct used by Mexican mestizos to characterize indigenous people in derogatory terms.

15. I thank one of the reviewers for the following comment: In California, the development of a Oaxacan identity in terms of a pan-ethnic Oaxacan indigenous identity is creatively expressed in the pan-Oaxacan festivals like the Guelaguetza, one that "is billed as Oaxacan, but with the inclusion of specific local/ethnic identities such as Mixtec, Mixe, Triqui, and Chatino within this larger frame."

CHAPTER 6 — *DANZAS CHUSCAS*

1. Michael Kearney coined this term in his work on Mixtec and Zapotec migration to the United States. He refers to Oaxacalifornia as a social, political, cultural, and public space in which Oaxacan indigenous immigrants connect their lives and community projects with their communities of origin. Oaxacalifornia constitutes a "third sociocultural and political space" because new forms of community, agency, politics, and ethnicity are

created. The name *Oaxacalifornia* "implies both a fusion of aspects of life and society in Oaxaca and in California and a transcendence of them" (2000, 182).

2. The *gwzon* or *guelaguetza* is a system of reciprocal aid. This type of relationship can be between individuals and/or groups, and also between people and patron saints. The latter is a *gwzon* of faith. For a more detailed discussion about this practice, see chapter 2.

3. Immigrants make also monetary *promesas* to other Yalálag patron saints: San Juan Bautista, Santa Rosa de Lima, Santa Catarina Mártir, and Santiago Apóstol.

4. Brettell 2003 and Levitt 2001a describe a similar phenomenon among Portuguese and Miraflores immigrants in Lahneses, Portugal, and Miraflores, Dominican Republic.

5. See Adler 2004, Brettell 2003, Glick Schiller and Fouron 2001, Ebaugh and Chafetz 2002, Levitt 2001a.

6. In the 1966, with the establishment of the first Protestant church in Yalálag, Yalaltecos divided into Catholics and Protestants. The latter do not participate in the religious life of the Catholic population and are not obliged to comply with religious posts. In the past, there were confrontations between these two groups because converting into Protestantism was a sign of rupture with the Catholic Church and its practitioners. Also, not complying with religious *cargos* began to create social disorganization—the Protestants stopped complying with their obligations to their community. Later, they began to fight against the Catholic population to establish their own church.

7. Brettell 2003, Goldring 1992, 1998, and Rouse 1995 described the same issue among immigrants in Mexico and Portugal.

8. For a discussion of other United States immigrants behaving this way, see Brettell 2003; Levitt 2001a; Mandel 1989, as cited in Brettell 2000, 101; and Smith 1995.

9. Zárate Rosales indicates that the participation of indigenous women in ritual dances has been restricted since the pre-Hispanic times. Currently, the Totonacs, Tenek, and Nahuas among other indigenous groups consider that only men should dance during ritual fiestas. This is so because it is believed that there is a unique "bond between men and gods." There is a series of requirements that men must fulfill to participate in ritual dances: sexual abstention, fasting, and isolation from society and women. Fertile women have been restricted from ritual dancing because they represent "all that can alter the states of purification and all that is susceptible to sin, sexual tension . . . they are associated with that which is 'dirty,' such as menstruation" (2009, 141).

10. Although all *danzas chuscas* are historically performed by men, in recent years, young single women or girls have started to participate in *chusca* and religious dances. In both Yalálag and Los Angeles, girls participate in the dances such as *Los Chinantecos*, the *Huenches*, *Los Serranos*, the *Malinches*, and *San José*. At this celebration, I saw a teenage girl performing as a male character in the dance of *Los Norteños* because a male dancer was missing. It is possible that women's participation in the dance is related to changes in gender ideology experienced in the migration context. As discussed elsewhere (Cruz-Manjarrez 2009), in the early 1990s, in Los Angeles, young Yalaltec women were integrated for the first time in ritual dances.

11. Although many parodic dances, as this one, are used to criticize immigrants, there are a great number of *danzas chuscas* that make fun of local people, children, local political leaders, Zapotecs from other villages, and neighboring indigenous groups such as the Mixes and the Chinantecos.

12. The *cholos* represent a new type of social identity in Yalálag, and the community criticizes them and feels upset about their behaviors but does not exclude them. That is, they participate in community and family fiestas. In this fiesta of San Antonio, for

example, some of them were doing community labor for the event such as helping the fiesta committee to bring the bulls for the bullfights and helping to build the bullring. They were also socializing with village people and relatives.

13. I thank Allen Roberts for pointing out that L.A. *cholo* fashion is an adaptation of African American hip-hop chic.

14. Hamilton and Stoltz Chinchilla 2001; Levitt 2001a; and Smith 1995 and 2006 have made the same argument.

15. For more information related to gangs in Los Angeles, see National Alliance of Gang Investigators' Association, www.nagla.org.

16. See Liebel 2005 for a discussion on barrio gangs of Latino origin in the United States.

17. It is important to point out that alcoholics also harm locals, but since residents feel more threatened by and afraid of the *cholos*, residents prefer to accuse them.

18. In other Zapotec villages, municipal authorities have tried to negotiate with *cholos* by asking them to leave the village or integrate themselves into the social life of the community. Nonetheless, heated discussions between local people and the *cholos* have led to violent confrontations. In last five years, the Zapotec village of San Mateo Cajonos has been burdened by the permanent establishment of *pandillas* and their hated acts of vandalism. In this village the level of violence escalated to a shocking degree when quarrels between locals and *cholos* turned into machete fights.

19. While they perform these group movements, they have to maintain a combination of four different steps. The majority of the Yalálag Zapotec *chusca* dances are based on a combination of step-hop-point/step-hop-point, hop-step/step, and a step-hop-point.

20. Vigil 1988 points out that multiple factors may lead to the development of a gang identity within the Mexican community in the United States. Immigrant teens and members of the second generation who cannot handle social adaptation to American society are victims of ethnic, cultural, class, and racial discrimination and exclusion. They may experience stressful family situations, economic instability, and social clashes with family members and peers, and they may lack opportunities for acquiring a good education. All these factors may lead to drugs and alcohol addiction and other antisocial behaviors.

21. Hondagneu-Sotelo 1994 and Mendoza 2000 have found similar experiences among Mexican mestizo migrants and Peruvian mestizo and indigenous migrants. Lynn Stephen 2002 shows similar patterns among Zapotec immigrants of the Central Valleys who live in California.

22. See Hondagneu-Sotelo 1994, 2003; Hirsch 2003, 2007; Malkin 2007; and Menjivar 2003 for further discussion of the changing gender roles and ideology of Mexican immigrant women in the United States.

23. As mentioned above, *danzas chuscas* are always performed by men in two lines, one of four female characters and the other of four male ones.

24. See Cruz-Manjarrez 2006, Fox and Rivera-Salgado 2004, Hulshof 1991, Klaver 1997, Stephen 2007c.

CHAPTER 7 — COMMUNITY AND CULTURE IN TRANSNATIONAL PERSPECTIVE

1. The *ermitas* are tiny chapels located in the Yalaltec hills. Each chapel is dedicated to specific patron saints. According to Molina, these chapels were built in pre-Hispanic religious sites.

2. This cultural center was founded in January of 1995. Its origin dates back to 1982, when a group of Yalaltecos organized the Taller de Lecto-Escritura de La Lengua Zapoteca.

Currently, it is a civic association, and its name is Taller de Investigación y Difusión de la Lengua y la Cultura Zapoteca Uken ke Uken A.C.

3. The peasant family was not asked to revive the ceremony. Rather, they were willing to be filmed during the corn ceremony they had planned.

4. During the fiesta of Santa Rosa de Lima, the barrio committee places the patron saint in the chapel patio. The image is not returned to its altar until the fiesta ends.

5. A drum player and a flutist accompany this dance. Yalaltecos consider these musicians sacred.

6. *Petates* are used to sit or to sleep on (as a bed). They are also used for drying grains, coffee, and chili. Yalaltecos, who are very poor, are still buried in *petates*. Families that can afford a coffin buy one to bury their relatives. The baskets used here usually store coffee, chili, beans, and corn.

7. The incorporation of plastic masks is related to the disappearance of wooden mask makers in Yalálag.

8. The dance ensemble of *Los Huenches* is usually invited to perform in private homes. Because some Yalaltecos have altars in their homes, they invite the *huenches* to perform for their sacred images in the days of the saint's fiestas.

9. Some Yalaltecos rent their fields to other Yalaltecos or Mixe immigrants.

10. CONASUPO (National Company of Popular Subsistance) is a Mexican state agency.

11. In Yalálag, there is a Mixe immigrant community. Unlike Yalálag Zapotecs, the Mixes have a great appreciation for the countryside and the value of working as peasants.

12. I used quotations for "original" to refer to the ways in which Zapotecs describe the loss of meaning of this dance.

13. Research on Mesoamerican cosmology suggests that Mexican indigenous groups such as the Nahuas, Huicholes, Yaquis, and Mayos have considered deer as sacred animals. López Austin 1980 mentions that the Aztecs did so because it was believed to be a messenger between the pre-Hispanic deities and human beings. Olmos Aguilera indicates that the deer is the symbol of the Yaqui identity. Yaquis believe that every night during Holy Week the deer transforms into man to teach the Yaquis their dance and the secrets of nature (1998, 79).

14. An old man in Yalálag told me that in the past, thirteen teenage boys and thirteen men performed this dance. The former represented the *maiz tierno* (baby corn) and the latter the *maiz maduro* (mature corn).

15. Yalaltecos do not bait and kill the bulls as mestizo bullfighters do.

16. According to the director of a brass band Filarmonica de Yalálag, each Yalaltec saint has its own sacred music.

17. The dance of San José is a religious dance of barrio Santa Catarina. It is thought of as the dance of Santa Catarina Mártir.

18. Perhaps the reader will think that there is a lot of hostility in this sketch toward the young maid and that it is unusual to use a sacred symbol like the Virgin Mary to make fun of someone. Although I do find this sketch somehow unpleasant with respect to the woman, I refrain from making an interpretation of this performance. After many years of interacting with the Yalaltecos, I found that they have a special sense of humor that I do not share and understand. They make fun of everything, especially themselves: men, women, children, elders, and youngsters. Thus, I leave open the reading of this sketch. Humor is a theme that needs further research.

GLOSSARY

baile. In Los Angeles, a *baile* is a community gathering. In Yalálag, it is a nighttime popular dance gathering.

barrio. A geopolitical area and social institution of Yalálag

bi gwlash. Zapotec term for countryman or countrywoman

cacicazgo. A sociopolitical institution ruled by a cacique and controlled by the state government

cacique. A local ruler or political boss

calenda. A late evening walk that starts around 10 p.m. and ends at 2 a.m. Along with the Zapotec brass bands, the residents and the visitors dance through the village as an invitation to the celebration of patron saint fiestas. It takes place two days before the major day patron saint fiesta takes place

calzón y camisa de manta. A white, long-sleeved shirt and white pants made of cotton

capitán de la danza. Dance leader

cargo. A religious, political, or civic post

cargo or *barrio-cargo* **system.** A local system of civil service or public service posts

carnicerías. Butcher shops

casa del barrio. Neighborhood cultural center

casa del pueblo. Community center of a village and the Kitchen village

Cerro Brujo. Bewitched Hill

caudillo. A military dictator

champurrado. A drink made of corn, sugar cane, and chocolate

Chicano. This term has various meanings. It denotes Mexicans born in the United States. It can also refer to Mexican gang members. It refers to a politicized identity of Mexicans born in the United States who reject the ideology of assimilation into Anglo-American mainstream culture and notions of Anglo superiority.

cholo. A Mexican American gang member

chuntis. Indian-looking or behaving

cirio. Paschal candle

cofradía. Sodality; a lay brotherhood responsible for financing religious services and maintaining the church

comisiones de festejos. Fiesta committees

comisiones de las iglesias. Church committees

comisiones de obras. Church reconstruction committees

compadrazgo. Godparenthood

convite. A late afternoon procession. Accompanied by the music of local brass bands, a delegation of children and the fiesta committee walk through the village announcing that the main day of the fiesta is about to start. The procession invites all Yalaltecos and visitors to attend all the events. This procession takes place on June 11, two days before the celebration of the festival of San Antonio de Padua.

corregidor. Spanish officer in charge of a local Indian district

corregimiento. Jurisdiction or office of a *corregidor*

coyote. **Smuggler**

danza chusca. Parodic dance

danzante. Dancer

FOCOICA. Oaxacan Federation of Indigenous Communities and Organizations in California

grupo tropical. A tropical music ensemble

gwzon. A system of reciprocity and mutual support in which person or group A does *gwzon* (gives or does a favor) for person or group B. Then, person(s) A trusts and expects that person(s) B will return this help in the future.

gwzon **of faith.** Relation of reciprocity with the Yalálag Catholic patron saints. It is an act of reciprocity with the Yalálag deities.

encomienda. Grant of an Indian town or towns, carrying the right to access tribute

El Norte. The United States

ermita. Small chapel

HTA (Hometown Association). A community organization of immigrants

huenche. A *nahuatl* word that means "old people." In Zapotec, the Yalálag Zapotec say *wench gure*, meaning "the ancient Zapotecs." The dance of *Los Huenches* translates as "the dance of the ancient Zapotecs."

INS. Immigration and Naturalization Service

IRCA. Immigration Reform and Control Act

jaripeo. Traditional bullfight

jarabe. A dance and a music genre. It is composed of a set of *sones* (dances) to be performed together.

'll xha. Zapotec dress

maítines. A mass that takes place on June 12. It is accompanied by one of the local brass bands and the church choir, who provide music and religious chants.

mayordomo. Sponsor of a religious celebration

mescal. An alcoholic drink made from the agave plant

NAFTA. North American Free Trade Agreement

Niño Dios. Christ child

norteño **music.** A popular music genre born in the 1940s in the U.S.-Mexico borderlands. Rooted in the Mexican Revolution, it currently stands as a symbol of Mexican national identity.

octava. A one-day fiesta a week after the festival of June 13

ORO. The transnational, multiethnic Oaxacan Regional Organization

paisano/a. Spanish word that means countryman or countrywoman

pandillerismo. Hooliganism, gang activity

PNR. Partido Nacional Revolucionario, forerunner to the PRI

pochos. A word used in the United States and in Mexico to describe Mexicans born in the United States. A word used in Central American to designate indigenous workers on banana plantations, viewed by white and *mestizo* workers as "unskilled, uncultured natives" (Enloe 1989, 134).

posada. Each of the nine days of celebration before Christmas

PRD. Democratic Revolutionary Party

PRI. Partido Revolucionario Institucional

progresistas or *castellanizados.* Progressives; Mexicanized

promesa. A sacred vow, an offering consisting of dancing, playing music, or offering food, flowers, candles, incense, and money for the realization of patron saint fiestas

quinceañera. A rite of passage into womanhood at the age of 15. In Mexico, it is known as *XV años* celebration.

radg be?. The Hill Where the Wind Cuts

rboz. A shawl

rezador(a). Someone who recites Catholic prayers or leads a rosary

rústicos or *cerrados.* Conservatives

servicio. Community work, *tequio*

son. A term used to describe a Zapotec dance piece or song

tequio. A system of mutual aid. It promotes communal work to benefit the community, the barrio, or the family.

tienditas. Little stores

tierra. Mother Earth

tortillerias. Tortilla stores

UNAM. Universidad Nacional Autónoma de México

vaqueros. Cowboys

vocales. Committee assistants

wench gure. Zapotec word that means "old people" or *huenche*

xhtap. Skirt

Yalálag. "Overflowing Hill," "Spread Hill," or "the Sliding Hill"

yope. A discriminatory term used by Oaxacan mestizos to discriminate against indigenous people. It means stupid, ignorant, brute, ugly, and stubborn.

Zapotec. "People from the clouds." In the Zapotec language, it reads as *ben' zaa.*

REFERENCES

Adler, Rachel. 2004. *Yucatecans in Dallas, Texas: Breaching the Border, Bridging the Distance.* Boston: Pearson.

Alcina F., José. 1993. *Calendario y religión entre los Zapotecos.* Mexico City: Universidad Nacional Autónoma de México, Instituto de Investigaciones Históricas.

Anderson, Benedict. 1983. "Introduction." In *Imagined Communities.* London: Verso.

Appadurai, Arjun. 1996. "Global Ethnoscapes: Notes and Queries for a Transnational Anthropology." In *Modernity at Large: Cultural Dimensions of Globalization.* Minneapolis: University of Minnesota Press.

Aquino, Alejandra. 2002. "Acción colectiva, autonomía, y conflicto: La reinvención de la identidad entre los Zapotcas de la Sierra Juárez." Masters thesis, Sociología, Instituto de Investigaciones Dr. José Luis Mora, Mexico City.

———. 2010. "Entre luttes indiennes et 'rêve américain': L'expérience migratoire des jeunes Indiens mexicains aux États-Unis." Doctoral dissertation, Sociologie, Ecole des Hautes Études en Sciences Sociales, Paris.

Arellanes M., Anselmo. 2005. "La Confederación de Partidos Socialistas." In *La Revolución en Oaxaca: 1900–1930,* edited by V. R. Martínez V. Oaxaca: Instituto de Administración Pública de Oaxaca. http://www.cseiio.edu.mx/biblioteca/libros/cienciassociales/historia _de_la_revolucion_en_oaxaca.pdf.

Avelino, Heriberto. 2004. "Topics in Yalálag Zapotec with Particular Reference to Its Phonetic Structures." Ph.D. dissertation, Linguistics, University of California Los Angeles.

Back, Les. 1995. "'Not something we're new to it's something we grow to . . .': Youth, Identification and Alliance." In *New Ethnicities and Urban Culture: Racisms and Multiculture in Young Lives.* London: University College London.

———. 1996. "'Ingland, nice up!': Black Music, Autonomy, and the Cultural Intermezzo." In *New Ethnicities.* London: University College London.

Barth, Frederick. 1969. "Introduction." In *Ethnic Groups and Boundaries: The Social Organization of Cultural Difference,* edited by F. Barth. London: George Allen & Unwin.

Bartolomé, M., and A. M. Barabas. 1986. "Los migrantes étnicos de Oaxaca." *México Indígena* 13 (2): 23–25.

Basch, Linda, Nina Glick Schiller, and Christine Blanc-Szanton. 1994. *Nations Unbound: Transnational Projects, Post-Colonial Predicaments, and Deterritorialized Nation-States.* Langhorne, Pa.: Gordon and Breach.

Baskes, Jeremy. 2000. *Indians, Merchants, and Markets: A Reinterpretation of the Repartimiento and Spanish-Indian Economic Relations in Colonial Oaxaca, 1750–1821*. Stanford: Stanford University Press.

Berg, Janine, Christoph Ernst, and Peter Auer. 2006. "The Evolution of the Labor Market in Argentina, Brazil, and Mexico." In *Meeting the Employment Challenge: Argentina, Brazil, and Mexico in the Global Economy*. Boulder, Col.: Lynne Rienner.

Bertely, Busquets Maria. 1996. *Aproximación histórica al estudio etnográfico de las relación indígenas migrantes y procesos escolares: Familias yalaltecas asentadas en la periferia metropolitana*. Edited by Instituto Superior de Ciencias de la Educación del Estado de México. Avances de Investigación 5. Toluca, Estado de México: Instituto Superior de la Educacion del Estado de México.

Besserer, Federico. 2002. "Contesting Community: Cultural Struggles of a Mixtec Transnational Community." Ph.D. dissertation, Anthropology, Stanford University.

Bonfil Batalla, Guillermo. 1996. *México Profundo: Reclaiming a Civilization*. Translated by P. A. Dennis. Austin: University of Texas Press.

Bourdieu, Pierre. 1983. "Ökonomisches Kapital, kulturelles Kapital soziales Kapital." In *Soziale Ungleichheiten, Soziale Welt*, edited by R. Kreckel. Göttingen: Otto Schwartz.

———. 1990. *In Other Words: Essays toward a Reflexive Sociology*. Stanford: Stanford University Press.

Brettell, Caroline. 2000. "Theorizing Migration in Anthropology: The Social Construction of Networks, Identities, Communities, and Globalscapes." In *Migration Theory: Talking across Disciplines*, edited by C. Brettell and J. F. Hollifield. New York: Routledge.

———. 2003. *Anthropology and Migration: Essays in Transnationalism, Ethnicity, and Identity*. Walnut Creek, Cal.: Altamira.

Calavita, Kitty. 1989. "The Immigration Policiy Debate: Critical Analysis and Future Options." In *Mexican Migration to the United States: Origins, Consequences, and Policy Options*, edited by W. A. Cornelius and J. A. Bustamante. La Jolla: University of California San Diego, Center for U.S.-Mexican Studies.

Calvo, Thomas. 2010. *Vencer la derrrota: Vivir en la Sierra Zapoteca de México (1674–1701)*. Mexico City: Colegio de Michoacán, Centro de Investigaciones y Estudios Superiores en Antropología Social and Instituto Oaxaqueño de las Culturas, Universidad Autónoma Benito Juárez.

Cameron, Maxwell A., and Brian W. Tomlin. 2002. "A Mexican Tragedy." In *The Making of NAFTA: How the Deal Was Done*. Ithaca: Cornell University Press.

Castles, Stephen, and Mark J. Miller. 1998. *The Age of Migration: International Population Movements in the Modern World*. 2nd. ed. New York: Guilford Press.

Center for International Finance and Development. 2001. "Has NAFTA Contributed to Economic Development in Mexico?," edited by E. Carrasco. Iowa: University of Iowa College of Law. http://blogs.law.uiowa.edu/ebook/issues/nafta/perspectives/has-nafta-contributed-to-economic-development-in-mexico.

Cerrutti, Marcela, and Douglas S. Massey. 2006. "Trends in Mexican Migration to the United States, 1965 to 1995." In *Crossing the Border: Research from the Mexican Migration Project*, edited by J. Durand and D. S. Massey. New York: Russell Sage Foundation.

Chance, John K. 1978. *Race and Class in Colonial Oaxaca*. Stanford: Stanford University Press.

———. 1989. *Conquest of the Sierra: Spaniards and Indians in the Colonial Oaxaca*. Norman: University of Oklahoma Press.

Chassen, Francis. 2005. "Los precursores de la revolución en Oaxaca." In *La revolución en Oaxaca, 1900–1930*, edited by V. R. Martínez V. Oaxaca: Instituto de Administración Pública de Oaxaca. http://www.cseiio.edu.mx/biblioteca/libros/cienciassociales/historia _de_la_revolucion_en_oaxaca.pdf.

Chavez, Leo R. 1985. "Households, Migration and Labor Market Participation: The Adaptation of Mexicans to Life in the United States." *Urban Anthropology* 14: 301–346.

Clifford, James. 1994. "Diasporas." *Cultural Anthropology* 9 (3): 302–338.

———. 1997. "Diasporas." In *Routes: Travel and Translation in the Late Twentieth Century*. Cambridge: Harvard University Press.

Cohen, Anthony P. 1985. *The Symbolic Construction of Community*. London: Ellis Horwood and Tavistock.

Cohen, Jeffrey. 2004. *The Culture of Migration in Southern Oaxaca*. Austin: University of Texas Press.

Coleman, James S. 1988. "Social Capital in the Creation of Human Capital." *American Journal of Sociology* 94: 95–120.

———. 1990. "Social Capital." In *Foundations of Social Theory*. Cambridge: Belknap Press of Harvard University Press.

CONAPO. 2005. *Proyecciones de la población indígena en México*. Consejo Nacional de Población 2006. http://www.cdi.gob.mx/cedulas/sintesis_resultados_2005.pdf.

Cornelius, Wayne A. 1989. "The U.S. Demand for Mexican Labor." In *Mexican Migration to the United States: Origins, Consequences, and Policy Options*, edited by W. A. Cornelius and J. A. Bustamante. La Jolla: University of California San Diego, Center for U.S.-Mexican Studies.

Cornelius, Wayne A., and Jorge A. Bustamante, eds. 1989. *Mexican Migration to the United States: Origins, Consequences, and Policy Options*. La Jolla: University of California San Diego, Center for U.S.-Mexican Studies.

Cornelius, Wayne A., and Jessa M. Lewis. 2007. *Impacts of Border Enforcement on Mexican Migration: The View from Sending Communities*. La Jolla, Cal.: Center for Comparative Immigration Studies and Lynne Rienner.

Cruz-Manjarrez, Adriana. 2001. "Performance, Ethnicity and Migration: Dance and Music in the Continuation of Ethnic Identity among Immigrant Zapotecs from the Oaxacan Highlands Village of Villa Hidalgo Yalálag to Los Angeles." Master's thesis, World Arts and Cultures, University of California Los Angeles.

———. 2005. "Performing Zapotec Identity: Aesthetics and Religiosity in the International Context of Migration." In *Dance and Society: Dancer as a Cultural Performer*, edited by D. E. Ivanich. Budapest: Akadémia Kiadó, European Folklore Institute Budapest.

———. 2006. "Transnational Identities and the Performance of Zapotec Culture." Ph.D. dissertation, World Arts and Cultures, University of California Los Angeles.

———. 2009. "Dancing to the Heights: Performing Zapotec Identity, Aesthetics, and Religiosity." In *Dancing across Borders: Danzas y bailes mexicanos*, edited by N.-R. Olga, N. E. Cantú, and B. Romero. Urbana: University of Illinois Press.

Debry, Joanna. 2010. *Divided by Borders: Mexican Migrants and Their Children*. Berkeley: University of California Press.

De Genova, Nicholas, and Ana Y. Ramos-Zayas. 2003. "Latino Rehearsals: Divergent Articulations of Latinidad." In *Latino Crossings: Mexicans, Puerto Ricans, and the Politics of Race and Citizenship*. New York: Routeledge.

De la Fuente, Julio. 1949. *Yalálag: Una villa zapoteca serrana*. Mexico City: Museo Nacional de Antropología.

———. 1994. "La cultura zapoteca." In *Los Zapotecos de la Sierra Norte de Oaxaca: Antología etnográfica*, edited by M. Ríos. Mexico City: Centro de Investigaciones y Estudios Superiores en Antropología Social and Instituto Oaxaqueño de las Culturas.

De Souza B., Xavier. 2004. "Social Capital: Easy Beauty or Meaningful Resource?" *Journal of the American Planning Association* 70 (2) (Spring): 151–158.

De Villa-Señor y Sánchez, José Antonio. 1994. "De la jurisdicción de Villa Alta y sus pueblos." In *Los Zapotecos de la Sierra Norte de Oaxaca: Antología etnográfica*, edited by M. Ríos. Mexico City: Centro de Investigaciones y Estudios Superiores en Antropología Social and Instituto Oaxaqueño de las Culturas.

Díaz Polanco, Héctor. 1991. *Autonomía regional: La autodeterminación de los pueblos indios*. Mexico City: Siglo XXI.

Drewal, Margaret. 1992. "Theory and Method in the Study of Ritual Performance." In *Yoruba Ritual: Performers, Play, Agency*. Bloomington: Indiana University Press.

Durand, Jorge. 2007. *Braceros: Las miradas mexicana y estadounidense. Antología (1945–1964)*. Mexico City: Miguel Ángel Porrúa.

Durkheim, Émile. 1964. *The Division of Labor in Society*. New York: Free Press.

Ebaugh, Rose Helen, and Janet Saltzaman Chafetz. 2002. *Religion across Borders: Transnational Immigrants Networks*. Walnut Creek, Cal.: Altamira.

Enloe, Cynthia. 1989. *Bananas, Beaches, and Bases: Making Feminist Sense of International Politics*. Berkeley: University of California Press.

Ennis, Sharon R., Merarys Ríos-Vargas, and Nora G Albert. 2011. "The Hispanic Population: 2010." 2010 Census briefs. http://www.census.gov/prod/cen2010/briefs/c2010br-04.pdf.

Equipo Pueblo. 1988. "Yalálag. Testimonios indígenas." Mexico City: Equipo Pueblo.

Esquivel, Paloma. 2012. "Epithet that Divides Mexicans Is Banned by Oxnard School District." *Los Angeles Times*, May 28.

Faist, Thomas. 2000a. "Transnationalization in International Migration: Implications for the Study of Citizenship and Culture." *Ethnic and Racial Studies* 23 (2): 447–563.

———. 2000b. "The Crucial Meso Link: Social Capital and Symbolic Ties." In *The Volume and Dynamics of Interntional Migration and Transnational Social Spaces*. Oxford: Oxford University Press.

———. 2000c. *The Volume and Dynamics of International Migration and Transnational Social Spaces*. Oxford: Oxford University Press.

Feld, Steven, and Keith H. Basso. 1996. "Introduction." In *Senses of Place*, edited by F. Steven and K. H. Basso. Santa Fe: School of American Research Press.

Fernandez, Raul E., and Gilbert G. Gonzalez. 2003. *A Century of Chicano History: Empire, Nations, and Migration*. New York: Routledge.

Fitzgerald, David. 2000. *Negotiating Extra-territorial Citizenship: Mexican Migration and the Transnational Politics of Community*. Berkeley: University of California Press.

Florescano, Enrique. 1999. *Memoria indígena*. Mexico City: Taurus and Pensamiento.

Fox, Jonathan. 2006. "Reframing Mexican Migration as a Multi-Ethnic Process." *Latino Studies* 4: 39–61.

Fox, Jonathan, and Gaspar Rivera-Salgado. 2004. *Indigenous Mexican Migrants in the United States*. La Jolla: University of California San Diego, Center for U.S.-Mexican Studies and Center for Comparative Immigration Studies.

Geertz, Clifford. 1973. "Thick Description: Toward an Interpretative Theory of Culture." In *The Interpretation of Cultures*. New York: Basic Books.

———. 1983. "Blurred Genres." In *Local Knowledge: Further Essays in Interpretative Anthropology*. Stanford: Stanford University Press.

Giménez, Gilberto. 1994. "Comunidades primordiales y modernización." In *Modernización e Identidades Sociales*. Mexico City: Universidad Nacional Autónoma de México, Instituto de Investigaciones Sociales, Instituto Francés de América Latina.

Glick Schiller, Nina. 1999. "Who Are These Guys?" In *Identities on the Move: Transnational Processes in North America and the Caribbean Basin*, edited by L. R. Goldin. Albany: University at Albany, Institute for Mesoamerican Studies.

Glick Schiller, Nina, Linda Basch, and Christine Blanc-Szanton. 1992. *Toward a Transnational Perspective on Migration. Race, Class, and Ethnicity: Nationalism Reconsidered.* New York: New York Academy of Sciences.

Glick Schiller, Nina, and George E. Fouron. 2001. *Georges Woke up Laughing*. Durham: Duke University Press.

Goldin, Liliana R. 1999. "Transnational Identities: The Search for Analytic Tools." In *Identities on the Move: Transnational Processes in North America and the Caribbean Basin*, edited by L. R. Goldin. Albany: University at Albany, Institute for Mesoamerican Studies.

Goldring, Luin. 1992. "Diversity and Community in Transnational Migration: A Comparative Study of Two Mexico-U.S. Migrant Circuits." Ph.D. dissertation, Sociology, Cornell University.

———. 1998. "The Power of Status in Transnational Social Fields." In *Transnationalism from Below*, edited by M. P. Smith and L. E. Guarnizo. New Brunswick, N.J.: Transaction.

———. 2001. "Disaggregating Transnational Social Spaces: Gender, Place, and Citizenship in Mexico-U.S. Transnational Spaces." In *New Transnational Social Spaces: International Migration and Transnational Companies in the Early Twenty-First Century*, edited by L. Pries. London: Routledge.

Gómez, Magdalena. 2005. "La autodeterminación comunitaria de Yalálag." *La Jornada*, December 6, 2005.

Grimes, Kimberly M. 1998. *Crossing Borders: Changing Social Identities in Southern Mexico*. Tucson: University of Arizona Press.

Griswold, Wendy. 1994. *Cultures and Societies in a Changing World*. Thousand Oaks, Cal.: Pine Forge Press.

Guarnizo, Luis. 1997. "The Emergence of a Transnational Social Formation and the Mirage of Return Migration among Dominican Transimmigrants." *Identities: Global Studies in Culture and Power* 4 (2): 281–332.

Gupta, Akhil, and James Ferguson. 1992. "Beyond Culture: Space, Identity, and the Politics of Difference." *Cultural Anthropology* 7 (1): 6–23.

Gutiérrez, David G. 1995. "Sin Fronteras? The Contemporary Debate." In *Walls and Mirrors: Mexican Americans, Mexican Immigrants, and the Politics of Ethnicty*. Berkeley: University of California Press.

Gutiérrez Nájera, Lourdes. 2007. "Yalálag Is No Longer Just Yalálag: Circulating Conflict and Contesting Community in a Zapotec Transnational Circuit." Ph.D. dissertation, Social Work and Anthropology, University of Michigan.

Hall, Stuart. 1998. "Introduction: Who Needs 'Identity?'" In *Questions of Cultural Identity*, edited by Stuart Hall and Paul du Gay. London: Sage.

Hamilton, Nora, and Norma Stoltz Chinchilla. 2001. *Seeking Community in a Global City: Guatemalans and Salvadorans in Los Angeles*. Philadelphia: Temple University Press.

Hannerz, Ulf. 1996. *Transnational Connections: Culture, People, and Places*. London: Routledge.

Harvey, D. 1989. "Time-Space Compression and the Post-modern Condition." In *The Conditions of Postmodernity*. Oxford: Basil Backwell.

Hernández, Kelly L. 2010. *Migra! A History of the Border Patrol*. Berkeley: University of California Press.

Herrera-Sobek, Maria. 2012. *Celbrating Latino Folklore: An Encliclopedia of Cultural Traditions*. 3 vols. Santa Barbara, Cal.: ABC-CLIO.

Hinojosa, Raul. 2003. "Transnational Migration, Remmittances, and Development in North America: Global Lessons for the OaxaCalifornia Transnational Village/Community Modeling Project." Unpublished paper, North American Integration and Development Center, University of California Los Angeles.

Hirabayashi, Lane Ryo. 1993. *Cultural Capital: Mountain Zapotec Migrant Associations in Mexico City, PROFMEX*. Tucson: University of Arizona Press.

Hirsch, Jennifer S. 2003. *A Courtship after Marriage: Sexuality and Love in Mexican Transnational Families*. Berkeley: University of California Press.

———. 2007. "'En el Norte manda la mujer': Gender, Generation, and Geography in a Mexican Transnational Community." In *Women and Migration in the U.S.-Mexico Borderlands: A Reader*, edited by D. A. Segura, P. Zavela, W. D. Mignolo, and I. Silverblatt. Durham: Duke University Press.

Hobsbawn, Eric. 2000. "Introduction." In *The Invention of Tradition*, edited by Hobsbawn and Terence Ranger. Cambridge: Cambridge University Press.

Hondagneu-Sotelo, Pierrette. 1994. *Gendered Transitions: Mexican Experiences of Immigration*. Berkeley: University of California Press.

———. 2003. "Gender and Immigration: A Retrospective and Introduction." In *Gender and U.S. Migration: Contemporary Trends*, edited by P. Hondagneu-Sotelo. Berkekey: Univesity of California Press.

Huizar Murillo, Javier, and Isidro Cerda. 2004. "Indigenous Mexican Migrants in the 2000 U.S. Census: Hispanic American Indians." In *Indigenous Mexican Migrants in the United States*, edited by J. Fox and G. Rivera-Salgado. La Jolla: University of California San Diego; Center for U.S.-Mexican Studies and Center for Comparative Immigration Studies.

Hulshof, Marije. 1991. *Zapotec Moves: Networks and Remittances of U.S.-Bound Migrants from Oaxaca, Mexico*. Amsterdam: Koninklijk Nederlands Aardrijkskundig Genootschap.

Humes, Karen R., Nicholas A. Jones, and Roberto R. Ramírez. 2011. "Overview of Race and Hispanic Origin: 2010." 2010 Census briefs. http://www.census.gov/prod/cen2010/briefs/c2010br-02.pdf.

Hylland Ericksen, Thomas. 2002. "What Is Ethnicity?" In *Ethnicity and Nationalism: Anthropological Perspectives*. London: Pluto.

IME (Instituto de los Mexicanos en el Exterior). 2005. *Matrícula Consular*. http://www.sre.gob.mx/index.php/matricula-consular.

INALI (Instituto Nacional de Lenguas Indígenas). 2011. Información General de las 11 Familias Lingüísticas Nacionales. http://www.inali.gob.mx/component/content/article/60-informacion-general.

INEGI (Instituto Nacional de Estadística y Geografía). 2000. *Estados Unidos Mexicanos. XII Censo General de Población y Vivienda, 2000. Resultados Preliminares*. Mexico City: INEGI.

———. 2004. *La Población Indígena en México*. Mexico City: INEGI.

———. 2005. *II Conteo de Población y Vivienda 2005. INEGI. Tabulados Básicos. Población de 5 años y más que hablan alguna lengua indígena por municipio y lengua indígena según*

su condición de habla española y sexo. http://www3.inegi.org.mx/sistemas/Tabulados
Basicos/LeerArchivo.aspx?ct=33591&c=27302&s=est&f=1.

———. 2010a. *XII Censo General de Población y Vivienda: Tabulados del Cuestionario
Básico. Población total por municipio, sexo, religión según grupos de edad.* Mexico City:
INEGI. http://www3.inegi.org.mx/sistemas/TabuladosBasicos/LeerArchivo.aspx?ct=336
20&c=27302&s=est&f=1.

———. 2010b. *Censo de Población y Vivienda 2010: Tabulados del Cuestionario Básico.
Población de 3 años y más que habla lengua indígena por sexo y lengua según grupos quin-
quenales de edad.* Mexico City: INEGI.

———. 2010c. Clasificación del Censo de Población y Vivienda 2010. Mexico City:
INEGI. http://www.inegi.org.mx/est/contenidos/espanol/metodologias/censos/cpv2010
_clasificaciones.pdf.

———. 2010d. Censo de Población y Vivienda 2010. Villa Hidalgo, Oaxaca. México en
Cifras. Información Nacional, por entidad Federativa y Municipios. http://www.inegi
.org.mx/sistemas/mexicocifras/default.aspx?e=20&mun=038&src=487.

———. 2010e. *Censo de Población y Vivienda 2010: Tabulados del Cuestionario Básico. Población
de 5 años y más que habla lengua indígena por entidad federativa y lengua según condición
de habla española y sexo.* Mexico City: INEGI. http://www3.inegi.org.mx/sistemas/
TabuladosBasicos/LeerArchivo.aspx?ct=27419&c=27302&s=est&f=1.

Jones-Correa, Michael. 2002. "The Study of Transnationalism among the Children of
Immigrants: Where We Are and Where We Should Be Headed." In *The Changing Face
of Home: The Transnational Lives of the Second Generation,* edited by Peggy Levitt and
Mary C. Waters. New York: Russel Sage Foundation.

Kearney, Michael. 1986. *The Winds of Ixtepeji: Worldview in a Zapotec Town.* Prospect
Heights, Ill: Waveland Press.

———. 1991. "Borders and Boundaries of State and Self at the End of Empire." *Journal of
Historical Sociology* 4 (1): 52–74.

———. 1995. "The Effects of Transnational Culture, Economy, and Migration on Mixtec
Identity in Oaxacalifornia." In *The Bubbling Cauldron: Race, Ethnicity, and the Urban Crisis,* edited by M. P. Smith and J. R. Feagin. Minneapolis: University of Minnesota Press.

———. 1999. "Neither Modern nor Traditional: Personal Identities in Global Perspec-
tives." In *Identities on the Move: Transnational Processes in North America and the
Caribbean Basin,* edited by L. R. Goldin. Albany: University at Albany, Institute for
Mesoamerican Studies.

———. 2000. "Transnational Oaxacan Indigenous Identity: The Case of Mixtecs and
Zapotecs." *Identities* 7 (2): 173–175.

Kearney, Michael, and Federico Besserer. 2004. "Oaxacan Municipal Governance in Transnational Context." In *Indigenous Mexican Migrants in the United States,* edited by J. Fox
and G. Rivera-Salgado. La Jolla: University of Caifornia, San Diego, Center for U.S.-
Mexican Studies and Center for Comparative Immigration Studies.

King, Anthony D. 1995. "The Times and Spaces of Modernity (or Who Needs Postmodernism?)." In *Global Modernities,* edited by Mike Featherstone, Scott Lash, and Roland
Robertson.Thousand Oaks, Cal.: Sage.

Kivisto, Peter. 2001. "Theorizing Transnational Immigration." *Ethnic and Racial Studies*
24 (4): 549–577.

Kivisto, Peter, and Thomas Faist. 2009. "Transnationalism and the Persistance of Homeland Ties." In *Beyond a Border: The Causes and Concequences of Contemporary Immigration.* Los Angeles: Pine Forge Press.

Klaver, Jeanine. 1997. *From the Land of the Sun to the City of Angels: The Migration Process of Zapoec Indians from Oaxaca, Mexico to Los Angeles, California*. Utrecht: Dutch Geographical Society, and Amsterdam: Department of Human Geography, University of Amsterdam.

Kluckhohn, Clyde. 1962. *Culture and Behavior*. New York: Free Press.

Kondo, Dorinne K. 1990. "Introduction." In *Crafting Selves: Power, Gender, and Discourses of Identity in a Japanese Workplace*. Chicago: University of Chicago Press.

Levitt, Peggy. 2001a. *Transnational Villagers*. Berkeley: University of California Press.

———. 2001b. "Transnational Migration: Taking Stock and Future Directions." *Global Networks* 1 (3): 195–216.

Levitt, Peggy, and Mary C. Waters. 2002. *The Changing Face of Home: The Transnational Lives of the Second Generation*. New York: Russell Sage Foundation.

Liebel, Manfred. 2005. "'Barrio Gangs' en Estados Unidos: Un reto a la sociedad excluyente." *Desacatos* 18 (May-August): 127–146.

Light, Ivan. 2004. "Social Capital's Unique Accesibility." *Journal of the American Planning Association* 7 (2) (Spring): 4–10.

López, Felipe H., and David Runsten. 2004. "Mixtecs and Zapotecs Working in California: Rural and Urban Experiences." In *Indigenous Mexican Migrants in the United States*, edited by J. Fox and G. Rivera-Salgado. La Jolla: University of California San Diego, Center for U.S.-Mexican Studies, and Center for Comparative Immigration Studies.

López Austin, Alfredo. 1980. *Cuerpo humano e ideología: Las concepciones de los antiguos nahuas*. Vol. 2. Mexico City: Universidad Nacional Autónoma de México and Instituto de Investigaciones Antropológicas.

López Castro, G. 2007. "Niños, socialización y migración a Estados Unidos." In *El país transnacional: Migración mexicana y cambio social a través de la frontera*, edited by M. Ariza and A. Portes. Mexico City: Instituto de Investigaciones Sociales-Universidad Nacional Autónoma de México.

MacAloon, John J. 1984. "Introduction: Cultural Performances, Cultural Theory." In *Rite, Drama, Festival, Spectacle. Rehearsals toward a Theory of Cultural Performance*, edited by J. J. MacAloon. Philadelphia: Insititute for the Study of Human Issues.

Mahler, Sara J. 1995. *Salvadoreans in Suburbia: Symbiosis and Conflict*. Boston: Allyn and Bacon.

———. 1998. "Theoretical and Empirical Contributions toward a Research Agenda for Transnationalism." In *Transnationalism from Below*, edited by M. P. Smith and L. E. Guarnizo. New Brunswick, N.J.: Transaction.

———. 2003. "Engendering Transnational Migration: A Case Study of Salvadoreans." In *Gender and U.S. Immigration: Contemporary Trends*, edited by P. Hondagneu-Sotelo. Berkeley: University of California Press.

Malkin, Victoria. 2007. "Reproduction of Gender Relations in the Mexican Migrant Community of New Rochelle, New York." In *Women and Migration in the U.S. Borderlands: A Reader*, edited by D. A. Segura, P. Zavela, W. D. Mignolo, and I. Silverblatt. Durham: Duke University Press.

Mandel, Ruth. 1989. "Ethnicity and Identity among Guestworkers in West Berlin." In *Conflict, Migration, and the Expression of Ethnicity*, edited by N. L. Gonzalez and C. S. McCommon. Boulder, Col.: Westview.

Malpica, Daniel. 2007. "Indigenous Mexican Immigrants in the City of Los Angeles." Ph.D. dissertation, Sociology, University of California Los Angeles.

Marcus, George. 1998. "Anthropology on the Move." In *Ethnography through Thick and Thin*. Princeton: Princeton University Press.

Margolis, Maxine L. 1994. *Little Brazil: An Ethnography of Brazilian Immigrants in New York City*. Princeton: Princeton University Press.

Martínez M., Héctor Gerardo. 2005. "Génesis y desarrollo del maderismo en Oaxaca (1902–1912)." In *La revolución en Oaxaca, 1900–1930*, edited by V. R. Martínez V. Oaxaca: Instituto de Administración Pública de Oaxaca. http://www.cseiio.edu.mx/biblioteca/libros/cienciassociales/historia_de_la_revolucion_en_oaxaca.pdf.

Martínez-Saldaña, Jesús. 2004. "Building the Future: The FIOB and Civic Participation of Mexican Immigrants in Fresno, California." In *Indigenous Mexican Migrants in the United States*, edited by J. Fox and G. Rivera-Salgado. La Jolla: University of California San Diego, Center for U.S.-Mexican Studies, and Center for Comparative Immigration Studies.

Massey, Douglas S., Rafael Alarcón, Jorge Durand, and Humberto González. 1987. *Return to Aztlán: The Social Process of International Migration from Western Mexico*. Berkeley: University of California Press.

Massey, Douglas S., Luin Goldring, and Jorge Duran. 1994. "Continuities in Transnational Migration: An Analysis of Nineteen Mexican Communities." *American Journal of Sociology* 99 (6): 1492–1533.

Massey, Douglas S., Arango G. Hugo, A. Kouaouci, A. Peregrino, and J. E. Taylor. 1998. *Worlds in Motion: Understanding International Migration at the End of the Millennium*. Oxford: Clarendon Press.

Matute-Bianche, Maria Eugenia. 1986. "Ethnic Identities and Patterns of School Sucess and Failure among Mexican-Descent and Japanese-American Students in a California High School: An Ethnographic Analysis." *American Journal of Education* 95 (1): 233–255.

Mendoza, Zoila. 2000. *Shaping Society through Dance: Mestizo Ritual Performance in the Peruvian Andes*. Chicago: University of Chicago Press.

Menjivar, Cecilia. 2000. *Fragmented Ties: Salvadorean Immigrant Networks in America*. Berkeley: University of California Press.

———. 2003. "The Intersection of Work and Gender: Central American Immigrant Women and Employment in California." In *Gender and U.S. Migration: Contemporary Trends*, edited by P. Hondagneu-Sotelo. Berkekey: Univesity of California Press.

Molina, Mario. 2003. *Primeras interpretaciones de simbolismos: Zapotecos de la Sierra de Oaxaca*. Vol. 1. Oaxaca: Casa de la Cultura Oaxaqueña and Watix Dillè Ediciones.

———. 2004. *Luá ke dillé, ofrenda de palabras, voces de nuestra tierra: Antología*. Oaxaca: Instituto Oaxaqueño de las Culturas.

Montes, García Olga. 1998. "El Indio visto por una oligarquía regional: El caso Oaxaca." In *Las imágenes del Indio en Oaxca*, edited by D.J.C. Hernández. Oaxaca: Instituto Oaxaqueño de las Culturas, Universidad Autónoma Benito Juárez de Oaxaca.

Moran-Taylor, Michelle. 2008. "When Mothers and Fathers Migrate North: Caretakers, Children, and Child Rearing in Guatemala." *Latin American Perspectives* 35: 79–95.

Muñoz, Carlos. 1989. "Introduction." In *Youth, Identity, Power: The Chicano Movement*. London: Verso.

Muntzel, Martha, and Benjamin Pérez González. 1987. "Panorama general de las lenguas indígenas." *America Indígena* 47: 571–605.

Nader, Laura. 1969. "The Zapotec of Oaxaca." In *Handbook of Middle American Indians*, edited by G. D. Robert Wauchope. Austin: University of Texas Press.

Nagengast, Carole, and Michael Kearney. 1990. "Mixtec Ethnciity: Social Identity, Political Consciousness and Political Activism." *Latin American Research Review* 25 (2): 61–91.

Oboler, Suzanne. 1999. "Racializing Latinos in the United States." In *Identities on the Move: Transnational Processes in North America and the Caribbean Basin*, edited by L. R. Goldin. Albany: University at Albany, Institute for Mesoamerican Studies.

Olivé, León. 1999. *Multiculturalismo y pluralismo*. Mexico City: Paidós, Universidad Nacional Autónoma de México.

Olmos Aguilera, Miguel. 1998. *El sabio de la fiesta: Música y mitología en la región cahita-tarahumara*. Mexico City: Instituto Nacional de Antropología e Historia.

Ong, Aihwa. 1996. "Cultural Citizenship as Subject-Making: Immigrants Negotiate Racial and Cultural Boundaries in the United States." *Current Anthropology* 37 (5) (December): 737–762.

Pessar, Patricia. 1995. *A Visa for a Dream: Dominicans in the United States*. Boston: Allyn and Bacon.

Portes, Alejandro. 1998a. "Globalization from Below: The Rise of Transnational Communities." Working paper, *Transnational Communities Program*. http://www.transcomm .ox.ac.uk/working%20papers/portes.pdf.

———. 1998b. "Social Capital: Its Origins and Applications in Modern Sociology." *Annual Review of Sociology* 24: 1–24.

———. 2000. "Globalization from Below: The Rise of Transnational Communities." In *The Ends of Globalization: Bringing Society Back In*, edited by Don Kalb, M. Van der Land, and R. Staring. Lanham, Md.: Rowman and Littlefield.

———. 2001. "Introduction: The Debates and Significance of Immigrant Transnational-ism." *Global Networks* 1 (3): 181–193.

Portes, Alejandro, Luis E. Guarnizo, and Patricia Landolt. 1999. "The Study of Transna-tionalism: Pitfalls and Promise of an Emergent Field Research." *Ethnic and Racial Studies* 22 (2): 217–237.

Portes, Alejandro, and Rubén Rumbaut. 2001a. *Legacies: The Story of Immigrant Second Generation*. Berkeley: University of California Press, and New York: Russell Sage Foundation.

———. 2001b. The Crucible Within: Family Schools, and the Psychology of the Second Generation. In *Legacies*. Berkeley, Los Angeles, London, and New York: University of California Press and Russel Sage Foundation.

Pries, Ludger. 1999. *Migration and Transnational Social Spaces*. Aldershot: Ashgate.

———. 2001. *New Transnational Social Spaces: International Migration and Transnational Companies in the Early Twenty-first Century*. London: Routledge.

Putnam, Robert. D. 1993. *Making Democracy Work: Civic Traditions in Modern Italy*. Princeton: Princeton University Press.

Ragland, Catherine. 2009. *Musica Norteña: Mexican Migrants Creating a Nation between Nations*. Philadelphia: Temple University Press.

Ríos, Manuel. 1994. *Los Zapotecos de la Sierra Norte de Oaxaca: Antología Etnográfica*. Mexico City: Centro de Investigaciones y Estudios Superiores en Antropología Social and Instituto Oaxaqueño de las Culturas.

Rivera-Salgado, Gaspar. 1999. "Migration and Political Activism: Mexican Transnational Indigenous Communities in a Comparative Perspective." Ph.D. dissertation, Sociology, University of California Santa Cruz.

Rivera-Salgado, Gaspar, and Luis Escala. 2004. "Collective Identity and Organizational Strategies of Indigenous and Mestizo Mexican Immigrants." In *Indigenous Mexican*

Migrants in the United States, edited by J. Fox and G. Rivera-Salgado. La Jolla: University of California San Diego, Center for U.S.-Mexican Studies, and Center for Comparative Immigration Studies.

Rodríguez, Clara E. 2000. *Changing Race: Latinos, the Census, and the History of Ethnicity in the United States*. New York: New York University Press.

Rodriguez, Sylvia. 1996. *The Matachines Dance: Ritual Symbolism and Interethnic Relations in the Upper Rio Grande Valley*. Albuquerque: University of New Mexico Press.

Rohe, Williams M. 2004. "Building Social Capital through Community Development." *Journal of the American Planning Association* 7 (2) (Spring): 17–23.

Rosaldo, Renato. 1989. *Culture and Truth: The Remaking of Social Analysis*. Boston: Beacon.

———. 1994. "Ciudadania cultural en San Jose California." In *De lo local a lo global. perspectivas desde la antropologia*. Mexico City: Universidad Autónoma Metropolitana Iztapalapa.

Rosales, Arturo F. 1997. *Chicano! The History of the Mexican American Civil Rights Movement*. 2nd. ed. Houston: Arte Público Press.

———. 1999. *Pobre Raza! Violence, Justice, and Mobilization among México Lindo Immigrants, 1900–1936*. Austin: University of Texas Press.

Rouse, Roger C. 1989. "Mexican Migration to the United States: Family Relations in the Development of a Transnational Migrant Circuit." Ph.D. dissertation, Anthropology, Stanford University.

———. 1991. "Mexican Migration and the Social Space of Postmodernism." *Diaspora* 1 (1): 8–23.

———. 1995. "Questions of Identity: Personhood and Collectivity in Transnational Migration to the United States." *Critique of Anthropology* 15 (4): 351–380.

Ruíz Arrazola, Víctor. 2000. "Violento enfrentamiento entre priístas y perredistas en Yalalag." *La Jornada*, March 3, 2005.

Ruiz C., José. 2005. "El movimiento de la sberanía en Oaxaca (1915–1920)." In *La revolución en Oaxaca, 1900–1930*, edited by V. R. Martínez V. Oaxaca: Instituto de Administración Pública de Oaxaca. http://www.cseiio.edu.mx/biblioteca/libros/cienciassociales/historia_de_la_revolucion_en_oaxaca.pdf.

Rumabut, Rubén G. 1999. "Assimilation and Its Discontents: Ironies and Paradoxes." In *The Handbook of International Migration: The American Experience*, edited by C. Hirschman, P. Kasinitz, and J. De Wind. New York: Russel Sage Foundation.

Sánchez, George J. 1993. *Becoming Mexican American: Ethnicity, Culture, and Identity in Chicano Los Angeles 1900–1945*. New York: Oxfrod University Press.

Sassen, Saskia. 1998. "Introduction: Whose City Is It? Globalization and the Formation of New Claims." In *Globalization and Its Discontents*. New York: New Press.

Schechner, Richard, and Willa Appel. 1985. "Restoration of Behavior." In *Between Theater and Anthropology*. Philadelphia: University of Pennsylvania Press.

———. 2002. "What Is Performance?" In *Performance Studies: An Introduction*. London: Routledge.

Sklar, Deidre. 2001. *Dancing with the Virgin: Body and Faith in the Fiesta of Tortugas, New Mexico*. Berkeley: University of California Press.

Smith, Robert C. 1995. "Los ausentes siempre presentes: The Imagining, Making, and Politics of a Transnational Community between Ticuani, Puebla, Mexico and New York City." Ph.D. dissertation, Sociology, Columbia University.

———. 2002. "Life Course, Generation, and Social Location as Factors Shaping Second-Generation Transnational Life." In *The Changing Face of Home: The Transnational Lives of the Second Generation*, edited by P. Levitt and M. C. Waters. New York: Russell Sage Foundation.

———. 2006. *Mexican New York: Transnational Lives of New Immigrants.* Berkeley: University of California Press.

Stavenhagen, Rodolfo. 2008. "Un mundo en el que caben muchos mundos: El reto de la globalización." In *Revisitar la etnicidad: Miradas cruzadas en torno a la diversidad.* Mexico City: El Colegio de Sonora, El Colegio Mexiquense.

Stephen, Lynn. 2002. "Sexualities and Genders in Zapotec Oaxaca." *Latin American Perspectives* 29 (2): 41–59.

———. 2005a. "Ethnicity and Class in the Changing Lives of Zapotec Women." In *Zapotec Women: Gender, Class, and Ethnicity in Globalized Oaxaca.* Durham: Duke University Press.

———. 2005b. *Zapotec Women: Gender, Class, and Ethnicity in Globalized Oaxaca.* Durham: Duke University Press.

———. 2007a. "Navigating the Borders of Racial and Ethnic Hierarchies." In *Transborder Lives. Indigenous Oaxacans in Mexico, California, and Oregon.* Durham: Duke University Press.

———. 2007b. *Transborder Lives: Indigenous Oaxacans in Mexico, California, and Oregon.* Durham: Duke University Press.

———. 2007c. "Women's Transborder Lives: Gender Relations in Work and Families." In *Transborder Lives: Indigenous Oaxacans in Mexico, California, and Oregon.* Durham: Duke University Press.

Stokes, Martin. 1994. "Introduction." In *Ethnicity, Identity and Music: The Musical Construction of Place.* Oxford: Berg.

Stout, Robert J. 2008. *Why Immigrants Come to America" Braceros, Indocumentados, and the Migra.* Westport, Conn.: Praeger.

Swadesh, Mauricio. 1949. "El idioma de los Zapotecos." In *Los Zapotecos: Monografía histórica, etnográfica, y económica,* edited by M. y. Nuñez. Mexico City: Universidad Nacional Autónoma de México.

Tavárez, David Eduardo. 2011. *The Invisible War: Indigenous Devotions, Discipline, and Dissent in Colonial Mexico.* Stanford: Stanford University Press.

Taylor, William B. 1972. *Landlord and Peasant in Colonial Oaxaca.* Stanford: Stanford University Press.

Thomas, W. I. , and Florian Znaniecki. [1894] 1920. *The Polish Peasant in Europe and America.* Chicago: University of Illinois Press.

Thompson D., Margaret. 1992. "Theory and Method in the Study of Ritual Performance." In *Yoruba Ritual: Performers, Play, Agency.* Bloomington: Indiana University Press.

Tienda, Marta. 1989. "Looking to the 1990s: Mexican Immigration in Sociological Perspective." In *Mexican Migration to the United States: Origins, Consequences, and Policy Options,* edited by W. A. Cornelius and J. A. Bustamante. La Jolla: University of California San Diego, Center for U.S.-Mexican Studies.

Tsuda, Takeyuki. 2003. *Strangers in the Ethnic Homeland: Japanese Brazilian Return Migration in Transnational Perspective.* New York: Columbia University Press.

Ueda, Reed. 1994. *Postwar Immigrant America: A Social History.* Boston: Bedford Books of St. Martin's Press.

———. 2002. "An Early Transnationalism? The Japanese American Second Generation of Hawaii in the Interwars Years." In *The Changing Face of Home: The Transnational Lives of the Second Generation*, edited by P. Levitt and M. C. Waters. New York: Russell Sage Foundation.

Van Gennep, Arnold. 1960. *The Rites of Passage*. Chicago: University of Chicago Press.

Velasco Ortiz, Laura. 2005. *Mixtec Transnational Identity*. Tucson: University of Arizona Press.

Velásquez C., Maria Cristina. 2004. "Migrant Communities, Gender, and Political Power in Oaxaca." In *Indigenous Mexican Migrants in the United States*, edited by J. Fox and G. Rivera-Salgado. La Jolla: University of California San Diego, Center for U.S.-Mexican Studies, and Center for Comparative Immigration Studies.

Vertovec, Steven. 2001. "Transnationalism and Identity." *Ethnic and Migration Studies* 27 (4): 573–582.

———. 2004. "Cheap Calls: The Social Glue of Migrant Transnationalism." *Global Networks* 4 (2): 219–224.

———. 2010. "Transnational Social Formations." In *Transnationalism*. London: Routledge.

Vigil, Diego. 1994. *Barrio Gangs: Street Life and Identity in Southern California*. Austin: University of Texas Press.

Villareal, M. Angeles. 2011. "U.S.-Mexico Economic Relations: Trends, Issues, and Implications." http://www.fas.org/sgp/crs/row/RL32934.pdf.

Waters, Mary C. 1990. *Ethnic Options: Choosing Identities in America*. Berkeley: University of California Press.

———. 2001a. *Black Identities: West Indian Immigrants Dreams and American Realities*. Cambridge: Harvard University Press, and New York: Russell Sage Foundation.

———. 2001b. "Identites of the Second Generation." In *Black Identities: West Indian Immigrants Dreams and American Realities*. Cambridge: Harvard University Press, and New York: Russell Sage Foundation.

———. 2001c. "Racial and Ethnic Identity Choices." In *Black Identities: West Indian Immigrants Dreams and American Realities*. Cambridge: Harvard University Press, and New York: Russell Sage Foundation.

Weismantel, Mary. 2001. "Sharp Trading." In *Cholas and Pishtacos: Stories of Race and Sex in the Andes*. Chicago: University of Chicago Press.

Whitecotton, Joseph. [1985] 2004. *Los Zapotecos: Principes, sacerdotes y campesinos*. Translated from English by S. Mastrangelo. Mexico City: Fondo de Cultura Económica.

Wimmer, Andreas. 2002. "Nationalism and Ethnic Mobilization in Mexico." In *Nationalist Exclusion and Ethnic Conflict: Shadows of Modernity*. Cambridge: Cambridge University Press.

Wimmer, Andreas, and Nina Glick Schiller. 2002. "Methodological Nationalism and Beyond: Nation-States Building, Migration and the Social Sciences." *Global Networks* 2 (4): 310–334.

Wolf, Diane L. 2002. "There's No Place Like 'Home': Emotional Transnationalism and the Struggles of Second Generation Filipinos." In *The Changing Face of Home. The Transnational Lives of the Second Generation*, edited by Peggy Levitt and Mary C. Waters. New York: Russell Sage Foundation.

Woodman Colby, Catherine. 1998. "Return Migration from Canada and the United States: Its Effects in the Mixteca Alta of Oaxaca." Ph.D. dissertation, Anthropology, Vanderbilt University.

Yannakakis, Yanna. 2008. *The Art of Being in-between: Native Intermediaries, Indian Identity, and Local Rule in Colonial Oaxaca*. Durham: Duke University Press.

Young, C. M. 1976. "The Social Setting of Migration: Factors Affecting Migration from a Sierra Zapotec Village in Oaxaca, Mexico." Doctoral dissertation, Anthropology, University of London.

Young, Kathe. 1979. "Modes of Appropriation and the Sexual Division of Labour: A Case of Study from Oaxaca, Mexico." In *Feminism and Materialism: Women and Modes of Production*, edited by A. Kuhn and A. Wolpe. London: Routledge and Kegan Paul.

Zárate Rosales, Alberto. 2009. "Dances of the Sierra Norte of Puebla." In *Dancing across Borders: Danzas y bailes mexicanos*, edited by O. Nájera-Ramírez, N. E. Cantú, and B. Romero. Urbana: University of Illinois Press.

Zilbermann, Ma. Cristina. 1994. "Idolatrías de Oaxaca en el Siglo XVIII." In *Los Zapotecos de la Sierra Norte de Oaxaca: Antología etnográfica*, edited by M. Ríos. Mexico City: Centro de Investigaciones y Estudios Superiores en Antropología Social and Instituto Oaxaqueño de las Culturas.

Zolberg, A. 1989. "The Next Waves: Migration Theory for a Changing World." *International Migration Review* 23: 402–430.

INDEX

The letter f following a page number denotes a figure; the letter t denotes a table.

cargo (*barrio-cargo*) system, 9–10; composition of, 213n31; immigrant participation in, 90, 91; obligation to participate in, 48

Carrancistas, 84, 85

Carranza, Venustiano, 84

casas del los barrios, 49, 57, 75

Castles, Stephen, 13

Catholic Church, influence on ideologies of gender/sexuality, 168, 169, 172

Catholics, in Yalálag, 75, 212n14, 214n2, 222n6

caudillo, 85, 217

Cerro Brujo, 73

Cerrutti, Marcela, 31

champurrado, 76, 80

Chance, John K., 47, 56, 71

Chiapas uprising, 36

Chicanos, 131, 133–134, 135–137

Chinese Americans, view of Yalaltecos, 151–152

cholos: clothing as symbol of identity of, 137, 162; identity as Mexican Americans, 134–135; as negative identity, 109–110; as negative social remittances, 162–163; and violence in Yalálag, 223n18; in Yalálag, 222n12

chuntis, 148, 161

churches in Yalálag, 72, 77, 212n15

chusca dances. See *danzas chuscas* (parodic dances)

cirios, 55, 159

citizenship: U.S., 202; in Yalálag, 213n29

code switching, 109

coffee trade, 157

cofradia, 47

Cohen, Anthony P., 51

colonialism, 47–48, 112, 181, 214n32

comisiones, 53

comisiones de festejos, 73, 74

comisiones de las iglesias, 73, 74

comisiones de los barrios, 92

comisiones de obras, 73, 74

Comité Municipal del PRI (Municipal Committee of the Institutional Revolutionary Party), 36, 85, 87, 88, 89

Communitarian Group (Grupo Comunitario), 79, 85, 87–88, 89

community: defining, 6–7; as social construct, 51; transnational perspective on, 6–13

community formation, social and symbolic processes in, 191–192

community service (*servicio*), 8, 56–60

compadrazgo, 204

comunidad fragmentada, 9

consonant acculturation, 16

convíte, 80, 215n15

corn ceremony, 175, 176–177

corregidor, 211n7

corregimiento, 211n7

cosmology, 224n13

Council of Elders, 85, 87, 88

coyotes, 23, 26, 28, 34, 38

Cuba, 32, 98

cultural performance, 17

culture of migration, 42, 121

cumbia, 81, 183, 215n19

Danza de Los Mixes (Dance of Los Mixes), 1–2

danzante, 49, 60–61, 161

danzas chuscas (parodic dances), 5, 10, 14, 17, 54; appeal and relevance of, 167; humor in, 17, 153, 167, 172–173, 175, 176, 185–187; reasons to perform, 153–154, 161, 162, 193–194; symbolism of, 166. See also *individual dances*

deer, significance of, 183

de la Fuente, Julio, 71, 73, 76–77, 87, 88

Democratic Revolutionary Party (PRD), 85

Desamortization Laws of 1856, 216n24

de Souza, Xavier, 51

deterritorialized nation-state building, 101

Día de los Muertos ("Day of the Death"), 94, 108

Díaz, Porfirio, 82–83, 84, 86

discrimination: and internal migration, 119–120, 127, 128; toward Latinos, 113–114; within Mexican community in U.S., 14–15, 16, 99, 111–112; against Zapotec language speakers, 104–105

dis-identification as Yalaltecos, 14, 16, 141–143, 150, 151, 197

dissonant acculturation, 16

domestic workers: in Mexico, 24, 28, 37; in U.S., 24–25, 28, 29, 32, 34, 38

Dominican migration, 10, 13

Durkheim, Émile, 156

economic crisis: in Mexico, 32, 36–37, 38, in Mexico, historical, 83

education: as reason for migration, 20, 34, 35, 38, 39; social effects of, 180; in Yalálag, 86–87, 180

18th Street gang, 163–164

El Regreso de los Mojados (The return of the wetbacks), 153

encomiendas, 211n7

endogamy, 39, 202, 210n9, 212n12

ABOUT THE AUTHOR

Adriana Cruz-Manjarrez is a research professor at University of Colima, Mexico. Her interdisciplinary work specializes on the study of Yalálag Zapotec and Yucatec Maya migration into the United States with a focus on transnational communities, identity, gender, race, ethnicity, and cultural practices.

www.ingramcontent.com/pod-product-compliance
Lightning Source LLC
Chambersburg PA
CBHW021812270326

41932CB00007B/159